THE
MYTHOLOGY
BOOK

THE
MYTHOLOGY
BOOK

DK LONDON

PROJECT ART EDITOR
Duncan Turner

ILLUSTRATIONS
James Graham

JACKET EDITOR
Claire Gell

SENIOR JACKET DESIGNER
Mark Cavanagh

JACKET DESIGN
DEVELOPMENT MANAGER
Sophia MTT

PRODUCER, PRE-PRODUCTION
Andy Hilliard

PRODUCER
Alex Bell

MANAGING EDITOR
Angeles Gavira

MANAGING ART EDITOR
Michael Duffy

ASSOCIATE PUBLISHING DIRECTOR
Liz Wheeler

ART DIRECTOR
Karen Self

DESIGN DIRECTOR
Philip Ormerod

PUBLISHING DIRECTOR
Jonathan Metcalf

DK DELHI

SENIOR ART EDITOR
Mahua Sharma

ART EDITORS
Rupanki Kaushik, Debjyoti Mukherjee

ASSISTANT ART EDITOR
Mridushmita Bose

SENIOR EDITOR
Anita Kakar

ASSISTANT EDITORS
Rishi Bryan, Aishvarya Misra

JACKET DESIGNERS
Suhita Dharamjit, Juhi Sheth

SENIOR DTP DESIGNERS
Harish Aggarwal, Shanker Prasad

DTP DESIGNER
Vikram Singh

PICTURE RESEARCHER
Aditya Katyal

JACKETS EDITORIAL COORDINATOR
Priyanka Sharma

MANAGING JACKETS EDITOR
Saloni Singh

PICTURE RESEARCH MANAGER
Taiyaba Khatoon

PRE-PRODUCTION MANAGER
Balwant Singh

PRODUCTION MANAGER
Pankaj Sharma

SENIOR MANAGING EDITOR
Rohan Sinha

MANAGING ART EDITOR
Sudakshina Basu

original styling by
STUDIO 8

TOUCAN BOOKS

EDITORIAL DIRECTOR
Ellen Dupont

SENIOR DESIGNER
Thomas Keenes

SENIOR EDITOR
Abigail Mitchell

EDITORS
John Andrews, Guy Croton, Sue George,
Larry Porges, Anna Southgate, Dorothy Stannard,
Rachel Warren Chadd

EDITORIAL ASSISTANT
Michael Clark

INDEXER
Marie Lorimer

PICTURE RESEARCHER
Sharon Southren

PROOFREADER
Marion Dent

ADDITIONAL TEXT
Andrea Jovanovic, Cynthia O'Brien,
Joan Strasbaugh

First published in Great Britain in 2018
by Dorling Kindersley Limited
DK, One Embassy Gardens,
8 Viaduct Gardens, London, SW11 7BW

The authorised representative in
the EEA is Dorling Kindersley Verlag GmbH.
Arnulfstr. 124, 80636 Munich, Germany

Copyright © 2018
Dorling Kindersley Limited
A Penguin Random House Company
12 11 10 9
032–305931–May/2018

A CIP catalogue record for this book is
available from the British Library.
ISBN: 978-0-2413-0191-3

Printed and bound in China

For the curious
www.dk.com

CONTRIBUTORS

PHILIP WILKINSON, CONSULTANT

Philip Wilkinson has written more than 50 books on history, religions, the arts, and mythology. His titles include *Mythology* and *Religions* in Dorling Kindersley's Eyewitness Companions series, *Myths and Legends*, and *A Celebration of Customs and Rituals* of the World, which was endorsed and adopted by the United Nations.

GEORGIE CARROLL

Georgie Carroll is a PhD candidate at SOAS University of London working on eco-aesthetics in Indian literature. She is author of *Mouse* (*Animal*) (2015), and a fiction writer.

DR MARK FAULKNER

Dr Mark Faulkner lived and worked in Africa for 17 years before returning to academia and gaining his PhD, which focused on the Boni hunter-gatherer community. He now lectures in Religions of Africa at SOAS (School of Oriental and African Studies), University of London.

DR JACOB F. FIELD

Dr Jacob F. Field is a historian, currently a research associate at the University of Cambridge. His academic work focuses on the Great Fire of London and British social and economic history. He has also written five books for a popular audience.

DR JOHN HAYWOOD

Dr John Haywood studied medieval history at the universities of Lancaster, Cambridge, and Copenhagen. He is the author of over 20 books including *Viking: the Norse Warrior's Unofficial Manual* (2013) and *Northmen: the Viking Saga 793-1241* (2015).

MICHAEL KERRIGAN

Michael Kerrigan contributed to the *Chambers Dictionary of Beliefs and Religion* (1993) and The Times World Religion (2002). His books include BBC *Ancient Civilizations: Greece* (2001) and *Ancient Rome* (2002); *The Ancients in their Own Words* (2009), and *Celtic Legends* (2016).

NEIL PHILIP

Neil Philip is the author of numerous books on folklore and mythology, including *Mythology of the World*; *The Great Mystery: Myths of Native America*; and Dorling Kindersley's Eyewitness Companion to Mythology.

DR NICHOLAUS PUMPHREY

Dr Nicholaus Pumphrey is the Assistant Professor of Religious Studies and Curator of the Quayle Bible Collection at Baker University in Baldwin City, Kansas. He specializes in Biblical Studies, Ancient Near Eastern History and Literature, and Islamic Studies. Currently, he is a senior staff member on the Tel Akko Total Archaeology project in Akko, Israel.

JULIETTE TOCINO-SMITH

Juliette Tocino-Smith is a postgraduate student at University College, London. During her undergraduate studies, she spent a semester in South Korea, where she became fascinated by the way in which fiction and mythology had come together in shaping contemporary Korean society.

CONTENTS

ANCIENT ROME

NORTHERN EUROPE

ANCIENT EGYPT AND AFRICA

OCEANIA

INTRODU

CTION

With rare exceptions – such as a recently discovered Amazonian tribe, the Pirahãs – every human culture has developed its own mythology to explain its origins and make sense of the phenomena observed in the natural world.

The word "mythology" comes from the Greek *muthos*, meaning "story" and *logia*, "knowledge". Myths tell of the creation of the world or predict its end; they explain how animals were made and the land formed; they bridge the world of humans and the world of the spirits or gods; they try to impose order on a terrifying chaos, and to confront the mysteries of death. Crucially, myths are also the foundation of religions: they define cultures and codify their values.

Ancient civilizations
The mythologies of the ancient world take up much of this book. In ancient Mesopotamia – in the crucible of civilization of the 4th millennium BCE, when humankind first learned to live in cities – the Sumerians developed the first recorded pantheon of deities. It was preserved in statues, carvings, and ancient texts – such as *The Epic of Gilgamesh*, in which the eponymous hero searches for

immortality. Such a quest was repeated in myths the world over. Subsequent Mesopotamian civilizations developed, demoted, or culled the Sumerian gods and the myths associated with them. The powerful goddess Inanna, for example, became Ishtar in the Babylonian pantheon and later the Phoenician goddess Astarte.

Like other civilizations, ancient Mesopotamia was shaped by the narratives it used to explain the cosmos. Its rulers were guided by the gods, whose capricious will was interpreted by priests. The gods had to be continually praised and placated. During the Akitu, a 12-day festival held in the great temple of Marduk, people chanted

Myth is the facts of the mind made manifest in a fiction of matter.
Maya Deren
Anthropologist

the *Enuma Elish*, the Babylonian myth of Creation, with the force of a magical incantation in their ritual re-energizing of the cosmos.

Great cultures
Myths had a great influence on the societal fabric of history's greatest civilizations. The rich and complex mythology of ancient Egypt emphasized the creation of order out of chaos. Such stories validated the governance of society and legitimized a status quo in which the pharaoh himself was viewed as divine and therefore worthy of being served. The Egyptians also saw time as cyclical; events that happened in their society were merely repeating what had happened before and had been recorded in their myths.

In ancient Greece and Rome, the foundation myths of city states were fundamental to the concepts of citizenship; they bound ideas of patriotism and common interest with divine authority. In Greece, which consisted of more than 1,000 city-states, each had a founding myth and a protective deity, which led to a highly complex set of myths that was often contradictory. It took the poets Homer and Hesiod to create a comprehensive, pan-Hellenic record of Greek mythology.

Homer's epic stories – the *Iliad* and *Odyssey* – and Hesiod's *Theogony* comprised the first and most authoritative attempts to weave the disparate Greek myths into one narrative thread.

In ancient Rome, the local myths of Italic peoples, such as the Latins and the Etruscans, blended with the Greek myths that had gone before them. The poet Virgil composed a foundation myth for Rome, the *Aeneid*, consciously modelled on the epics of Homer, while Ovid retold many Greek myths in his narrative poem *Metamorphoses*, and recorded the myths of a number of purely Roman deities in his poem on the religious year, *Fasti*. The Romans enriched the mix by adding deities from Phrygia (such as the Great Mother Cybele), Egypt (the goddess Isis), and Syria (Elagabal, or Sol Invictus, briefly the chief god of Rome).

Preserving myths

The line between literature, myth, and folktale is blurry; many myths have been preserved as literary works. The popular tales of King Arthur are rooted in Celtic myth; while the *Ramayana* and the *Mahabharata*, the great works of Hindu mythology, are celebrated masterpieces of epic poetry.

In preliterate societies, myths were recited and passed along orally. The written recording of a myth depended on luck, which probably led to the disappearance of a great many mythologies. Even in literate societies, such as the Viking-Age Norse, some myths survived through only a single source. Had the manuscripts of the mythological poems known as the *Edda* – and of Snorri Sturluson's later *Prose Edda* – been destroyed, we would know as little about Norse mythology as we do about the myths of the ancient Britons.

Living religions

Many tribal peoples – including the Dogon of Mali, the Baiga of central India, the Tikopia of the Solomon Islands, and the Ifugaos of the Philippines – still live in a world suffused by what outsiders might call myths. Oral tradition in these societies is remarkably enduring: as proven by the abundant myths or Dreamings of the Aboriginal Australians, the myths of the déma (creation spirits) among the Marind-Anim people of New Guinea, or the eloquent Chantways of the Navajo in North America. Many myths from these peoples, however, have not reached the outside world because they are secret, or they have not been collected or translated, or they have been lost as exposure to outsiders has attacked and destroyed indigenous cultures.

Mythology is the territory of poetic imagination, and the stories individual cultures tell are a profound expression of the creative impulse. Yet myths are more than simply stories; they are the stories cultures tell themselves about the great mysteries that perplex and intrigue us all: questions of birth and death and everything in between. Even now, myths remain the bearers of tradition and the spiritual and moral guide of peoples all across the globe. ∎

Myth ... takes all the things you know and restores to them the rich significance hidden by the veil of familiarity.
C. S. Lewis
Writer, scholar, and author of
The Chronicles of Narnia

ANCIENT

GREECE

In the Bronze Age collapse of Aegean and Mediterranean kingdoms, **Troy is destroyed** by war.

Hesiod's *Theogony* tracks the origins and **genealogies** of a wide array of Greek deities.

In *On Nature*, **Heraclitus** discourses on ethics, theology, and the universe.

Aeschylus stages the *Oresteia*, a trilogy that retells a **blood-soaked cycle** of myths.

c.1200 BCE   **c.700 BCE**   **c.500 BCE**   **c.458–430 BCE**

c.800 BCE   **c.600 BCE**   **432 BCE**   **c.450–400 BCE**

Homer's epic poems, the **Iliad and Odyssey**, are among the oldest surviving works in Western literature.

The *Homeric Hymns*, written anonymously, are **devoted to the praise** of 33 gods.

The Parthenon temple is dedicated to the goddess Athena, and marks the zenith of **Classical Greece**.

In **Oedipus Rex**, Sophocles contrasts fate and free will in a sinister tale of murder and incest.

The ancient Greeks first entered the territory now associated with them in about 2000 BCE, when Egypt was still a great power and the Minoans of Crete were evolving into a highly sophisticated society. The first migrants, who probably came from Russia and central Asia, settled in the mountainous north and the Peloponnese to the south, where the city of Mycenae was founded c.1600 BCE. Described by Homer as "rich in gold", the Mycenaean civilization prospered thanks to trade networks across the Aegean and Mediterranean seas.

With the Bronze Age collapse of palace culture and the end of Mycenaean civilization c.1100 BCE, Greece entered its Dark Age. By the 8th century BCE, *poleis* ("city-states") began to emerge as agricultural and trading hubs. Greece became a collection of separate city-states – such as Athens, Sparta, and Corinth – united by a shared language and the worship of common gods. However, Greek religion was not standardized; there was no book of doctrine to tell people how they should worship. Their mythology borrowed from their ancestors – the myth of the Minotaur came from the Minoans in Crete, and the Mycenaean era was the setting for the Trojan War, immortalized in Homer's *Iliad*.

Athenian dominance
The Classical era in Greece began with the fall of the powerful Persian empire in 479 BCE. Having defeated the Persians, the city-states of Athens and Sparta fought each other for dominion over Greece. As the pre-eminent power, Athens was the setting for many Greek myths, from its origins under the care of its patron goddess, Athena, to tales such as Jason and Medea.

Many of the surviving Greek myths come to us via Athenian dramatists: from the tragedies of Aeschylus, Sophocles, and Euripides in the 5th century BCE to the comedies of Aristophanes (c.446–c.386 BCE) and Menander (c.342–c.291 BCE). These works told stories about the gods and heroes of Greek mythology and inspired later writers such as Shakespeare (1564–1616), whose *A Midsummer Night's Dream* and *Romeo and Juliet* borrow from Greek myth.

The era of Athenian dominance ended in the 4th century BCE, when the Macedonian ruler Alexander

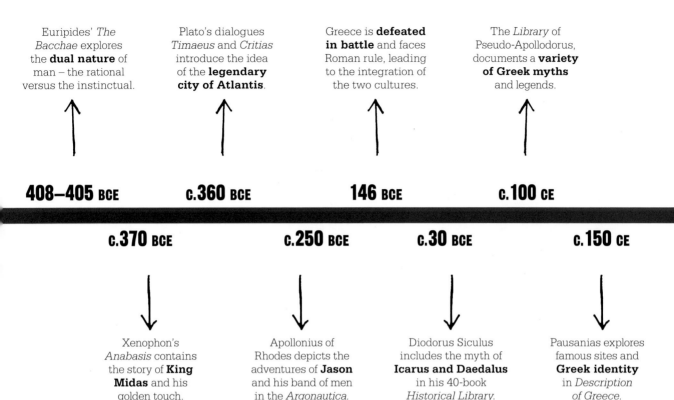

Euripides' *The Bacchae* explores the **dual nature** of man – the rational versus the instinctual.

Plato's dialogues *Timaeus* and *Critias* introduce the idea of the **legendary city of Atlantis**.

Greece is **defeated in battle** and faces Roman rule, leading to the integration of the two cultures.

The *Library* of Pseudo-Apollodorus, documents a **variety of Greek myths** and legends.

408–405 BCE **c.360** BCE **146** BCE **c.100** CE

c.370 BCE **c.250** BCE **c.30** BCE **c.150** CE

Xenophon's *Anabasis* contains the story of **King Midas** and his golden touch.

Apollonius of Rhodes depicts the adventures of **Jason** and his band of men in the *Argonautica*.

Diodorus Siculus includes the myth of **Icarus and Daedalus** in his 40-book *Historical Library*.

Pausanias explores famous sites and **Greek identity** in *Description of Greece*.

the Great built his empire. Thanks to Alexander's conquests, Greek culture and mythology were exported as far as Asia Minor, Egypt, Mesopotamia, and India.

The major deities

It was the poets Homer and Hesiod who imposed order upon the myriad gods and beliefs inherited from earlier times. Homer set down his poetry from oral tradition around 800 BCE, after the migrations that followed the collapse of the Mycenaean culture. His two epic poems, the *Iliad* and *Odyssey*, gave the Greeks a history, a pantheon, and guidelines for how to live their lives. As the Olympian family of 12 principal gods dwelling on Mount Olympus gradually replaced older beliefs, Homer and Hesiod gave them distinct characters and

appearances. Because Homer's epic poems were set in an aristocratic and feudal society – which preceded the birth of democracy in Athens in the 5th century BCE – his gods behaved like chieftains, motivated solely by their own desires.

Like other ancient agrarian peoples, the Greeks were local in their focus. They ordered their religious life around local places, identifying different hills, streams, and plains with different deities. This mythic lore invested every corner of the land with spiritual significance. The earth was the source of existence: divine power originated in its depths, as did the crops. Myths sought to explain aspects of agrarian life. The tale of Persephone – daughter of the harvest goddess Demeter – and her imprisonment in the Underworld by

Hades was a way of accounting for the changing cycles of the agricultural year.

The rise of the cult

At the end of the 5th century BCE, various mystery cults arose in the Greek-speaking world. Chief among these were the Eleusinian mysteries, an ancient agrarian cult honouring Demeter and Persephone and promising paradise for the dead. The Dionysian cult, which originated in Asia, worshipped Dionysus and involved wild dancing, drinking, and ecstasy. Unlike the public worship of the gods, which was well documented, these mystery cults consisted of secret rites and doctrines that remain enigmatic to this day, but would go on to influence the beliefs and myths of ancient Rome. ■

GAIA FIRST GAVE BIRTH TO HER EQUAL, OURANOS

ORIGIN OF THE UNIVERSE

IN BRIEF

THEME
Creation by Mother Earth

SOURCES
Theogony, Hesiod, c.700 BCE;
Argonautica, Apollonius of
Rhodes, c.250 BCE; *Natural
History*, Pliny the Elder, 79 CE;
Library, Pseudo-Apollodorus,
c.100 CE.

SETTING
Chaos – a vast and infinitely
dark void at the origin of the
universe.

KEY FIGURES
Gaia The primordial earth-
mother goddess, and
personification of the
solid world.

Ouranos The sky god, Gaia's
spontaneously conceived
son; later father of the Titans,
the Hecatoncheires, the
Kyklopes, the Erinyes,
Aphrodite, and many other
gods and goddesses.

Kronos A Titan who castrated
his father, Ouranos; also
associated with the harvest.

Out of the Chasm came
Night, and from Night in
turn came Day.
Theogony

In the beginning was Chaos,
an open chasm of emptiness –
infinitely deep, dark, and
silent. In his vision of the universe's
origin, set down in *Theogony*, the
Greek poet Hesiod saw creation as
the imposition of a positive reality
on this negativity and absence. Key
to that reality was the capacity for
change. The nothingness of Chaos
could have continued, eternally
unaltered, but existence, once
created, brought with it endless
cycles – the comings and goings
of the seasons, generations of
humans, birth, and death. These
cycles were set in motion by the
making of the original division
between night and day; time was
now measurable and meaningful.

Earth mother
The first Greek goddess, Gaia, was
the earth in its mineral form – its
rocks and soils, its mountains and
its plains. From its solid and
seemingly inert state, it became
vibrant with the potential for new
life. The first manifestation of that
new vitality was Ouranos, god of
the sky, spontaneously conceived
within the womb of the great Earth
Mother Gaia, with whom he would
subsequently father children.

Though Gaia's son, Ouranos was
her equal. Hesiod wrote that she
bore him specifically so that he
could "cover her". While this was a
statement of fact – the sky being
above the earth – it adds more than
a hint of sexuality to the relationship
between the earth and heaven. In
real life, the Greeks were as horrified
at the idea of incest as we are. Its
function in their mythology appears
to have been to show that all the
different aspects of existence are
intensely conflicted, yet intimately
linked. The sky was not simply
positioned above the earth; it
conjoined with it dynamically and,

Gaia, the Earth Mother, sits with
her two godly progeny at her side in
an ancient Greek stone relief. It was
said that an oath sworn by Gaia
would prove irrevocable.

ultimately, creatively, just as night
did with day, darkness with light,
and death with life.

Kinship and conflict
While creative, these conjunctions
inevitably cast opposing principles
into a never-ending struggle for
supremacy. Hesiod's portrayal
of primal sexual relations was
essentially violent; male and female
forces as complementary but also
competing. It was far from an
idealized world view, and the
depiction of Ouranos was even
more extreme; the despotic
patriarch would brook no rival –
not even his own children.

Ouranos's jealousy of his sons
and daughters was such that, at
each birth, he took them away and
stowed each one in some hidden
recess of the earth – which was
actually his wife's body. He did this
to establish his ownership of Gaia.

See also: The Olympian gods 24–31 ▪ The war of gods and Titans 32–33 ▪ The many affairs of Zeus 42–47 ▪ The fate of Oedipus 86–87

The sky god Ouranos is depicted as a benign father with offspring draped around him in a wood engraving after a fresco by the Prussian artist Karl Friedrich Schinkel (1781–1841).

Her sexual attentions had to be entirely and eternally available to him, so their offspring could not be allowed to see the light of day. Successive infants were consigned to subterranean depths.

First came the 12 Titans – the sisters Theia, Mnemosyne, Phoebe, Themis, Tethys, and Rhea, and their brothers Oceanus, Coeus, Crius, Hyperion, Iapetus, and Kronos. Each in his or her turn was rammed into some convenient crack or crevice of the earth and left there, trapped. After the Titans came three giant brothers, the Kyklopes, each of whom had a single eye at the centre of his forehead. Like their siblings, they were consigned at birth to be buried in the heart of the earth. Then came three more giants of even greater strength– the Hecatoncheires, whose name »

Hesiod and his *Theogony*

The ancient Greek poet Hesiod may well be a myth in his own right for there is no evidence that any such person actually existed. The works attributed to him – assorted poetry from the eighth and seventh centuries BCE – may simply have been conveniently bundled together. They include a miscellany of poems, from brief narratives to genealogies that record the heroic ancestries of important families.

The importance of these works in tracing back traditions and uncovering origins is undeniable. The genealogical poems discuss human beginnings, while the *Theogony*, Hesiod's most famous work, focuses on the birth of the gods and is the source for much of what we know about Greek myth. Hesiod was not the only available authority; other more mystic-minded thinkers and writers promoted an alternative "Orphic" tradition, built around the myth of Orpheus, the bard and musician. For the most part, however – and for well over 2,000 years now – it has been the version of mythical events attributed to Hesiod that has held sway.

means "hundred-handed" in Greek. Each was also said to have 50 heads, making them formidable – they too were incarcerated by Ouranos deep inside the earth.

The upstart son

As for Gaia, the Earth Mother felt both physically burdened by the number of infant bodies literally forced back inside her and also deeply upset by the attempted suppression of her children. Finally, she rebelled and appealed to her sons for help. She secretly made a sickle out of adamant – by legend an unbreakable mineral – and gave it to Kronos. The next time Ouranos spread himself over her, attempting to force her into intercourse, Kronos leapt out from his hiding-place to aid his mother. Wielding his sickle, and with one fell swoop, he sliced off his father's genitals.

It was the ultimate patriarchal nightmare – the father not just supplanted by his son but castrated by him, with the connivance of his wife. Even now, however, Ouranos's potency was not quite spent. The splashes of blood and semen that flew from his wound sowed spirit life wherever they landed, bringing into being a vast assortment of new-born nymphs and giants, good and bad. The Erinyes, three baleful sisters better known to us now as the Furies, were angry and avenging spirits. Aphrodite was a deity of a very different kind. Where Ouranos's wound-spatter landed in

> A white foam arose where the immortal skin touched water: amidst the waves, a beautiful maiden took form.
> ***Theogony***

the ocean, this most beautiful of goddesses was born. She stepped from the waves, bringing with her all the delights of erotic love.

Titans of all trades

When Kronos had finally freed his brothers and sisters from captivity in the earth, the Titans were to serve a twofold mythic function. First, they were living, breathing, loving, and fighting personalities. Each of them symbolized a different aspect of existence, so that collectively they represented a way of ordering and enriching the world. The eldest daughter Mnemosyne, for instance, stood for the faculty of memory and all it brought with it in terms of history, culture, and heritage. Later, having lain with her nephew Zeus, she would give birth to the nine Muses – divine patronesses of scientific study, historical study, poetry, and the performing arts.

Tethys, who married her brother Oceanus, went on to bear him 3,000 sons – all river gods – and as

Beautiful Aphrodite emerges from the ocean, where the seed of her brutal father had fallen. *The Birth of Venus* (her name in Roman mythology) was painted by Peter Paul Rubens (c.1637).

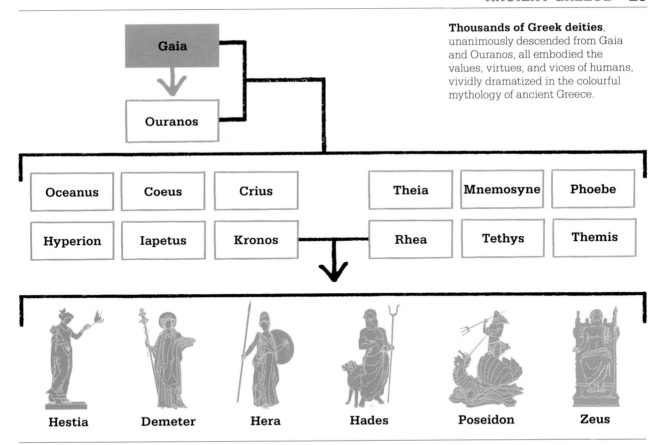

Gaia

Ouranos

Oceanus | Coeus | Crius | Theia | Mnemosyne | Phoebe

Hyperion | Iapetus | Kronos | Rhea | Tethys | Themis

Hestia | Demeter | Hera | Hades | Poseidon | Zeus

Thousands of Greek deities, unanimously descended from Gaia and Ouranos, all embodied the values, virtues, and vices of humans, vividly dramatized in the colourful mythology of ancient Greece.

many daughters, the Oceanids, who were nymphs of springs, rivers, lakes, and seas. Her younger sister Theia, too, took a brother, Hyperion, for her husband; she bore him Helios, the sun, and his sister Eos, goddess of dawn. Helios and Eos had a sister, Selene, who was a goddess of the moon, though her aunt Phoebe – sister to Tethys, Mnemosyne, and Theia – also had lunar associations.

Themis, the youngest female Titan, was associated with reason, justice, and with the orderly conduct of existence in the universe. Like her sister Mnemosyne, she would for a time become consort to her nephew Zeus. Of their children, the Horae ("Hours") would oversee the measurement and passage of the seasons and of time. Another daughter, Nemesis, took her mother's association with justice to violent extremes; as her name suggests, she became notorious as the personification of punishment and divine retribution.

The name of the youngest male Titan, Iapetus, comes from *iapto*, a Greek word meaning "wound" or "pierce". The implications of this translation have long been debated. Ancient poets seem to have been unsure whether he was given this name because he sustained an injury or because he made the weapon that inflicted it. Meanwhile, in classical literature, Iapetus appears both as a deity of mortality and of skill in crafts.

Patricidal patriarch

Artists in ancient Greece almost invariably represented Kronos carrying a sickle – an emblem of his attack upon his father. The sickle also has more mundane and practical associations. Kronos came to be seen as the godly guarantor of a successful harvest. The connection between these two functions – the idea that one generation had effectively to be destroyed for its successor to survive and thrive, took an early hold on the Greek consciousness.

Kronos, having killed his father, now replaced him as the head of the household: he then married his sister Rhea and began to produce children of his own. Much like his father, Kronos would soon confront the idea that human life can only advance through intergenerational struggle. This theme runs through the Greek mythological tradition, and is most notoriously associated with the story of King Oedipus. ■

RHEA SWADDLED UP A STONE AND PASSED IT TO KRONOS TO SWALLOW

THE OLYMPIAN GODS

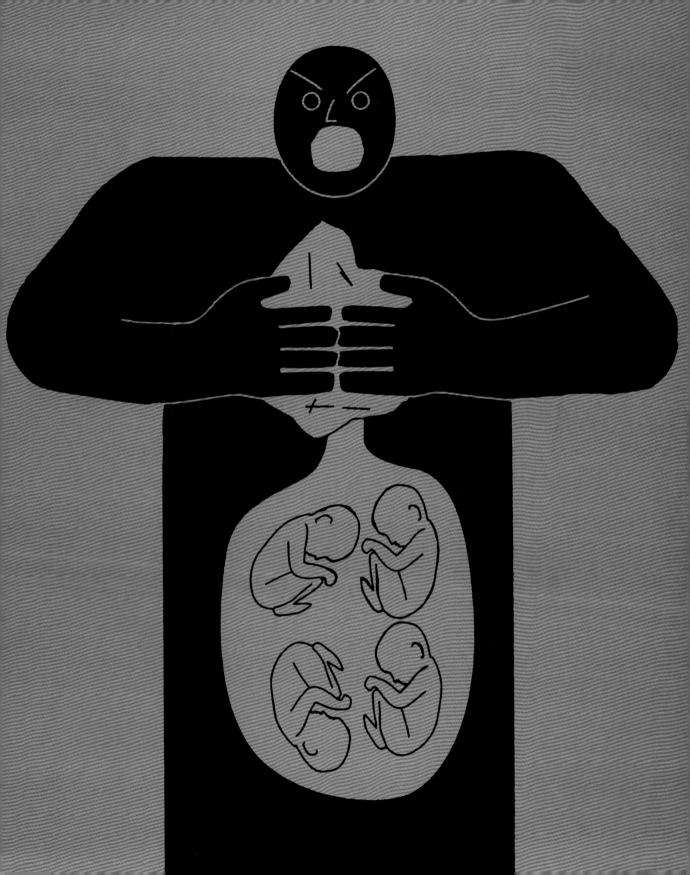

IN BRIEF

THEME
Origin of the Olympian gods

SOURCES
Theogony, Hesiod, c.700 BCE; *Library*, Pseudo-Apollodorus, c.100 CE.

SETTING
Crete.

KEY FIGURES
Kronos King of the Titans; son of Gaia and Ouranos.

Rhea Sister and wife of Kronos.

Hestia Goddess of the hearth.

Demeter Goddess of the harvest.

Hera Queen of the Olympian gods.

Hades Lord of the Underworld.

Poseidon God of the seas.

Zeus King of the Olympian gods; killer of Kronos.

Both Earth and Sky foretold him that he would be dethroned by his own son.
Library

Kronos, Titan son of the earth goddess Gaia and the sky god Ouranos, proved every bit as possessive a patriarch as his father had been. After just one generation, a dismal pattern of godly conduct was emerging; just as Ouranos had dominated Gaia, Kronos required his wife and sister Rhea to be exclusively and endlessly available to him in order to meet his sexual needs. No one else, least of all his children, would be allowed to compete for her attention. Having deposed his own father to become king of the Titans, Kronos knew how dangerous it was to let a child grow in envy and rage.

Determined that no one should pose such a threat to him, Kronos ensured that the children Rhea bore him were destroyed just as quickly as they were conceived.

As soon as she gave birth to a new baby, he would swallow it whole. Hestia, the first child that Rhea bore, was gone in a single gulp, before her mother could even cradle her in her arms. Another daughter, Demeter, soon followed: she too was swallowed promptly. Hera, the third daughter, went the same way, and Kronos's sons fared no better. First came Hades – bolted down

Kronos, known as Saturn by the Romans, as depicted in *Saturn Devouring His Son*, Francisco Goya, (1821–23). The work is part of the artist's "Black Paintings" series.

before he could utter his first helpless cry – swiftly followed by the next son, Poseidon, who met the same fate.

The despairing Rhea finally turned to her mother, the elderly Gaia, and her neutered father

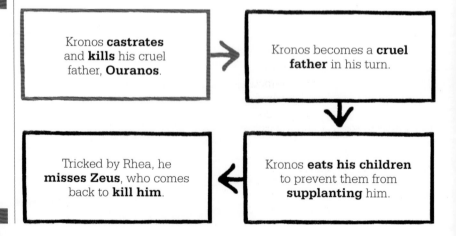

Kronos **castrates** and **kills** his cruel father, **Ouranos**.

Kronos becomes a **cruel father** in his turn.

Kronos **eats his children** to prevent them from **supplanting** him.

Tricked by Rhea, he **misses Zeus**, who comes back to **kill him**.

See also: Origin of the universe 18–23 ▪ The war of the gods and Titans 32–33 ▪ Mount Olympus 34–35 ▪ The founding of Athens 56–57 ▪ The sybil of Cumae 110–11

Ouranos, for help. Together they hatched a devious plan to save their daughter's next child.

Switched with a stone

Rhea followed her parents' advice. As soon as she had given birth to Zeus, the last of her sons, and before his father Kronos had a chance to see him, she hid the baby away. Then she wrapped a stone in swaddling clothes and handed it to her unsuspecting husband in place of the infant.

Kronos, in his rapacious greed, did not even look at the bundle before he tipped back his head, opened his mouth wide, and dropped it in. The "baby" tumbled straight down into his stomach, ready to join the jostling crowd of children already there. Unknown to Kronos, they had all survived in the deep darkness of his belly. There they grew in size and resentment.

Brought up in safety

Meanwhile, Rhea, on the recommendation of the child's grandmother, Gaia, spirited the infant Zeus away, carrying him across the sea to the fertile island of Crete. There, in a concealed cave on the thickly wooded slopes of Mount Ida (now known as Psiloritis, the highest mountain on Crete), Rhea left her son in the care of a warlike tribe called the Kouretes. They, in turn, gave the baby to a nymph named Adamanthea (Amalthea in some sources), who nursed Zeus in secret. According to Hesiod, the nymph

Zeus is protected from all-seeing Kronos by his attentive nymph carers and the noise of the Kouretes, as shown in this 17th-century painting *The Childhood of Zeus on Mount Ida.*

was frightened that Kronos – thanks to his universal authority over the earth, sea, and sky – would be able to see where his son was being hidden. To prevent Kronos from finding him, she hung Zeus from a rope that dangled between the earth and the heavens but was in neither one realm nor the other.

Adamanthea cared for Zeus and nursed him with milk from a herd of goats that grazed nearby. Whenever the baby gurgled,

squealed, or cried, the Kouretes danced and chanted to disguise the sound. As a result, Kronos was completely unaware that his youngest son was still alive.

Zeus seeks his father

In no time at all, it seemed, Zeus grew to manhood. He was hungry for revenge against his cruel father. Yet, if Zeus was ever to emerge from hiding, some sort of showdown between them would »

be inevitable. Kronos could not afford to let a potential usurper live. If he became aware of Zeus's existence, he would view his son only as a threat to his power.

Kronos's fear of being usurped was fully justified. When he finally met his son, whom he believed to be dead, he was forced to yield to Zeus in the most brutal way: Zeus simply turned up one day and, with the help of his grandmother, Gaia, ambushed his father. He kicked Kronos violently in the stomach and forced his father to vomit up the contents of his stomach. First to emerge was the stone Kronos had swallowed, believing it to be the infant Zeus. The young god took this stone and set it upright in the earth as a monument to Kronos's cruelty, and a symbol of his triumph over the wicked god.

Zeus placed the stone at the *omphalos* or "navel" of the Greek ancient world – at Delphi, in the very centre of Greece. In future ages, the stone would become a shrine, renowned for its oracle. Pilgrims would visit it to seek the guidance of the priestess, or Sibyl, regarding their personal problems, and the Sibyl would

> First he vomited up the stone, which he had swallowed last. Zeus set it up to be a sign … a wonder to mortal men.
> ***Theogony***

provide them messages of wisdom, which were said to come directly from the gods.

Great deities disgorged

After vomiting up the stone, Kronos began to disgorge his offspring. One by one, Zeus's elder brothers and sisters came out of their father's mouth – no longer babies, now, but fully grown. Once reborn, they became the Olympian gods and were revered for their powers.

Soon after their rebirth, the sons and daughters of Kronos went to war with the mighty Titans for control of the cosmos. After their

victory, the gods set up their seat of power on Mount Olympus and drew lots to decide who would take which role in ruling the universe. The three sons of Kronos divided the cosmos up between them; one would take control of the sky, another would have the sea, and the third would preside over the Underworld. Zeus, whose weapon of choice was the thunderbolt, became ruler of the sky and leader of all the Olympian gods.

Hades, the first son to be born, and the last to be regurgitated, became lord of the Underworld. His name came to stand for both the deity and his unseen realm, where souls go after death. Hades was not happy to have been allocated this dismal domain, but there was nothing he could do about it. Meanwhile, Poseidon, who had been the tiniest baby, became the almighty "Earth-Shaker", the god of the sea in all its awesome power.

Disparate goddesses

The three female children of Kronos also had important roles to play. Hestia, goddess of the hearth, ruled over people's domestic life. As

---

Hestia

Kronos and Rhea's eldest child, Hestia ("hearth"), was the first to be swallowed by her father – and the last to reappear when Zeus forced him to vomit up his offspring. Given that she was both the oldest and youngest of the children, she was widely referred to as "Hestia, First and Last". Like the later Roman god Janus, Hestia was seen as the embodiment of all of life's ambiguities and ambivalences. Like Janus, too, she quickly came to be associated with the

home, with domesticity and all its blessings. In particular, her realm was that of the hearth – the fire that was a household's warm and hospitable centre. The hearth was also the site of the altar where sacrifices were offered to any domestic gods; she presided over these rituals, too.

Though herself a sworn virgin, having refused all proposals of marriage, Hestia was considered the protector of the family. The metaphorical family of the state was also part of her realm, and she would look after the public altar or hearth within a city.

Zeus and Hera become man and wife in a scene from a decorative, marble-and-limestone frieze that was part of a temple in Selinunte, Sicily, dating from the 5th century BCE.

goddess of the harvest, Demeter was a life-giver to the worshippers who relied on her annual bounty. She proved a fickle protectress, however, ready not just to cross swords with her siblings but to withhold favours from humankind at any perceived slight.

Hera's role was more prominent than that of her sisters, and she became the foremost female deity following her marriage to her brother Zeus. To her great dismay, however, Hera never quite received the recognition and honours she expected as the queen of the gods. As the goddess of women and marriage, Hera was supposed to represent the archetypal wedded state, but she became known for her marital troubles.

Nor was Hera the goddess who inspired men's passions. While Hera was portrayed as a wifely figure, Aphrodite was the goddess

Aphrodite had an illicit affair with another Olympian – Ares, the god of war. They were caught in bed by her husband, Hephaistos, the blacksmith god, who threw a net over the pair.

associated with feminine beauty, sexuality, and erotic pleasures. The Greeks had these two different deities for what, in ancient times, were considered two separate spheres of affection. One deity represented marital love, the other romantic and erotic love. While this distinction may now be alien to many people, in most cultures and at most times in history, the majority of marriages were arranged – as transactions for the management and transmission of property and land. The idea of "companionate" marriage – in which the love between a husband and wife is the driving factor – is a relatively modern convention.

The *Dodekatheon*

Aphrodite was the only member of this first generation of Olympians who was not a child of Kronos and Rhea; some accounts suggest she was the daughter of Zeus, but Hesiod, Pausanius, and Ovid all described her as Kronos's sister who was born from sea foam after the castration of Ouranos. Despite being the same generation as Kronos and Rhea, she was always considered an Olympian, rather than a Titan, and one of the gods and goddesses who eventually made up the *Dodekatheon* – the 12 most important Olympians in the Greek pantheon. The *Dodekatheon* included Zeus, Demeter, Hera, Poseidon, and Aphrodite from the first generation of Olympians. The hearth goddess Hestia was not among them, as she later chose to live on earth to avoid her siblings' squabbles; Hades, similarly, was not included because he resided permanently in the Underworld.

After the war between the gods and the Titans established the Olympians as rulers of the cosmos, the first generation of gods went on to have many children. Many of the gods and other figures in Greek mythology were children of Zeus. »

Of the second generation of gods, several joined the *Dodekatheon*, and were powerful deities in their own right. The gods Apollo, Ares, Hestia, Hephaistos, and Hermes all joined the ranks of Zeus and his siblings on Mount Olympus, as did the goddesses Artemis and Athena. The *Dodekatheon* met as a council to discuss matters in their ruling of the cosmos, and Dionysus, god of wine, attained his seat at the table only after Hestia left Olympus to reside on Earth.

Human personalities

The Olympian gods were all too human in their personalities, and often lacked the lofty transcendence of the supreme beings in later religions. In a dramatic soap opera of fierce rivalries and petty spats, their actions were influenced not by a desire to work for the good of humankind, but by their own selfish desires and whims. The Greeks therefore did not worship the gods by attempting to emulate them, instead treating them as they might a powerful human ruler, by offering sacrifices and celebrating the deities at regular festivals.

At its core, this was a system of exchange: people offered gifts to the gods in the hope that the gods would give them what they asked for. The gods often rewarded mortals who treated them well and showed them the appropriate deference and respect.

Zeus and his siblings could be needlessly cruel and were often subject to jealousies and petty fights. His brothers Poseidon and Hades often used humans as pawns in these squabbles, which usually stemmed from a reluctance to accept the supreme god's authority as unquestionable.

Still more reluctant was his sister Demeter, a strong-willed deity in her own right. After she was pursued and raped by Poseidon, and Hades abducted her daughter Persephone, Demeter wreaked havoc across the world.

Marble sculptures from the Parthenon temple on the Acropolis in Athens show the gods – from left to right: Dionysus, Demeter, Persephone, and Artemis – reacting to the birth of Athena.

Demeter was wroth
with the gods and
quitted heaven.
Library

Infidelity, too, was a major theme in all Greek myths – not just in the affairs (and assaults) committed by Zeus that riled the jealous Hera.

Twixt god and mortals

Despite their power, in many ways Greek deities appear to have an intermediate status, hovering somewhere between the spiritual and the real. Their attributes reflect the countless aspects of Greek everyday life in which the gods played an implicit part. All the gods had specific areas of influence, such as Zeus and Athena, who were among the *theoi agoraioi* (gods of the *agora* – the marketplace and people's assembly). Both Zeus and the goddess Hestia were also gods of the home (*theoi ktesioi*). Hestia, Dionysius, and Aphrodite were among the *theoi daitioi*, who presided over feasts and banquets.

The gods themselves also needed sustenance. According to Greek tradition, they lived on a diet of nectar and ambrosia, carried up Mount Olympus by doves. To later belief systems, the notion that deities needed material sustenance seems at odds with their divinity. Ancient Greek authorities, however, agreed on the importance of this nourishment for the gods to empower and sustain them. ∎

The 12 Olympians	
Description	**Symbols of the gods**
Aphrodite, the goddess of love and beauty, was often shown with a sceptre, myrtle, and dove.	Sceptre Myrtle Dove
Apollo was an archer, but also played the lyre, while the laurel symbolized his love for Daphne.	Bow Lyre Laurel
Ares was the bloodthirsty god of war. His love of arms was usually represented by a spear.	Spear
Artemis, the hunting goddess and Apollo's twin, was shown with a bow and her sacred deer.	Bow Deer
Athena, goddess of wisdom, bore the Aegis shield; her bird was the owl, her tree the olive.	Aegis Owl Olive
Demeter, the sceptre-wielding harvest goddess, carried a torch in a bid to find her daughter.	Sceptre Torch Grain
Dionysus, god of wine, was crowned with ivy and bore a *thyrsos* – a symbol of pleasure.	Grapevine Ivy Thyrsos
Hephaistos was the god of smiths, craftsmen, and fire. His axe was never far from his side.	Axe
Hera, Zeus's queen, carried a sceptre and wore a regal crown. Her bird was the peacock.	Sceptre Diadem Peacock
Hermes, the gods' messenger, wore winged boots and carried a *caduceus*, a magical staff.	Caduceus Winged boots
Poseidon, the sea god, wielded a trident to shake the earth. Bulls and horses were sacred to him.	Trident Bull Horse
Zeus, the supreme god, tossed thunderbolts at foes. The eagle was his bird, the oak his tree.	Thunderbolt Eagle Oak

ZEUS IN HIS FIRST YOUTH BATTERED THE EARTHBORN TITANS

THE WAR OF THE GODS AND TITANS

IN BRIEF

THEME
Olympians take power

SOURCES
Iliad, Homer, 8th century BCE;
Theogony, Hesiod, c.700 BCE;
Library, Pseudo-Apollodorus,
c.100 CE.

SETTING
The slopes of Mount Olympus
and plains of Thessaly,
northern Greece.

KEY FIGURES
Olympians The gods Zeus,
Poseidon, Hades, Hera,
Demeter, and Hestia.

Titans Oceanus, Hyperion,
Coeus, Tethys, Phoebe, Rhea,
Mnemosyne, Themis, Theia
Crius, Kronos, and Iapetus.

Kyklopes The one-eyed
giants Brontes, Steropes,
and Arges; sons of Ouranos.

Hecatoncheires The giants
Briareos, Kottos, and Gyges;
sons of Ouranos and Gaia.

Zeus slipped easily into a position of authority over his brothers and sisters: though the youngest, he had been in the world by far the longest. His siblings supported him as he strove to overthrow his father and assert his primacy across the cosmos. So began the Titanomachy – the War of the Gods and Titans.

Zeus, with the support of his siblings, launched a concerted and determined attack against the Titan gods. The siblings were joined by some of Ouranos's cast-out sons. The three Kyklopes – the one-eyed giants Brontes, Steropes, and Arges – sided with Zeus after he freed them from the Underworld. They were skilled craftstmen who made weapons for the gods: a mighty thunderbolt for Zeus, a cloak of invisibility for Hades, and a trident for Poseidon. The Hecatoncheires – Briareos, Kottos, and Gyges – also fought for the gods. Each of these terrifying giants had 50 heads and 100 hands, and howled as they rampaged across the battlefield.

Total war

The war was fought on the lower slopes of Mount Olympus and across the open plains of Thessaly, but the earth-shattering conflict encompassed the entire world. Huge rocks were hurled around;

Zeus, leader of the gods, stands beside an eagle in this 4th-century statue. The eagle, Zeus's messenger, remained a symbol of power from ancient Rome to Nazi Germany.

See also: The Olympian gods 24–31 ■ War of the gods 140–41 ■ A complex god 164 ■ The game of dice 202–03

entire mountaintops were ripped up and sent flying back and forth as projectiles; bolts of lightning flashed like javelins across the sky. Flames rose up to the farthest heights of heaven; the thud of marching feet caused quakes in the most remote reaches of the Underworld; swirling dust clouds darkened the sky, and the din of conflict was deafening.

According to Hesiod, the intensity of the fighting "pained the soul". The advantage tipped back and forth without any real interval for a full ten years. Neither side would yield, so finally Zeus rallied his cohorts. He refreshed the Hecatoncheires with nectar and ambrosia – the divine and exclusive sustenance of the gods, which conferred immortality on any mortal who consumed it. This may not have been the effect it had on the Hecatoncheires, but according

The Fall of the Titans by Giulio Romano (1532–35). Depicting the war of the Titans, this continuous fresco covers the walls and ceiling of the *Sala dei Giganti* in the Palazzo Te, Italy.

to Hesiod, "the heroic spirits grew in all their hearts" after Zeus gave it to the giants.

Ultimate triumph

Reinvigorated, the Hecatoncheires proved the tipping point. With such formidable allies and weapons, the gods were at last able to defeat the Titans. They banished them to Tartarus, the lowest pit of the Underworld, where the Titans were imprisoned for all eternity under the watch of the Hecatoncheires. Zeus and his siblings now had full control over the cosmos. They set up their imperial seat on the top of Mount Olympus, from where they ruled the universe. ■

Warfare in ancient Greece

After the rise of the city states of Athens, Sparta, and beyond, warfare became a way of life for the people of ancient Greece. The states fought each other for territory, trade, and power in highly ritualized wars – both sides would consult with oracles and sing hymns to the gods before meeting for set-piece battles. Scholars use the term "limited warfare" to describe the ancient Greek model, in which cities were destroyed but the victors were honourable, fighting within a set of rules of conduct.

Some city states, such as Sparta, became very militaristic. This perhaps explains the recurrence of the idea of a war in heaven. Such stories dramatized real-life shifts in theological and spiritual thinking in ancient societies: for example, the Titanomachy could explain the shift from an earth-cult, centred around deities who lived in the Underworld, to the more sky-based theology found in ancient Greece.

Zeus's bolts flew thick and fast from his mighty hands, with flash and thunder and flame.
Theogony

NO WIND BEATS ROUGHLY HERE, NO SNOW NOR RAIN

MOUNT OLYMPUS

IN BRIEF

THEME
Home of the gods

SOURCES
Theogony, Hesiod, c.700 BCE;
Illiad and *Odyssey*, Homer,
c.800 BCE; *Description of
Greece*, Pausanias, c.150 CE.

SETTING
Mount Olympus,
northeastern Greece.

KEY FIGURES
Zeus King of the Greek gods.

Hera Wife and sister of Zeus;
queen of the gods.

Hephaistos The blacksmith
god; son of Hera.

The Muses Children of Zeus.

The Horai Three sisters;
goddesses of time and
the seasons.

The Moirae Three sisters;
goddesses of fate.

Originally, the dwellings of ancient Greek deities were not in the heavens but in the heart of the earth. Once Zeus and his siblings defeated the Titans, however, the Greeks turned their eyes heavenward to worship the new generation of gods and goddesses. Hephaistos, god of fire and the forge, built them palaces in the sheltered ravines of Mount Olympus. Hesiod described the mountain as "many-folded", a phrase suggestive of a sky-high stronghold full of secrets.

The palaces were built of stone on bronze foundations. They were both gigantic and luxurious, their floors inlaid with gold and precious stones. Zeus set up his throne at the top of the peak of Stefani. From here he hurled his thunderbolts at those who displeased him in the world below.

Life on Olympus

The council of the gods typically met in Zeus's golden courtyard to discuss their rule of the cosmos, and gathered in Zeus's hall to while away the evenings with feasting. Apollo sang to them, accompanying himself upon his lyre. Sometimes the Muses came up from their home at the foot of Olympus to sing, dance, and tell stories.

Mount Olympus, home of the Greek gods, rises from the Plain of Thessaly. Thessaly was the site of the decade-long war fought between the Titans, and Zeus and his siblings.

See also: The Olympian gods 24–31 ▪ The war of the gods and Titans 32–33 ▪ Cupid and Psyche 112–13 ▪ Pangu and the creation of the world 214–15 ▪ The legendary foundation of Korea 228–29

> The gods pressed far-seeing Zeus of Olympus to reign over them.
> *Theogony*

The council of the gods meets amongst the clouds on Olympus in this fresco by Italian Renaissance master Raphael (1518), which shows Zeus conferring immortality on Psyche.

There were separate stables for the creatures that drew the gods' chariots – most famously, those that pulled the blazing car of Apollo, the sun god. Zeus had a chariot drawn by the four Anemoi, gods of the winds – Boreas (north), Euros (east), Notos (south), and Zephyros (west). Poseidon's chariot was pulled along by fishtailed horses of the sea, while Aphrodite's was drawn by a team of doves.

The Horai – the sisters Eirene, Eunomia, and Dike – guarded the gates to Olympus and saw to the orderly passage of time and the seasons. Another trio of goddesses, the Moirae (Fates), sat at the foot of Zeus's throne and watched over the lives of mortals.

Physical and symbolic

What we refer to today as "Mount" Olympus is actually a massif, with over 50 distinct peaks almost 3,000m (9,850ft) above sea level.

Much of the time, its upper slopes are wreathed in snow or dense cloud, cutting off the summit from the view of mortals down below. It is no wonder that the ancient Greeks held this to be the royal seat of their reigning dynasty of gods.

The idea of the sacred mountain existed long before the Greeks began to worship the Olympians, and is found in many other cultures. Mount Meru, for example, towered at the cosmological centre of Indian religions; Mount Fuji dominated the Japanese religious scheme; and Inca priests in Peru offered sacrifice high up on the Andean summits.

In mythology, the mountain peak has often seemed to occupy a separate physical space from the earth. Homer underlined this by showing Mount Olympus from different perspectives. Viewed from earth, it was described as "snow-topped" or "cloud-enveloped"; for the gods, however, their home was a place of permanent sunshine and clear blue sky. ∎

Changing gods

Anthropologists use the term "syncretism" to describe the merging of strands from different religious systems. Ancient Greece had many examples of this. The sanctuary of Dodona, in northwestern Greece, lay in a valley surrounded by a grove of oak trees. The site seems to have been sacred to a matriarchal earth goddess since at least the second millennium BCE – before the idea of Zeus took root. After the ascendancy of the Olympians, the earth goddess was supplanted and one of Zeus's many wives, Dione, was worshipped at Dodona.

Isthmia – on the narrow land connecting the Peloponnese peninsula with the rest of Greece – was the obvious site for a shrine to Poseidon, god of the sea, beset on the narrow strip of land by roaring waves on either side. Yet archaeologists have found remains at Isthmia dating back long before the era of the Olympians, dedicated to a deity or deities unknown.

HE BOUND CUNNING PROMETHEUS IN INESCAPABLE FETTERS

PROMETHEUS HELPS MANKIND

IN BRIEF

THEME
Origin of humanity

SOURCES
Theogony and *Works and Days*, Hesiod, c.700 BCE; *Library*, Apollodorus, c.100 CE

SETTING
Greece, the Aegean, and the Caucasus Mountains, Western Asia.

KEY FIGURES
Zeus King of the gods.

Iapetus The youngest Titan, son of Ouranos and Gaia.

Klymene A sea nymph, daughter of the Titan Oceanus.

Prometheus Son of Iapetus and Klymene.

Deukalion Human son of Prometheus.

Pyrrha Wife of Deukalion.

Hephaistos The blacksmith god.

Zeus's victory in the war with the Titans had been hard won but decisive. He and his brothers held unchallenged sway over the heavens, earth, and sea. The usurper of a usurper, he had seized supremacy by dethroning Kronos, who had himself toppled the tyrant Ouranos. No ruler could afford to become complacent, however seemingly unassailable their position – and a challenge to the authority of Zeus was fast approaching.

Spirit of rebellion
Prometheus, a young Titan and therefore a survivor of the old regime, was the son of Iapetus and

See also: Origin of the universe 18–23 ▪ The war of the gods and Titans 32–33 ▪ Pandora's box 40–41 ▪ The many affairs of Zeus 42–47

Klymene, celebrated for quick intelligence, dexterity, and skill. Prometheus's very name meant "Thinking Ahead": he was an inventor and a strategist. Different sources disagree on the precise part Prometheus played in the continuing struggle between

Prometheus Carrying Fire, by Flemish painter Jan Cossiers (1671), shows the young Titan stealing the precious resource for mankind.

Zeus and his subjects. Despite this, all sources regard him as a central part of the conflict.

Self-confident in his cleverness, Prometheus was independent-minded, irreverent, and defiant. His contempt for Zeus's authority was all too clear. Worse still, he appeared to pass on this rebellious spirit to Zeus's human subjects.

From clay to stone

According to Apollodorus's *Library*, Prometheus was the creator of humanity, shaping the first man and woman from moist clay. This first race of humans walked the earth for only a single generation before being swept away by an angry Zeus in a worldwide flood. Prometheus's human son Deukalion and his wife Pyrrha were the only survivors. Typically, Prometheus had out-manoeuvred Zeus, prompting his son and his

> Prometheus shaped men out of water and clay.
> *Library*

daughter-in-law to save themselves by building a floating wooden chest in which to ride out the deluge.

Deukalion survived the great flood and its aftermath by showing more tact than his father. He thanked Zeus for letting him and Pyrrha live, built an altar, and offered sacrifice. Zeus was so pleased to see this submissive spirit that he not only allowed Deukalion and Pyrrha to go on living but told Deukalion how he could re-create humanity. He and his wife were told to »

Klymene's children

According to Hesiod's *Theogony*, "Iapetus took Klymene, Oceanus's elegant-ankled daughter to his bed". Other ancient authors, however, referred to her as "Asia". With Iapetus, Klymene bore four sons, each of whom was, ultimately, fated for misery.

During the war of the Titans, Zeus killed Klymene's prideful son Menoetius, by hurling him into the underworld with a lightning-bolt. Following the victory of the Olympian gods,

another of Klymene's sons, Atlas, was made to suffer for his role in leading the Titan forces. He was sentenced by Zeus to carry the heavens on his shoulders as punishment for resisting the Olympian ascendancy.

Epimetheus, Klymene's third son, was every bit as foolish as Prometheus was cunning. Against his brother's advice, he was duped into accepting Pandora as a gift and marrying her. He had no idea that she had been created to be both beautiful and deceitful, and was sent by Zeus to bring all manner of sorrows into the world.

Atlas carries the heavens on his shoulders. Although commonly mistaken for an earth globe, the round structure weighing on Atlas represents the celestial sphere.

Mortal men and women sprung up fully formed from the stones thrown by Deukalion and Pyrrha, as shown in Peter Paul Rubens's 1636 painting, and repopulated the earth.

pick up stones and throw them backwards over their heads. They did so and wherever Deukalion's stones landed, the bodies of living men immediately took form; where Pyrrha's came to rest, women sprang up out of the ground.

A trick backfires

Unlike Appolodorus, Hesiod's genealogy incorporated mortal humans almost from the beginning, though he said little about their origins. They were mentioned as existing during the reign of Kronos, but only incidentally, emerging into the foreground only in the age of the Olympian gods.

When Zeus summoned humans for a meeting on the sort of sacrifices they would have to offer him, Prometheus intervened on their behalf. Wrapping some choice beef inside an ugly oxhide, and a bundle of bones inside some of the most delicious meat, he offered Zeus the choice of which sacrifices should be made to him thenceforth. Zeus appeared to have fallen for the trick, asking for the outwardly appealing bag of bones – though Hesiod hints the king of the gods may have chosen this deliberately, to have an excuse for hating humans.

Either way, Zeus was enraged. Far from easing people's plight as he had intended, Prometheus's cunning made them victims of Zeus's rage. The angry god hid the secret of fire from his human subjects. This not only deprived them of warmth and comfort but also hindered human progress.

Out in the cold

Without fire or the technologies it makes possible, mortals existed in a miserable state of subsistence. They foraged for food in darkness, damp, and cold, with only animal skins for clothes, surviving on raw roots, berries, and fruits (when they were in season) and uncooked carrion. They used twigs as

The stones which Deucalion threw became men; the stones which Pyrrha threw became women.
Library

The Five Ages

Kronos's reign may have been unpleasant for the Titan's children but was, says Hesiod, a "Golden Age" for mortal humans. Sickness, war, and discord were unknown; men and women lived for centuries, trees and fields yielded their produce freely through an endless Spring. The rise of Zeus saw an immediate decline in human fortunes. The men and women of this "Silver Age" lived only a hundred years, most of it spent in an extended childhood; when they finally grew up, they were foolish and quarrelsome. An "Age of Bronze" came next: its men were warriors, who spent their short lives squabbling and fighting. The "Heroic Age" which followed was an improvement on the Bronze Age in the sense that its perennial wars took on a noble and epic character. This was the age of Homer's Trojan War, and very different from Hesiod's "Iron Age" in which he himself lived – and in which we all live now – in fearfulness, scarcity, misery, and toil.

rudimentary tools and old bones for weaponry, in what could scarcely be qualified even as a "primitive" existence. As they fought a daily battle to stave off starvation, any possibility of shaping their wider destiny was unthinkable.

Stolen fire

Prometheus came to humanity's rescue. He took some glowing embers from a blaze built by the gods high up on Mount Olympus and, secreting this fire inside a hollow fennel-stalk, he carried it down to the little encampments where mortal men and women shivered on the plains below. Soon, "visible from afar", fires twinkled across the length and breadth of the peopled world. In that moment, human life was instantly and permanently transformed.

Heat, warmth, light, and safety from predatory beasts was just the start. In no time at all, mankind began to thrive – smelting metal, fashioning the finest jewellery and the strongest tools, blacksmithing all kinds of weapons, from hoes

and hammers to spears and swords. Each new innovation opened the way to others – suddenly, humanity was progressing at a breakneck pace.

Harsh punishment

Zeus was enraged by Prometheus's theft of fire. Not only had he been defied in the most public way, but his power over humanity had been significantly weakened. Zeus decided that Prometheus deserved an eternal and painful punishment. He had the thief seized by his henchmen Bia ("Violence") and Kratos ("Power") and carried to a high mountain peak. Here, with the help of Hephaistos, the blacksmith god, they chained Prometheus to a rock. An eagle flew down, tore at his abdomen, then pulled out the living, pulsing liver, and gorged on it. Despite the agony of this torture, it was no more than a beginning for the rebellious Titan. Each night his internal organs and his skin grew back, ready to be attacked afresh by the eagle the next day.

For centuries, Prometheus was tied to the rock. He was finally rescued from his torments by Herakles, who found him while hunting for the elusive apples of the Hesperides. Prometheus would only give Herakles the apples' location after he killed the eagle and set Prometheus free. Prometheus was not the only one punished for stealing fire from the gods. Zeus also inflicted his rage upon humankind, instructing Hephaistos to create the woman Pandora to punish the humans by bringing them hardship, war, and death. ■

Prometheus was punished by the gods for giving humans fire. He was chained to Mount Caucasus to endure constant torture, as depicted by Jacob Jordaens (1640).

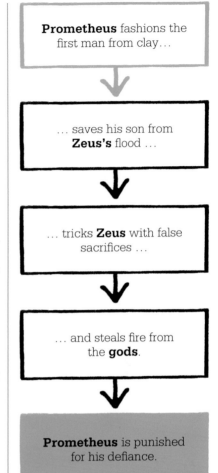

Prometheus fashions the first man from clay…

… saves his son from **Zeus's** flood …

… tricks **Zeus** with false sacrifices …

… and steals fire from the **gods**.

Prometheus is punished for his defiance.

It stung anew Zeus, high thunderer in his spirit, and he raged in his heart when he saw among men the far-seen beam of fire.
Theogony

HER IMPULSE INTRODUCED SORROW AND MISCHIEF TO THE LIVES OF MEN
PANDORA'S BOX

IN BRIEF

THEME
Origins of evil

SOURCE
Works and Days, Hesiod,
c.700 BCE.

SETTING
The foot of Mount Olympus,
Greece.

KEY FIGURES
Prometheus Titan brother
of Epimetheus; creator
of humanity – and its
greatest benefactor.

Zeus King of the gods
of Mount Olympus.

Hephaistos Olympian
blacksmith god and creator
of the first woman.

Pandora The first woman;
created on Zeus's instruction.

Epimetheus Titan brother
of Prometheus.

In Hesiod's account of humanity's mythic origins, *Works and Days*, man was first created alone, with no female mate to accompany him on his journey through the world. Woman would make her first appearance not as man's helpmate and partner, but as his punishment.

A jealous god

When the Titan Prometheus stole fire from the gods, he did much to empower humanity, at high personal cost. In an existence that had been largely trouble-free, humanity, to whom he gave the gift of fire, continued to thrive and

The glorious lame god moulded clay into the shape of a demure and decorous young maiden.
Works and Days

prosper. In punishment, however, Prometheus would be held captive and tortured eternally at the hands of Zeus, who was a jealous and grudging deity. Far from rejoicing in man's improving fortunes, the god felt threatened by humanity's growing confidence.

Zeus concluded that in order to correct the balance between divine and human power, some great calamity in the world was required. That calamity was woman. On Zeus's orders, the blacksmith and fire god Hephaistos set to work, shaping soft clay into a female mate for man.

Gilding the lily

The other Olympians then added their own contributions to the woman's make-up: Aphrodite gave her beauty and attractiveness; Athena gave her skill in sewing; Hera gave her curiosity; and so on. Hermes, the gods' messenger, gave woman the power of speech to help her communicate – but he also gave her the dangerous gift of guile. This new woman was enchanting in her beauty, seductive in her softness, inspiring in her smile, and soothing in her gentleness. In light of these traits,

See also: The Olympian gods 24–31 ▪ Prometheus helps mankind 36–39 ▪ The Mead of Poetry 142–43 ▪
Nanga Baiga 212–13

> Prometheus had warned
> him never to accept
> a gift from Zeus.
> ***Works and Days***

she was given the name Pandora
(literally meaning "all gifts"). Her
name alone would have caused
Prometheus concern. He had
previously warned his brother
Epimetheus not to accept any
offering from Zeus, in case it
unleashed "some evil thing for
mortal men". However, due to
the punishment of Prometheus,
Epimetheus had been left in charge
in the world of men. Whereas
Prometheus's name meant
"Thinking Ahead" or "Foresight",
Epimetheus's meant "Thinking

Pandora, as depicted by the British
Pre-Raphaelite artist Dante Gabriel
Rossetti (1828–1882). She is holding the
infamous box from which all the
troubles of the world poured forth.

After". He was gullible and did
not stop to think when Zeus's
messenger Hermes presented him
with Pandora as a goodwill present
to humanity from Zeus. Nor did he
give a second glance to the present
that she herself brought with her –
a *pithos* or ceramic jar (usually
re-imagined as a richly ornamented
box in modern retellings). The all-
gifted girl was both gift and giver.

Fatal curiosity
There was nothing inherently evil
about Pandora. Although she had
been warned against opening the
pithon, it was her innocent
curiosity – itself a characteristic
given by Hera – that led to her
downfall. When she could not
resist peeping inside the jar, she
pulled back the lid, all the ills and
misfortunes of the world flew out:
Hunger, Sickness, Loss, Loneliness,

and Death. Horrified, Pandora
hastily pushed the lid back on
– just in time to prevent Hope from
escaping. With hope, the world
could still persevere, despite the
adversity that the jealous Zeus
had inflicted on mankind. ▪

Hephaistos

At least one source states that
Hephaistos was ugly and squat
from birth, which explains why he
was thrown from the top of Mount
Olympus by his disgusted mother,
Hera. Landing further down the
mountain with a crash, he was
then rendered lame as well.

The unprepossessing
appearance of this first divine
artisan was in sharp and highly
symbolic contrast to the beauty of
the many things that he created.
He was often aided by attendants
such as Cedalion, who helped
with his creations. Hephaistos
is widely known as the Greek

"blacksmith god" and presided
over manufacture in its broadest
sense – perfecting his craft in
everything from metalwork and
the manufacture of weapons
to fine jewellery and intricate
items of clothing.

Of all his many creations,
Pandora is certainly the most
wonderful – and the most
flawed. According to Hesiod, it
was Hephaistos who created the
first woman, thereby enabling
each generation of humanity to
repeatedly replicate itself. In this
sense, the craft of Hephaistos
gave birth to humanity's future.

ZEUS HAD MANY WOMEN, BOTH MORTAL AND IMMORTAL

THE MANY AFFAIRS OF ZEUS

IN BRIEF

THEME
Lovers of the gods

SOURCES
Iliad, Homer, 8th century BCE;
*Theogony, Works and Days,
The Shield of Heracles,* Hesiod,
c.700 BCE; *Library,* Pseudo-
Apollodorus, c.100 CE.

SETTING
Greece and the Aegean.

KEY FIGURES
Zeus Father of the gods.

Hera Zeus's wife; queen of
the gods.

Mnemosyne Goddess of
memory.

Europa Phoenician princess.

Antiope Daughter of the river
god Asopos.

Leda A Spartan princess.

Metis Daughter of Oceanus.

Athena Daughter of Metis.

The Muses gladden
the great spirit of
their father Zeus
in Olympus
with their songs,
telling of things
that shall be.
Theogony

The sexual adventures of Zeus, the king of the gods, made up a significant strand of ancient Greek mythology. Without Zeus's many infidelities, the myths suggest that knowledge and artistic expression of any kind – poetry, music, drama, or works of art – would not exist.

One of Zeus's first affairs was with Mnemosyne, the Titan goddess of memory. After he slept with her on nine consecutive nights, nine daughters were born. Collectively known as the Muses, each of these daughters became responsible for inspiring mortals in a particular area of artistic endeavour: Calliope inspired epic poetry; Clio history; Euterpe lyric poetry and song; Erato love poetry; and Polyhymnia sacred poetry. Melpomene became responsible for inspiring tragic drama, Thalia took charge of comedy and pastoral poetry; Terpsichore inspired dance, and Urania astronomy.

All through the classical period, musicians and poets called on the Muses for assistance as they worked. "Blessed is he whom the Muses love," said the Greek poet Hesiod after invoking their help in *Theogony*, his poem about the genealogy of the gods. With the inspiration of the Muses, Hesiod said, musicians and poets could relieve a suffering mind of its cares.

Hera and the cuckoo

Zeus's instinct for trickery was an integral part of his character and informed all of his erotic exploits. He had assumed the form of a mortal – a handsome shepherd – to seduce Mnemosyne, and many of his other love affairs involved similar sorts of shape-shifting.

Hera, Zeus's wife, had also been won this way. The notoriously formidable goddess had dismissed Zeus disdainfully when he had first approached her, forcing him to take deceptive measures to win her affections. First, he summoned a thunderstorm, then he stood outside her window and took on the form of a fledgling cuckoo, its

The nine Muses lived on Mount Helicon, central Greece. In this scene by Jacques Stella (c. 1640) they are visited by Minerva (Athena), goddess of wisdom and patron of the arts.

See also: The birth of Zeus 20–23 ▪ The war of the god and the Titans 24–31 ▪ The Olympian gods 24–31

Zeus in disguise

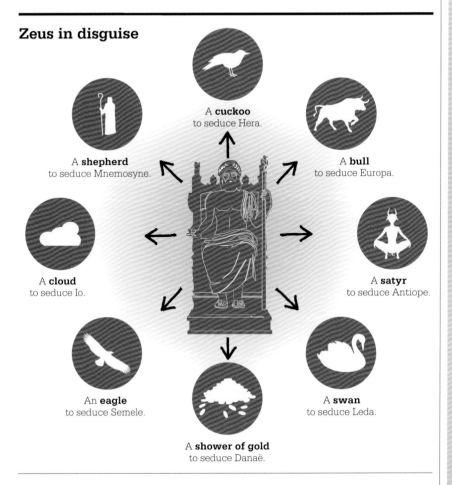

A **cuckoo**
to seduce Hera.

A **shepherd**
to seduce Mnemosyne.

A **bull**
to seduce Europa.

A **cloud**
to seduce Io.

A **satyr**
to seduce Antiope.

An **eagle**
to seduce Semele.

A **swan**
to seduce Leda.

A **shower of gold**
to seduce Danaë.

Hera

As the daughter of the Titans Kronos and Rhea, and wife and sister of the mighty Zeus, it might seem odd that Hera was commonly associated with cattle. She was often pictured with a sacred cow and in the *Iliad* is described as "cow-faced" or "ox-eyed". Such imagery was probably more flattering than it sounds. To the ancient Greeks, the cow was an emblem of motherhood and prosperity; wealth was often measured in the number of livestock owned.

While Hera was clearly no sex symbol – a role more associated with the goddess of beauty, Aphrodite – she did exemplify the importance of women in everyday life in Greece. She was celebrated as a goddess of both marriage and virginity. At Kanathos, in the Peloponnese, she was worshipped as Hera *Parthenos* ("Virgin") and was said to renew her virginity by bathing in the spring every year. The Heraion of Argos – possibly the first of many temples dedicated to Hera – honoured her as Zeus's consort and queen. Argos, Sparta, and Mycenae, according to Homer, were the cities she loved best.

expression helpless and its feathers ruffled up as if chilled and battered by the wind-blown hail. Hera could not bear to see this tiny creature suffering. She cupped the cuckoo in her hand and placed it inside her dress against her bosom, so that it could get warm. At this point, Zeus assumed his normal quasi-human form and seduced her.

The conquest of Hera was not the only time Zeus took the form of a bird. Zeus took on the shape of a swan in order to seduce the Spartan princess Leda. As with Hera, he took advantage of his victim's compassion. Apparently fleeing from an attacking eagle, he fell into her arms, but when she cradled him protectively, Zeus raped her. In the case of the Theban princess Semele, his choice of species – a raptor – clearly signalled his predatory intentions. Taking the form of an eagle, his royal emblem, he visited Semele and made her pregnant. Dionysus, god of wine and festivity, was the result of their union.

Ruined innocence

Zeus's conquest of Alcmene – a mortal princess with whom he fathered Herakles – was more sinister. Alcmene was a paragon of beauty, charm, and wisdom. She » was betrothed to Amphitryon, the son of a Theban general. Zeus assumed his guise to approach Alcmene while her fiance was away avenging the deaths of her brothers.

King Acrisius of Argos was particularly anxious to keep his only daughter Danaë chaste. He had been warned by an oracle that she was destined to bear a son who would one day slay him. To avoid this fate, he placed her in a cell so that no one could come near her. However, Zeus took the form of a shower of gold to pour himself through her prison skylight. The child of the encounter, Perseus, would later unwittingly cause her father's death.

Zeus as beast

Despite her name, Europa was a child of Asia, a princess from Phoenicia, a region covering parts of Israel, Syria, and Lebanon. Smitten by her charms, Zeus took on the form of a fine, white bull and mingled among her father's cattle. Picking flowers, Europa noticed the new bull and was struck by its beauty and its seeming gentleness. When she drew near to pet it, the bull lay down and she climbed onto its back. Suddenly, the bull leapt up and sped away across the fields and over the sea while the terrified girl clung on for dear life. The bull only stopped when it reached the island of Crete, where Zeus at last revealed himself and bedded his young victim. Zeus rewarded Europa by making her Crete's first queen. In time, she gave birth to Minos, the island's first king. Scholars think the story of Europa may have originated in Crete, where the cult of the bull also produced the story of Theseus and the Minotaur.

For his assault on Antiope, the daughter of Asopos, a river god from Attica in central Greece,

> Suddenly, the bull, possessed of his desire, jumped up and galloped off towards the sea.
> *Europa*

Zeus took the shape of a satyr – a half-man, half-goat who roamed the wild woods. Usually associated with the idea of lechery, satyrs were often depicted with erections in ancient art: Zeus had disguised his identity, not his lust.

Hiding from Hera

In some stories, it was Zeus's quarry who had to take a different shape. In the case of Io – the daughter of the king of Argos, and a priestess in the temple of Zeus's wife Hera – Zeus transformed himself into a cloud to make his approach and conceal it from the watchful Hera. Once he had raped Io, he turned her into a beautiful white heifer, to hide her from his wife. Hera saw through the trick and asked if she could have the heifer as a gift. Zeus had no option but to agree. Hera consigned Io to the care of the hundred-eyed giant Argus to watch over.

Maddened with frustration, Zeus sent his son Hermes to slay the all-seeing herdsman; the divine messenger blinded Argus with a

A fearful Europa rides the waves, clinging to Zeus, who took the form of a bull to abduct her. The powerful image was painted in 1910 by the Russian artist Valentin Serov.

Athena springs from a gash in Zeus's head, in a scene decorating an amphora (c.500 BCE) from Attica, Greece. Behind Zeus, Prometheus holds the axe that made the wound.

touch from his *kerykeion*, or staff. As the giant lay there dead, Hermes collected up his hundred eyes and set them in a peacock's tail: the bird was sacred to Hera from that time on.

If Zeus thought the way was now clear for him to pursue Io, he was wrong. Hera sent a fly to attack her. Buzzing about, and biting her again and again, the insect put Io to flight and chased her across the earth. Io was never to find rest.

The birth of Athena

Metis, Zeus's cousin – and in some accounts, his first wife – wrought her own transformation in a bid to shake off Zeus's pursuit. Metis assumed a series of different forms to avoid him, but Zeus eventually succeeded in catching her and making her pregnant. Nevertheless, Zeus was worried: Metis was renowned for her sharp intellect and wiliness, and an oracle had told him that Metis was destined to bear a child who matched her strength and cunning. Zeus – a usurper who had overthrown his

Asteria in the form of a quail flew across the sea, with Zeus in pursuit.
Library

own father – was on his guard against this child. Just before Metis was due to give birth, Zeus challenged her to a shape-shifting match. She was vain enough to agree. When Zeus told her that he did not believe she could transform herself into a tiny fly, she promptly did – and was swallowed by a triumphant Zeus.

It was a clever trick, but it did not succeed. When Zeus developed an unbearable headache, the Titan god Prometheus swung an axe at his head, splitting it wide open. Out from the wound sprang Athena, the goddess of war and wisdom, in a full suit of armour. She became one of the most important deities on Olympus and the patron goddess of the powerful city state of Athens.

Both transformed

In some stories, both predator and prey underwent changes. Zeus again disguised himself as an eagle to pursue Asteria, the Titan goddess of shooting stars. She transformed into another bird – the timid quail – in a desperate bid to escape and finally dived into the sea. There she changed her shape again and was preserved forever as an island, later variously identified as Delos, or Ortygia in Syracuse, Sicily. It was on this island that Asteria's younger sister Leto was to find sanctuary some years later, after she too caught the lecherous eye of Zeus. Here she gave birth to twins: Apollo, the god of the sun and of poetry, prophecy, and healing; and the divine huntress Artemis, goddess of the moon.

Mythology relates scores of Zeus's exploits, highlighting a sexual appetite that apparently drew little censure in ancient Greece. Despite his countless acts of rape, deception, and infidelity, the king of the gods was not seen as a villain. In his dialogue *Euthyphro*, the ancient Greek philosopher Plato, declared: "Do not men regard Zeus as the best and most righteous of the gods?" ■

MIGHTY HADES WHO DWELLS IN HOUSES BENEATH THE EARTH
HADES AND THE UNDERWORLD

IN BRIEF

THEME
The Underworld

SOURCES
Iliad and *Odyssey,* Homer, 8th century BCE; *Theogony,* Hesiod c.700 BCE.

SETTING
The Underworld.

KEY FIGURES
Hades Brother of Zeus; god of the Underworld.

Charon Ferryman of the River Styx.

Cerberus Three-headed guardian of the Underworld; son of the serpentine Typhon and Echidna.

Tantalus A Phrygian king held captive by Hades.

Sisyphus King of Corinth, who tricked Hades into letting him go free.

Hekate Goddess of witchcraft and necromancy.

While Zeus ruled over the skies and Poseidon over the seas, their brother Hades guarded his subject-souls in the Underworld – the kingdom that bore his name, where mortal humans went when they died.

Five dark rivers marked the boundaries of Hades's kingdom. Acheron was the river of sadness, Cocytus of mourning. Lethe was the river of forgetfulness, and Phlegethon an impassable river of fire. The River Styx marked the main border between Earth and the Underworld. The dead queued on one side of the river and paid the ferryman, Charon, with a coin to grant them passage into Hades. Because of this belief, the ancient Greeks were sometimes buried with a coin in their mouth, known as "Charon's obol".

On the other side of the river lay a dark and dismal realm. There, the new arrivals had to go through a large gate, guarded by the three-headed, snake-tailed monster,

Hades and his abducted bride, Persephone, watch over the tortured souls of the dead in François de Nomé's 17th-century depiction of the Underworld.

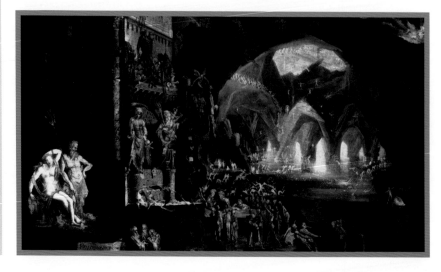

See also: The war of the gods and the Titans 32–33 ■ The abduction of Persephone 50–51 ■ The quest of Odysseus 64–69 ■ The Sibyl of Cumae 108–09

Cerberus. Though loosely described as a dog, this creature was born of the union between the giant snake-man, Typhon, and the man-eating serpent-maiden, Echidna. Cerberus turned this same ferocity on those who attempted to escape.

Charon and Cerberus were not the only non-human residents of Hades. Nyx, the goddess of night, lived there – as did Eurynomos, a flesh-eating demon, and the goddess Hekate. The Furies served Hades as his torturers, while Tartarus was both a deity and the pit where Titans were punished.

Hellish punishments

Some souls faced hideous torments in Hades. The crimes of Tantalus, a Phrygian ruler, were twofold: to test the gods, he had cooked and served up his son at a banquet he was hosting for them; and, as a guest at Zeus's table, he had tried to steal nectar and ambrosia, which would make him immortal, to take back with him to Earth. For this, he was imprisoned in Hades, wracked with thirst and hunger, surrounded by a pool of water, and with fruit-

Round the pit from every side the crowd thronged, with strange cries, and I turned pale with fear.
Odyssey

Once Death has caught hold of a man, he never lets him go.
Theogony

laden branches that dangled inches from his face. When he leaned over to taste either the water or the fruit, they withdrew from his reach, driving him into a frenzy.

Sisyphus, King of Corinth, had tricked Hades into thinking that he had been taken to the Underworld prematurely, and managed to get himself returned to Earth. As punishment, he was sentenced to push an enormous boulder up a hill. Each time he got to the top, the stone rolled back down to the bottom and he had to start all over again – and again, and again, for the rest of all time.

The Greek afterlife

Hades was not the only realm for the dead. According to the ancient writers, fallen heroes and the most virtuous were sent to the Elysian Fields – paradisiacal islands where they could live in bliss. Neither Hades nor Elysium, however, were representative of the ancient Greek view of the afterlife. Stories about Elysium, or the punishment of Sisyphus, were isolated tales: there is no sense that the ancient Greeks, as a whole, believed in a systematic judgement of the dead. ■

Hekate

Despite Zeus's victory over Kronos and his Titans, and his otherwise unchallenged authority over the universe, Hesiod's *Theogony* tells us that the goddess Hekate, associated with darkness, was honoured "above all others". Darkness and death were seen as powerful, immutable elements.

Hekate was conventionally depicted with three heads, representing the full moon, the crescent moon, and the empty dead-black sky. She was often identified with crossroads, especially those where three different paths met. Associated with liminal spaces and transitions, she was often worshipped by those wishing loved ones a safe crossing into the realm of the dead. Hekate was invited to stay in the Underworld as a companion to Hades's wife, Persephone, but was allowed to come and go as she wished. In myth, Persephone is often seen as the maiden and Demeter the mother; Hekate is the crone to complete the trio.

HE SLIPPED A POMEGRANATE, SWEET AS HONEY, INTO HER HAND
THE ABDUCTION OF PERSEPHONE

IN BRIEF

THEME
Life, death, and the seasons

SOURCES
Theogony, Hesiod, c.700 BCE; *Hymn to Demeter*, Homer, c.600 BCE; *Description of Greece*, Pausanias, c.150 CE.

SETTING
Sicily; the Underworld.

KEY FIGURES
Demeter Goddess of the harvest, sister of Zeus and Hades.

Persephone Demeter's daughter, who became the queen of the Underworld.

Hades God of the Underworld and Demeter's brother.

One of classical Greece's *Homeric Hymns* refers to Demeter as the "sacred goddess with the glorious hair" – her thick and lustrous golden tresses were emblematic of the abundance of the harvest. Demeter was the goddess of the harvest, charged with ensuring that the fields were rich and fertile. Before tragedy struck, there was no winter, cold, or decay.

Stolen away

One day, Demeter's beloved daughter Persephone was out with some nymphs in one of Sicily's prettiest vales, picking flowers. Persephone marvelled at the "roses, crocuses, lovely violets … irises,

Hades kidnaps Persephone in a field of daffodils in British artist Walter Crane's *The Fate of Persephone* (1877). Two of his four horses rear up between a sunlit world and ominous darkness.

hyacinths, and narcissi", exulting in the beautiful colours and heady fragrances of the scene.

When Persephone pulled a narcissus from the ground, the earth split and opened up beneath her. A huge chariot thundered forth, drawn by sable-black horses. As her companions fled, Persephone stood transfixed. A tall, shadowy figure leaned down from the chariot and scooped her up. Persephone's uncle, Hades, had come up from the Underworld to take her as his bride.

See also: The Olympian gods 24–31 ▪ Hades and the Underworld 48–49 ▪ Cupid and Psyche 112–13

> Hades dragged
> Persiphone into his
> speeding chariot
> and she screamed
> out loud.
> **Hymn to Demeter**

Persephone struggled and wept, crying out for her father, Zeus. But her pleas went unanswered. Some versions of the myth suggest that Zeus himself had played a part in the abduction by conspiring with his brother. Hades took Persephone with him down into the gloomy Underworld. He promised that she would be queen of his subterranean kingdom, revered and beloved by all – but she was inconsolable.

Demeter's despair

Persephone's mother, Demeter, was equally distraught. Frantically combing the forests, fields, and hills in search of her daughter, she called out Persephone's name over and over again – but received no reply. In her grief, Demeter blighted the countryside, causing the crops to die and all the leaves to turn brown. It seemed as if the entire earth had died. Eventually, the sun god, Helios, told Demeter that her brother Hades had snatched her daughter and spirited her off to his dismal realm. At this news, Demeter was filled with rage, and wrought yet more destruction upon the earth. Hades's abduction of Persephone had set all of creation askew. At last, Zeus was forced to intervene in the quarrel between his siblings. He ruled that, so long as Persephone had not taken food or drink since she arrived in the Underworld, Hades must agree to release her.

A seasonal solution

Unfortunately, Persephone had eaten something in the Underworld. Hades had given her a pomegranate, the fruit of the dead, and she had consumed several of the sweet seeds. This resulted in a fresh judgement from Zeus, who decided that Persephone could return to the world above – but she would have to go back down to the Underworld and reside with Hades for three months of every year.

Persephone's sentence explained why, with the onset of winter, the world appears to fade and die, as Demeter mourns her daughter's absence. Then, as spring approaches and Persephone returns to the surface of the earth, its fields and forests once again come into bloom. ▪

> Stealthily, though, Hades
> slipped a pomegranate,
> sweet as honey, into
> Persephone's hand.
> **Hymn to Demeter**

Eleusian mysteries

Priests at the shrine of Eleusis, a settlement near Athens in the region of Attica, developed an elaborate set of ceremonies based on the story of the abduction of Persephone. The "Eleusinian Mysteries" are among the oldest and best known of the secret religious rites of the ancient Greeks. By the Greek classical period (5th–4th century BCE), the Eleusinian Mysteries were already ancient. The cult spread to Athens soon after the annexation of Eleusis in 600 BCE. As with similar rituals in other early societies, the Eleusinian cult strove to assert a sense of control over the growing cycle and the seasons.

The highpoint of the Eleusinian calendar came toward the end of winter, with ceremonies designed to ensure the return of the sun and the renewal of the earth. The ceremonies involved rites of personal purification, animal sacrifices, libations (the ritual pouring of wine onto the earth), fasting, and feasting.

The priests of Eleusia honoured Demeter, Kybele, and Persephone on this altar from Chalandri, Attica, c. 360 CE. The male figure is Iakhos, leader of the Eleusinian Mysteries.

THE RAVING LADIES STREAMED OUT OF THEIR HOMES
THE CULT OF DIONYSUS

IN BRIEF

THEME
Passion versus restraint

SOURCES
Homeric Hymns to Dionysus, Homer, c.600 BCE; *On Nature*, Heraclitus, c.500 BCE; *The Bacchae*, Euripides, 405 BCE.

SETTING
The countryside around Thebes, central Greece, during the reign of King Pentheus.

KEY FIGURES
Dionysus God of fertility, wine, and madness.

Zeus King of the gods.

Semele Dionysus's mortal mother.

Hera Zeus's wife; goddess of women and marriage.

Maenads Delirious, drunken female followers of Dionysus.

Pentheus King of Thebes.

D ionysus, the god of wine and ecstasy, was born after Zeus's liaison with a mortal named Semele. Her insistence on seeing Zeus revealed in his full divine glory resulted in her death, because a mere mortal was not permitted to see an undisguised god. Zeus rescued the fetus and sewed the unborn child into his thigh. After this, Dionysus was born again – both as a boy-deity and as an emblem of fertility. Zeus's wife Hera then cursed Dionysus, sending Titans to dismember and kill him. Zeus, however, brought his son back to life once more.

Women, here he is: the man who mocks you and me and our unruly rituals.
The Bacchae

The Maenads
Dionysus presided over fertility both for the vineyards and for women's wombs. His followers, predominantly female, were known as Maenads – meaning "raving ones". These women shared their god's love of wine and raucous behaviour, and he encouraged them to indulge in both. Marauding bands of Maenads terrorized the Theban countryside so much that Pentheus, the King of Thebes, banned the cult of Dionysus. The king's decree was angrily rejected by many women – including the king's own mother – who went out into the countryside to praise the wine-god in one last, climactic rite.

Dionysus convinced Pentheus to climb a tree to enjoy the view of the final orgy. Dressed in women's clothes, the king went to watch, but was seen by the ecstatic Maenads. Mistaking him for a wild animal, they tore him limb from limb. ∎

See also: The Olympian gods 24–31 ▪ The many affairs of Zeus 42–47 ▪ Vesta and Priapus 108–09 ▪ A complex god 164

TURNING ROUND, HE CAUGHT A GLIMPSE OF HIS WIFE AND SHE HAD TO RETURN BELOW
ORPHEUS AND EURYDICE

IN BRIEF

THEME
The finality of death

SOURCES
Argonautica, Apollonius of Rhodes, c.250 BCE; *Library*, Pseudo-Apollodorus, c.100 CE.

SETTING
Greece and the Underworld.

KEY FIGURES
Orpheus A renowned musician; the son of Calliope and Oeagrus.

Eurydice The bride of Orpheus; killed on her wedding day

Hades The king of the Underworld.

Persephone The young wife of Hades and queen of the Underworld.

reek mythology's great bard, Orpheus, was born of the relationship between Calliope, the Muse of poetry, and Oeagrus, a Thracian river god. Orpheus's most heartfelt verses were dedicated to Eurydice, who became his wife – only to be killed by a snakebite on her wedding day.

Lyrical lamentation

Wandering through the woods, Orpheus mourned Eurydice in impassioned song, which surpassed anything he had ever composed. The music was so moving that the nymphs and gods wept to hear it. Eventually, Orpheus decided to travel to the Underworld to beg Hades and his queen to take mercy on him and return Eurydice to life.

In the Underworld, Orpheus played for Hades and Persephone. The queen was so touched by the music that she begged her husband to break the rules of the Underworld and release Eurydice. Hades agreed, on the condition that Orpheus did not lay eyes on Eurydice while she remained in the Underworld.

Orpheus led his bride through the caverns of darkness and despair, slowly winding upwards towards the earth's surface. Eurydice followed after him at a distance, so that he would not look upon her.

At last, Orpheus caught a glimpse of daylight up ahead. Happily, he glanced back at his wife, only to realize even as he saw her that she was lost to him – pulled back down, despairing, into the realms of death. ∎

Orpheus plays his lyre in a 3rd-century CE Roman mosaic from Antakya, Turkey. The bard is surrounded by wild animals that are entranced by his sublime music.

See also: Hades and the Underworld 48–49 ▪ The abduction of Persephone 50–51 ▪ The descent of Inanna 182–87 ▪ Osiris and the Underworld 276–83

A BRINGER OF DREAMS
HERMES' FIRST DAY

Hermes, generally described as the "messenger of the gods", was that and much more. Famously, he was able to flit from one place to another in an instant, carried through the air on winged sandals that would become emblematic of the god himself. His ability to fly was key to his role as courier. Symbolically, though, the god's rapid travel

The god Hermes, with a painted whiplash in his right hand, leads a chariot carrying Echelos and the nymph Basile in this marble votive relief dating from 410 BCE.

suggested his quickness of thought and his heedlessness of the normal restrictions of time and space.

Springing to life
Hermes was the son of Zeus and Maia, daughter of the Titan Atlas and the sea nymph Pleione. Known to the Romans as Mercury, he showed his mercurial character from the very beginning of his life, when (according to the *Homeric Hymn* to Hermes) he "jumped straight from his mother's womb" and landed in his cradle. The young god did not lie there long, but instead leapt out of the cave that

See also: The war of the gods and Titans 32–33 ▪ The many affairs of Zeus 42–47 ▪ The quest of Odysseus 66–71 ▪ Arachne and Minerva 115 ▪ The adventures of Thor and Loki in Jötunheim 146–47 ▪ Ananse the spider 286–87

The seven daughters of Atlas and Pleione – depicted here by Elihu Vedder (1885) – fly to the heavens and become the Pleiades.

Maia and the Pleiades

Hermes' mother was one of Zeus's many amatory conquests. According to Hesiod's *Theogony*, Maia, daughter of Atlas the Titan and Pleione the sea nymph, had gone up to Zeus's "holy bed", slept with him, and bore him a son – the messenger god. Maia in turn would be rewarded with her own winged transformation.

After the war of the gods with the Titans, while Atlas was forced to carry the sky and heavens upon his shoulders, his wife Pleione was romantically pursued by Orion, the great huntsman. For seven years Orion harassed not only the sea nymph but her seven daughters as well. At last Zeus answered their prayers and intervened, first turning Orion into the group of stars now associated with his name – Orion's belt. He then transformed Pleione and her daughters – including Maia – into doves. They flew into the night sky to become the Pleiades, a cluster of stars whose appearance is traditionally associated with the onset of rainy weather.

had been his mother's refuge – despite being only one hour old – to find and steal the cattle of the sun god, Apollo. Hermes had barely stepped outside the cave when he was diverted by the sight of a tortoise. Scooping out the animal, he turned the hollow shell "into a singer". He covered the opening with cowhide, leaving a sounding-hole; he then stretched strings across it and built a little wooden bridge to make the world's first lyre. Plucking the strings, he burst into song, recounting epic stories of the world and its creation – of Titans, Olympians, nymphs, men and women, and other beings.

Multi-faceted god

Not yet a day old, Hermes was already the world's first musician, poet, and historian. His multi-faceted genius was also capricious. The *Homeric Hymn* states that, even as he sang, he was "inwardly attending to other matters": as Apollo's sun went down, Hermes crept onto the lands of the god and took his cattle. Walking the beasts backwards, so their trail seemed to lead in the opposite direction, he herded them back to his home.

The quick cunning displayed by Hermes had much in common with "trickster" spirits of other mythologies, such as West Africa's Ananse, or the Loki of Norse legend. Despite his love of pranks, Hermes also possessed a capacity for more serious deeds. For example, he is held to have invented the ritual sacrifice when he slew two of Apollo's cows, skinned, and roasted

[Hermes] fastened on his feet the immortal golden sandals which carried him faster than the breeze.
Odyssey

And Maia bore to Zeus glorious Hermes, the herald of the deathless gods.
Theogony

them, and – hungry though he was – left the aromatic flesh on a platform to atone for his theft.

The *caduceus*, the rod that Hermes carried in his left hand, could confer sleep and healing at a touch. The two symmetrically coiling serpents that wound around the *caduceus* suggested its ability to balance and reconcile opposing sides, whether through changing them from one form to another or through negotiation and trade – Hermes was also believed to be the god of commerce. ▪

ATHENA PRESENTS THE OLIVE TREE, POSEIDON THE WAVE

THE FOUNDING OF ATHENS

IN BRIEF

THEME
Origins of the state

SOURCES
Homeric Hymns, Anonymous,
c.600 BCE; *Library*, Pseudo-
Apollodorus, c.100 CE;
Description of Greece,
Pausanias, c.150 CE.

SETTING
Athens, Greece.

KEY FIGURES
Athena Goddess of wisdom
and patron deity of Athens.

Hephaistos The god of
blacksmiths and craftworkers;
father of Erichthonius.

Erichthonius Founder of the
city of Athens.

Poseidon God of the seas and
contender for patron of Athens.

Cecrops First king of Athens.

The *Homeric Hymn* to
Athena begins with
the words, "Of Athena,
guardian of the city, I sing". No
other Greek deity was so closely
identified with a particular location,
nor does any other location loom so
large in our modern-day perceptions
of Greek culture. When we think
of ancient Greece – its literature,
its art, its democracy – we are
thinking largely of ancient Athens.

The mythological associations of
Athens with the goddess of wisdom
are reflected in its reputation as
a cultural and intellectual haven
full of philosophers, artists, and
playwrights. This dazzling legacy
arose from the solid foundations

The Parthenon ("Temple of the
Virgin Goddess") was built at the
top of the Acropolis of Athens in the
mid-5th century BCE. It replaced an
earlier temple dedicated to Athena.

of trade and industry, as the
prosperity, confidence, and
technical expertise of its people
came together to make the city
grow and prosper.

Work and pleasure
One foundation myth makes
this connection between beauty
and technology explicit, linking
the beginnings of Athens with
the craftsman-god Hephaistos.
Lame and ugly though he was,

See also: The Olympian gods 24–31 ▪ The many affairs of Zeus 42–47 ▪ Cupid and Psyche 112–13 ▪ Arachne and the spider 115

Hephaistos was married to the lovely Aphrodite. This union was symbolically suggestive of the marriage of utility and beauty, of work and pleasure, that was prevalent in Greek culture. However, in common with other Olympian marriages, their union also featured frequent infidelities.

A son is born

At one point, Aphrodite deserted her husband entirely for the war god, Ares. After she left, Hephaistos fell passionately in love with Athena, then pursued her and attempted to rape her.

Athena put up a furious resistance and pushed Hephaistos away just as he ejaculated. His semen struck Athena's thigh, and she brushed it off disdainfully. It landed in the Greek soil, and there produced a new life; in some retellings, this offspring

was Erichthonius ("born of the very soil"), who would go on to found the city of Athens.

By land and sea

Athena played a central role in another of the city's foundation myths. When Erichthonius was establishing his community on the coast of Attica, he called on the gods for a divine patron to come forward. With Athena and Poseidon both eagerly desiring the role, a contest was arranged to see what each deity could offer the future city and its people. Its victor would be decided – fittingly, for the birthplace of democracy – by a vote.

In the contest, Poseidon shook the earth, smiting it with his trident and making a vast wave come rolling forth. This was a bounteous spring – but its waters salty. In response, Athena then poked the ground, which produced

The Athenians are far more devoted to religion than other men.
Description of Greece

an olive tree, laden with its abundant and valuable fruit. The goddess of wisdom was confirmed by Cecrops, king of the city, as the people's choice. However, Poseidon's gift ensured that the seaport status of Athens was as important to its prosperity as its fertile fields and groves. "Look kindly on those who make their way in ships", says the *Homeric Hymn* to Poseidon. The sea god remained in the city's prayers. ▪

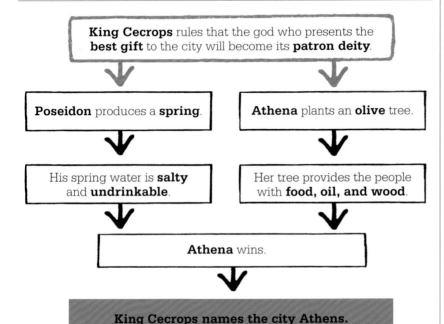

King Cecrops rules that the god who presents the **best gift** to the city will become its **patron deity**.

↓   ↓

Poseidon produces a **spring**.   **Athena** plants an **olive** tree.

↓   ↓

His spring water is **salty** and **undrinkable**.   Her tree provides the people with **food, oil, and wood**.

↓   ↓

Athena wins.

↓

King Cecrops names the city Athens.

Athena and Poseidon's contest is depicted on an amphora created by the Amasis Painter, c.540 BCE. The signature between the two gods reads *Amasis mepoiesen* ("Amasis made me").

I WILL GIVE INFALLIBLE COUNSEL TO ALL WHO SEEK IT

APOLLO AND THE ORACLE OF DELPHI

IN BRIEF

THEME
Inspiration, poetry, and wisdom

SOURCES
Homeric Hymn, author anonymous, c.600 BCE; *Description of Greece,* Pausanias, c.150 CE.

SETTING
Delphi, on the slopes of Mount Parnassus in central Greece.

KEY FIGURES
Apollo God of the sun and the arts, who was also associated with wisdom.

The Pythia Apollo's high priestess at Delphi.

Hera The wife of Zeus.

Zeus King of the Olympian gods; father of Apollo.

Leto Mother of Apollo and Artemis.

Artemis Sister of Apollo.

Asclepius Son of Apollo.

The Temple of Apollo at Delphi, on the slopes of Mount Parnassus, in central Greece, was the site of the most important oracle in the ancient world. It was believed that the god Apollo channelled prophecies through the Pythia, the high priestess of the temple.

Raising a temple
Apollo's association with Delphi began when he was just four days old. Taking the form of a dolphin, he left his birthplace on the island of Delos in the Cyclades, a group of islands in the Aegean Sea, to seek out and kill the feared Python, a huge and ferocious dragon that lived in the innards of the earth, beneath what was regarded as its *omphalos*, or "navel", near the town of Delphi. An enraged Hera, the wife of Zeus, had sent the monster

The Pythia sits on a sacred tripod as she receives a message from Apollo in Camillo Miola's *The Oracle* (1880). The figures in the foreground shake bay leaves as part of the ritual.

See also: The war of gods and the titans 32–33 ▪ Mount Olympus 34–35 ▪ The many affairs of Zeus 42–47 ▪
Apollo and Daphne 60–61 ▪ The Sybil of Cumae 110–11

to hunt down Apollo's mother, the goddess Leto, who had become pregnant by Zeus.

Although Leto escaped and gave birth to Apollo and his twin sister Artemis on Delos, Apollo wished to avenge the attempt to destroy his mother. Apollo slayed the Python with a bow and arrows made for him by the blacksmith god, Hephaistos. He buried the creature beneath the omphalos stone, which marked the geographical centre of the earth, and established his temple to symbolize the resounding triumph of heaven over earth.

Joy and wisdom

By the fifth century BCE, Apollo had supplanted Helios the Titan as the sun god in the Greek pantheon. The *Homeric Hymn to Apollo* acclaims the "splendour of his radiance". It also says the god was born to be "the joy of men" and would "declare to men the unfailing will of Zeus", references to his role as the god of poetry and music, and

to his association with wisdom. The invention of medicine was also ascribed to Apollo – although he devolved most of his medical role to Asclepius, one of his sons. He was also a protector of shepherds, who were identified with the pastoral idyll celebrated in Greek poetry. Pan, a god of fertility and shepherds, who played the pipes, challenged Apollo to a musical duel. Apollo, who played a golden lyre (one of the god's many attributes with which

The child leapt forth into the light, and all the goddesses raised up a cry.
Homeric Hymn to Apollo

Delphi's Temple of Apollo
dates from the fourth century BCE. According to Pausanias, previous temples on the site were made of laurel leaves, beeswax, or bronze.

he is often shown) captivated the audience, and was unanimously proclaimed the victor.

Apollo communicated his wisdom through the Oracle at Delphi. People flocked to Delphi from every corner of Greece to gain knowledge of future events and discover the will of Zeus, especially in times of national crisis, such as war, when more than one Pythia performed the role of Apollo's mouthpiece. The people offered animal sacrifices to Apollo, then waited patiently as the Pythia, seated over a cauldron, with volcanic vapour rising around her, channelled his response. The Pythia's utterances were copious but often incoherent. Shrine officials interpreted and then recorded Apollo's precious words of wisdom in verse hexameters. ▪

ONE LOVED; THE OTHER FLED THE NAME OF LOVE
APOLLO AND DAPHNE

IN BRIEF

THEME
Desire and transformation

SOURCES
Description of Greece,
Pausanias, c.150 CE;
Metamorphoses, Ovid, 8 CE.

SETTING
Thessaly or the Peloponese,
Greece.

KEY FIGURES
Apollo God of the sun,
archery, magic, music,
and more.

Eros The young god of desire;
a troublemaker.

Daphne A beautiful nymph
dedicated to chastity; the
daughter of Peneus.

Peneus A river god; father
of Daphne

Apollo was among the
greatest of the gods, his
prestige unimpeachable,
his person radiant with all the
splendour of the sun. By contrast,
Eros personnified sexual desire
in all its indignity and neediness.
Like an overgrown infant, he was
a caprious troublemaker who
acted on his every whim.

Apollo was the god of archery
and a skilled archer. His silver
bow was as much a symbol of
power as a weapon, the arrows
rarely used. Eros also had bow and
arrows, which he used regularly
to make his conquests. His sharp,
gold-tipped darts made the target
they struck fall in love immediately.
He had a second set of arrows, too:
their heads were blunt and tipped
with lead, and they killed affection
in anyone they hit. The weapons
made Eros giddy with power.

Gods at odds
Seeing Eros strutting around,
Apollo could not help sneering.
Fresh from his glorious triumph
over the monstrous Python – killed
by a thousand arrows from his
quiver – Apollo laughed to see this
infant-at-arms give himself such
grand airs. Apollo believed that

such an impudent boy was not fit to
carry bow and arrows – and he said
as much to the young Eros.

Puffed up with petulant rage,
the boy yelled back that he would
get even; he would make the sun
god sorry that he had shown such
scorn. The passions his gold-tipped
arrows aroused could prevail over
the most powerful of individuals.
Even Apollo was not immune, as
the sun god was soon to learn.

Eros takes revenge
Depending upon which account
you read, the spat took place by
the River Peneus on the Plain of
Thessaly, central Greece, or by
the river Ladon in the Pelopponese,

You don't know who
you're fleeing from,
thoughtless nymph.
Metamorphoses

See also: The Olympian gods 24–31 ▪ Apollo and the Oracle of Delphi 58–59 ▪ Venus and Adonis 88–89 ▪ Cupid and Psyche 112–13

southern Greece. Eros spotted Daphne, a beautiful, virginal Naiad (a water nymph) and daughter of the river god – named by Ovid as Peneus – upon the banks of her father's stream. Eros took aim and pierced Daphne with a lead-tipped bolt. Spinning around, he shot another arrow, this time with a golden tip, which pierced Apollo. The sun god hardly had time to register the pain: seeing Daphne, he was instantly and sublimely smitten with desire.

Daphne, however, had been hit just as hard by Eros's leaden dart. Seeing Apollo, even in all

Daphne recoils from Apollo in this mid-18th-century painting by Italian artist Giovanni Battista Tiepolo. Eros hides and Peneus watches on as the nymph is transformed into a laurel tree.

his beauty, she recoiled. As he approached her with vows of eternal love, she turned and fled. Pursued by Apollo, she cried out to her father as she ran, and just as Apollo caught and grabbed Daphne and held her in his arms, Peneus answered her pleas and turned his daughter into a laurel tree.

Apollo, his desire still burning, declared that even though Daphne could not be his bride, he would claim the laurel as his own. From then on, laurel leaves would always adorn his hair, his lyre, and quiver. Laurel wreaths would be used to honour victorious generals in triumphal processions and, matching Apollo's immortality and always lustrous hair, laurel leaves would never fade. The laurel tree then inclined its branches as if nodding in agreement. ▪

Eros

Usually a relatively minor character in the stories of Greek mythology, Eros was the son of Aphrodite, the goddess of love. Eros also represented love – but, more specifically, he personified "erotic", sexual desire. Often portrayed as a slender and brattish boy, he could be touchy and quick to take offence, as he was when Apollo teased him. He could also be immature, thoughtless, and capricious, even perverse; the revenge he inflicts on Apollo has the cruellest of consequences for Daphne. Eros was sometimes depicted with a blindfold to show his lack of discrimination – lust typically does not exercise much logic or judgement.

Eros is perhaps better known today by his Roman name, Cupid. Depictions of the god gradually changed from the slender youth of Greek tradition to the pudgy, cherubic young boy familiar from classical western art and modern Valentine's Day cards.

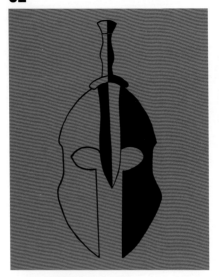

LIFE AND DEATH ARE BALANCED ON THE EDGE OF A RAZOR

THE TROJAN WAR

The Trojan War inspired some of the greatest ancient Greek poetry, particularly Homer's *Iliad* and *Odyssey*. Although the story has mythical aspects, it may have been based on a conflict between the Mycenaeans and the Hittites that took place in the 12th century BCE.

The chain of events that led to the war began when the goddess Aphrodite offered Paris, a Trojan prince, the love of Helen, the world's most beautiful woman. Helen was already married to King Menelaus of Sparta, but Paris did not consider this an obstacle and abducted her. Her husband was furious. Menelaus persuaded his brother Agamemnon, King of Mycenae, to lead a Greek alliance to Troy and recapture her. The Greek army included the semi-divine warrior Achilles, son of the sea nymph Thetis, and Odysseus, the cunning king of Ithaca. They crossed the sea to Troy but were unable to breach the city's walls.

After nine years away from home, the Greek alliance was fracturing. The men were on the verge of mutiny and a plague diminished their ranks. Achilles

Helen was abducted by Paris and taken away on his ship, but smitten by his beauty, she may have left willingly. This alabaster carving decorates an Etrurian funerary urn, 2nd century BCE.

See also: The quest of Odysseus 66–71 ▪ Aeneas, founder of Rome 96–101 ▪ The cattle raid of Cooley 166–67

The giant wooden horse, filled with Greek warriors, is brought inside the walls of the city in *The Procession of the Trojan Horse into Troy* by Giovanni Battista Tiepolo (c.1760).

refused to fight after Agamemnon took one of his concubines. Despite the great warrior's absence, the Greeks rallied, and fought a pitched battle with the Trojans. Menelaus was close to killing Paris when Aphrodite intervened to save him.

Attacking the city walls

The Trojans regathered and drove back the Greeks. Achilles refused to fight but allowed his close companion Patroclus to borrow his armour. Patroclus inspired a Greek counter-attack and forced the Trojans back to the city walls. He was slain by Hector, the greatest of the Trojan warriors, who stripped him of his borrowed armour.

Devastated, Achilles built a towering funeral pyre for his beloved Patroclus, held funeral games in his honour, and returned to the fray with a vengeance. Killing Hector in single combat, he refused to return his body for a royal burial; instead, he dragged Hector's corpse behind his chariot around Troy's walls. Soon after, Achilles was mortally wounded when Paris fired an arrow at his heel – the only part of his body that was not immortal.

Now in its tenth year, the war was won not by force but trickery. Odysseus had the Greeks build a giant hollow wooden horse, secretly fill it with Greek soldiers, and leave it outside the gates of Troy. The rest of the Greeks sailed out of sight, so that the Trojans believed they had left. Thinking the war was over, the Trojans dragged the horse inside the city walls. As the inhabitants slept, oblivious to their imminent doom, the Greeks inside the horse sneaked out and murdered Troy's guards. These soldiers let in the rest of the Greek army, which had secretly returned to Troy under cover of night.

A savage massacre followed and Troy was burned to the ground. Menelaus had regained Helen, but both sides had lost some of their most famous warriors, and much of their population. The Greeks, due to their wanton destruction of temples during the Sack of Troy, had also lost the goodwill of the gods. ▪

Achilles

The warrior Achilles was the son of the sea nymph Thetis and King Peleus of Phthia. When he was born his mother wanted to make him immortal so she dipped him into the River Styx, which ran between earth and Hades. She held him by his left heel, which left Achilles with one vulnerable spot. Growing up, Achilles was taught by the wise centaur Chiron to become a warrior. When the Trojan War began, Chiron gave Achilles a mighty shield, but Thetis intervened before her son could join the fray. Calchas had prophesied that Achilles would help the Greeks take Troy and, fearing for his life, Thetis disguised Achilles as a girl in the home of the king of Scyros. Odysseus, however, soon found Achilles and revealed his true identity. After marrying the king's daughter, Achilles left Scyros to lead Odysseus's army.

THIS PAIR OF TYRANTS. THEY MURDERED MY FATHER

ORESTES AVENGES AGAMEMNON

IN BRIEF

THEME
Revenge versus justice

SOURCES
Odyssey, Homer, 8th century BCE
Oresteia, Aeschylus, 458 BCE;
Orestes, Euripides, 408 BCE;
Electra, Sophocles, c.400 BCE.

SETTING
Agamemnon's palace,
Mycenae, Argos, Greece.

KEY FIGURES
Agamemnon The murdered
king of Argos.

Iphigenia Agamemnon's
sacrificed daughter.

Clytemnestra Agamemnon's
wife.

Aegisthus Clytemnestra's
lover; Agamemnon's successor
as king.

Orestes Agamemnon's son,
who killed Aegisthus.

Electra Agamemnon's
daughter.

Agamemnon, King of Argos, was commander of the Greek forces during the legendary Trojan War. His family history was steeped in blood and betrayal. A ruthless feud between his father, Atreus, and his uncle, Thyestes, had already precipitated adultery, multiple murders, and enduring enmity by the time the Trojan conflict in Asia Minor had broken out. That grisly lineage was set to pass on to a new generation.

Iphigenia's sacrifice
Agamemnon's departure for Troy with his fleet of a thousand ships was delayed for weeks by adverse winds, sent by the goddess

This man, Agamemnon, my husband, is dead, the work of this right hand.
Oresteia

Artemis, whom he had offended by killing a sacred deer. To banish these winds, the king reluctantly heeded the advice of a prophet, and sacrificed his own innocent daughter, Iphigenia, whom he had lured to the coast with the false promise of a husband. This was an act that his wife, Clytemnestra, would neither forgive nor forget.

The king is murdered
While Agamemnon was away at war, his queen took a lover named Aegisthus, who was Agamemnon's first cousin. They had been bitter enemies since the king's father had slain Aegisthus's siblings. Having gained access to the bed of Agamemnon, Aegisthus quickly helped himself to his crown as well: soon he and Clytemnestra were reigning together as king and queen in Argos, openly displaying their adulterous union.

Such was the situation to which Agamemnon returned, victorious at last after ten long years of war. No longer lord in his own house, he faced a fight to reclaim what was his. This was a fight he quickly lost, when he was murdered by his wife and her lover. Different versions of the story offer varying details: some

See also: The many affairs of Zeus 42–47 ▪ The founding of Athens 56–57 ▪ The quest of Odysseus 66–71

Orestes slays his mother to avenge his father's death in this painting by Bernardino Mei (1655). Clytemnestra's lover, Aegisthus, lies beside her, also slaughtered at the hand of Orestes.

say the king was killed at a feast celebrating his return from the war; others say he was murdered while naked and helpless after his bath.

Crime and punishment

The varying accounts also cite several possible motivations for Agamemnon's murder. Some place the guilt squarely with Aegisthus, Agamemnon's longstanding enemy, as an act of vengeance for the crimes of the king's father. Other versions lay the blame firmly at Clytemnestra's feet, presenting her as a fearless and defiant woman who murdered her husband as retribution for killing their daughter.

Other accounts cite Clytemnestra's ungovernable female sexuality and her passion.

Agamemnon's children – his son, Orestes, and his daughter Electra – were both away from home when their father was killed. They returned to Argos to find their mother and Aegisthus reigning in his place. Orestes felt it the duty of a son to avenge his father, so – with his sister's help and encouragement – he disguised himself and gained access to the palace, where he killed Aegisthus.

The spirit of vengeance demanded that Clytemnestra too should pay the price for her role in the crime. Orestes slew her also, but carried her dying curse on his head: relentless furies, the Erinyes, hunted him across the face of the earth for the rest of his days for his crime of matricide. Electra escaped the curse, marrying Orestes's friend and co-conspirator Pylades. ▪

Aeschylus

Revered as the father of tragedy, Aeschylus was an early Greek dramatist – one of three, along with Euripides and Sophocles, whose works survive and are still performed. He was born around 525 BCE in Eleusis, a town northwest of Athens, and grew up to fight against two Persian invasions. When not at war, Aeschylus regularly took part in Athens's annual "Dionysia" playwriting contest.

He claimed that the god of theatre, Dionysus himself, visited him while he was asleep and persuaded him to take up the art.

Aeschylus was known to be a prolific playwright, yet only seven of his plays survive, each one believed to have won first prize at the Dionysia. The Oresteia trilogy – *Agamemnon*, *Choephoroi*, and *Eumenides* – are now his best-known plays. Aeschylus was credited with writing *Prometheus Bound*, though his authorship of that play is now disputed.

TELL ME
OH MUSE, THE HERO'S
STORY
THE QUEST OF ODYSSEUS

IN BRIEF

THEME
Heroic journeys

SOURCE
Odyssey, Homer, 8th
century BCE.

SETTING
The Trojan War, 13th–12th
century BCE. The Aegean Sea;
Asia Minor (western Turkey);
the Peloponnese peninsula of
southern Greece.

KEY FIGURES
Odysseus A cunning warrior.

Poseidon God of the sea.

Telemachus Odysseus's son.

Penelope Odysseus's
faithful wife.

Calypso A nymph.

Alcinous King of Phaecia;
father of Nausicaa.

Polyphemus The one-eyed
giant, or Cyclops.

Circe A sorceress.

Of all those creatures
which exist on earth,
none is more weak
or worthless than
a man.
Odyssey

One of several Greek heroes who fought at Troy, as related in Homer's first epic poem, the *Iliad*, Odysseus stands out by virtue of his cunning and resourcefulness. When he becomes the subject of Homer's second great epic, the *Odyssey*, those qualities are tested to the limit. The fateful events related in both works are thought to be part of a long oral tradition that arose hundreds of years before they were written down and later attributed to Homer, their legendary author.

Odysseus's return from Asia Minor to his kingdom on the Ionian isle of Ithaca – off the west coast of Greece – should have taken a week at most by sea. No matter how strong or weak the wind was, an ancient Greek galley could make good headway, thanks to its bank of 25 oars on each side. Odysseus's voyage, however, took him some ten years – a consequence of the obstacles and challenges that the sea god Poseidon set in his way. As an indication of the forces that stood against Odysseus, Homer wrote that the hero's very name means "victim of enmity".

Stitches in time

The *Odyssey* is a drama of delay; each step forward is followed almost immediately by a setback. At the story's beginning, actually set more than midway through Odysseus's journey, the action was already at a standstill. Calypso, a seductive nymph, held Odysseus captive on her island (possibly Gozo, off Malta). Between bouts of lovemaking with the captive hero, she worked away at her loom using a golden shuttle.

Ironically, Calypso's weaving echoed the heroic handiwork of Odysseus's wife Penelope at home in Ithaca. She too was extremely

Calypso displays the charms with which she entraps Odysseus on her isle in a painting by the 16th-century Flemish artist Hendrik van Balen.

busy at her loom. Although many on the island despaired of ever seeing the return of Odysseus, and despite the failure of his son Telemachus's searches, Penelope remained devoted to her husband's memory. She kept her many eager and increasingly insistent suitors at bay by promising she would decide which to marry once her tapestry was complete. Each night, however, she toiled for hours unpicking all her stitches from the day before; like Calypso, Penelope held up time, but her delaying tactics also showed her to be her husband's counterpart in cunning.

Double standards

An admirer of Odysseus as a man of action, Athena, goddess of war, decided to intervene on his behalf with her father, Zeus. Calypso was compelled to let Odysseus go, and he built a ship to escape the nymph's island and return home. When Poseidon discovered this, he stirred up a storm to thwart

See also: The Olympian gods 24–31 ▪ The war of the gods and Titans 32–33 ▪ The many affairs of Zeus 42–47 ▪ The founding of Athens 56–57

the hero. Shipwrecked and cast ashore alone on the coast of Phaecia (perhaps Corfu), Odysseus was discovered by Nausicaa, the daughter of Alcinous, the country's king. Encouraged by Nausicaa, who brought him clothes, Odysseus made his way to the king's palace to seek help and was welcomed as a guest. While he was entertained in the hall of King Alcinous, the hero told the king the impressive story of his wanderings to date.

Sweet stupor

Odysseus began with the tale of his sojourn in the land of the Lotus-Eaters; he had gone there after his men sacked Ismarus, their first stop after Troy. The Lotus-Eaters lived in a permanent trance. The lotus fruits they ate not only provided nutritional sustenance; they also induced a daze of calmness and contentment. Only Odysseus was sufficiently quick-thinking and self-disciplined to recognize the danger when his shipmates fell upon the narcotic fruits. Seizing the men by force, he frogmarched them back to their ship and ordered his crew to set sail.

Cyclops and sea god

Hungry and tired after further days at sea, Odysseus and his men reached another coast, where they dropped anchor. Going ashore to forage, the men stumbled on a cave and were thrilled to find »

The 14 books of the *Odyssey*

I–IV
Struggles of Telemachus
to hold on to his father's house

V–VIII
Odysseus is freed
from captivity with Calypso but struggles to return home

IX–XII
Wanderings of Odysseus
as his voyage home to Ithaca is dogged by setbacks

XII–XIV
Odysseus returns home,
reunites with his son, and reclaims his house

Who was Homer?

The poet credited with both the *Iliad* and the *Odyssey* was almost certainly mythical. Ancient tradition portrayed him as a blind and bearded bard, strumming on a lyre. It was said he came from Ionia, on the coast of Asia Minor, in modern day Turkey. It is unlikely that such a person existed, and that a single poet created the *Iliad* or the *Odyssey*, let alone both.

Instead, "Homer" appears to have been an after-the-fact rationalization to account for the existence of the two great works. They are probably a compilation of stories told by innumerable anonymous bards, working in an "oral tradition" that dated back as far as the 12th century BCE. Such narrators could memorize vast screeds of narrative verse and fluently improvise new storylines; they would have used many formulaic narrative elements and ready-made images that were widely accepted and are strongly evident in the *Iliad* and *Odyssey*. The "writing" of the two works in the 8th century BCE was most probably a conclusive setting down, rather than an originating act.

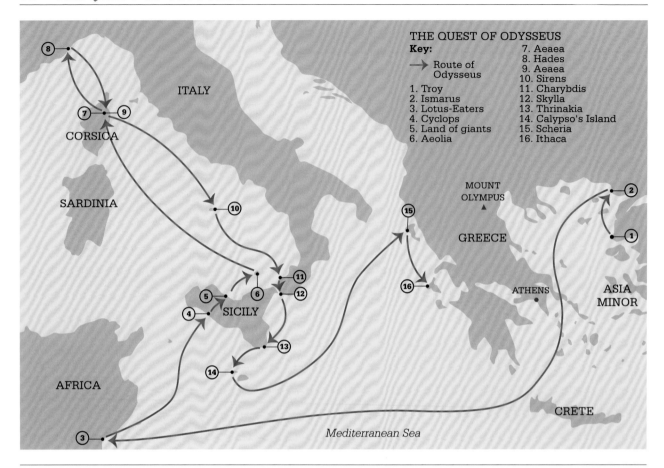

THE QUEST OF ODYSSEUS
Key:

→ Route of Odysseus

1. Troy
2. Ismarus
3. Lotus-Eaters
4. Cyclops
5. Land of giants
6. Aeolia
7. Aeaea
8. Hades
9. Aeaea
10. Sirens
11. Charybdis
12. Skylla
13. Thrinakia
14. Calypso's Island
15. Scheria
16. Ithaca

ITALY

CORSICA

SARDINIA

MOUNT OLYMPUS ▲

GREECE

ATHENS

ASIA MINOR

SICILY

AFRICA

CRETE

Mediterranean Sea

great quantities of food, wine, and other supplies stored within it. They began to help themselves, only to be interrupted when the owner of the cave returned. This was the terrifying Cyclops – a one-eyed giant named Polyphemus, who drove before him a flock of giant sheep. Polyphemus was a son of the sea god Poseidon.

Wounding Polyphemus
When the Cyclops discovered Odysseus and his crew inside his cave, he was furious. He rolled a huge boulder across the entrance, sealing it shut and trapping the men inside. He then snatched two of the men and devoured them. Desperate to escape, a terrified Odysseus and his remaining crew

came up with a plan. Waiting until the giant shepherd was drunk and drowsy, they heated up a massive tree-sized stake in the fire, then thrust it forcefully into the giant's single eye, blinding him.

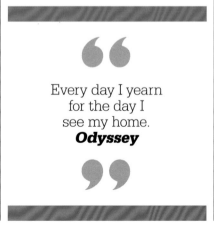

❝
Every day I yearn for the day I see my home.
Odyssey
❞

Groping about in agonized rage, Polyphemus could not find his attackers. They plotted their escape and, next morning, when the giant rolled back the boulder to take out his flock, the men hid beneath the bellies of the giant sheep, clinging on to their fleece. The giant felt each animal as it came out, but did not check underneath them. Reaching the safety of their ship, Odysseus jeered at the Cyclops. Hearing his voice, Polyphemus hurled boulders after Odysseus and his crew as they sailed away.

By wounding Polyphemus, however, Odysseus and his men had incurred the wrath of Poseidon, who would prove an implacable foe from this moment on. Every wind, wave, and current was against them. Even an apparent stroke of luck – when Aeolus gave Odysseus a leather bag in which all the winds of the world were stored – only delayed them further. The ship was in sight of Ithaca when the crew, thinking the bag might contain gold, opened it. The winds blew out, taking them away from Ithaca and into the unknown, where they wandered for several more years.

Witchcraft and prophecy

Next, Odysseus travelled to Aeaea, where the witch-goddess Circe turned a band of his men into pigs. He forced her to change them back and became her lover. After a year, Odysseus asked Circe how to get back to Ithaca; she advised him to sail to Hades to seek direction from a blind prophet named Tiresius.

Odysseus and his crew set off from Aeaea and he blocked his men's ears to save them from the seductive songs of the Sirens as they sailed past their isle. They then steered a course through a fiendishly narrow strait (Messina). On one side was the whirlpool Charybdis, eager to suck ships down; on the other was a crag, on which the six-headed maiden-monster Skylla sat, ready to seize and swallow passing sailors. When Odysseus finally met Tiresius, the seer explained Poseidon's grudge.

Against Tiresius's advice, Odysseus and his crew stopped to rest in Thrinakia (Helios). Odysseus told his men not to eat the sacred cattle, but they disobeyed and Zeus sent a mighty storm in punishment. Odysseus was the sole survivor; he swam to the island of Calypso, but

Odysseus's waiting wife, seated at her loom, is besieged by requests for her hand in marriage. *Penelope with the Suitors* was painted by the Italian Renaissance artist Pinturicchio (1509).

was captured by the nymph. After leaving Calypso, Odysseus was caught in a storm sent by Poseidon; he was washed up on Scheria, and rescued by the goddess Athena.

A hero's homecoming

When he finally made it home to Ithaca, Odysseus disguised himself to avoid recognition by Penelope's suitors and win back his "widow". He was taken in by Eumaeus, his old swineherd, and reunited with his son Telemachus in the servant's cottage.

By this time, the suitors had tired of Penelope's tapestry ruse, and so she set a new challenge. She agreed to marry only the man who could string her husband's bow and shoot an arrow accurately through a row of 12 axeheads. Penelope knew that Odysseus alone had the skill and strength for this. Still disguised, Odysseus succeeded with his first arrow and killed a suitor with his next. The angry suitors drew their weapons against the hero, who, with his son's help, killed them all. ∎

AFTER THE LABOURS HAD BEEN ACCOMPLISHED, HE WOULD BE IMMORTAL

THE LABOURS OF HERAKLES

Although he would grow up to become a hero, Herakles owed his existence to a deception. Zeus tricked the lovely Alcmene into having sex with him by disguising himself as her husband Amphitryon. When Alcmene gave birth to Zeus's son Herakles, the god ignored him. Amphitryon brought up the baby as his own. When she heard about Zeus's misdeeds, the goddess Hera went into a jealous rage and sent two giant serpents to kill baby Herakles. But not only was Herakles huge in size, his strength was already superhuman. He strangled the serpents with his bare hands. Later, Herakles married Princess

See also: The Olympian gods 24–31 ▪ Prometheus helps mankind 36–39 ▪
The many affairs of Zeus 42–47 ▪ The madness of Dionysus 52

Herakles strangles the serpents
sent by Hera to murder him in his
cradle. His parents Alcmene and
Amphitryon look on in awe in this
1743 painting by Pompeo Batoni.

Megara of Thebes and the couple
had a son and daughter. But Hera
was still jealous of Zeus's behaviour
and temporarily sent Herakles mad.
Losing all control, he slaughtered
his wife and his two children.

The labours begin
Grief-stricken Herakles was now
branded a murderer, and would
have to be punished. Hera coerced
the Delphic Oracle into imposing a
series of tasks as punishment.
Herakles was sentenced to serve
King Eurystheus of Mycenae and
perform 12 labours of his choosing.
Devising the most challenging and
dangerous tasks imaginable, the
king first ordered Herakles to find

and kill the Nemean lion. The beast
had been abducting women from
the area of Nemea and imprisoning
them in its den nearby. Herakles
tracked down the lion and shot it
with his bow and arrows, but the
arrow tips merely bounced off the
lion's impervious hide. Cornering
the lion in its cave, he knocked it
down with his club, then strangled
it. As a result, Herakles is always
depicted with his club and the skin
from the lion he had killed.

The Hydra
Next, Herakles faced an even more
dreadful monster. Living in Lake
Lerna, near the city of Argos, the
Hydra was a giant water snake
with nine heads waving, hissing,
and spitting poison. Its very breath
was venomous; its blood corroded
everything it came into contact
with; its skin was deadly to the
touch. When Herakles chopped off
one head, two new ones would
spring back in its place.

Unable to defeat the creature,
Herakles begged his nephew Iolaus
for help. Iolaus brought a blazing
brand so Herakles could cauterize
the wound as he cut off each head.
Stopping the blood prevented a »

The Hydra had a gigantic
body, with nine huge heads –
eight of them mortal.
Library

Alcmene

The daughter of Electryon,
Perseus's and Andromeda's
son, Alcmene was celebrated
as a paragon of feminine
beauty and virtue in ancient
Greece. Despite the duplicity
that led to Herakles's
conception, she and her
husband Amphitryon loved
her son and brought him up
alongside their own two
children, Iphicles – Herakles's
half-twin brother, who later
died in battle – and their
daughter Laonome, who
married an Argonaut.

According to Pausanias,
the jealous Hera sought to
punish Alcmene for carrying
Zeus's child, sending witches
to make her childbirth as
difficult as possible. In Ovid's
account, Alcmene struggled to
give birth to the enormous
Herakles, but the goddess of
childbirth, Eileithyia, refused
to help – terrified of upsetting
Hera, Eileithyia crossed
Alcmene's legs to hinder the
birth. In both versions of the
myth, Alcmene was saved by
a maidservant, who tricked
Hera's minions into believing
the baby was already born.

new head springing up. He finally succeeded in slaying the Hydra by cutting off and then burying its final, immortal head. Herakles then armed himself for future struggles by dipping the tips of his arrows in the monster's blood as it lay dying. His triumph was brief: Eurystheus ruled that the killing did not count, as he had relied on outside help.

A hind and other animals

The Ceryneian hind – also known as the Golden hind – was a deer with golden antlers, sacred to Artemis. The creature was so fast, it could outrun a speeding arrow. Herakles was told to bring it back for Eurystheus's menagerie. He had no trouble finding this extraordinary animal – the glint of the sun on its golden antlers gave it away – but catching it was harder. He chased it for a year across the whole of Greece before he finally caught it in a net and headed home.

Herakles's next target – the Erymanthian boar – was not just fast but ferocious, and Eurystheus

The labours of Herakles were a popular subject in Greek and Roman carvings. This frieze covered one side of a sarcophagus (c.240–250 CE), now in Rome's Palazzo Altemps.

> When he had chased the boar with shouts from a certain thicket, Herakles drove the exhausted animal into deep snow.
> *Library*

was terrified of it. The boar lived in Mount Erymanthos, where it was laying waste to farmers' fields. After a hunt which took him the length and breadth of Greece – and across the uplands of the Near East – Herakles drove the boar into a mountain snowdrift where he could tie up the floundering beast. Eurystheus begged him to get rid of it, and so Herakles flung the boar into the sea.

Herakles's fifth labour was to clean the Augean stables, which housed not horses but the cattle of King Augeas, who ruled Elis. Home to 1,000 cows, the shed had not been cleared for over 30 years. Herakles undertook this dirty and

degrading job with miraculous ease by diverting two rivers through the site to flush it clean. Eurystheus cried foul: Herakles had not done the work himself and he would not count this as a completed task.

Next, Herakles was sent into a swamp outside the town of Stymphalos, not far from Corinth, where birds – metal-beaked fowl that fed on human flesh – went to roost. Herakles struggled to make his way on the soft and soggy ground so Athena gave him a rattle. When swung, the rattle made a terrifying sound, startling the birds into flight. He could then pick them off with his bow and arrows.

More beasts, and a belt

After the Stymphalian birds were dispatched, Herakles was given the task of capturing the Cretan bull: the animal which had mated with Pasiphaë, wife of King Minos. Driven mad by Poseidon, the bull rampaged across the entire island of Crete. Herakles caught the great beast unawares by sneaking up behind it and strangling it with his mighty hands. He took the bull to Eurystheus's court in chains, but Eurystheus later set it free.

Next, Herakles had to steal the man-eating mares of Diomedes, king of Thrace. They were reputed

The 12 labours of Herakles

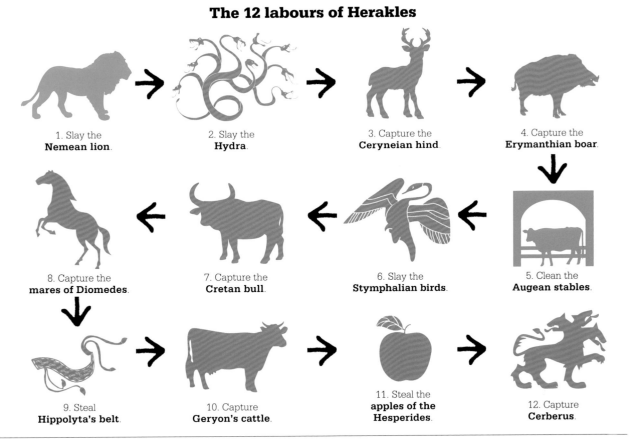

1. Slay the **Nemean lion**.

2. Slay the **Hydra**.

3. Capture the **Ceryneian hind**.

4. Capture the **Erymanthian boar**.

8. Capture the **mares of Diomedes**.

7. Capture the **Cretan bull**.

6. Slay the **Stymphalian birds**.

5. Clean the **Augean stables**.

9. Steal **Hippolyta's belt**.

10. Capture **Geryon's cattle**.

11. Steal the **apples of the Hesperides**.

12. Capture **Cerberus**.

to be uncontrollable, and Herakles's companion Abderus had previously been eaten by them. Herakles killed the king to avenge Abderus, and fed Diomedes's flesh to his horses. This briefly satisfied their hunger, making them calm enough for Herakles to bind their muzzles, put the horses in harness, and lead them back to Mycenae.

The ninth labour turned out to be the easiest. Herakles had to steal the belt of Hippolyta, Queen of the Amazons – a tribe of ferocious women warriors who lived in the Greek town of Themiscyra. Queen Hippolyta was so charmed by Herakles that she offered him her girdle of her own free will, but then Hera intervened. Determined to pursue her grudge against Herakles, the vengeful goddess

stirred up hostility amongst the Amazons, forcing Herakles to kill Hippolyta in order to escape.

Further burdens

Herakles's next labour took him to the very edge of the western ocean, to the island of Erytheia, near Libya. There, he had to steal the red cattle of Geryon, the three-headed giant. He also killed Geryon's herdsman Eurytion and his dog Orthrus – a two-headed monster with a writhing snake for its tail. Then, with great difficulty, he drove Geryon's cattle home to Greece.

For his eleventh task, Herakles headed west again to obtain the apples of the Hesperides: nymphs of the setting sun. Mysteriously unable to pick the apples himself, he convinced Atlas to do so in his

place. The Titan agreed – as long as Herakles held up the heavens for him. Atlas returned with the apples, but threatened to leave Herakles there for good. Herakles asked him to take the strain just for a moment and – when Atlas unthinkingly agreed – escaped with his prize.

Back in Mycenae, Herakles was given his final task: to go down deep into the earth and bring back Hades's many-headed watchdog, Cerberus. Herakles could have Cerberus, Hades said, only if he could capture him without using any of his weapons – so Herakles swept the hell hound up inside his lionskin cloak. Herakles had atoned for his sins and, redeemed, was finally released from his oath to serve Eurystheus. ∎

HE HAD THE FACE OF A BULL, BUT THE REST OF HIM WAS HUMAN
THESEUS AND THE MINOTAUR

IN BRIEF

THEME
Man and monster

SOURCES
Life of Theseus, Plutarch, 75 CE;
Library, Pseudo-Apollodorus,
c.100 CE.

SETTING
King Minos's palace,
Knossos, Crete.

KEY FIGURES
Aegeus King of Athens.

Minos King of Crete; son
of Zeus and Europa.

Pasiphaë Queen of Crete;
wife of Minos.

Poseidon God of the sea.

Minotaur A monster that is
half-man, half-bull.

Daedalus Inventor.

Theseus Son of King Aegeus
and Aethra.

Ariadne Daughter of Minos
and Pasiphaë.

The island of Crete was at the heart of the Minoan civilization that dominated the Aegean and Mediterranean world in the second millennium BCE. The Minoans were keen traders and had a sophisticated culture. Their rivalry with mainland Greeks may have been the origin of the myth of the Minotaur.

Sacrificial tribute

When King Aegeus of Athens had King Minos's son, Androgeos, murdered, the Delphic Oracle ordered him to atone for the crime. Every seven years Aegeus had to send seven of the city's finest

Daedalus built a labyrinth, whose complicated windings confounded whoever tried to leave.
Library

youths and seven of its loveliest maidens, drawn by lots, to Minos's capital of Knossos to be fed to the Minotaur, a monster that lived in a complex maze called the Labyrinth.

Half-man, half-bull, the Minotaur was the son of Minos's wife, Pasiphaë, and a white bull sent to King Minos by Poseidon. Rather than sacrifice the bull, as the sea god had intended, King Minos had kept it for his herd. Cursing the king, Poseidon had made Pasiphaë fall in love with the creature. When the queen, who disguised herself as a cow in order to visit the bull, then conceived and bore the Minotaur, King Minos ordered Daedalus to build the maze to hide the monster.

Theseus's mission

By the time Athens drew lots for the third sacrifice, King Aegeus's son Theseus had come of age. Determined to kill the Minotaur, he asked his father if he could join the sacrificial party bound for Crete. He promised to change his ship's sails from black to white for the return journey, as a signal of his success.

When Theseus arrived in Knossos, King Minos's daughter Ariadne fell madly in love with him.

See also: The many affairs of Zeus 42–47 ▪ Apollo and the Oracle of Delphi 58–59 ▪ Daedalus and Icarus 76–77 ▪ Mithras slays the bull 118–19 ▪ The epic of Gilgamesh 190–97

Theseus defeats the Minotaur in a scene on a *kylix* (drinking cup) from c.420 BCE. Decorated with Theseus's heroic deeds, the cup is signed by the Greek vase painter Aison.

She begged Daedalus to help her lover in his quest. To ensure Theseus would find his way out of the maze, Daedalus gave her a ball of wool for him to attach at the entrance to the maze and then unwind as he went deeper in. After an epic struggle, he killed the bull and followed Ariadne's thread back to safety.

Hasty exit

With Ariadne at his side, Theseus set sail for Athens, but Athena intervened, ordering him to leave Ariadne on the island of Naxos. In his distress at abandoning his lover, Theseus forgot to change the sail to white. Waiting on a clifftop, Aegeus saw the black-sailed ship return and in his grief – believing his son to be dead – hurled himself into the sea below. The sea has been the "Aegean" ever since. ▪

The bull

None held the bull in higher regard than the people who inhabited Crete for several centuries during the second millennium BCE. In a sense, King Minos, the mythical first king of Crete, was a half-bull like the Minotaur: his father, Zeus, had taken the form of a bull to rape his mother, Europa.

The bull cult was at the centre of Minoan culture: art depicting bulls abound in the palace-complex of Knossos, including one in which athletes leap over a bull. Excavated in the early 20th century by British archaeologist Arthur Evans, the palace is the most elaborate of several such complexes on the island of Crete. Evans called the culture "Minoan" on account of the culture's obsession with the bull, and due to the mazelike architecture of the excavated royal palace, which Evans referred to as the Labyrinth.

This Minoan *rhyton* (a carved libation vessel in the shape of an animal's head) from c.1500 BCE was found in a palace in Knossos.

DISDAINING HIS FATHER'S WARNINGS, THE EXHILARATED ICARUS SOARED EVER HIGHER
DAEDALUS AND ICARUS

IN BRIEF

THEME
Man's pride and punishment

SOURCES
Historical Library, Diodorus Siculus, c.30 BCE; *Library*, Pseudo-Apollodorus c.100 CE; *Metamorphoses*, Ovid, 8 CE; *Natural History*, Pliny, c.78 CE.

SETTING
Crete and the Aegean.

KEY FIGURES
Minos King of Crete; son of Zeus and Europa.

Daedalus Greek inventor employed by King Minos.

Icarus Son of Daedalus by Naucrate, an Egyptian slave.

Cocalos King of Kamikos, Sicily; Daedalus's protector.

Daedalus was an inventor and was responsible for a host of innovations: he equipped ships with masts, sails, and prows with battering rams to outpace and outfight rival fleets; he made lifelike statues and automata that could think and feel like men; and invented new tools for construction. Originally from Athens, he worked for King Minos in Crete and built not only the Labyrinth that concealed the Minotaur but also the wooden cow in which the monster's mother had hidden in order to mate with the king's prized bull. Minos valued Daedalus so much that he did not want to let him of his sight.

See also: Theseus and the Minotaur 76–77 ▪ Arachne and the spider 115 ▪ The epic of Gilgamesh 190–97

Daedalus and Icarus build a wooden cow for Queen Pasiphaë (far left) in this floor mosaic from Zeugma, Turkey. Hidden inside the cow, Pasiphaë mated with her husband's bull.

Daedalus's inventions made him indispensable, but dangerous – he knew the king's deepest secrets, and Minos dreaded losing him. After Daedalus helped Theseus escape from the Labyrinth, Minos installed the inventor in a tower where he lived as a pampered prisoner, enjoying every luxury except his freedom. With him was Icarus, Daedalus's son by Minos's Egyptian slave Naucrate.

Taking wing

Daedalus resolved to flee his gilded cage. Escape routes from the tower and off the island were barred, first by the dizzying drop beneath the window; then by Minos's men below; and lastly by the waves of the Aegean Sea. Watching from his window as the birds flew by,

Daedalus realized that the sky was still open to him as a highway – if only he could fly.

Daedalus devoted hours of study to the birds; he examined the anatomy of their wings and the aerodynamics of their flight. Day and night he toiled to construct two pairs of wings – one pair for him and one for his son.

The wings were complex: their frames had to be strong but flexible and light, and they had to provide »

Daedalus's dark past

Originally from Athens, Daedalus fled to Crete after the murder of his nephew Talos (sometimes identified as Perdix), who was also his talented apprentice. Daedalus was believed to have felt threatened by Talos's growing powers of invention, which seemed set to outshine his own. By the age of 12, Talos had already invented the potter's wheel, the chisel, and the first compass, which he made out of two pieces of iron that he pivoted on a pin.

Overcome with jealousy, Daedalus pushed Talos off the top of the Acropolis. In Ovid's version of the myth, Pallas Minerva (Athena) witnessed the incident and intervened to catch Talos in mid-air, transforming him into a partridge – a bird, the poet notes, that likes to live close to the ground. Seeking to escape trial, Daedalus then fled to Crete, while Talos's mother, Daedalus's sister, took her own life.

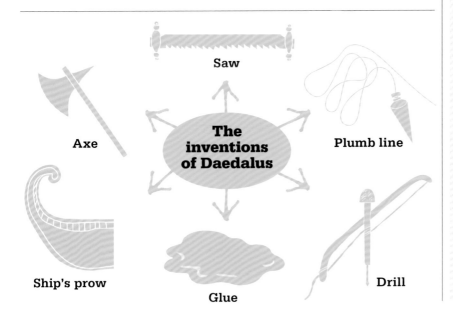

Saw

Axe

The inventions of Daedalus

Plumb line

Ship's prow

Glue

Drill

Daedalus and Icarus by the Genoese master Domenico Piola (c. 1670) shows Daedalus strapping wings to his son's back as he points to the sky and the hazardous journey ahead.

enough lift to defy gravity and keep Daedalus and Icarus airborne. Daedalus covered the wings with real feathers, but puzzled over how to attach them. The answer, he decided, was wax: strong and yielding at the same time, it held the feathers firmly while still allowing flexibility. Daedalus set to work. Row on row and layer upon layer, every plume had to be carefully placed and precisely anchored to re-create the contours of a real wing.

Risky flight
Finally, the wings were completed. The results were astounding: the man-made wings perfectly replicated the movement of the birds. Yet the inventor knew that the wings were fragile, and he gave his son strict instructions: on no account should he to fly too low, in case the waves should splash his wings and the extra weight of the water then drag him in to the ocean. Nor should he fly too high, in case the rays of the sun melted the wax holding his wings together. Daedalus urged Icarus to pursue the middle way instead.

Wearing his father's inventions, the young boy stepped from the tower and, instead of plunging to his death, was borne aloft by the slow sweep of the wings through the air. Icarus was exhilarated; he had never felt so powerful or free. His father was more apprehensive and cautiously led the way towards the clouds, assessing his height at every stage in the journey and using landmarks on the ground to steer a safe course.

Icarus did not feel his father's fear. With every wingbeat, he grew more masterful and more audacious, swooping and soaring through the air, oblivious to his father's repeated warnings. Well out over the Aegean, he flew ever higher, and laughed to see his father flapping slowly below.

The boy's descent
Icarus rejoiced at the warmth of the sun upon his face, but then suddenly remembered his father's warnings. Seeing a feathered wing tip loosen and fall away, he realized the wax was softening in the heat. Alarmed, he dipped into a descent. As he did so, the feathers streamed away from his wings as the wax melted, and he plunged towards the sea.

Daedalus heard his son's despairing cry and looked back only to see the flurry of feathers and foam where he had hit the surface of the water – the nearby island of Icaria is named for the place where he fell. Devastated by the loss of his son, Daedalus had no option but to continue on alone. Although Icaria lies northeast of Crete off the coast of Turkey, sources say that

Virtue both finds and chooses that which is intermediate.
Aristotle
Nicomachaean Ethics

Hubris

The myth of Daedalus and Icarus warns against over-confidence, or hubris. Mortals who were considered guilty of hubris were severely punished in Greek myths and in the poetry and plays those stories inspired. The offence was considered grave because it threatened the order of the cosmos and the limitations placed on mortals by the gods.

Aristotle proclaimed the desirability of the "golden mean" – the middle way between two extremes. The advisability of this ideal applied to all aspects of life and was considered an attribute of beauty. In architecture, the golden mean was expressed in terms of ideal proportions derived from mathematics. For example, the Parthenon, built in 447–432 BCE in thanks for an Athenian victory over Persian invaders, was the crowning glory of a city at its political and military zenith, but it was also a stone-built hymn to symmetry and balance – the embodiment of moderation and beauty.

Daedalus eventually landed in Sicily, far to the west. There, King Cocalus of Kamikos took him in.

Tested by a riddle

Meanwhile, King Minos was intent on finding his ingenious inventor and returning him to Crete. He pursued Daedalus to Sicily, where he combed the island with a riddle he knew only Daedalus would be able to solve – threading a spiral seashell with a silken cord. When King Cocalus returned the shell neatly strung, Minos guessed that Daedalus had assisted him. He was correct: Daedalus had tied the thread to an ant and let the tiny creature draw it through the shell.

Minos demanded Daedalus's surrender, but Cocalus played for time and asked his visitor to wait

Icarus falls from the sky as his father looks on in this engraving by Jean Matheus (c.1610), from a translation of Ovid's *Metamorphoses* by Frenchman Nicholas Renouard.

> " Because of the ignorance of youth, he made his flight too far aloft and fell into the sea.
> **Historical Library**

and enjoy his hospitality for a while. Some say that his daughters attacked and killed King Minos as he took a bath, others that Daedalus himself took a hand in killing him by pouring boiling water into the bath through secret pipes. Some versions of the myth say that after his death, the gods took Minos to Olympus, where he worked with Hephaestus, the god of metalworking and blacksmiths. ∎

Phaëton and Helios

The myth of Icarus and Daedalus is often compared to that of Phaëton and Helios. Helios, the Titan sun god, drove westwards across the sky each day in a golden chariot drawn by flaming horses and plunged over the western horizon by nightfall. Every day, Helios's son, Phaëton ("Shining One"), watched in awe and envy, begging his father to let him drive the chariot. Despite misgivings, Helios eventually agreed and Phaëton took off, laughing exultantly.

Soon, however, Phaëton panicked; his horses pulled him far off course, bucking, diving, and swerving through the sky. Flying low, they scorched the earth; then soaring into space, they left the fields frozen and barren. Finally, Zeus had seen enough: he hurled a thunderbolt and sent Phaëton falling to his death, as a punishment for trying to fly too high. While the story of Icarus is most often viewed as a warning against hubris, Ovid's account of Phaëton's downfall can be read as a tale of both the nobility of man's aspirations and their folly.

WATCHING THE GORGON'S HEAD IN THE POLISHED SHIELD, HE BEHEADED HER

PERSEUS AND MEDUSA

IN BRIEF

THEME
The threat of female sexuality

SOURCES
Theogony, Hesiod, c.700 BCE; *Prometheus Bound*, Aeschylus, c.430 BCE; *Library*, Pseudo-Apollodorus, c.100 CE; *Description of Greece*, Pausanias, c.150 CE.

SETTING
Argos; Asia; Aethiopia.

KEY FIGURES
Perseus A hero; son of Zeus and Danaë.

Danaë Daughter of Acrisius; mother of Perseus.

Zeus King of the gods; father of Perseus.

Medusa One of three Gorgons.

Andromeda Daughter of Queen Cassiopeia and King Cepheus of Aethiopia.

The origins of Perseus were both unlikely and extraordinary: Zeus impregnated his mother, Danaë, with a shower of gold. Perseus was born in Argos, in Greece, but because Acrisius, his grandfather, had been warned that he would one day be killed by his grandson, Perseus and Danaë were cast adrift in a wooden chest to drown. They landed on the Aegean island of Serifos, where the king took them in.

Perseus's quest
Years passed and the king, Polydectes, wanted to marry the beautiful Danaë, but she refused.

In some versions of the story, the king sent Perseus away with the deadly task of slaying the monster Medusa, leaving Polydectes free to marry Danaë. In others, Perseus volunteered as a dare. In any case, Perseus set off to kill Medusa and bring back her head as evidence.

Medusa was one of a trio of Gorgons: creatures who had snakes for hair, and faces so hideous that the slightest glimpse would turn any onlooker into stone. According to some myths, Medusa had been born monstrous, but in others she had been cursed by the goddess Athena for her vanity. Medusa's two sisters were immortal, but Medusa herself had been specially punished by Athena with mortality and could therefore be killed.

Divine assistance
Faced with the challenge of killing Medusa, Perseus turned to the gods for assistance. Athena gave him a gleaming shield of bronze; his father Zeus suppled him with a

The beheading of Medusa by Perseus, accompanied by Athena, as depicted in a 6th-century BCE limestone relief carved in Temple C, Selinunte, Sicily.

See also: Prometheus helps mankind 28–31 ▪ The many affairs of Zeus 39–47 ▪ The labours of Herakles 70–73 ▪ Theseus and the Minotaur 74–75

> They turned
> to stone all those
> who beheld them.
> *Library*

sword; Hades provided a helmet of invisibility; and Hermes granted him winged sandals. At Athena's prompting, Perseus also visited the Hesperides, who gave him a bag with which to safely carry the head of Medusa: even in death, her petrifying stare and her hissing hair could prove fatal.

Finally, Perseus reached the Gorgons' island of Sarpedon, near Cisthene. The Gorgons slept in a cave guarded by the Graeae: three hags who shared a single tooth and one eye. While they were switching their shared tooth and eye from one

hag to another, he snatched them both and slipped past. Finding Medusa asleep, Perseus crept up on her undetected and looked not at her actual face but at her reflection in his shield. Raising his sword high, he swung it down with all his might, cut off her head, and put it into his bag – never once looking directly at Medusa's petrifying face.

New life

Medusa had been made pregnant by Poseidon, and from the gaping wound left by her decapitation, the winged horse Pegasus came galloping out, followed by his giant brother Chrysaor, named for the golden sword he brandished. Perseus rode off on Pegasus and, during his return voyage home, he rescued the maiden Andromeda from a sea monster. When he finally reached home, Perseus entered the palace victoriously bearing Medusa's head. Polydectes looked upon it and was turned to stone. Perseus then returned his gifts to the gods, giving the Gorgon's head as a gift to Athena. ▪

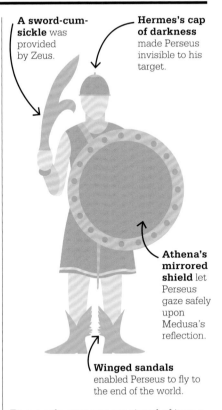

A sword-cum-sickle was provided by Zeus.

Hermes's cap of darkness made Perseus invisible to his target.

Athena's mirrored shield let Perseus gaze safely upon Medusa's reflection.

Winged sandals enabled Perseus to fly to the end of the world.

Perseus's armour consisted of items given to him by several different gods. Often, in ancient Greek mythology, enchanted items imbued with magical powers would aid a hero in his quest.

Andromeda

The daughter of the king and queen of the ancient kingdom of Aethiopia – Africa's upper Nile region – Andromeda was renowned for her beauty. She was humble, but her mother – the sea-nymph Cassiopeia – was not. Boasting that her daughter's allure surpassed even that of the Nereids – the nymphs who attended Poseidon – she caused the god of the sea unpardonable offence. Every day, he sent the giant sea monster Cetus to attack Aethiopia's fields and

villages. Andromeda's father, Cepheus, begged Poseidon to spare his kingdom further persecution. Poseidon replied that he would only call off the monster if Cepheus offered it his daughter as a sacrifice.

Andromeda was stripped naked, chained to a rock beside the sea, and left to her fate when Perseus chanced upon this scene and swooped down to intervene. He killed Cetus, freed Andromeda from her chains, and took her to be his bride and live with him at his home on the isle of Serifos.

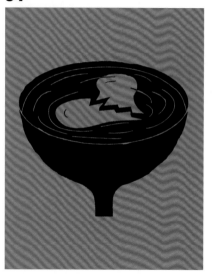

HATE IS A BOTTOMLESS CUP, I WILL POUR AND POUR
JASON AND MEDEA

IN BRIEF

THEME
Betrayal and revenge

SOURCES
Medea, Euripides, 431 BCE; *Argonautica*, Apollonius of Rhodes, c.250 BCE; *Library*, Pseudo-Apollodorus, c.100 CE; *Description of Greece*, Pausanias, c.150 CE.

SETTING
Iolcos, Thessaly; Colchis, on the Black Sea; Corinth, the Peloponnese.

KEY FIGURES
Jason Son of Aeson; rightful heir to the throne.

Pelias King of Iolcos.

King Aeëtes Son of the sun god Helios; king of Colchis.

The Argonauts Jason's band of warriors, who command a ship named the *Argo*.

Medea Sorceress, and daughter of King Aeëtes.

Jason, the rightful heir to the throne of Iolcos, grew up in exile, displaced by his father's half-brother Pelias. As soon as Jason was old enough, he made the return voyage to his Thessalian kingdom to take back his crown. Pelias conceded Jason's claim but insisted that, to be the king of Iolcus, he would first have to journey east to the Caucasus and bring the magical Golden Fleece back from King Aeëtes of Colchis.

The Argonauts
Pelias was confident that the mission would be suicidal and that Jason would never return, but Jason

had the goddess Athena on his side. Guided by her instructions, a ship – the *Argo* – was constructed and named after Argus, its builder. Meanwhile Jason gathered together a group of warriors to help in his quest. Calling themselves the "Argonauts", they set out to sea, and after many adventures, they arrived in Colchis – a land the Greeks considered to be the edge of the Earth. Making their way upstream into a wild mountain region, the Argonauts found the fabled fleece hanging from a branch in a sacred grove, guarded by a ferocious dragon that never slept.

Medea's obsession
On Jason's arrival, capricious Eros, god of desire, struck the king's daughter, Medea, with one of his gold-tipped arrows. The young princess instantly fell madly in love. Though she was a niece of the witch Circe, and a sorceress in her own right, Medea was powerless to resist. Consumed by desire, all she

Medea holds her deadly potion as the unwitting daughters of Pelias bring in a cauldron for his fatal bath. This is a Roman copy of a Greek marble stele (funerary monument) from c. 420 BCE.

See also: The Labours of Herakles 70–73 ▪ Theseus and the Minotaur 74–75 ▪ Perseus and Medusa 80–81 ▪ Cupid and Psyche 110–11

Medea prepares to murder Absyrtus and throw his remains overboard, as she and Jason flee Colchis together on board the *Argo* in this painting by Herbert James Draper (1904).

wanted was to be with Jason and help him in any way she could. She prepared a potion that would send the dragon into a long, deep sleep, so that Jason could step over its resting body and take the fleece.

Having cheated her father of the fleece, Medea then resorted to a gruesome murder in order to escape with Jason and the Argonauts. As she fled Colchis on board the *Argo*, she butchered her younger brother and threw his body parts into the sea, so that her pursuing father would have to stop to gather them up for burial.

A woman scorned

When Jason reached Iolcos with the Golden Fleece, Pelias refused to keep his side of the contract. Medea tricked him into taking a deadly potion she claimed would give him eternal youth. After this second murder, Jason, Medea, and

their children had to flee to Corinth. There, in pursuit of political advantage, Jason betrayed Medea and left her for Glauce, a princess of the city's ruling house.

Medea soon took her revenge. She gave the new bride a wedding gown steeped in poison that burst into flames when she put it on, killing her and her father. Medea then slew two of her three children, leaving only Thessalus alive. Before Jason could punish her for this terrible crime, she fled to Athens, flying in the golden chariot of her grandfather, Helios. ▪

Stronger than lover's love is lover's hate. Incurable, in each, the wounds they make.
Medea

Euripides

The three greatest playwrights of ancient Greece turned myths into tragedies that are still performed to this day and eloquently articulate the helplessness of humanity in the face of an unforgiving fate. Aeschylus (c.525–455 BCE) and Sophocles (c.496–405 BCE) wrote about the existential anguish of mankind, but Euripides (c.480–406 BCE) went further, revealing the harrowing inner lives of compelling individuals, both men and women. More of his works survive than of Aeschylus and Sophocles combined – his popularity grew in the Hellenistic period that followed the death of Alexander in 323 BCE, and he is regarded as a cornerstone of Western literature.

Euripides's *Medea* is particularly striking for its psychological sophistication and its compassion for Medea. Her fury is evoked in all its horror. So too is the torment she feels at her abandonment, and the pain she faces as a woman and a mother: "I would sooner stand in the front line of the battle phalanx three times", she says, "than go through the sufferings of childbirth even once".

UNFORTUNATE OEDIPUS – OF ALL MEN, LEAST TO BE ENVIED!

THE FATE OF OEDIPUS

IN BRIEF

THEME
Fate

SOURCE
Oedipus Tyrannus, Sophocles, c.430 BCE.

SETTING
Thebes.

KEY FIGURES
Laius King of Thebes.

Jocasta Queen of Thebes; wife of Laius, then Oedipus.

Oedipus Son of Laius and Jocasta.

Polybus and Merope The king and queen of Corinth.

The Oracle Also known as the Pythia; a woman widely revered for her prophecies.

The Sphinx A creature that asked riddles and punished any who answered incorrectly.

Tiresias The blind prophet of Thebes.

King Laius of Thebes was warned by his soothsayer (a psychic) never to father a child. If he did, the soothsayer prophesied, the king's son would grow up to kill him, and then marry his wife. However, Laius's queen, Jocasta, was irresistibly beautiful. Eventually he was overcome with desire and they slept together. Nine months later, Jocasta gave birth to a son, Oedipus.

Home from home

Mindful of the prophecy, Laius gave the baby to a servant, and told him to leave Oedipus on the mountainside to die. But a shepherd family found the baby and took care of him, later handing him over to King Polybus and Queen Merope of Corinth, who had no children of their own. Oedipus grew up happily but one day heard it muttered that he wasn't his parents' child. He went to Delphi to ask the Oracle, and discovered that he was fated to kill his father and

Oedipus answers the Sphinx in this detail of a sarcophagus from the Hellenistic Period (c. 323–31 BCE), now displayed in the National Archaeological Museum in Athens.

wed his mother. Distraught at the thought of killing Polybus and marrying Merope, Oedipus left Corinth and fled towards Thebes – unaware that this was the home of his biological family.

Prophecy fulfilled

On the road to Thebes, Oedipus met a self-important dignitary, who demanded that Oedipus make way for him. He quarrelled with the man and killed him, not realizing that he was King Laius, his father. When he then fell in love with the King's widow Jocasta, Oedipus had no idea she was his own mother.

Any man who hoped to marry Jocasta and become the new king of Thebes had to solve a riddle

See also: The Olympian gods 24–31 ▪ Orestes avenges Agamemnon 64–65 ▪ The quest of Odysseus 66–71 ▪ Eshu the trickster 294–97

Oedipus blinds himself upon learning his wife's identity in this miniature from *De Casibus Virorum Illustrium* ("On the Fates of Famous Men"), Giovanni Boccaccio (1313–1375).

What man's misfortunes ever threw his successes into so violent a reverse?
Oedipus Tyrannus

posed by the human-headed, lion-bodied, and bird-winged creature known as the Sphinx. "What," the Sphinx asked, "goes on four legs in the morning, two legs at noon, and three legs in the evening?" Oedipus did not hesitate: "Man," he replied. As an infant, man crawls on all fours; then he walks upright; finally, in old age, he shuffles along with the help of a stick.

Doomed by destiny

Oedipus and Jocasta were wed, lived happily in the palace, and had several children before Thebes was struck by a devastating plague. When all rituals and sacrifices failed to provide a cure, the blind prophet Tiresias told the astonished king that he had doomed the city with his own actions. When

Tiresias explained to Oedipus that the man he had fought and killed was his father, Oedipus realized that Jocasta was his mother. At this revelation, Jocasta committed suicide, and when Oedipus found her body, he drove her dress pins into his eyes, blinding himself.

Although Oedipus had not been aware that he was committing patricide or incest, his behaviour had to be punished. Despite his royal birth, integrity, and ability to answer the hardest riddle, Oedipus was as unable as any of us to escape his destiny. ▪

The Oedipus Complex

Sigmund Freud (1856–1939), the founder of psychoanalysis, shocked the world with his theories of the unconscious. His idea that people were driven by parts of their personality of which they had no knowledge was profoundly upsetting at that time. Special outrage was reserved for his theory of the "Oedipus Complex", named after the characters in Sophocles' play. In every family, said Freud, the son subconsciously yearns to possess his mother – his first love from infancy – and oust his father from first place in her affections.

Freud's theories were unfalsifiable – impossible to prove or disprove – and many are discounted by modern psychiatrists. Yet the idea of the Oedipus Complex persists in popular culture, as it helps to make emotional sense of seemingly irrational rivalries and jealousies within families.

SHE WANTS ADONIS MORE THAN SHE DOES HEAVEN ITSELF
APHRODITE AND ADONIS

IN BRIEF

THEME
Unrequited love

SOURCES
Metamorphoses, Ovid, 8 CE;
Library, Pseudo-Apollodorus,
c.100 CE.

SETTING
Ancient Greece.

KEY FIGURES
Aphrodite Goddess of love;
known as Venus in Roman
myth, she pursued Adonis
relentlessly.

Eros Son of Aphrodite; god
of sexual attraction.

Cinyras King of Cyprus;
deceived, seduced, and then
disgusted by his daughter.

Myrrha Daughter of Cinyras;
pitying her, the gods later
turned her into a myrrh tree.

Adonis Son of Cinyras and
Myrrha; a beautiful and
chaste youth.

E ven Aphrodite, the great
goddess of love, was not
immune to the darts of
desire. One day, as Eros played in
his mother's arms, one of his arrows
brushed against her breast. When
she looked up, the first person that
Aphrodite chanced to see was the
beautiful Adonis, as he sprinted
past with his pack of hounds in
pursuit of a lone deer.

Aphrodite was instantly smitten.
Adonis, Myrrha's son, was not only
the fairest youth of all – to this day
his name is a byword for male
beauty – but also the least

Adonis rejects Aphrodite as he
hurries off to hunt. In Titian's *Venus
and Adonis* (1554), this is no time for
love – Eros is asleep, dawn is breaking,
and the hounds yearn to leave.

See also: Orpheus and Eurydice 53 ▪ Perseus and Medusa 82–83 ▪ Cupid and Psyche 112–13 ▪ Echo and Narcissus 114 ▪ Pomona and Vertumnus 122–123 ▪ Pyramus and Thisbe 124

Myrrha

Adonis was conceived through his mother Myrrha's unnatural desire for her father Cinyras, king of Cyprus. This happened when Myrrha slipped into his bed one night, after he had drunk too much wine, tricking him into believing she was her mother. Her incestuous passion was punishment from the Furies, Cinyras's unwitting involvement an act of spite by Aphrodite, who had taken great offense when Myrrha's mother, Kenkhreis, had boasted about

her daughter's beauty. Fleeing her outraged father, Myrrha was turned into a tree at her own request, after praying for transformation from the gods as a punishment for her actions. Shedding tears of myrrh, she gave birth to Adonis, who was perversely chaste. Classical writers wrote that Myrrha's lust for her father came from an obsesssion with her virginity.

Myrrha hides her face in shame as the poets Dante and Virgil journey through Hell, in an illustration by Gustave Doré (1885).

attainable. Resolutely chaste, he had no interest in romantic love – hunting was the only passion that stirred his cold heart. Day and night, he ran through dense dark forest in search of every sort of quarry.

Inflamed by desire, Aphrodite set off in pursuit of Adonis, her long hair streaming behind, and her garments flying open as she ran. Each time she caught Adonis, he struggled free. He would not submit to her embraces, however much she called after him to stay.

Unheeded warnings

Pursuing Adonis through the woods, Aphrodite took care to steer clear of savage boars and other wild animals that might attack, and urged Adonis to do the same.

Adonis dismissed Aphrodite's fears, rejected her pleas and caresses, and returned to his hunt – only to be charged by a giant and ferocious wild boar. Its sharp tusk sliced into his groin – a symbolic castration regarded as punishment for his rejection of sexual love. As

Adonis lay dying in the arms of weeping Aphrodite, his blood spilled out. At her command, the bloody drops stained the lovely petals of the anemone a deep red, and the flower sprung up afresh each year.

Adonis and the seasons

Athenian women held an annual festival in memory of Adonis, called the Adonia. Plato disapproved, but the overwhelmingly male official chroniclers of Greek life said little about this festival of female

My dear Adonis, keep away from savage beasts.
Metamorphoses

sexuality. Women openly celebrated male physical beauty and mourned its fleeting nature. They and their daughters made miniature gardens in pots packed with fast-growing plants and carried them up to the rooftops. When the Adonia's eight days of dance and song ended, the plants were thrown into streams or the ocean – a symbolic act seen by some scholars as an attempt to generate plentiful rain for the coming harvest.

In myths and festivals alike, Adonis was not only remembered for his cold beauty but linked to fertility, the seasons, and the cycle of decay and regeneration. One myth, for example, tells of a conflict between Aphrodite and Persephone over who should be allowed to keep the infant Adonis. Zeus ordered Adonis to divide his time equally between the two, spending spring and summer with Aphrodite (amongst the living) and autumn and winter with Persephone (in the Underworld). This tale emphasizes Adonis's connection to fertility and the cycle of death and revival in crops. ▪

WHATEVER I TOUCH, MAY IT BE TRANSFORMED INTO TAWNY GOLD

KING MIDAS

IN BRIEF

THEME
A cursed gift

SOURCES
Anabasis ("The March of the 10,000"), Xenophon, c.370 BCE; *Metamorphoses*, Ovid, 8 CE.

SETTING
Ancyra (now Ankara), in Phrygia (central Turkey).

KEY FIGURES
Midas King of Phrygia; cursed with a golden touch.

Silenus Half-man, half-horse; god of wine-making and drunkenness; companion and tutor of Dionysos.

Dionysus The god of fertility and wine, who brought both ecstasy and rage.

King Midas generously entertained Silenus, the companion of Dionysus, for ten days after saving him from a village mob. Although Xenophon's account claimed Midas captured Silenus to steal his wisdom, in Ovid's tale Dionysus was grateful for his friend's safe return and offered Midas anything he wanted.

Midas asked that whatever he touched should turn to gold, and the god granted his wish. The king

was thrilled and instantly touched everything he saw – a twig, a stone, an ear of wheat, an apple on a branch. All immediately turned into glowing, solid gold. As he reached home, the wooden doors and sills of his own palace were transformed where he touched them. What good fortune!

Soon, though, Midas realized how hungry he felt, and told his servants to bring him food. At his touch, the bread turned to gold and the wine turned to molten gold. Could he ever eat or drink again?

Midas fled his home, hating what he had wished for. Seeking refuge in the wilderness, he cried out to Dionysus, begging his benefactor to take back his gift. The god told him to bathe up in the hills at the source of the Pactolus; washing away the curse, Midas was freed from his golden touch. ■

As Midas bathed at the river's source, shown here in a work by Bartolomeo Manfredi (1617–19), the gold he washed away was said to have seeped into the sand, later enriching King Croesus.

See also: The many affairs of Zeus 42–47 ▪ The cult of Dionysus 52 ▪ Vesta and Priapus 108–109

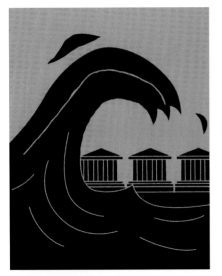

IN A SINGLE DAY AND NIGHT THE ISLAND OF ATLANTIS DISAPPEARED BENEATH THE WAVES
THE LEGEND OF ATLANTIS

IN BRIEF

THEME
Lost city

SOURCES
Timaeus and *Critias*,
Plato, c.360 BCE.

SETTING
Beyond the Pillars of Herakles (now known as the Strait of Gibraltar), which marked the edge of the ancient Greek world.

A confederacy of kings, of great and marvellous power.
Critias

Atlantis was a mythical civilization that flourished before an ill-fated war and natural forces destroyed it. It is described in two dialogues by the Athenian philosopher Plato as an imaginative illustration of his beliefs about how an ideal state should be run and the dangers of the arrogant use of power.

Though an island, Atlantis was "larger than Libya and Asia". It was an advanced society, technically accomplished and well governed. Yet when this wealthy aggressor waged an unprovoked war, it was the small, democratic Athens that prevailed through her "virtue and strength". The seemingly utopian Atlantis failed, Plato notes, because its people became corrupt. For this, the great god Zeus punished them, sending earthquakes and floods until finally Atlantis was swallowed up in the sea.

Minoan memories
So vividly suggestive was this one fable that the quest to find a site that inspired Plato's story never

[Athens] shone forth, in the excellence of her virtue and strength.
Critias

ceased. There was a historical precedent for the loss of Atlantis: the eruption of the island-volcano of Thera (Santorini), in the Aegean, south of mainland Greece, around 1500 BCE. Not only did most of the island sink into the sea, but the darkening effect of the ash across the sky created a "winter" which lasted several years. This disaster likely brought about the end of the Minoan civilization, and some scholars believe that the story of Atlantis represented a sort of folk memory of these events. ■

See also: The founding of Athens 56–57 ▪ The Trojan War 62–63 ▪ The quest of Odysseus 66–71

ANCIENT

ROME

Rome is **founded** (according to tradition celebrated in the annual *Parilia* festival).

Virgil's **national epic** the *Aeneid* recounts Aeneas's flight from Troy and long journey to Italy.

Livy's ***History of Rome*** intertwines foundational myths with historical records of Rome.

753 BCE   **30–19** BCE   **27–9** BCE

509 BCE   **27** BCE   **7** BCE

The last king of Rome, Tarquin the Proud, is overthrown; Rome becomes a **republic**.

After **civil war** ends in victory for Octavian, he becomes Rome's first emperor, Augustus.

Roman Antiquities by Dionysius traces Rome's **history and legends** up until c.240 BCE.

The city of Rome is said to have been founded in 753 BCE by Romulus and Remus – two descendants of the Trojan prince Aeneas, whose voyage from the sacked city of Troy was the subject of the *Aeneid*. Rome became a great imperial power, at its greatest extent under Trajan (c.100 CE), encompassing 20 per cent of the world's population.

Greece and Rome

Roman culture absorbed that of Italy's various tribes – the Latins, the Etruscans, the Sabines – whose gods were adopted by Roman mythology. However, Romans also appropriated the myths of the ancient Greeks, whose colonies, culture, and myths they had taken on, aligning many of their own gods with Greek counterparts.

The Roman gods were not, however, simply Greek gods by different names. Bacchus, the lighthearted Roman god of wine and inspiration, is more similar to the pleasure-seeking Etruscan god Fufluns than to the Greek Dionysos. The "Capitoline Triad" of Jupiter, Juno, and Minerva developed from the Etruscan gods Tinia, Uni, and Menvra. Only later were these Roman gods aligned with Zeus, Hera, and Athena.

Many Roman writers took pains to emphasize the moral superiority of the Roman gods over their Greek counterparts. The Romans disliked the wanton amorality of the Greek gods, preferring to stress the moral rectitude of the gods of Rome. A myth such as that of Arachne – the spinner and weaver who criticized the gods by depicting their most

shameful deeds and was turned into a spider as a result – appealed to Roman values because it both condemned the gods' immorality and punished a human for daring to reproach them. The story of Arachne was recorded by the poet Ovid, one of the key authorities for Roman mythology, but he probably took it from a lost Greek source, as *arachne* means "spider" in Greek.

Ancient Roman religion revolved around pleasing the gods. Before Christianity was recognized by Constantine in 313 CE, the Roman calendar was full of feast days, sacrifices, and rituals to the numerous deities. While Romans shared and celebrated the myths of their various gods, their religion was based around the practice of ritual acts, rather than beliefs in doctrine or mythological narratives.

Ovid explores the creation, deities, history, and rituals of Rome in his poems, *Fasti* and *Metamorphoses*.

Plutarch pens 23 **biographies** of legendary Greeks and Romans in *Parallel Lives*.

Under Emperor Constantine, Rome begins to transition to **Christianity** as its official religion.

The Eastern Roman (or Byzantine) Empire, formed in 330 CE, **falls to the Ottoman Turks**.

8 CE   **c.100–120 CE**   **306–337 CE**   **1453 CE**

c.80 CE   **c.158–180 CE**   **476 CE**

The *Thebaid* by Statius depicts the **assault of Argos's champions** on the city of Thebes.

Apuleius's *Metamorphoses*, known as *The Golden Ass*, tells the story of **Cupid and Psyche**.

Germanic leader Odoacer deposes Emperor Romulus, and the **Roman empire falls**.

Origin stories

Much of the mythology that can be called authentically Roman – such as the tale of Romulus and Remus – concerns the founding of Rome. Virgil's epic poem The *Aeneid*, consciously modelled on the Greek works of Homer, explains how the Trojan Prince Aeneas fled the sack of Troy and travelled to Italy to found a new nation.

Another myth, recorded by Dionysius of Halicarnassus, told of a fleet of warships from Achaea (Greece), that was sailing back from Troy with some captured Trojan women. Its triumphant journey was interrupted when a storm forced them onto the Italian coast. The Acheans hauled up their ships for the winter, and in the spring, just as they were preparing to leave, the Trojan women made their move.

Fearing they would be sold into slavery, they set fire to the ships, making them unseaworthy. The Achaeans were therefore forced to settle there in Italy rather than return to Greece.

Whichever myth they favoured, the Romans were proud to trace their culture back to that of ancient Greece, via the victorious Achaeans or the defeated Trojans. One account, by Hellanicus of Lesbos, even unified the two: in this version, Aeneas travelled to Italy alongside Odysseus, and named the city of Rome after Romê (or Rhome), the Trojan woman who had encouraged the others to burn the ships.

Other influences

Roman mythology was also coloured by the influence of deities and cults from lands beyond Italy and Greece; it absorbed the stories of the Great Mother, Cybele, from Anatolia; of the Egyptian goddess Isis; and of Syrian deities such as Jupiter Heliopolitanus. As the poet Juvenal wrote in his *Satires*, "The Syrian Orontes has been disgorging into the Tiber for a good while now". One god who gained a huge following among Roman soldiers was Mithras. His origins may have been Persian, but the cult of the bull-slayer was distinctively Roman.

Ruling over a vast empire, the Romans kept extensive records, which may explain why so much of their mythology has survived. Art and literature – poems, letters, and satires – preserved and transformed Greek, Etruscan, and eastern myths in vivid reimaginings that still influence Western artists today. ∎

I SING OF ARMS AND THE MAN

AENEAS, FOUNDER OF ROME

IN BRIEF

THEME
National epic

SOURCES
Aeneid, Virgil, c.30–19 BCE;
Metamorphoses, Ovid, 8 CE.

SETTING
From Troy to Italy, c.1000 BCE.

KEY FIGURES
Aeneas A prince of Troy.

Venus Goddess of love and
mother of Aeneas.

Anchises Father of Aeneas.

Juno Queen of the gods;
enemy of the Trojans.

Dido Queen of Carthage; lover
of Aeneas.

Jupiter King of the gods.

Lavinia Princess of Latium;
future wife of Aeneas.

Turnus Ruler of Rutuli; enemy
of Aeneas.

Neptune God of the sea.

The Trojan prince Aeneas, the son of the mortal Anchises and the goddess Venus (Aphrodite), first featured in Homer's *Iliad*, but was elevated to the role of founding father of Rome in Virgil's powerful epic, the *Aeneid*. His story begins at the end of the Trojan War. Aeneas was forced to flee Troy when the city fell to the Greeks. The *Aeneid* describes Aeneas's subsequent voyage to Italy, beset with drama and misfortune.

Escape from Troy

The poem begins with Aeneas storm-bound in Carthage, telling the queen about the events that had led to his flight from Troy. He explained how the Trojans had been duped by a giant wooden horse that the Greeks had left outside Troy. The Trojans brought it within the city walls, unaware that Greek warriors hid inside. That night, they crept out and opened the city gates to the rest of the Greek forces, who destroyed Troy.

Aeneas initially joined the fight, but his slain cousin Hector called on him in a dream to found a new Trojan city. His mother Venus also

Bearing Anchises, his father, on his shoulders, Aeneas flees Troy with his son Ascanius. His wife Creusa is still beside them in this image, painted in 1598 by Federico Fiori Barocci.

urged him to flee and take his family, Troy's sacred relics, and the household gods with him. Aeneas escaped with his son Ascanius, and his father Anchises, but his wife Creusa became separated from the group. When he went back, Aeneas found only her ghost, who told him he was destined to found a new city in Italy.

Fleeing by sea, Aeneas and his followers went to Thrace and then Delos, where Apollo, the god of

Virgil

The poet Publius Vergilius Maro was born near Mantua in 70 BCE, and died in Brundisium in 19 BCE. He wrote three major works: the *Eclogues*, the *Georgics*, and the *Aeneid*. While the first two deal with pastoral themes, Virgil was inspired by Homer's *Iliad* and *Odyssey* to create the *Aeneid* as a Roman national epic and foundational myth. Although the *Aeneid* follows immediately on from the events of the *Iliad*, its hero is not one of the victorious Greeks but Aeneas, a fleeing prince of the vanquished Trojans. Nor is Aeneas wily, like Homer's

Odysseus; Aeneas is often described as *pater* ("father") and *pius* ("pious") to emphasize his noble quest.

According to his biographer, Aelius Donatus, Virgil recited much of the *Aeneid* to the emperor Augustus, causing Augustus's sister Octavia to faint at the prophetic mention of her son Marcellus in book VI.

After Virgil finished writing the *Aeneid*, he planned to make corrections, but he fell ill. Despite his dying wish that the manuscript be burned, the emperor ordered its publication.

See also: Hades and the Underworld 48–49 ▪ The quest of Odysseus 66–71 ▪ The labours of Herakles 72–75 ▪ The founding of Rome 102–03 ▪ The Sibyl of Cumae 110–11

Prophecies about Aeneas

5. Dido condemns Rome and Carthage to eternal **enmity** after Aeneas abandons her.

1. Hector comes to Aeneas in a dream and tells him to **flee** Troy and found Lavinium.

4. Jupiter tells Venus that **Aeneas** will wage war in Italy and **crush** his enemies.

2. Creusa's ghost tells Aeneas that he is destined to found a city in **Italy**.

3. A harpy prophesies that the Trojans will face **starvation** and eat their own tables.

prophecy, advised him to seek the land of his ancestors. Aeneas therefore sailed to Crete, home of the Trojan ancestor Teucrus, but he was directed by the gods in a vision to go instead to Italy, home of his ancestor Dardanus.

Next, Aeneas met the Harpies, fierce female-faced bird creatures. One cursed Aeneas, prophesying that he would reach his goal only when dire hunger forced the group to eat their tables. They sailed to Sicily, where Aeneas's elderly father died, and then set off for Italy, but the wind god Aeolus – by order of Juno, who hated the Trojans – sent their ships wildly off course.

Taking shelter in the north African city of Carthage, Aeneas met the queen, Dido; it was to her that he told the story of his flight from Troy. Encouraged by Venus, Aeneas and Dido fell in love and consummated their passion in a cave during a storm. When Jupiter, king of the gods, heard of this, he sent his messenger Mercury to remind Aeneas to leave Carthage to found a new city.

The tragic queen

On hearing of her lover's departure, Dido asked her sister Anna to build a sacrificial pyre and threw herself upon it. From the flames, she could see Aeneas's ships leaving, so the queen thrust his sword through her

Dido stabs herself as Aeneas and his followers set sail from Carthage, bound for Italy. This miniature is from a vellum copy of the *Aeneid* made in France in 1469.

body. To end her agony, Juno sent Iris, the rainbow, down to earth, to release her soul by snipping a lock of Dido's hair as an offering to Dis, ruler of the underworld. As Aeneas sailed away from Carthage, he looked back and saw the smoke of the funeral pyre. He did not learn of Dido's suicide until later, when he met her shade in the Underworld.

Aeneas seeks his father

Returning to Sicily, Aeneas held funeral games to commemorate his dead father, Anchises. Meanwhile, Juno, still bearing her ancient grudge and anxious to delay Aeneas's quest, inspired the Trojan women to set fire to the ships. Jupiter sent down torrential rain to extinguish the flames and, in a vision, Anchises urged Aeneas to pursue his quest and to meet him in the underworld. Aeneas sailed on and – despite the loss of his helmsman Palinurus, who fell overboard – finally reached Italy.

Anxious to see his dead father again, Aeneas was advised by the Sibyl of Cumae to pluck a golden »

Timeline of events in the *Aeneid*

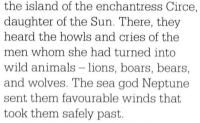

In Delos, Aeneas offers sacrifices to Apollo but misunderstands clues about the site of his future city.

The Harpies attack Aeneas after he is blown off course to their home on the Strophades islands.

Aeneas flees Troy, with his father Anchises after his wife's ghost tells him he must find the land of the Tiber.

In Crete, Aeneas has a vision in which the gods tell him to travel to Italy.

In love with Dido, queen of Carthage, Aeneas only leaves her when the gods remind him of his fate.

---

bough to give to Proserpina, queen of the underworld and wife of Dis; the bough ensured them safe passage with the ferryman Charon across the River Styx. The Sibyl then sedated the guard dog Cerberus with a drugged honey cake. In the underworld, Aeneas spoke to the ghost of Dido, but she turned away from him without a word. Anchises was overjoyed to see his son, however, and stretched out his arms. Aeneas tried in vain to embrace his father, but his arms closed on empty air. Then, as they walked with the Sibyl beside the river Lethe, Anchises prophesied the founding of Rome. To further impress on his son the importance of his mission, Anchises showed him a parade of the spirits of the great Romans who would be born, including Romulus, Julius Caesar, and Augustus. Aeneas then returned to the world of light.

The promised land

As they sailed up the west coast of Italy towards the River Tiber, Aeneas and his followers skirted the island of the enchantress Circe, daughter of the Sun. There, they heard the howls and cries of the men whom she had turned into wild animals – lions, boars, bears, and wolves. The sea god Neptune sent them favourable winds that took them safely past.

The Trojans landed in Latium, at the Tiber's mouth, and laid out their first meal on platters of crusty bread, piling them high with freshly harvested fruit and vegetables. They were so ravenous that they ate not only the meal but the bread platters too. Aeneas's son Ascanius joked that they were even eating the tables. Realizing that this fulfilled the harpy's prophetic curse, Aeneas and his followers knew they had found the place to build their city, and Jupiter thundered three times in confirmation.

Aeneas did not plan to conquer Latium with a hostile invasion. Instead, he paid court to Lavinia, the daughter of King Latinus, who was said to be the son of the god

Aeneas descends into a nightmarish underworld, depicted here by Flemish painter Jacob Isaacsz van Swanenburg (c.1600 CE). Virgil's vision influenced many Christian images of hell.

In Sicily, Aeneas performs funeral games following the death of his father, Anchises.

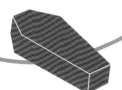

Landing in Latium, Aeneas is welcomed at the mouth of the River Tiber by King Latinus who offers his daughter Lavinia in marriage.

In a duel with Turnus, Aeneas is the victor and ends the war.

The Sibyl of Cumae leads Aeneas to the underworld, where he talks to several spirits including Dido and Anchises. The future of Rome is revealed to him.

The Trojans go to war in Italy. Aeneas initially sustains heavy losses, before enlisting King Evander and his people as allies.

Faunus. Once again, however, the enmity of Juno worked against him. The goddess persuaded Lavinia's mother, Queen Amata, that her daughter must marry Turnus, ruler of the neighbouring Rutuli. Juno then called on Alecto, one of the three Furies (or goddesses of retribution) to foment war.

The final conflict

Vastly outnumbered by Turnus's forces, Aeneas initially despaired, but was then visited by the river god Tiberinus in a dream. The god told him that he should find a place on the river bank where a white sow was nursing 30 piglets; there his son Ascanius would one day

Against my own wishes I have abandoned Turnus and abandoned the earth.
Aeneid

found a city called Alba Longa. Encouraged by Tiberinus, Aeneas then gained the support of the aged Evander, king of Pallanteum on the Palatine Hill, where Rome would later be founded, and of Tarchon, the king of the Etruscans.

With new allies – and help from the gods – Aeneas began to gain ground. When the enemy tried to set fire to the Trojan fleet, the goddess Cybele turned the ships into nymphs, who swam away. However, Turnus had Juno on his side and killed King Evander's son Pallas, taking his belt as a trophy.

Finally, Aeneas and Turnus met in single combat; Venus supported Aeneas while Turnus had his sister, the water nymph Juturna, at his side. Jupiter then persuaded Juno to abandon Turnus and cease her opposition to Aeneas, assuring her that the Latin name ("Latium") and language would be preserved. Jupiter then sent a snake-haired Fury to drive off Juturna and harry Turnus. Aeneas wounded Turnus but was about to spare his life until he saw that he was wearing Pallas's belt. In fury he drove his sword through Turnus's heart. The epic poem ends in Turnus's death, which also ended the war. ∎

New cities

Aeneas founded the city of Lavinium in Latium and named it for his wife, Lavinia. After Aeneas's death, his son Ascanius founded the city of Alba Longa, at the spot prophesied by the river god Tiberinus, in the Alban hills southeast of Rome. For 400 years, the descendents of Aeneas ruled Alba Longa until Romulus and Remus founded Rome. According to legend, war between the two cities broke out in the 7th century BCE. Livy described how two pairs of triplets – the Horatii for Rome and the Curiatii for Alba Longa – did battle. The Romans emerged victorious.

Historically, the Romans and the people of Latium were part of a confederation known as the Latin League, which fought together against enemies. When the Albans deserted the Romans in a war against the Etruscans, the Romans killed the Alban leader, Mettius, razed Alba Longa to the ground, and brought its people to Rome.

A DESIRE SEIZED ROMULUS AND REMUS TO BUILD A CITY

THE FOUNDING OF ROME

IN BRIEF

THEME
Birth of a nation

SOURCES
Roman Antiquities, Dionysius of Halicarnassus, c.7 BCE; *Fasti* ("The Book of Days"), Ovid, 8 CE; *Romulus,* Plutarch, c.70–110 CE.

SETTING
Rome, c.753 BCE.

KEY FIGURES
Romulus Founder of Rome.

Remus Brother of Romulus.

Amulius King of Alba Longa.

Numitor Deposed brother of Amulius.

Rhea Silvia Daughter of Numitor.

Mars God of war.

Faustulus A shepherd.

Larentia Wife of Faustulus.

The myth of the brothers Romulus and Remus was not the only story of the founding of Rome, but it became the widely accepted one. Early accounts claimed that the twins were the sons of the Trojan hero Aeneas, but most versions set the story fifteen generations later.

Aeneas's son, Ascanius, founded the ancient city of Alba Longa about 19 km (12 miles) from the site that was later to become Rome. Centuries later, Alba Longa was inherited by two brothers, Amulius and Numitor. Amulius suggested to his brother that they divide their inheritance in two, one taking the reins of the kingdom and

See also: The Olympian gods 24–31 ▪ Aeneas, founder of Rome 96–101 ▪ Vesta and Priapus 108-09

Ancestry of Romulus and Remus

```
        Aeneas, prince of Troy
        and hero of the Aeneid
                 ⋮
          Proca, king of
           Alba Longa
            ↓          ↓
       Amulius      Numitor
          ↓             ↓
    Mars, the war   Rhea Silvia
         god
          ↓             ↓
       Romulus       Remus
```

The exposure of Roman children

The element of the myth of Romulus and Remus that repels modern readers would not have shocked Romans. Infanticide by means of exposure was commonplace in ancient societies. The surprise in Rome's foundation myth lay in the survival of the infants, not their rejection.

Roman fathers had absolute control over their children and could simply choose not to rear them. In some instances babies would be left at recognized sites, where they could be adopted. But many others were simply abandoned. Girls, who would in the event of marriage require a dowry – a legally enforced monetary donation to their husband – were more often victims of exposure than boys as a result. The extent of the practice in ancient Rome is a matter of scholarly debate, but it was made illegal in 374 CE.

---

the other the treasures brought by their ancestor Aeneas from Troy. Numitor agreed and chose the kingdom, while Amulius took the treasure. But with the wealth brought by that treasure, Amulius schemed against his brother, and deposed and imprisoned him.

Birth of the twins

Fearing a challenge from any descendants of Numitor, Amulius killed Numitor's son Aegestus and forced his daughter Rhea Silvia to become a Vestal Virgin. According to most accounts, Mars, the god of war, seduced her as she lay sleeping on a riverbank, or in a sacred grove, telling her that she would bear two

sons who would exceed all men in bravery; other accounts said that the true father was a masked Amulius himself. When her twin children Romulus and Remus were born, Rhea Silvia was either put to death for breaking her virginal vows, or locked up for life. As for the babies, Amulius ordered a servant to drown them in the River Tiber. Instead, the servant cast them adrift in a basket, and then the river god brought them safely to the bank. A female wolf who had just

The Capitoline Wolf shows Romulus and Remus suckling from the she-wolf. The bronze wolf dates to the 11th or 12th century and the twins to the 15th.

whelped found the babies and suckled them to health. They were then discovered by Faustulus, a shepherd (or in some accounts a swineherd or cowherd) who brought up the children with the help of his wife, Larentia. According to some »

sources, the story of the she-wolf came about because Larentia had been a *lupa,* a Latin slang word for prostitute that also meant wolf.

Rome is founded

The boys grew handsome and strong. Famous for their feats of courage and generosity, they became leaders among the local farmers and huntsmen. When Romulus and Remus were grown men, they learned of their history – from either Faustulus or Mars – and launched a revolt. The usurper Amulius was killed and King Numitor was restored to his throne.

The twins then decided to found a great city of their own. They declared that, in obedience to an oracle from Delphi, their city would be the sanctuary of the god of asylum, and they gathered around them a great band of fugitives, outlaws, and runaway slaves. When it came to choosing the exact site of the city, Romulus preferred the Palatine Hill and Remus the Aventine Hill. To determine the site and which of them would be the city's first ruler, they agreed to seek a sign from the gods by observing birds of omen – Romulus, in contrast to his brother, carried a crooked staff known as a *lituus,* used by diviners to interpret future events by studying the flight of birds. This marked Romulus out symbolically as more conscientious than his brother and, therefore, the more deserving of victory. When Remus saw six vultures, he claimed the gods favoured him. Romulus then saw 12 vultures – though, according to Dionysius's account, Romulus was trying to dupe Remus and hadn't seen any birds at all.

The followers of each brother pronounced their respective champion as king. When Romulus started to plough a furrow to mark the city's boundary, an argument arose that quickly got out of hand. Remus jeered his brother and mocked him by jumping over the furrow, at which point Romulus (or, some say, his follower Celer) killed him. Romulus then founded the city of Rome in 753 BCE.

The Sabine women

The tale of Rome's initial foundation emphasizes the warlike nature of Romulus, inherited from his war-god father, and has a brutal theme

> When the signal was given, they drew their swords, rushed in with shouts, and ravished away the daughters of the Sabines.
> *Romulus*

that would come to define the Roman empire's expansion for centuries to come. On the Palatine Hill, as soon as Rome was built, Romulus placed all his men in legions to defend against surrounding peoples such as the Sabines.

The first problem facing the new city was the lack of women, for the refugees and outlaws attracted by Romulus and Remus were all men. To solve this, Romulus announced that he had discovered the altar of the harvest god Consus beneath the city, and instituted a festival, the Consualia,

The Greco-Roman author Plutarch (45CE–c. 120 CE) composed more than 225 works on Greek and Roman history and culture.

Plutarch's *Romulus*

Among the sacred treasures guarded by the Vestal Virgins was a phallus that relates to a curious alternative story of the birth of Romulus and Remus.

According to Plutarch, there was a wicked king of Alba Longa named Tarchetius, in whose hearth a phallus appeared. An oracle prophesied that if a virgin had relations with this phallus, she would bear a child of unparalleled strength and good fortune. Tarchetius commanded his daughter to obey the oracle, but she sent her slave instead. When Tarchetius discovered his daughter's deceit, he ordered both girls put to death. However, Vesta, goddess of the hearth, appeared to the king in his sleep and warned him not to kill the girls – so he imprisoned them instead.

When the slave girl gave birth to twins, Tarchetius ordered them to be exposed (left outside to die); but, as in the usual story, Romulus and Remus were suckled and saved by a she-wolf before being found by the peasants who raised them.

The rape of the Sabine women has been depicted by many artists. This detail is from a vast fresco by Luca Cambiaso (c. 1565) for a salon at the Villa Imperiale in Genoa, Italy.

in the god's honour. He invited the Sabines to the festival but, while the Sabine men watched the chariot races, Romulus gave a signal, throwing his cloak over his shoulders, and with this, his men took up arms. They seized the Sabine women, carrying them over the thresholds of their houses and claiming them as their wives.

War and reconciliation

Hoodwinked and humiliated, the Sabine men resolved to wage war against the Romans. After Romulus killed the Sabine king Acron, the Sabines united under Titus Tatius and laid siege to Rome. Tarpeia, the daughter of the commander of Rome's citadel, betrayed the city: in exchange for the Sabines gold armlets, she opened the gates and let in the foreign army.

The Forum was the centre of everyday life in ancient Rome. Among other shrines, it contained the Temple of Vesta – one of its oldest shrines, dating back to the 7th century BCE.

During the bloody fight that followed, Romulus was knocked down by a stone thrown at his head. The Romans began to retreat, rallying only when Romulus rose and prayed to Jupiter Stator ("the stayer") for help. The battle was halted by the Sabine women, who ran between the two armies and begged their Sabine fathers and Roman husbands not to kill each other. Peace was made between the two sides under the joint leadership of Romulus and Tatius.

Romulus ruled Rome for 40 years, establishing it as a mighty city. Many stories were told of his superior strength. In one display of power, Romulus stood on the Aventine Hill and hurled his spear into the earth. It sank so deep that no man could pull it out. The shaft was made of hard cornel wood, and the tree that grew from it was treated with great reverence. In the time of Gaius Caesar, who reigned from 27 BCE–14 CE, the roots of Romulus's cornel tree were inadvertently cut by workmen repairing some nearby steps, and the tree withered and died.

The city of Rome grew in power and prestige, but not without conflict. When ambassadors from the city of Laurentum were murdered by Tatius's kinsmen, Tatius was slain in revenge. A plague afflicted both Rome and Laurentum, as both sides were seen to be at fault in not pursuing justice for their murderers. Taking advantage of the plague, the people of Cameria attacked Rome, but Romulus defeated them, taking their city and half of its inhabitants.

Ascension

One day when Romulus was mustering his troops in the Field of Mars, a storm arose. The air rang with peals of thunder, and Romulus was wrapped in cloud and carried up to heaven in the chariot of his father Mars to become a god himself. Thereafter, Romulus was worshipped under the name of Quirinus, the Sabine god of war. The next king after Romulus, Numa Pompilius, was a Sabine, showing that the union of the two peoples lasted beyond the reigns of Romulus and Tatius. ∎

THE FATHER OF GODS SPURTS RED FLAMES THROUGH THE CLOUDS

NUMA OUTWITS JUPITER

IN BRIEF

THEME
Prophecy and destiny

SOURCES
History of Rome, Livy, 1st
century BCE; *Fasti* (*"The Book
of Days"*), Ovid, 8 CE; *Parallel
Lives*, Plutarch, early 2nd
century CE.

SETTING
The Aventine Hill, Rome,
c.715–673 BCE.

KEY FIGURES
Jupiter The Roman god of
thunder; ruler of the gods.

Numa The second king
of Rome (715–673 BCE).

Egeria A nymph and queen;
wife of King Numa.

Faunus and Picus Woodland
gods, captured by Numa.

Salii Dancing priests and
guardians of the sacred shield
of Rome.

When angry Jupiter sent lightning flaming from the sky with torrents of rain, King Numa – the second king of Rome – was alarmed. However, his wife, the nymph Egeria, told him, "You must appease Jupiter and deflect his anger. Seek out Picus and his son Faunus, gods of the Roman soil, for they know how it can be done".

These woodland gods could be found on the Aventine Hill, which was then a pastoral place of springs and dells, and not yet part of the city. Numa mixed wine and honey

When captured, they dropped
their own forms and assumed
many different shapes,
presenting hideous and
dreadful appearances.
**Plutarch,
Life of Numa**

with water in the spring where the two gods drank. When they fell asleep, Numa bound their hands tight with ropes.

Upon awakening, Picus and Faunus tried to escape by changing from one fantastical shape to another, but they could not free themselves from Numa's bonds. Numa told them he meant no harm – he simply wanted to learn how to appease Jupiter. The gods, while unable to offer this knowledge, were willing to bring Jupiter to him: "You ask what is not lawful for a man to know. Release us, and we will lure Jupiter down from the sky."

Man versus god

Jupiter descended, as promised, the earth sinking beneath his weight. Numa was so afraid that his face drained of blood and his hair stood on end, but he entreated the god, "King of heaven, call back your thunderbolts, I pray. Tell me what offering you desire". Jupiter replied, "Cut off the head …" "Of an onion," answered Numa, quick as a flash. "A man's …", said Jupiter. "Hair," Numa cut in. "The life of a …" "Sprat." At this, Jupiter roared with laughter. It delighted him to meet a mortal fit to converse with

See also: The Olympian gods 24–31 ▪ The founding of Rome 102–05 ▪ The Sibyl of Cumae 110–11 ▪ Philemon and Baucis 125

Numa consults Egeria in her sacred grove, while an unknown figure sits hunched in the background, in *Pompilius and the Nymph Egeria* (1631–1633) by artist Nicolas Poussin.

a god – despite only possessing human faculties, Numa's quick wits were a match for his own.

Jupiter then told Numa, "When Apollo is at his highest point in the sky tomorrow, I will send you signs of empire". With these last words, Jupiter rose again into the sky with loud claps of thunder, leaving the awed Numa on the hillside. When Numa returned to the city in high spirits, the citizens were reluctant to believe his story. "Actions speak louder than words", he said. "Let us gather tomorrow and see what omens Jupiter will send". The next morning, the people of Rome came to Numa's door. The king sat among them on his throne, and they watched Apollo rise into the sky and travel across it. When the sun reached its zenith, Numa raised his hands to the sky and said, "The time has come, Jupiter, to fulfil your vow".

Omnipotent Jupiter

Jupiter answered King Numa from heaven by hurling three thunderbolts. Then a shield fell out of the sky, and a voice declared that so long as the shield was preserved, Rome would rule the world.

Wily Numa asked the craftsman Mamurius to make eleven more shields exactly like it – to confuse any would-be thief. These 12 sacred objects were kept in the Temple of Mars, in the care of the dancing priests, the Salii. ▪

Roman Trinity

The Capitoline Triad of Jupiter, his wife Juno, and his daughter Minerva, shared a temple on the Capitoline Hill in Rome known as the Temple of Jupiter. They were regarded as the ruling gods of Rome. This trio of supreme gods succeeded an earlier triad, known to scholars as the Archaic Triad – which consisted of the gods Jupiter, Mars, and Quirinus.

Both triads were central to the public religion of ancient Rome. Capitolia temples were built across Italy and the provinces. In them, Jupiter was revered as Jupiter Optimus Maximus ("Jupiter Best and Greatest"), alongside Juno, his queen, and Minerva, the goddess of war.

The temple of Jupiter was regarded as one of the most important of all temples in ancient Rome. Within its walls lay the Jupiter Stone, which was used by political officials to swear oaths. Its Latin name – *Iuppiter Lapis* – became the title for a cult that came to regard the stone itself as a god.

Three Capitoline temples, built in the 2nd century CE in Sufetula (now Sbeitla, Tunisia), are just some of the many capitolia temples that were built across the Roman world.

CONCEIVE OF VESTA AS NAUGHT BUT THE LIVING FLAME
VESTA AND PRIAPUS

IN BRIEF

THEME
Virgin goddesses

SOURCES
Fasti ("The Book of Days"),
Ovid, 8 CE.

SETTING
Mount Ida – the Mountain of
the Goddess, Cybele; Anatolia,
in modern day Turkey.

KEY FIGURES
Saturn Roman god of wealth;
Roman equivalent of Kronos.

Ops Earth goddess; wife of
Saturn.

Vesta Virgin goddess of the
hearth.

Cybele Anatolian mother
goddess – the "Great Mother"
of Roman mythology.

Priapus God of sexuality
and fertility; a cast-out son
of Venus.

Silenus A drunken old satyr
riding a donkey.

The daughters of Saturn
and Ops were Juno, Ceres,
and Vesta, the goddess of
the hearth. All three were major
Roman goddesses, but Vesta, in
contrast to her sisters, was rarely
depicted in myth.

The concept of the hearth
god originated in the proto-Indo-
European religion based in ancient
Anatolia, from which a number of
Roman and Greek gods would
ultimately be derived. The Latin
word Vesta came from the proto-
Indo-European word meaning "to
burn", underlining the goddess's
ancestral roots.

The relatively small number of
myths focusing on Vesta is largely
due to the fact that the goddess
rarely strayed from her house or her
temple. In one myth, told by Ovid,
Vesta was tempted out to a party
thrown by the mother goddess,
Cybele, on Mount Ida, a central
location of worship for Cybele's
orgiastic cult following. With her
turreted mural crown, which

Nymphs and satyrs cavort together
in *A Bacchanal Before a Statue of Pan*
(1632–33) by the French artist Nicolas
Poussin. In the foreground to the right,
Priapus attempts to molest Vesta.

See also: The Olympian gods 24–31 ▪ The mad cult of Dionysus 52 ▪ Cybele and Attis 116–17

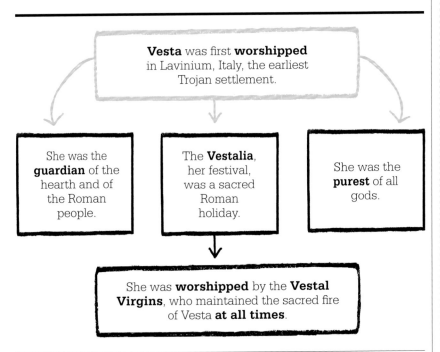

Vesta was first **worshipped** in Lavinium, Italy, the earliest Trojan settlement.

She was the **guardian** of the hearth and of the Roman people.

The **Vestalia**, her festival, was a sacred Roman holiday.

She was the **purest** of all gods.

She was **worshipped** by the **Vestal Virgins**, who maintained the sacred fire of Vesta **at all times**.

The Vestal Virgins

The six Vestal Virgins, Rome's only female priesthood, tended the fire of Vesta, the symbolic hearth of the city in the Temple of Vesta, in the Forum. If the fire was ever allowed to go out, it was regarded as a bad omen, and the negligent Vestal was whipped by the high priest. The chastity of the Vestals was essential to the safety of Rome itself, and any Vestal who lost her virginity would be buried alive, with meagre rations of food and water, so that her blood was not spilled, and her death was by the will of the underworld gods.

The six priestesses were chosen in childhood, between the ages of six and ten years. They then served for thirty years, after which they were free to leave the order – and even to marry, if they so desired. However, Vestal Virgins who married lost their unusual degree of independence, including the freedom to make a will.

designated her as a patron and protector of Rome, Cybele was constantly surrounded by revelling female followers (Maenads), and males (Corybantes), who provided her with musicical entertainment.

Cybele invited all the gods to her party, together with the satyrs, nymphs, and spirits of the countryside. These included the lustful Priapus, who was afflicted with a permanent, over-sized erection. Priapus's mother Venus was so ashamed of this deformity that she abandoned him in the mountains to be brought up by shepherds. Priapus became a god of gardens, bees, and herds. The party's final guest was the drunken satyr Silenus, who came to the event despite lacking an invitation.

Priapus is denied

The gods ate and drank their fill, and as the party wound down, some went out strolling on Mount Ida, while some began to dance, and others lay down on the grass to sleep off their excesses. Vesta found a quiet spot by a stream and fell asleep, unaware that Priapus lurked nearby. The always lecherous Priapus was on the prowl, looking for a goddess or nymph to bed. Spying the virgin goddess Vesta as she lay asleep, he tiptoed up to her. However, just as Priapus was about to take Vesta's virginity, Silenus's donkey let out a loud bray nearby, and startled her awake. The other gods ran to Vesta's aid, quickly driving Priapus away.

At his cult centre in Lampsacus, in the northern Troad, the donkey was Priapus's sacrificial animal. During the Vestalia, held every June in honour of Vesta, loaves of bread baked in the ash of the Vestal hearth were hung from donkeys, and grindstones that they turned were also garlanded with flowers in honour of the goddess. ▪

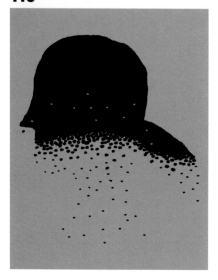

THE FATES WILL LEAVE ME MY VOICE, AND BY MY VOICE I SHALL BE KNOWN

THE SIBYL OF CUMAE

IN BRIEF

THEME
Prophecy and destiny

SOURCES
Aeneid, Virgil, c.20 BCE;
Roman Antiquities, Dionysius
of Halicarnassus, c.7 BCE;
Metamorphoses, Ovid, 8 CE;
Satyricon, Petronius, c.60 CE.

SETTING
Cumae, in the times of Aeneas
(c.1200 BCE) and Trimalchio
(1st century CE); Rome during
the reign of Tarquinius
Superbus (535–509 BCE).

KEY FIGURES
Aeneas A Trojan hero of
Greco-Roman mythology.

The Sibyl of Cumae A
prophetess of Apollo.

Apollo The god of prophecy,
music, and the sun.

Tarquinius Superbus The
last king of Rome before
the birth of the Republic.

In Greek and Roman lore, the
Trojan hero Aeneas wished to
visit his father's ghost, so he
travelled to the gateway of the
Underworld – the cave of the aged
Sibyl of Cumae. Cumae was a
Greek colony in Campania, in
southern Italy. There, the Sibyl, a
divinely inspired prophetess of the
god Apollo, safely guided Aeneas
to the Underworld and back. As
Aeneas and the Sibyl climbed back
up into the world of the living, he
told her that he owed her his life,
that he would always regard her as
a goddess, and that he would build
a temple in her honour.

The Sibyl said she was no
goddess, and that no human being
was worthy of being worshipped.
To prove that she too was fallible,
she recounted the story of how, as
a young woman, she was wooed by
the god Apollo. When she rejected
him, she sealed her sad fate.

Apollo and the Sibyl
Apollo, desperate to win the Sibyl's
favour, promised her anything she
desired. She pointed at a heap of
dust and asked to live as many
years as there were grains of dust.
Apollo offered her both the years
and eternal youth if she would
submit to him. But she spurned
him, so the god granted her the
years but not the youth.

By the time she met Aeneas,
the Sibyl was a withered old
woman. She had spent seven
centuries singing the fates and
spelling her prophecies out on palm

Authors depict the Sibyl in three ways:

| As a **young woman**, beloved by **Apollo**. | At **700 years of age**, when she meets **Aeneas**. | Ancient but not **immortal**, wishing for **death**. |

See also: Hades and the Underworld 48–49 ▪ Apollo and the Oracle of Delphi 58–59 ▪ Aeneas 96–101 ▪ The founding of Rome 102–05

The three books of prophecies known as the Sibylline Books were one of ancient Rome's greatest treasures. They were kept in the temple of Jupiter on the Capitoline Hill and consulted at times of crisis.

The original books were burnt in a temple fire in 83 BCE, but the prophecies that they contained were carefully gathered together from across the Roman Empire and placed back in the temple. The Emperor Augustus later had them moved to the temple of Apollo on the Palatine Hill.

The Sibylline Books had ten custodians who interpreted the obscure and ambiguous prophecies. These men also directed the Romans on how to worship the gods Apollo, Cybele, and Ceres. Apollo had inspired the Sibyl's prophecies and the Sibylline Books gave advice on the worship of Cybele and Ceres. However, the books were intentionally destroyed in 405 CE by Flavius Stilicho, a Roman general who believed that they were being used against him.

leaves, which she would arrange at the mouth of her cave; if the wind blew the leaves about, the Sibyl would refuse to rearrange them, and the prophecy would be lost.

Final prophesies

The Sibyl of Cumae approached Tarquinius Superbus (Tarquin the Proud), the last king of Rome before the Republic, with nine books of prophecies, which she offered to sell him for a high price.

Aeneas greets the Sibyl at the Temple of Apollo, accompanied by Achates, a fellow exile from Troy, before his descent into the Underworld in this manuscript illustration (c. 400 CE).

Tarquinius, seeing merely a withered old woman, haughtily turned her away. The Sibyl burned three of the books, and offered him the remaining six for the same price. Again he refused. The Sibyl burned another three books and offered the king the remaining three for the same price as the original nine. He was so intrigued that he paid her what she asked.

After selling her books, the Sibyl disappeared and was not mentioned again until she was spotted by Trimalchio, a former slave, in the 1st-century CE *Satyricon* of Petronius. By then, her withered body was so tiny that she was hung up in a jar. When some local boys asked her what she wanted, she replied, "I want to die". Eventually, only her voice was left. ▪

Tis time to ask the oracles; the god, lo! The god!
The Sybil of Cumae, Aeneid

The Sibyl of Cumae is portrayed in the Vatican's Sistine Chapel in Rome, painted by Michelangelo (1510), to illustrate that pagans can enter the kingdom of God.

I LOVE YOU AS I LOVE MY OWN SOUL

CUPID AND PSYCHE

IN BRIEF

THEME
True love

SOURCE
Metamorphoses (also known
as *The Golden Ass)*, Apuleius,
c.158–180 CE.

SETTING
Ancient Greece.

KEY CHARACTERS
Venus The goddess of love,
who is jealous of Psyche.

Psyche A beautiful mortal
princess; becomes the goddess
of the spirit.

Cupid Venus's son, the god of
love; a troublemaker who falls
in love with Psyche.

Apollo The sun god; also the
god of wisdom and prophecy.

Jupiter King of the gods.

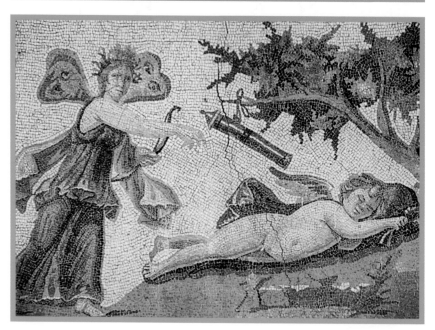

Psyche reaches for Cupid's arrows
in this 3rd-century CE Roman mosaic.
She is portrayed with butterfly wings,
as butterflies represented the soul.

The mortal princess Psyche
was said to be so beautiful
that people began to
worship her and neglect Venus,
the true goddess of love, and her
temples. Venus was angered by
this and called upon her son,
Cupid – a mischievous youth who
constantly caused mayhem with
his arrows of love and his torch of
desire. She urged him to punish
Psyche by making her fall in love
with a vile and wretched man, but

Cupid clumsily scratched himself
with his own arrow of passion, and
instead fell in love with Psyche.
Meanwhile, Apollo warned
Psyche's father that she was
destined to marry no mortal man,
but instead a terrible winged
serpent. Psyche's distraught

See also: Hades and the Underworld 48–49 ▪ The abduction of Persephone 50–51 ▪ Apollo and Daphne 60–61 ▪ Venus and Adonis 88–89

Tasks given to Psyche by Venus

Sort a pile of mixed grains. A horde of ants pity Psyche and sort the barley, wheat, lentils, millet, poppy-seeds, chickpeas, and beans into separate piles.

Obtain the fleece of a golden ram. A reed by the river magically tells Psyche how to safely gather up the golden strands.

Fill a flask with water from the River Styx. Jupiter's royal eagle flies above the dangers and fills Psyche's vial.

Gather a jar of Properina's beauty from Hades. A castle turret speaks and guides Psyche's way.

parents prepared her for this dreadful wedding and, as Apollo demanded, led her to the top of a crag, where she was left alone to meet her fate.

Secret husband

No winged serpent came; instead, the west wind Zephyrus picked Psyche up and carried her down to a wonderful palace so magnificent that she knew it must be the home of a god. An invisible voice told Psyche the palace was hers, and invisible servants washed and dressed her, brought her food, and played music.

However, in the darkness that night, Psyche's unseen husband got into her bed, made love to her, and left before the light of dawn. This became the pattern of her nights – sleeping with a husband she never set eyes upon. Lonely and now pregnant, Psyche persuaded her husband to allow her two older sisters to visit. He warned her not to let them convince her to find out what he looked like. If she did, her happiness would be over.

Psyche's jealous sisters arrived and reminded her of Apollo's prophecy, that she would marry a monstrous beast. That night, when

her husband was asleep, Psyche approached him with a lit oil lamp and a knife, intending to kill him. However, to her shock, the light revealed him to be Cupid. When she reached for an arrow of his, she accidentally pricked her thumb with its tip, falling deeply in love with him. Her hand trembled, and a drop of hot oil spilled on his shoulder. Injured and betrayed, he fled.

Lover's quest

Psyche travelled far and wide searching for her lost husband. She went to the palace of Venus herself,

where the hostile goddess set Psyche a series of near-impossible tasks. Her final task was to enter the Underworld and fetch a jar of beauty from its queen, Proserpina. On her return, Psyche forgot the warning she had received to not open the jar. When she unsealed it, a deep sleep overcame her and she fell as if dead.

Cupid flew to Psyche and woke her from her slumber. Jupiter consented to their marriage and made Psyche immortal, after which Venus finally accepted her. The child born of Psyche and Cupid was Voluptas, goddess of pleasure. ∎

Folklore and fairy tale

The ancient Greeks, Romans, and Egyptians all told fairy tales with recognizable connections to the ones we know today. The allegorical element of the story of Cupid and Psyche – with Cupid (love) marrying Psyche (soul) and conceiving Voluptas (pleasure) – is built on a fairy tale foundation. There are clear similarities between the stories of *Cinderella* and *Beauty and the Beast* and the myth of Cupid and Psyche, which is a tale of the widely-dispersed type

known by folklorists as the "search for the lost husband" and the "animal bridegroom".

The story of Cupid and Psyche is an unusual blend of fairy tale and myth – most fairy tales of this genre highlight a human husband who has been enchanted into animal form, rather than featuring a god. In Ovid's *Metamorphoses*, however, when the daughters of Minyas tell fairy tales, some involve gods, so the boundaries between myth and fairy tale may have been more porous in Rome than in other cultures.

I AM ON FIRE WITH LOVE FOR MY OWN SELF
NARCISSUS AND ECHO

IN BRIEF

THEME
Self-love

SOURCES
Metamorphoses, Ovid, 8 CE.

SETTING
Mount Helicon, Greece.

KEY FIGURES
Liriope A river nymph, the mother of Narcissus.

Cephisus A river god, who raped Liriope and fathered Narcissus.

Tiresias A seer.

Narcissus Son of Liriope and Cephisus, who fell in love with his own beauty.

Echo A mountain nymph, cursed by Juno only to repeat the words of others.

Juno Goddess of marriage; the jealous consort of Jupiter.

Nemesis Goddess of revenge, who punishes Narcissus.

After the nymph Liriope was raped by the river god Cephisus, she gave birth to a son so beautiful that everyone fell in love with him. Liriope asked the blind seer Tiresias if her son Narcissus would live to grow old, and he answered, "If he does not come to know himself".

Unrequited love

When Narcissus was 16, he was seen by the nymph Echo, who fell in love with him. Echo could not speak to Narcissus – as punishment for aiding Zeus in his extra-marital affairs, she had been cursed by the goddess Juno to be able only to repeat the last few words anyone else had said. She followed Narcissus into the wild, where he called, "Is there anybody here?" Echo replied, "here". As she continued to repeat his words, he grew more and more impatient. When Echo came out of the woods to embrace him, he cried, "Don't touch me!" Humiliated, Echo retreated to a cave, and dwindled away until only her voice was left.

One day, the goddess Nemesis decided to avenge the scorned Echo and led Narcissus to a pool, where he finally fell in love – with his own reflection. He reached out, but could not touch the partner of his dreams. Burning with an impossible love, and with one last "farewell", he died of sorrow. Echo, watching, moaned "farewell" back. Narcissus then transformed into the flower that now bears his name. ■

Echo watches as Narcissus reaches for his one true love in a 1903 painting by J W Waterhouse. After his death, Narcissus turns into a daffodil leaning over the water's edge.

See also: The Olympian gods 24–31 ■ Ikarus 78–81 ■ King Midas 90

SHE YET SPINS HER THREAD, AS A SPIDER

ARACHNE AND MINERVA

IN BRIEF

THEME
Challenging the gods

SOURCES
Metamorphoses, Ovid, c.8 CE.

SETTING
Lydia, Asia Minor (in modern-day Turkey).

KEY FIGURES
Arachne A young woman from Lydia, a skilled weaver, with little respect for the Greek gods and their actions.

Nymphs Beautiful female spirits associated with the natural world.

Minerva The goddess of wisdom, medicine, and the arts, including weaving and other handicrafts.

Neptune The god of the sea, who had a violent temper.

Jupiter King of the gods; brother of Neptune.

O vid's *Metamorphoses* tells the story of a young woman named Arachne from Lydia. She was so skilled at weaving that nymphs used to come from the sides of Mount Tmolus and the shores of the River Pactolus just to watch her work. The nymphs thought she must have been taught by Minerva, goddess of weaving, but Arachne was offended by this suggestion. Proudly, she challenged the goddess to a weaving match.

Minerva, equally proud, then disguised herself as an old woman and confronted Arachne. While she applauded Arachne's skills, Minerva also suggested that she should show some humility and honour the goddess of weaving. Arachne insulted both the old woman and Minerva – so the goddess threw off her disguise and challenged Arachne to a contest.

The weaving match

Minerva wove a tapestry depicting the competition between herself and Neptune to be the protector of Athens. Arachne wove one showing

Arachne was not of noble family but her talent had made her famous.
Metamorphoses

the immorality of the gods, with scenes of the lustful Jupiter and Neptune deceiving and seducing their conquests in one disguise after another. Minerva could find no fault in Arachne's work except its string of insults to the gods and so, in a fit of rage, Minerva struck her repeatedly with a wooden weaving shuttle. Unable to bear this torment, Arachne hanged herself. Minerva then felt guilty and brought Arachne back to life as the world's first spider. ∎

See also: The Olympian gods 24–31 ▪ The many affairs of Zeus 42–47 ▪ The founding of Athens 56–57

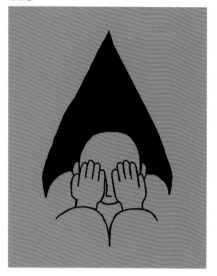

I PAY THE DUE PENALTY IN BLOOD

CYBELE AND ATTIS

IN BRIEF

THEME
Cults

SOURCE
Fasti and *Metamorphoses*,
Ovid, 8 CE.

SETTING
Phrygia, part of the ancient
kingdom of Anatolia.

KEY FIGURES
Cybele The Phrygian great
mother goddess, who
represented all of womankind.

Atalanta A huntress turned
into a lion by Cybele as
punishment.

Hippomenes Atalanta's
husband, also a lion.

Attis Companion and
devotee of Cybele.

Sagaritis A tree nymph; she
seduced Attis and was
punished by death.

The ancient Greeks saw
the goddess Cybele as the
mother of the gods and of
mankind. She first appeared in
Phrygia, now part of west-central
Turkey. The Greeks associated her
with the mother goddess Rhea, as
did the Romans, who made Cybele
the centre of a popular cult from the
4th century BCE onwards. Cybele
played a key role in the foundation
of Rome: she gave Aeneas her
sacred pines to build his ships,
begged her son Jupiter to make
them unsinkable, and turned them
into sea nymphs at journey's end.

Cybele's worship was usually
accompanied by frenetic, orgiastic
rites. She was attended by ecstatic
women called Maenads, who were
known for their frenzied dancing.
Her male attendants were called
Corybantes. These wild beings
made loud, discordant music with
cymbals, pipes, and drums,
drowning out all other sounds.

In this altar dedicated to Cybele
and Attis, Cybele is pulled in her lion
chariot, while the beautiful Attis
leans against a tree. Detail of relief,
Roman altar, 295 CE.

See also: The cult of Dionysus 52 ▪ Aphrodite and Adonis 88–89 ▪ Vesta and Priapus 108–09 ▪ Mithras and the bull 118–19

Foreign goddesses

Cybele was not the only imported goddess to play a crucial role in Roman religion. The Egyptian goddess Isis had a cult following in Rome, especially among courtesans and the lower classes. When the hero of Apuleius's novel *Metamorphoses (The Golden Ass)* had his religious revelation, it was with a vision of the goddess Isis.

The priests of Isis conduct a ritual banquet in this fresco from the Temple of Isis at Herculeaneum – a Roman town destroyed by a volcanic eruption.

Devotees of Isis were initiated into secret rites that promised a life after death, and festivals in Spring and Autumn celebrated rebirth and resurrection.

The emperors Augustus and Tiberius opposed Isis worship because she was not a Roman goddess. They ordered her temples to be destroyed and her statues thrown into the Tiber. Caligula made the cult legal again as part of his strategy to undo Tiberius's policies. After this, Isis remained popular until the rise of Christianity in the 4th century CE.

Cybele drove a chariot drawn by two lions – the huntress Atalanta and her husband Hippomenes, who had been transformed into wild animals for defiling Cybele's sanctuary with their lovemaking. On her head, she wore a turreted crown, because she built the first city walls and towers.

Cybele's beloved

Attis, a Phrygian mortal, won Cybele's favour with the purity of his love. Cybele made him her consort and the guardian of her shrine. He in turn promised to remain chaste and boyish forever. "If I break my promise," he said, "may the first woman I sleep with be my last". Alas, this promise proved too hard to keep. When Attis was tempted by a dryad, the tree nymph Sagaritis, he was unable to resist her advances and lost his virginity to her. In her fury, Cybele hacked at Sagaritis's tree, thus fatally wounding the nymph herself, who died in Attis's arms. As a dryad, her very life force was connected to the tree.

Insane with grief, Attis believed the roof of his chamber was falling in, and that the Furies – who represented the pangs of conscience that plagued the guilty – were coming to attack him. He ran screaming in terror to the top of Cybele's sacred Mount Dindymus. He dragged his long, beautiful hair through the dirt, and shouted that he deserved his fate, and should pay the penalty in blood.

Taking up a jagged stone, Attis cut off his genitals, which had been the cause of his downfall. His

I deserved this! I pay the due penalty in blood! Let the parts that harmed me perish!
Attis, *Fasti*

blood, which had seeped down at the foot of a pine tree, turned into violets. Attis himself died of his wounds. Following his example, his manservants also dragged their hair and castrated themselves. The sorrowing Cybele buried him where he fell, and he was reborn as a pine – the tree that ever after was sacred to Cybele.

Worship of Attis

Due to Attis's self-mutilation, death, and resurrection, he also came to represent fertility. Like other gods reflecting the seasons, he could be seen as dying in winter, and being reborn in the spring. After his death, Cybele's priests were always eunuchs who had castrated themselves in memory of Attis. This castration also ensured they kept his vow of chastity that he himself had broken.

In the Roman calendar, several days of the festival of Cybele honoured Attis; March 15 was the day Cybele met him, March 22 his self-mutilation, March 24 his death, and March 25 his resurrection. ▪

MITHRAS IS THE LORD OF GENERATION
MITHRAS AND THE BULL

IN BRIEF

THEME
Renewal

SOURCES
Thebaid, Statius, c.80 CE;
De antro nympharum
(On the Cave of the Nymphs),
Porphyry, c.234–305 CE.

SETTING
The cosmos.

KEY FIGURES
Mithras A god of the
cosmos; ruler of time.

Cautes and Cautopates
Torchbearers present at the
birth of Mithras.

Sol The sun god.

A cosmic bull The mythical
beast central to the myth.

A powerful deity called
Mithras was at the
centre of a secretive and
exclusively male religion practised
throughout the Roman Empire from
the late 1st century to the 4th
century CE. He bore the imposing
title, *Deus Sol Invictus Mithras*
("Mithras god of the Invincible
Sun"), yet his temples were always
underground in caves.

Mithras was a saviour who
rescued earthly creation from a
deadly drought. At his birth, he
burst forth from a rock, already a
youth, and holding a dagger in
one hand and a torch in the other.
These two implements foreshadow
his greatest achievements: the
bringing of light by means of the
sun, and the bringing of life by
means of slaying a bull. At his birth
he was attended by a serpent, dog,
and raven, and by two torchbearers,

Mithras kills the bull in a
2nd-century CE Roman fresco from
Marino, south of Rome. The size of his
torchbearers, Cautes and Cautopates,
emphasizes his strength.

See also: Theseus and the Minotaur 76–77 ▪ The founding of Rome 102–105 ▪ The Hero Twins 242–45

> He who beneath the rocks of the Persian cavern twists the horns of the stubborn bull: Mithras!
> ***Thebaid***

Cautes and Cautopates. Mithras then shot an arrow into a rock, causing a spring to gush forth to water the parched land. Yet the world was still under threat. Via his raven messenger, Sol, the sun god, told Mithras to hunt down and sacrifice the cosmic bull, which was associated with the moon, the ultimate source of moisture.

Mithras tracked down the bull, and, seizing it by the horns, rode it until the beast was subdued. He dragged it back into a cavern, then seized it by its muzzle and plunged his dagger into its neck. At its death, wheat and fruitful vines sprang from the wound, showing that the sacrifice of the cosmic bull had resulted in world regeneration and fecundity.

Master of the cosmos

Sol and Mithras feasted together on the bull's flesh, but the mythology suggests a rivalry. Both were sun gods, but it was Mithras who was titled "invincible". In temples to Mithras, the moon goddess Luna is often positioned over his left shoulder, and Sol over his right.

Mithras and his helpers are also often depicted wearing Phrygian caps – most likely an attempt to distinguish the cult of Mithras from other religions of its day. Two scenes at the Hawarte sanctuary in Syria show Mithras conquering evil, too – standing over a fettered devil and attacking a city of demons.

Images of the signs of the zodiac in Mithraic scenes further reinforce the cosmic symbolism of the myth. In the seven-day week standardized in ancient Rome, and based on the names of planets, the worship of Mithras on Sundays supports the idea that Mithras was viewed as the sun at the centre of the cosmos.

Every sanctuary, or *mithraeum*, included the essential bull-slaying scene (a "tauroctony"). Throughout these scenes, Mithras is always depicted looking back over his right shoulder in the same way that the hero Perseus did when he beheaded Medusa. In this way, some scholars believe that Mithras represents the constellation of Perseus, which, in its astronomical location above that of Taurus, is said to "slay" the bull, and bring in a new age. ▪

> Hail, O Master of the water!
> Hail, O Founder of the earth!
> Hail, O Ruler of the wind!
> ***De antro nympharum***

The cult of Mithras

The name Mithras is Persian, but scholars debate how closely the Roman cult and a similar Greek mystery religion are related to the older cult of Mithra, the Persian god of light, the sun, and war. The almost total lack of written evidence has led to a reliance on archaeological findings to support divergent theories. It is generally accepted that in Rome the cult first arose in the 1st century BCE and appeared to have some parallels with later Christian belief, such as the promise of new life after death; this appealed especially to soldiers, who were among its first recorded followers.

Initiates worshipped in underground temples known as *mithraea,* which Porphyry described. As all initiates were sworn to secrecy, it is only from surviving carvings and frescoes that the central myth in which Mithras slew a bull in a symbolic act of renewal can be reconstructed. The images celebrate his cosmic power in shaping the universe and heralding in the spring equinox.

The Sanctuary of the Mithraeum of Dura, in Syria, is renowned for its well preserved stone reliefs dating from the 3rd-century CE.

HE CARVED A STATUE OUT OF SNOW-WHITE IVORY
PYGMALION

IN BRIEF

THEME
Ideal love

SOURCE
Metamorphoses, Ovid, 8 CE.

SETTING
Cyprus, the birthplace
of Venus.

KEY FIGURES
Pygmalion A young sculptor
who vowed not to marry
any of the young women
of his time.

Venus The Roman goddess
of love and beauty; known as
Aphrodite in Greek mythology.

Galatea An ivory statue
expertly carved by Pygmalion,
turned into a living woman
by Venus.

Pygmalion is mentioned in Greek sources as a king of Cyprus who fell in love with a cult statue of Aphrodite, but the familiar myth of Pygmalion the sculptor is only known to us from the Roman poet, Ovid.

Pygmalion's creation

Pygmalion was so disenchanted by the wicked behaviour of the women of his day – who defied the authority of Venus, the goddess of love – that he vowed never to marry.

The sculptor devoted his hours to carving a life-sized, snow-white, ivory statue of a woman more beautiful than any who ever lived. This statue was so lifelike that even Pygmalion often had to touch it to check that it was still ivory, not living flesh. He soon fell in love with his creation – he kissed it, embraced it, spoke to it lovingly,

Pygmalion's ivory statue is brought to life by Venus – represented by a cupid in this 1763 marble sculpture by Étienne Falconet – and gazes tenderly at her creator.

and even brought it gifts. At the festival of Venus, after he had made his offering, Pygmalion prayed that the gods would grant him a woman as beautiful as his statue.

On returning home, Pygmalion embraced his statue. To his amazement, the flesh was warm – the statue had come to life. She opened her eyes and saw both daylight and her true love for the first time. The goddess Venus herself attended the wedding. ∎

See also: The Olympian gods 24–31 ▪ The fate of Oedipus 86–87 ▪ Cupid and Psyche 112–13 ▪ Pomona and Vertumnus 122–23

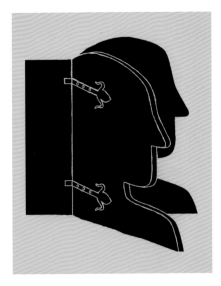

FOR LYING WITH ME, TAKE CONTROL OF THE HINGE
CARNA AND JANUS

IN BRIEF

THEME
Seduction and reward

SOURCE
Fasti ("The Book of Days"),
Ovid, 8 CE.

SETTING
The grove of Alernus on the
banks of the River Tiber.

KEY FIGURES
Carna A beautiful nymph,
who became Cardea, goddess
of the door hinge.

Phoebus God of the sun,
known as Apollo in Greek
mythology.

Janus The god of gateways
and doorways, who raped
Carna before making her
into a goddess.

Proca A baby; the ancestor
of Romulus and Remus, the
founders of Rome.

I n Roman tradition, a nymph
named Carna was born in the
ancient and sacred grove of
Alernus (a god of the underworld)
on the banks of the River Tiber.
She spent her time hunting deer
across the fields with her spear
and trapping them in nets. All the
young men were dazzled by her
beauty, and thought she must be
the sister of Phoebus (Apollo), the
god of the sun. To each of these
suitors who pursued her, Carna
would say, "It's too bright out here,
and with light comes shame. Lead
me to a secluded cave". While the
young man led the way, Carna
would hide among the trees and
vanish from sight.

Janus and the nymph
Carna then caught the attention
of the two-faced god of doorways,
Janus, who desired her as the
others had. When he spoke softly
to her, as usual she suggested
retiring to a cave. But when she
disappeared into the thicket, Janus
saw where she was hiding, for he
had eyes in the back of his head.

Lead me [Carna]
to a secluded cave;
I'll come.
Fasti

He pounced on her and took his
pleasure. To reward her, he made
her Cardea, the goddess of the door
hinge, who opens what is shut and
shuts what is open, and gave her a
branch of flowering white hawthorn
to drive evil spirits away.

The ability to banish evil would
prove useful in Cardea's role as the
protector of babies in the cradle.
She saved the five-day-old Proca
(the great-grandfather-to-be of
Romulus and Remus) from an
attack by shrieking owls that
preyed like vampires on infants. ■

See also: Hades and the Underworld 48–49 ▪ Apollo and the Oracle of
Delphi 58–59 ▪ The founding of Rome 102–05

NO WOOD NYMPH COULD TEND A GARDEN MORE SKILFULLY THAN SHE

POMONA AND VERTUMNUS

IN BRIEF

THEME
Love and fertility

SOURCE
Metamorphoses, Ovid, 8 CE.

SETTING
Roman countryside.

KEY FIGURES
Pomona Nurturing goddess of fruit trees, orchards, and gardens.

Silenus Old and lecherous god, often helplessly drunk.

Priapus God of fertility, a very small man with an oversized phallus.

Vertumnus God of the changing seasons, able to change his appearance however he wanted.

Pomona was a wood nymph who became the goddess of fruit trees, orchards, and gardens. She was a nurturing goddess, representing abundance, and was one of very few deities who had no counterpart in Greek mythology. Her name was taken from the Latin word *pomum*, or orchard fruit.

Pomona always carried her curved pruning knife with her, and used it to cut back unruly growth or encourage growth in the desired direction, and would direct water from the streams for her trees to drink. She feared no one and nothing, except that some malevolent god or satyr would rape her. To prevent this, she fenced herself inside her orchards, and allowed no man inside.

Despite her precautions, many of the young gods tried to seduce her; so did drunken old Silenus, the companion of Bacchus, and Priapus. Without exception, she shunned them all.

Hard to persuade

When Vertumnus, god of the changing seasons, saw Pomona, he fell deeply in love – but no matter what gifts he offered, she told him to go away. So he tried to trick her into marrying him. He could change his shape into anything he wanted, but no matter how he disguised himself, Pomona would not let him in. Every day he found some fresh disguise in which to approach his love. Finally, in

Vertumnus and Pomona (1807), lounge in an abundant orchard in this painting by British artist Richard Westall, commissioned by wealthy classics scholar Richard Payne Knight.

See also: The abduction of Persephone 50–51 ▪ Cupid and Psyche 112–13 ▪ Carna and Janus 121 ▪ Pyramus and Thisbe 124 ▪ Blodeuwedd 170–71

Vertumnus's disguises were many and varied. When one did not persuade Pomona to talk to him, he moved on to another.

Harvester	Oxherd	Vine-dresser	Fruit-picker	Soldier	Fisherman	Old woman
Vertumnus dressed as a reaper with a basket of corn.	He pretended to be an oxherd, holding a goad to drive cattle.	He posed as a vine-dresser carrying a pruning knife.	He also arrived to pick fruit, a ladder over his shoulder.	He disguised himself as a soldier in full armour.	He turned up with a rod and line; still she sent him away.	Pomona spoke to Vertumnus when he wore this disguise.

desperation, he let his hair grow grey, and arrived disguised as an old woman. The scheme worked; Pomona let in the old woman – and was startled to find herself being kissed in a passionate embrace.

Sinking to the ground, withered and bent, Vertumnus gestured to an elm tree around which a grapevine was twined. He tried to persuade Pomona of the advantages of marriage, and the perils of rejecting a suitor. "If this tree stood alone", he said, "and was not married to the vine, it would be of little interest. You shun marriage, when really you should follow the example of the tree. If you will take the advice of an old woman, you should reject all others and choose Vertumnus to share your bed. He loves the fruits you grow, though not as much as he loves you".

Eventual love

Pomona would not listen to the old woman's reasoning and so finally, Vertumnus shed his disguise, to reveal himself to her in the full glory of his divine youth. When she saw his true shape, Pomona fell for Vertumnus as deeply as he had for her, and told him that she never wanted him to take any shape again but his own.

Pomona and Vertumnus were a good match: together they held sway over fruits, orchards, growth, and the changing seasons. The annual Vertumnalias, their joint festival, occurred on 13 August and marked an opportunity for Roman citizens to give their thanks for the year's bountiful harvest. It was celebrated by the *flamen Pomonalis* ("priest of Pomona") in the *Pomonal*, a sacred grove near Ostia, the principal port of Rome. ▪

Ovid

The myth of Pomona and Vertumnus comes down to us from the *Metamorphoses* of the Roman poet Ovid. The *Metamorphoses* is a long narrative poem comprising 15 books and more than 250 myths. One of the most influential texts in literature, it has inspired masterpieces by writers, artists, and composers, from Dante, Chaucer, Shakespeare, and Kafka to Titian, Richard Strauss, and many more.

Publius Ovidius Naso was born into an important family in Sulmo (modern Sulmona, east of Rome) in 43 BCE. By the age of 18, he was already a poet. Ovid's fascination with both Greek and Roman mythology found expression in the *Heroides*, letters from mythological heroines to their lovers. This was followed by *Metamorphoses*, and his long poem on the Roman ritual calendar, *Fasti*.

In 8 CE, Ovid was exiled by the Emperor Augustus to Tomis on the Black Sea, where he died in 17 CE, unreprieved. Exactly why Ovid was exiled in this manner is not known. Ovid himself said it was due to "a poem and a mistake".

EVEN DEATH SHALL NOT PART US
PYRAMUS AND THISBE

IN BRIEF

THEME
Tragic lovers

SOURCE
Metamorphoses, Ovid, 8 CE.

SETTING
Ancient Babylon (modern Iraq).

KEY FIGURES
Pyramus A handsome young man from Babylon; in (forbidden) love with his neighbour, Thisbe.

Thisbe A beautiful young woman; forbidden from meeting with her love, Pyramus.

Pyramus and Thisbe grew up next door to each other in Babylon. They fell in love, but their parents forbade the union; the two were not allowed to meet or even talk. Only a chink in the wall between their two houses allowed them to whisper sweet nothings, and each kissed the wall on their own side to wish the other good night. They decided to sneak out at night and meet under a mulberry tree outside the city walls.

A tragic twist

Thisbe arrived first, but she was terrified by a lioness, fresh from a kill, who came to drink at a nearby pool. Thisbe ran into a cave, her veil slipping from her shoulders. The lioness pounced on the veil, ripping it to shreds and staining it with blood. When Pyramus arrived to find the bloody veil and pawprints in the sand, he believed that Thisbe had been devoured. Weeping, he stabbed himself with his sword; the blood gushed out from his wound and stained the mulberry tree's fruits a dark purple.

When Thisbe crept back and found Pyramus dying, she took his sword and killed herself, begging that the pair, parted in life, should be united in death. Her dying wish was that mulberries should always retain a bloodstained hue to commemorate their love. The gods granted this wish, and their parents buried the lovers' ashes in a single urn.

The tale of Pyramus and Thisbe had a lasting influence, inspiring both Shakespeare's *Romeo and Juliet* and the play within a play in *A Midsummer Night's Dream*. ∎

Jealous wall, why do you stand in the way of lovers?
Metamorphoses

See also: Apollo and Daphne 60–61 ▪ Echo and Narcissus 114 ▪ Cupid and Psyche 112–13

THOSE WHOM THE GODS CARE FOR ARE GODS

PHILEMON AND BAUCIS

IN BRIEF

THEME
Gods reward deserving mortals

SOURCE
Metamorphoses, Ovid, 8 CE.

SETTING
Phrygia, ancient Greece.

KEY FIGURES
Jupiter King of the gods; god of the sky and thunder.

Mercury God of commerce, communication, travellers, luck, and trickery; one of the 12 major Roman gods.

Philemon and Baucis A poor cottage owner and his wife, who were spared when the gods flooded their part of Phrygia to punish the people.

Jupiter and Mercury once visited the hill country of Phrygia, both disguised as mortal men. They went to a thousand doors, looking for a meal and a place to rest, and were turned away a thousand times. At last they came to the poorest, most dilapidated cottage of all, the home of an old woman, Baucis, and her husband Philemon, who welcomed the two travellers inside.

Gracious hosts

While Baucis set a fire, Philemon gathered vegetables from his garden, and together they provided the best feast they could for their guests. When the couple noticed their flagon of wine was magically refilling itself, they realized they were entertaining gods. "This wicked area will be punished for its unkindness to strangers", said Jupiter, "but you will be safe".

The old pair followed the gods up a mountain, and looked back. They saw the countryside flooded, but also their little cottage transformed into a glorious temple.

Philemon and Baucis humbly offer fruit, cheese, and wine to Jupiter and Mercury in this neoclassical painting by Andrea Appiani or a member of his circle in Milan (c.1800).

Philemon and Baucis asked to be guardians of the temple, and also to die at the same moment, so that neither would be left alone.

The gods granted their wish. One day, Baucis noticed leaves shooting out from Philemon's body – and from her own. With only time for a goodbye, they were turned into an oak and linden tree, intertwined in a single trunk. ∎

See also: The Olympian gods 24–31 ▪ Numa outwits Jupiter 106-07

NORTHE
EUROPE

RN

The fall of the **Roman Empire** heralds the beginning of the **Middle Ages**.

The *Poetic Edda* records **oral tradition** about the **Norse gods**.

Anglo-Saxon and German missionaries **convert** the people of **Scandinavia** to Christianity.

Geoffrey of Monmouth's *History of the Kings of Britain* popularizes the **Arthurian legend**.

476 CE **8TH–11TH CENTURY CE** **10TH–11TH CENTURY CE** **1136 CE**

597 CE **7TH-8TH CENTURY CE** **12TH CENTURY CE**

St Augustine goes to Britain, beginning the **conversion** of the **Anglo-Saxons** to Christianity.

The *Cattle Raid of Cooley* tells the story of the legend of **Cúchulainn**.

The *Four Branches of the Mabinogi*, a collection of **early prose tales**, is written in Wales.

The pre-Christian myths of northern Europe are less well recorded than those of the Greeks and Romans. Unlike these classical civilizations, the peoples of northern Europe did not have literate cultures until after they became Christian in the early Middle Ages. In its zeal to impose the new faith, the Christian Church did not sanction the recording of old myths and practices; much, perhaps most, has therefore been lost. Those Christian writers who did record pre-Christian myths were frequently unsympathetic towards them and often lacked any understanding of their original religious significance, so their meanings are now obscure.

Even writers who were not hostile, such as the 13th-century Icelander Snorri Sturluson, were careful to present the old myths in ways that would be acceptable to the Church, to protect themselves from accusations of heresy. Other myths went underground and continued to be passed on among the people. Over time, as myths lost their original pagan significance, they evolved into folkloric tales.

The old religions

Before they became Christians, the peoples of northern Europe were mostly divided into tribes and chiefdoms. They lacked centralized political and religious institutions that could impose uniformity of belief. Consequently, there was considerable regional diversity. At their peak in the last centuries BCE, the Celts inhabited Britain, Ireland, and large swathes of western and central Europe. They had no common pantheon of gods; while the worship of some deities, such as the thunder god Taranis and the horse goddess Epona, was widespread, none were universally worshipped by all Celtic peoples.

Across northern Europe, only the Celts are known to have had a professional priesthood. These priests, called Druids, served long apprenticeships during which they were expected to memorize all of their tribe's laws, history, myths, and religious practices. Among the pre-Christian Norse, on the other hand, religious rituals were conducted by local chiefs and kings. These old Norse religions lacked systematic theologies, and instead focussed on ritual sacrifices – of treasure, animals, or sometimes humans – in order to win the favour or avert the wrath of the gods.

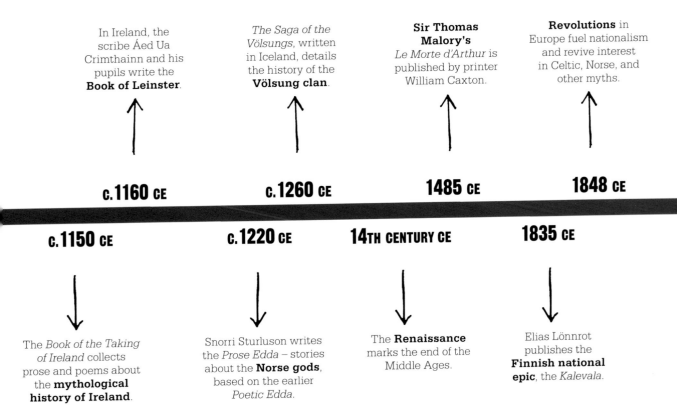

In Ireland, the scribe Áed Ua Crimthainn and his pupils write the **Book of Leinster**.

c. 1160 CE

The Saga of the Völsungs, written in Iceland, details the history of the **Völsung clan**.

c. 1260 CE

Sir Thomas Malory's *Le Morte d'Arthur* is published by printer William Caxton.

1485 CE

Revolutions in Europe fuel nationalism and revive interest in Celtic, Norse, and other myths.

1848 CE

c. 1150 CE

The *Book of the Taking of Ireland* collects prose and poems about the **mythological history of Ireland**.

c. 1220 CE

Snorri Sturluson writes the *Prose Edda* – stories about the **Norse gods**, based on the earlier *Poetic Edda*.

14TH CENTURY CE

The **Renaissance** marks the end of the Middle Ages.

1835 CE

Elias Lönnrot publishes the **Finnish national epic**, the *Kalevala*.

Historical origins

Some of the best known myths and legends from northern Europe are set, and probably originated, in the years after the fall of the Roman Empire in the 5th century CE. The earliest legends of King Arthur, for example, presented him as a heroic warlord defending the Celtic Britons against the Germanic Anglo-Saxons, who invaded Britain after the withdrawal of Roman forces in 410 CE. After the Norman conquest in 1066, Arthur was appropriated by French and English writers who depicted him as an idealized and chivalric king of all England.

The Norse legend of the dragon-slaying hero Sigurd includes real historical figures, testifying to its origins in the 5th or 6th century CE. While the Irish myths and legends have much more ancient origins,

many of these, too, can be placed in a historical context. The Ulster Cycle of myths, which features the hero Cúchulainn, centres on Emain Macha, a hillfort near Armagh, which was a major power centre in the Iron Age (500 BCE–400 CE).

The appeal of the Norse and Celtic legends, with their tales of heroes and dragon-slayers, remains strong in the modern world. They have inspired many works of art, music, and literature – from pre-Raphaelite paintings of Arthurian tales to Richard Wagner's *The Ring of the Nibelung* operas and J. R. R. Tolkein's *The Lord of the Rings*.

Nationalist purpose

While what we know of the Celtic and Norse myths and legends was written down during the Middle Ages, Finland's mythology was not

recorded until the 19th century. For most of their recorded history, the Finnish people were ruled by outsiders – first the Swedes, then the Russians – and literacy in the Finnish language was very limited until the early 19th century.

The collection of extant Finnish mythology and folklore began in the 1820s and was closely linked to the growth of Finnish nationalism. Under Russian rule from 1815, the Finns found their national identity increasingly threatened by policies of "Russification" and reacted by developing distinctively Finnish schools of art, music, and literature. One of the greatest achievements of this cultural movement was Elias Lönnrot's *Kalevala*, which wove together Finnish myths and legends to create a defining national epic for his people. ■

FRøM YMIR'S FLESH THE EARTH WAS MADE

CREATION OF THE UNIVERSE

Before the Christianization of Scandinavia in the 10th and 11th centuries, the Norse had an oral tradition rich with their own mythologies, which were frequently epic and violent. Even in their creation myth, an act of murder committed by the gods plays a central role.

The fullest version of the Norse creation myth is told in Snorri Sturluson's *Prose Edda*. According to Snorri, before the beginning of time, only the world of Muspelheim existed, guarded by the primeval fire giant Surt. Ages passed before the world of Niflheim was made. While the myths do not say who or

See also: Origin of the universe 18–23 ▪ Pangu and the creation of the world 214–15 ▪ Cherokee creation 236–37 ▪ Ta'aroa gives birth to the gods 316–17

Ymir suckles from the teat of the cow, Audhumla in this 1777 depiction by Nicolai Abildgaard. This neoclassical Danish painting also shows other frost giants, descendants of Ymir, being born from the ice of Ginnungagap.

what created the two worlds, they do highlight the contrast between Muspelheim, a world of fire, and Niflheim, a world of ice.

Between the two worlds was Ginnungagap, the primordial void. Eleven rivers rose from a spring called Hvergelmir and flowed into this void from Niflheim, carrying with them streams of poison. The rivers froze as they reached the void, and poisonous vapours rising from them formed rime (frozen fog). The northern part of Ginnungagap therefore became choked with layers of ice and rime.

The southern part of the void, close to Muspelheim, was hot enough to melt rock but the middle, halfway between the ice of the north and fire of the south, was mild: here the ice began to melt and drip. The heat from the south

caused life to quicken in the drops and they took the form of a giant named Ymir. He became the ancestor of the race of frost giants.

Ymir's descendants

While Ymir slept, a male and a female giant formed from the sweat under his left armpit and one of his legs fathered a son on the other leg. This was not all: as the ice in Ginnungagap continued to melt, a cow emerged. She was called

Audhumla, and she was nourished by licking the salty ice. The four rivers of milk that flowed from her teats fed Ymir.

By the evening of the first day, Audhumla's licking had revealed the hair of another giant. During the second day, his head emerged and, on the third day, the whole giant arose. His name was Búri. Búri was big, strong, and beautiful. He fathered a son called Bor – no mother is mentioned but she was »

The *Prose Edda*

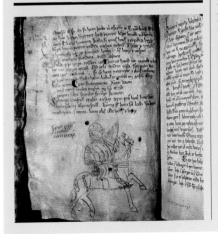

The *Prose Edda* was written by the Icelandic historian and politician Snorri Sturluson (1179–1241) as a handbook for composing skaldic verse: a form of bloodthirsty heroic poetry popular in the Viking age (c. 800–1100CE). Skaldic verse relied heavily on allusions to Norse mythology for its imagery, but knowledge of such myths had declined since the introduction of Christianity, and with it, so had the popularity of skaldic verse. Snorri hoped that by recording the myths he could revive the genre, but his attempts were largely unsuccessful.

Most of Snorri's sources are unknown – some were oral traditions which are now lost – but his work shows a knowledge of the older *Poetic Edda*. Snorri, himself a devout Christian, framed these stories so as to avoid any charges of heresy: his myths were interepreted as stories originally told about ancient *human* heroes, who used a variety of tricks to pass themselves off as gods. This approach to interpreting mythology, called euhemerism, interprets characters from myth as having origins in real people.

Loki, whose face decorates this forge stone, had his lips sewn together as punishment for using cunning wordplay to renege on a wager.

Giants and gods

The relationship between the giants and the gods was a complex one. In the Norse myths, giants usually appeared in an oppositional relationship to the gods. At the same time, myths also showed them to be similar to the gods. "Giant" is the usual English translation of the Norse *jötunn* but it is misleading: size is not their defining characteristic.

Although Ymir must have been huge for the gods to fashion the world from his body, most giants were like the gods. They had superhuman powers, and while some were hideous monsters, others were so beautiful that they became the gods' lovers or spouses: the god Thor was Odin's son by a giantess and all the gods were, ultimately, descended from giants. Giants could become gods – like Loki, who was born to giant parents. The distinction between giants and gods was primarily one of status rather than power: gods were entitled to be worshipped, while giants were not.

presumably a frost giantess as no other beings had yet been created. Bor took Bestla, the daughter of another frost giant of unknown origin named Bölthorn, as his wife. Together they had three sons, the first of the gods.

The eldest son was Odin, the second was Vili, and the youngest was Vé. These three gods, however, thought the giants were rough and uncouth. They killed Ymir and when he fell, so much blood gushed out of his body that all the frost giants were drowned except for his grandson Bergelmir, who escaped with his family in a boat and eventually re-founded the entire

They bore [Ymir] into the middle of the Yawning Void, and made of him the earth.
Prose Edda

giant race. Many commentators have suspected biblical influence in this story – with Bergelmir as a giant Noah. It is not clear if this is a genuine myth or an invention of the Christian Snorri's.

Heavens and earth

Because of Ymir's murder, the giants were, thereafter, invariably hostile to the gods. The three gods took Ymir's corspe to the middle of Ginnungagap and made the world from his body, encircling it with the sea, which they made from his blood. Ymir's flesh was used to make earth, his bones made the rocks, and his teeth formed smaller stones. The gods found maggots burrowing through Ymir's flesh. From these they created the dwarves and gave these beings consciousness, intelligence, and the appearance of men.

The gods used Ymir to make not only the earth but the heavens. They took Ymir's skull and placed it over the earth to make the sky. At each of the sky's four corners they set a dwarf. Their names were Austri (East), Vestri (West), Nordri (North) and Sudri (South). The gods also caught some of the sparks and molten embers that were blowing out of Muspelheim and set them in the sky to light the heavens. They fixed some of the sparks in the sky and these became the stars. Other sparks, the planets, moved about on courses set by the gods.

This myth also accounts for the creation of day and night, both of which are personified as giants. The gods placed the dark giantess Nótt ("night") and her bright and beautiful son Dag ("day") in the sky: they followed each other around the

Ymir is killed by the sons of Bor in the 19th-century drawing by Danish artist Lorenz Frølich. The frost giant is portrayed as ugly and rough, in comparison to the three beautiful gods.

The origin of the Gods

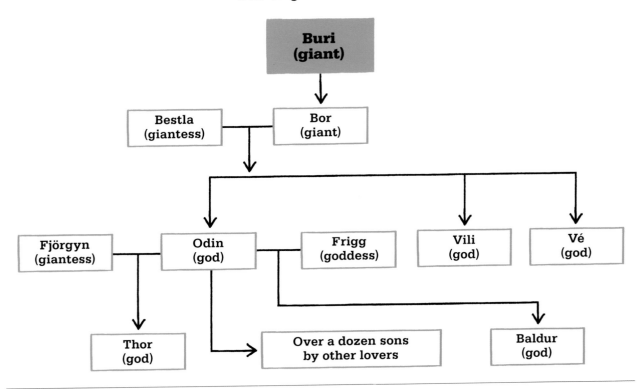

**Buri
(giant)**

**Bestla
(giantess)** — **Bor
(giant)**

**Fjörgyn
(giantess)** — **Odin
(god)** — **Frigg
(goddess)** | **Vili
(god)** | **Vé
(god)**

**Thor
(god)** | **Over a dozen sons
by other lovers** | **Baldur
(god)**

world once every 24 hours. The gods also took the beautiful brother and sister, Máni ("moon") and Sól ("sun"), and put them in the sky as well. According to Snorri's myth, both Máni and Sól move quickly across the sky because they are pursued by wolves. Ragnarök, the end of the world, will follow not long after the day when the wolves, children of a giantess, finally catch and devour them.

Fortress of Midgard
The gods made the earth circular, and gave the part around the shores to the giants as a home. This was called Jötunheim (from *jötunn*, the Old Norse name for the giants, and *heim*, meaning "home"). In the middle of the earth, the gods used Ymir's eyelashes to build a fortress to keep the giants out. They called this place Midgard.

The gods' final step was to take Ymir's brains and cast them into the sky to make the clouds. With this, the gods finished their brutal creation of the world.

The creation of man
Creation was not truly complete until one day, Odin, Vili, and Vé found two driftwood logs while walking along the seashore. From these logs, the gods created the first two humans, giving them life, consciousness, movement, faces, hearing, speech and sight. Finally, they gave them clothes and named the man Ask (ash) and the woman Embla (elm). The gods gave them and their descendants the realm of Midgard to live in.

After they had created humans, the gods created their own realm of Asgard, high above Midgard. There, they built their halls, the

most magnificent of which was Odin's own Valhalla: a heaven-like place where dead warriors would be entertained with feasting. To link Asgard and Midgard, the gods built a fiery rainbow bridge named Bifröst. Humans often fleetingly glimpse Bifröst in the sky but only the gods may cross it. ■

Then of his brows the blithe gods made Midgard for sons of men.
Prose Edda

THE ASH OF YGGDRASIL IS THE NOBLEST OF TREES

ODIN AND THE WORLD TREE

IN BRIEF

THEME
The Norse cosmos

SOURCES
Poetic Edda, Anonymous,
8th–11th century CE; *Prose
Edda*, Snorri Sturluson,
c.1220 CE.

SETTING
The nine worlds.

KEY FIGURES
Odin The leader of the gods.

Yggdrasil The world tree.

Nidhogg A serpent.

Ratatosk A squirrel.

Norns Three deities with
power over fate.

Valkyries Choosers of
the Slain.

Einherjar Dead warriors.

Hugin and Mumin Two
ravens who attend Odin.

Geri and Freki Two wolves.

Known as the Skog Tapestry,
this 13th–14th century textile was
discovered at Skog Church, Sweden,
in 1912. It is thought to represent the
Norse gods Odin, Thor, and Freyr.

The Norse believed that the
universe was made up of
nine worlds, or realms, with
Yggdrasil – a towering evergreen
ash tree – at its centre. According to
the "Völuspá" ("The Seeress's
Prophecy"), an Eddic poem, this tree
linked the nine worlds forming the
universe. The poem did not name
the nine worlds, but it is generally
accepted that they were Asgard,
Vanaheim, Álfheim, Jötunheim,
Midgard, Svartálfheim, Niflheim,
Muspelheim, and Hel.

Each world was home to a
different type of being. Asgard was
the realm of the Aesir family of
gods, led by Odin. Vanaheim was
home to the Vanir family of fertility
gods; Álfheim was the home of
the light elves; Jötunheim was the
realm of the frost giants. Midgard
was the world of humans;
Svartálfaheim was inhabited by
black elves and dwarves; and
Muspelheim was the world of the
fire giants. Niflheim was a realm of
ice, freezing mists, and dead souls.
Finally, Hel was the Underworld
realm of the goddess by the same
name, who ruled over those who
had died of sickness and old age.

Navigating the worlds
Norse sources often contradicted
one another, and it remains unclear
where each of these realms was in
relation to the others. It is likely
that the Norse themselves had no
settled understanding of this.
The description of the realms as
dwelling in Yggdrasil's roots and
branches gives little indication as
to their actual spatial positioning.
Asgard is usually considered to be
a celestial world, linked to Midgard
by the rainbow bridge Bifröst.
Álfheim was also probably a higher
realm in close proximity to Asgard.
We have no clues from the extant
sources as to the location of
Vanaheim but, because the Vanir
were associated with growth and
fertility, it may have been part
of the Underworld. As its name
implies, Midgard (meaning "Middle

See also: Creation of the universe 130–33 ▪ War of the gods 140–41 ▪ The death of Baldur 148–49 ▪ The twilight of the gods 150–57

World") lay between Asgard and the Underworld and was apparently surrounded by an ocean. It is unclear whether Jötunheim and Svartálfaheim lay inside this encircling ocean, or were outside it. In one Eddic poem, the land of the giants is separated from the human realm only by a river.

As black elves and dwarves lived underground, Svartálfaheim was probably subterranean, though not part of the Underworld, which Niflheim and Hel both belonged to. Hel was linked to Niflheim by Gjallarbrú, a golden-roofed bridge over the river Gjöll, which ran between the two realms.

Roots and skies

To complicate matters, Snorri wrote that Yggdrasil was supported by three enormous roots. One reached into Asgard, another into Jötunheim, and the third into Niflheim. In Snorri's account, there was a well, or spring, beneath each root: Urdarbrunn in Asgard; Mímir's Well in Jötunheim; and Hvergelmir in Niflheim. Each well had different properties. Urdarbrunn (the "Well of Fate") was where the gods met daily to hold their law court and settle disputes; the waters of Mímir's Well contained understanding and wisdom; Hvergelmir was the source of all the rivers of the nine worlds.

Things often came in multiples of three in Norse myths; three and nine, in particular, were sacred numbers. Adding to the mystery of the nine worlds, there were also nine heavens. The lowest was variously called Vindbláin ("Wind Dark"), Heidthornir ("Cloud Brightness), or Hréggmímir ("Storm Mímir"). The second-lowest heaven was Anlang ("Very Long"), and the

third, Vídbláin ("Wide Dark"); these were followed by Vídfedmir ("Wide Embracer"), Hrjód ("Cloaker"), Hlynir ("Double Lit"), Gimir ("Jewelled"), and Vetmímir ("Winter-Mímir"). Higher than all the clouds, and beyond all the worlds, was Skatyrnir ("Rich Wetter"). According to Snorri Sturluson, the only inhabitants of the heavens were the light elves who, perhaps influenced by his own Christian beliefs, he saw essentially as angelic beings. Although they came from Álfheim, they also protected the heavens.

Creatures of the tree

Yggdrasil was home to a number of creatures that fed on it, causing the tree constant suffering – it was seen as being sentient in some way. The serpent Nidhogg ("Vicious Blow"), which lived by Hvergelmir, constantly gnawed at Yggdrasil's roots. Four stags, called Dáinn, Dvalinn, Duneyrr, and Durathrór, ran between its branches feeding on its freshest leaves.

In the tree's highest branches sat a wise but unnamed eagle, »

> The squirrel that runneth on lofty Yggdrasil, and down to Nidhöggr bringeth the eagle's words, is Ratatosk.
> **Poetic Edda**

The Norns

Like the Fates of Greek mythology, the Norns were three female deities who determined the fate of the universe and every being in it. Not even the gods could challenge a verdict made by the Norns, who thereby represented the highest power in the universe.

The Norns dwelled by Urdarbrunn, the "Well of Fate" that lay beneath the root of Yggdrasil in Asgard, land of the Aesir gods. "Völuspá", a poem from Snorri's Prose Edda, named the Norns as Urd ("Past"), Verdandi ("Present") and Skuld ("Future"). They were present at the birth of every child in order to shape its life. Their art was described either as spinning the threads of life or engravings scored into wood.

Belief in the Norns gave the Norse a fatalistic outlook that encouraged taking risks. Nothing was to be gained by playing safe: you would die at your appointed time, no matter how far from danger you stayed. It was better by far to die in a blaze of glory and earn posthumous fame than to be forgotten because of your lack of achievements.

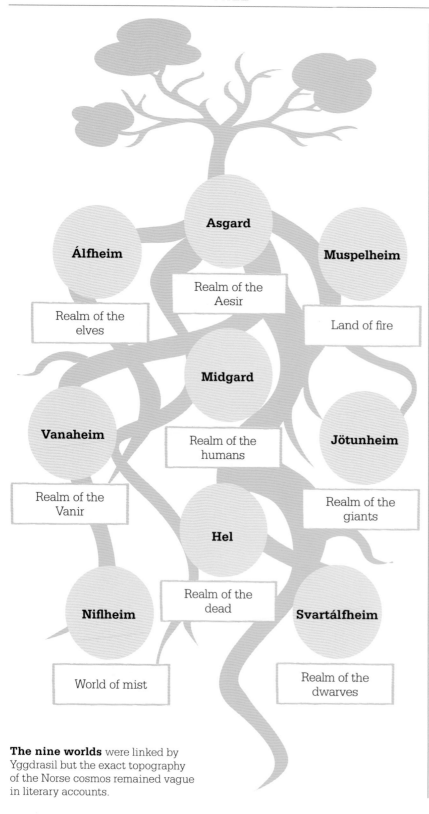

Asgard

Realm of the Aesir

Álfheim

Realm of the elves

Muspelheim

Land of fire

Midgard

Realm of the humans

Vanaheim

Realm of the Vanir

Jötunheim

Realm of the giants

Hel

Realm of the dead

Niflheim

World of mist

Svartálfheim

Realm of the dwarves

The nine worlds were linked by Yggdrasil but the exact topography of the Norse cosmos remained vague in literary accounts.

whose flapping wings caused the winds to blow. The eagle and Nidhogg were old enemies and their feud was enabled by a squirrel called Ratatosk, which scurried up and down Yggdrasil carrying hostile messages between them.

Because of the attacks made on the tree, Yggdrasil was decaying. It was tended by the Norns, three fate-making deities, who sprinkled it with holy water from Urdarbrunn and whitened its boughs with clay gathered from around the well to preserve them. Their actions kept the cosmos in balance between the forces of destruction and creation. Despite Yggdrasil's importance, no Norse myth told of either its creation or demise. At Ragnarök – the prophesied end of the world – Yggdrasil would tremble and groan, but it would not fall; the tree was thought to be eternal.

Odin's knowledge

Odin ruled the nine worlds from his throne Hlidskjálf in Asgard. Two ravens, Hugin (Thought) and Mumin (Memory), were symbols of his mind and sat on his shoulders. Each dawn Odin sent them out to fly over the worlds; they returned in the evening

I know that I hung, on a wind-rocked tree, nine whole nights, with a spear wounded, and to Odin offered, myself to myself.
Odin, *Poetic Edda*

Odin hangs from the branches of the World Tree. It is possibly from this episode that Yggdrasil gets its name. It means "Ygg's horse", Ygg being one of many alternative names for Odin.

to report what they had discovered. Yggdrasil was also a source of knowledge for Odin. Key to this, was Odin's knowledge of runes, gained through an act of auto-sacrifice: he hung himself from Yggdrasil for nine days, impaled on his own spear. The

water of Mímir's Well gave wisdom. For a single drink from the well, Odin tore out one of his eyes and left it in the well as a pledge. His search for knowledge had one purpose: he had foreseen his death at Ragnarök and was seeking a way to defy fate. From his ordeal, Odin gained the ability to use runes, which granted him powers far beyond other gods'.

Valhalla

Odin became a great warrior who was known for his "Hall of the Slain", Valhalla. The vast hall, roofed with spears, had 540 doors, each so wide that 800 warriors could march abreast through it. It was a paradise where the *einherjar*, fallen warriors, could feast on pork and mead. The promise of Valhalla must have been a comfort to a Viking warrior facing death in battle, but most preferred to live and enjoy the spoils of victory. Only "berserkers" actively sought death in battle so as to be guaranteed entry to Valhalla. These animalistic warriors worked themselves into a trance-like fury before each battle.

Odin's bloodlust was immense. Two wolves, Geri and Freki, were Odin's companions. Symbols of his

All those men who have fallen in battle from the beginning of the world are now come to Odin in Valhalla.
Prose Edda

cruelty, their names both meant "ravenous" or "greedy". They roamed battlefields feeding on corpses. At feasts, Odin gave his food to his pet wolves, subsisting only on wine himself. He was also accompanied by the Valkyries ("Choosers of the Slain"), who conducted the souls of the bravest men killed in combat to Valhalla to join his personal band of dead warriors. In this way the cosmic order mirrored the human order: for the Viking age Norse, the chief and his personal retinue were at the centre of society. ■

Runes

Runes were the individual letters of the runic alphabet, the indigenous writing system of the early Germanic peoples. The Norse believed that Odin gave runes to the world, but in reality they were probably derived from the Latin alphabet.

It is likely that the runic alphabet, known as the *futhark* after its first six letters, was originally designed to be inscribed on wood. Runes avoided curved lines, which were awkward to carve, and

horizontal lines, which would have been difficult to distinguish from the grain of the wood.

Runes were more than just letters. They were powerful symbols, each of which had its own meaningful, magical name. Norse priests used runes both to write spells and in their memorials to the dead. Runes slowly fell out of use after the conversion of the Norse to Christianity in the 10th and 11th centuries because of their pagan associations. By the 15th century, Runes had been replaced by the Latin alphabet in Scandinavia.

These runic letters feature on one of two 11th-century memorial rune stones found at Bjärby on the island of Öland, Sweden.

THE FIRST WAR IN THE WORLD
WAR OF THE GODS

IN BRIEF

THEME
Warring gods

SOURCES
Poetic Edda, Anonymous,
10th–13th century CE;
Heimskringla ("History
of the Norse Kings"),
Snorri Sturluson, c.1230 CE;
Prose Edda, Snorri Sturluson,
c.1220 CE.

SETTING
Asgard and Vanaheim –
separate realms inhabited by
two distinct families of gods:
the Aesir and the Vanir.

KEY FIGURES
Odin Leader of the Aesir.

Gullveig A witch and seeress.

Njord Leader of the Vanir.

Kvasir A wise being created
from the spittle of the gods.

Mímir A disembodied head,
source of wisdom.

Honir Odin's companion.

The Norse described their gods collectively as the Aesir, from which Asgard, the realm of the gods, was named. However, they believed that there had originally been two families of gods: the Aesir and the Vanir. The Norse believed that at the dawn of history, the Aesir and Vanir fought a war over who had the right to receive tribute (worship and sacrifices) from humans.

The goddess Freyja was seized by giants in *Das Rheingold*, the first opera in Wagner's *Ring Cycle*. This 1910 illustration shows her being dragged away from the gods.

The war of the gods began because of the Aesir's treatment of a witch called Gullveig during her visit to Odin's hall in Asgard. Three times the Aesir tried to burn her, but each time she came back to life. Gullveig could create magic wands and cast spells, and had the gift of prophecy. This marked her out as one of the Vanir goddesses. After the Vanir complained about Gullveig's treatment, both sides met at Urdarbrunn (the "Well of Fate") to settle their differences.

Peace and war
At Urdarbrunn, Odin threw a spear at the Vanir and the war broke out. The Vanir stormed Asgard; in return, the Aesir ravaged the Vanir's home, Vanaheim. Neither side could win, so the gods agreed to exchange hostages and live in peace, sealing the treaty by all spitting into one bowl. From their spit, the gods created Kvasir, a being of exceptional wisdom.

After the war, the sea god Njord, who was leader of the Vanir, his son Freyr and daughter Freyja, went to live with the Aesir, as did Kvasir. In return, Honir and the wise god Mímir, from the Aesir, went to live in Vanaheim. However, the Vanir

See also: The war of the gods and Titans 32–33 ▪ A complex god 164 ▪
The twilight of the gods 150–57 ▪ The game of dice 202–03

The Aesir

Lived in Asgard, one of the nine worlds.

Descended from **Vili, Vé, and Odin**.

Key figures include **Thor and Loki**.

Associated with **power and war**.

The Vanir

Lived in **Vanaheim**, one of the nine worlds.

Origins shrouded in **mystery**.

Key figures include **Freyja, Freyr, and Njord**.

Associated with **fertility and nature**.

were unhappy with their hostages. When Mímir was there to tell him what to say, Honir gave good advice, but when Mímir was away, he could only reply "Let others decide". Feeling they had been cheated, the Vanir beheaded Mímir and sent Honir, with his head, back to Asgard. Odin preserved Mímir's head and gave it the power of speech so that he could benefit from its wisdom. The distinction between the gods eventually faded when the Vanir became Aesir and shared the tribute from humans.

Clash between cults

The story of the war of the gods could be interpreted as a mythic representation of a clash between two religious cults. It is possible that the Vanir were the gods of Stone Age Scandinavian farmers (c. 11,000–1800 BCE), while the Aesir were the gods of Indo-Europeans who migrated into the region in the Bronze Age (c. 1800–500 BCE). ▪

They made a truce by this procedure, that both sides went to a pot and spat into it.
Prose Edda

The walls of Asgard

The gods hired a giant to rebuild the walls of Asgard after their war with the Vanir. They agreed to give him the sun, moon, and the goddess Freyja if he completed the task in a single winter, believing this was impossible. For his part, the giant agreed to work alone, aided only by his stallion. When they saw that the giant would finish on time, the gods ordered Loki to find a way to get out of keeping their promise. Turning himself into a mare, Loki lured the giant's stallion away, so that the giant missed his deadline. Realizing he had been cheated, the giant flew into a rage, and Thor killed him. The gods had become oath-breakers, corrupted by power. Odin also received an unexpected gift from Loki as a result of the deception – an eight-legged foal, Sleipnir, fathered by the giant's stallion.

Odin sits astride Sleipnir in this 18th-century Icelandic illumination. Sleipnir was born to Loki while the trickster took the form of a mare.

THEY MIXED HONEY WITH THE BLOOD AND IT TURNED INTO MEAD
THE MEAD OF POETRY

IN BRIEF

THEME
Origins of poetry

SOURCE
Prose Edda, Snorri Sturluson, c.1220 CE.

SETTING
Jötunheim, the homeland of the giants.

CHARACTERS
Odin The leader of the gods, who turned into a handsome man named Bolverk.

Kvasir A male being of extraordinary wisdom.

Gilling A frost giant.

Fjalar and Galar Dwarves, murderers of Kvasir and Gilling.

Suttung Gilling's son.

Gunnlod Suttung's daughter, who was seduced by Odin.

Baugi Suttung's brother, who helped Odin reach the mead.

Odin was primarily a god of kingship, war, and wisdom but he was also the god of poetry. All human poets owe their inspiration to Odin's theft of the Mead of Poetry from the giant Suttung. In the story of this theft, Odin fulfilled the role of a "culture hero", a mythological figure who brings a valuable gift to humankind.

Like many other treasures, the Mead of Poetry, which is a metaphor for poetic inspiration, was created by dwarves. The wise being Kvasir innocently accepted the hospitality of the dwarves, Fjalar and Galar, only to be murdered by them. The dwarves poured Kvasir's blood into three vessels and mixed the blood with honey, turning it into a mead that made anyone who drank it either a poet or a scholar. They told the gods that Kvasir had suffocated in his own intelligence because he could not find anyone learned enough to talk to.

Baugi drilled into a mountain to reach the Mead of Poetry with an auger named Rati. Baugi did not truly want Odin to obtain the mead, and tried but failed to kill the god with the auger.

The dwarves lost the Mead of Poetry after they killed the giant Gilling and his wife. Gilling's son, Suttung, seized the dwarves, took them to a skerry and threatened to leave them to drown as the tide came in. The dwarves then gave Suttung the mead as compensation for the death of his parents. Suttung hid it in a mountain and set his daughter Gunnlod to guard it.

Stealing the mead
Odin, a master of disguise as well as a shape-shifter, wanted to steal the mead for himself. Disguised as a handsome labourer named

See also: Pandora's box 40–41 ▪ The many affairs of Zeus 42–47 ▪ Odin and the world tree 134–39 ▪ Nanga Baiga 212–13

Odin sits embracing Gunnlod and holding a drinking horn, in this 19th-century illustration by German artist Johannes Gehrts. The Mead of Poetry is in vessels around them.

Bolverk, he hired himself out to Suttung's brother Baugi and agreed to do the work of nine men for a summer in return for a single drink of Suttung's mead. When winter came, Baugi asked his brother to give Odin a drink of the mead. Suttung refused, so Baugi agreed to help Odin by drilling a hole in the mountain, allowing him to enter in the form of a snake.

Odin's escape

Turning himself back into Bolverk, Odin seduced the lonely Gunnlod. After he had spent three nights with her, Gunnlod gratefully allowed Odin three drinks of the mead. He took the first vessel and emptied it in one gulp. After doing the same with the remaining two vessels of mead, Odin made his escape by turning himself into an eagle and flying away, leaving a heartbroken Gunnlod behind.

Discovering the theft, Suttung too took the shape of an eagle and set off in hot pursuit. When Odin flew over Asgard, he spat the mead out into containers the gods had placed in the courtyard. But he was so closely pursued by Suttung that he accidentally spat some of the mead from his backside. This less pure mead fell to the ground and was free to take for anyone who could make a simple rhyme. The rest of the mead, Odin kept for the gods and to inspire those who were skilled at making verse. ▪

Norse poetry

There are two surviving genres of Norse poetry – skaldic verse and Eddic verse. Both styles made considerable use of poetic similes called kennings – for example, calling a ship a "sea-stallion". Each genre relied on alliteration, rather than rhyme, for rhythm but Eddic verse used simpler metres.

Skaldic verse was composed by court poets called skalds whose main duty was to praise their aristocratic patrons' courage, wisdom, wealth, and generosity. Not surprisingly, war was the main subject of skaldic verse: it was full of violent imagery and has been compared by some scholars to modern day gangsta rap. Most skalds were warriors, expected to compose verse in the heat of battle to encourage warriors to fight bravely. Eddic verse, on the other hand, was always about religious or legendary subjects. While the authors of most skaldic poems are known, Eddic verse was always anonymous.

Odin gave Suttung's mead to the Aesir and to those people who are skilled at composing poetry.
Prose Edda

THOR MIGHT SMITE AS HARD AS HE DESIRED AND THE HAMMER WOULD NOT FAIL

THE TREASURES OF THE GODS

IN BRIEF

THEME
Magical weapons

SOURCES
The *Poetic Edda*, Anonymous, 10th–13th century CE; The *Prose Edda*, Snorri Sturluson, c.1220 CE.

SETTING
Svartálfheim, the realm of the dwarves and black elves.

KEY FIGURES
Thor The thunder and weather god, worshipped by farmers.

Loki The enigmatic and mischievous trickster god.

The sons of Ivaldi A group of dwarf craftsmen; Norse myth does not specify the identity of Ivaldi himself.

Brokk and Eitri Dwarf brothers, and skilled craftsmen.

The most important of the Norse gods were often closely identified with magical possessions, all crafted by dwarves, who were skilled blacksmiths. The gods originally acquired these treasures with the help of the trickster Loki. Unbeknownst to Thor's wife, Sif, Loki had cut her beautiful hair as a joke. When Thor found out, he threatened to break every bone in Loki's body unless Loki asked the dwarves to craft hair of gold for Sif.

Loki's contest

Loki went to the group of dwarves called the sons of Ivaldi, and they made Sif perfect golden hair. They also made the spear Gungnir, which, once thrown, never missed its mark, and the ship Skidbladnir, which could carry all the Aesir, yet also be carried in a pocket. Then Loki bet the dwarf Brokk that his brother Eitri could not make finer treasures than the Ivaldis. Whoever lost the bet, it was agreed, would forfeit their head.

Eitri went to his forge and, setting Brokk to work the bellows, said he must not stop blowing until the work was finished or it would be flawed. Loki, a shape-shifter like

Finding Sif asleep, Loki cuts off her long and beautiful golden hair, in this 1894 illustration by A. Chase.

See also: Odin and the world tree 134–39 ▪ War of the gods 140–41 ▪ The Mead of Poetry 141–42 ▪ The adventures of Thor and Loki in Jötunheim 146–47

Odin, turned himself into a fly and tried to distract Brokk by biting him. Despite this, Brokk blew steadily while Eitri made a golden boar that could run faster than a horse, and a golden arm-ring called Draupnir, from which eight equally heavy rings dropped every ninth night. Only when Eitri was forging the hammer Mjölnir did Loki cause Brokk to stop blowing for a moment by biting his eyelids. As a result, the handle was a little short, but Mjölnir retained its great power.

The finest work

Loki and Brokk went to Asgard to ask the gods whose work was the finest: Eitri's or the sons of Ivaldi. Judging Mjölnir the finest of the treasures, the gods declared Brokk the winner. After a failed attempt to bribe Brokk to save his own life, Loki ran off in his magic shoes, but Thor caught him. Quick-thinking Loki declared that his head might be Brokk's but his neck was not part of the bargain. The dwarf saw he had been outwitted and settled for sewing Loki's mouth shut. ▪

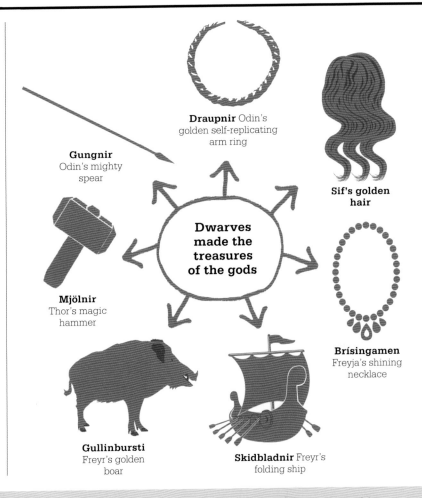

Draupnir Odin's golden self-replicating arm ring

Gungnir Odin's mighty spear

Sif's golden hair

Dwarves made the treasures of the gods

Mjölnir Thor's magic hammer

Brísingamen Freyja's shining necklace

Gullinbursti Freyr's golden boar

Skidbladnir Freyr's folding ship

Thor wields his mighty hammer against the giants in this 1872 painting by Swedish artist Mårten Eskil Winge.

Thor's hammer

Unlike most of the gods, Thor was believed to be unambiguously well-intentioned towards humans. While Odin was the god of kings, warriors, and poets, the ordinary farmers favoured Thor. Vikings commonly invoked his protection by wearing hammer amulets.

Thanks to its overwhelming power, Thor's magic hammer Mjölnir defended the gods and humans from the hostility of the giants and created order from chaos. Mjölnir was able to strike with as much force as Thor wished; it never missed its mark, and no matter how far it was thrown, it always returned to Thor's hand.

Thor delighted in using his hammer to smash giants' skulls. In one myth, the giant Thrym managed to steal Mjölnir and hid it deep underground. He hoped it would be beyond the reach of the gods, and used the hammer to bargain for Freyja in exchange for its safe return. A combination of Thor's strength and Loki's cunning, however, soon recovered it to restore Asgard's defences.

AM I WRONG IN THINKING THAT THIS LITTLE FELLOW IS THOR?
THE ADVENTURES OF THOR AND LOKI IN JÖTUNHEIM

IN BRIEF

THEME
The limitations of the gods

SOURCE
Prose Edda, Snorri Sturluson, c.1220 CE.

SETTING
Jötunheim, the land of the giants.

KEY FIGURES
Thor The thunder god.

Loki Thor's brother; the trickster god.

Thialfi Thor's human slave; a farmer's son.

Utgarda-Loki A strong giant, who Thor wished to test his strength against.

Logi A giant who bested Loki in an eating contest.

Hugi A small man who beat Thialfi in a series of races.

Elli An old woman; nursemaid to Utgarda-Loki.

lthough Thor's strength, bravery, and dependability were renowned, the Norse god was also portrayed as rather slow-witted and easy to deceive. Many of the myths concerning Thor were humorous examinations of the limitations of brute strength. He was often paired with Loki, who was cunning and clever, but also cowardly, malicious, and deceitful. Thor and Loki had an antagonistic relationship, but they made a good team and were frequent travelling companions.

The combination of Thor's brute strength and Loki's cleverness often brought success, but not always. In one story in the *Prose Edda*, Thor decided to travel to Jötunheim, a land of giants, to test his strength against Utgarda-Loki. He took with him Loki and a human bondservant, a slave called Thialfi.

Giant's challenge
When Thor, Loki, and Thialfi arrived in Jötunheim, the giant Utgarda-Loki expressed disappointment with Thor, complaining that he had expected

Loki travelled to Jötunheim many times. On one occasion, he tricked Idun, the goddess of spring, and she was kidnapped by a giant. Disguised as a falcon, Loki flew to her rescue.

See also: Prometheus helps mankind 36–39 ▪ Hermes' first day 54–55 ▪ Creation of the universe 130–33 ▪ The Mead of Poetry 142–43 ▪ Ananse and the spider 286–87

Tricksters

Tricks played a prominent role in the mythologies of many cultures. Whether a trickster was human, a god, a demigod, or even an anthropomorphized animal, they all broke rules and defied normal expectations of accepted behaviour. Many, such as Loki, had the ability to shape-shift. Stories of tricksters who achieved their ends through guile and cleverness rather than strength invited audiences to identify with them as the underdogs, even when their subterfuges were considered immoral. The trickster spider Ananse, originally from the mythology of the Akan people of Ghana, became a symbol of resistance when transported to the West Indies via the slave trade.

When a trickster's actions benefitted the human race, he or she sometimes became a culture hero. Examples include the tale of the Norse god Odin, when he stole the Mead of Poetry and, in ancient Greek mythology, Prometheus's theft of fire from the gods.

Thor strives in vain to lift Utgarda-Loki's cat in this 1930 illustration from a book of Norse tales retold and illustrated by the American artist Katharine Pyle.

the god to be bigger. The giant went on to explain that the three visitors could only stay in Jötunheim if they each managed to excel in some art or skill.

Loki offered to take part in an eating competition against Logi, one of the giants of Jötunheim. Loki ate all the meat placed before him, whereas Logi ate his meat, the bones, and the wooden plate, too. Next, Thialfi had to race against a small man called Hugi, but lost three times in succession.

Then Utgarda-Loki challenged Thor to drain a large drinking horn in one go. After taking three huge draughts, Thor discovered that the level of the liquid had only lowered slightly. Utgarda-Loki next asked Thor if he was even strong enough to pick up the giant's cat. Thor barely managed to lift just one of the feline's feet off the ground.

Frustrated, Thor offered to fight anyone in the giant's hall. Utgarda-Loki's response was that, in view of Thor's weakness, he would only be allowed to wrestle with the giant's nursemaid, an old lady called Elli. When Elli forced Thor down onto one knee, the god believed he had lost his strength completely.

Trickery of the giants

As the crestfallen trio set out for home, Utgarda-Loki revealed that everything they had experienced had been an illusion. The trickster Loki had competed with fire, which consumes everything. Thialfi had raced against thought, for which his speed could be no match. Utgarda-Loki's drinking horn had been connected to the sea and

Small as you say I am, just let someone come out and fight me. Now I am angry!
Thor, *Prose Edda*

Thor had drunk enough of it to create the tides. Utgarda-Loki's cat had really been the monstrous Midgard serpent, a creature so large, it encircled the whole world; Thor had lifted the serpent up almost to the sky. The ancient nursemaid was old age; while age would defeat everyone in time, it had only managed to force Thor down onto one knee.

As Utgarda-Loki explained, the giants had been so terrified by Thor's strength that they could only fight him with trickery. Enraged, Thor reached for his hammer, but before he could strike, Utgarda-Loki had disappeared. He, too, had been an illusion. So ended a myth that exposed the limitations of the Norse gods, proving that there are forces in the universe over which neither strength nor cunning can prevail. ▪

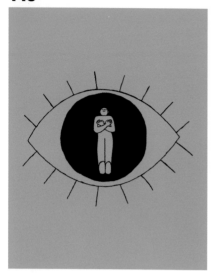

THE UNLUCKIEST DEED EVER DONE AMONGST GODS AND MEN
THE DEATH OF BALDUR

IN BRIEF

THEME
Fate

SOURCES
Poetic Edda, Anonymous,
10th–13th century CE;
Prose Edda, Snorri Sturluson,
c.1220 CE.

SETTING
Asgard, land of the gods,
and Hel, the underworld.

KEY FIGURES
Odin The leader of the gods.

Baldur Odin's son.

Frigg Odin's wife; the mother
of Baldur and Hod.

A seeress Prophesier of
Baldur's death.

Loki A trickster.

Sigyn Loki's wife.

Hod The blind god; brother
of Baldur.

Hel Ruler of the Underworld.

The Norse myths recount a complete history of the world, from its creation to its ultimate destruction at the cataclysm of Ragnarök, at which even the gods themselves would perish. The Eddic poem "Völuspá" ("The Seeress's Prophecy"), made it clear that Ragnarök had been inevitable since the beginning of time, but it was the death of Odin's son, Baldur, that forced the gods to face their mortality. Baldur, Odin's son by his wife Frigg, was noted for his good looks. Everyone praised him – his appearance was so brilliant that light flashed from him; his voice was mellifluous; and he was the kindest of all the Aesir. Baldur was also ineffectual: no one took any notice of anything he said or did. His role in the myths was simply to be beautiful and loved – and to die in tragic circumstances.

Prophecy of death
After Baldur reported experiencing disturbing dreams, Odin rode to the underworld and revived a long-dead seeress to ask her what the dreams meant. She told him that Baldur would soon be killed by his

Loki

An enigmatic character, Loki was a giant by birth, but Aesir by adoption. He was just as at home in Jötunheim, land of the giants, as in Asgard. Brimming with malice, deceit, and spite, he was amoral rather than pure evil. There is no evidence that he was ever worshipped and no one has yet satisfactorily explained his place in the Norse pantheon. One theory is that he was a personification of fire, which can both help and harm.

Despite his mischief, Loki was tolerated by the Aesir who found his cunning useful. His most common role was to create a crisis by his mischief-making and then to resolve it by his quick thinking. All of Loki's children were monsters: the eight-legged wonder-horse Sleipnir; Hel, the decaying goddess who ruled the Underworld; the giant wolf Fenrir; and the world-circling serpent Jörmungand. The last two, fighting alongside Loki, would play a major role in the demise of the Aesir gods at Ragnarök.

See also: Creation of the universe 130–33 ▪ War of the gods 140–41 ▪ The adventures of Thor and Loki in Jötunheim 146–47 ▪ The twilight of the gods 150–57

brother, the blind Hod. To prevent this from coming to pass, Frigg sought promises from everything in the world not to harm Baldur. Loki, who was jealous of Baldur's popularity, learned that Frigg had failed to extract a promise from the unobtrusive mistletoe. Unaware of this, the Aesir gods entertained themselves by playing a game in which they threw all manner of things at Baldur, who always remained unharmed. Loki then fashioned an arrow from mistletoe, placed it in Hod's hand, and guided the blind god's aim so that the mistletoe struck and killed Baldur.

Frigg hoped to save her son and sent the god Hermod to Hel to plead for Baldur's release from the Underworld (Hel was both the name of the realm and the being who presided over it). She agreed to release Baldur, but only if all things wept for him.

Loki's punishment

All things did weep for Baldur, bar one – a giantess who was none other than Loki in disguise. Baldur was thereby forced to stay in the underworld. The Aesir gods took vengeance on Loki by chaining him to a rock beneath the open jaws of a serpent so that the snake's venom dripped onto his face. Loki's faithful wife, Sigyn, held a bowl over him to catch the venom, but whenever she turned to empty the bowl, the venom dripped onto Loki's face, causing earthquakes as he writhed in agony, punished for his trick. ▪

Loki causes the death of Baldur, as depicted in a 17th-century manuscript of the *Prose Edda* by Icelandic farmer Jakob Sigurdsson for his foster father, the Reverend Ólafur Brynjólfsson.

He convinced the Aesir to **offer the goddess Freyja** in return for the building of a defensive wall.

He **tricked** the goddess Idun into taking her apples of youth to the Aesir, thus allowing her to be **kidnapped**.

Loki's tricks often hurt the other gods.

He **cut the golden hair** of **Sif**, the wife of Thor, who forced Loki to replace it.

He made **Hod kill Baldur** and refused to join the Aesir gods in **weeping** for him.

BROTHER WILL FIGHT BROTHER AND BE HIS SLAYER

THE TWILIGHT OF THE GODS

IN BRIEF

THEME
The end of the world

SOURCES
Poetic Edda, Anonymous,
10th–13th century CE;
Prose Edda, Snorri Sturluson,
c.1220 CE.

SETTING
The nine worlds.

KEY FIGURES
Heimdall Watchman of the
Aesir gods.

Odin The high god.

Jörmungand The Midgard
serpent; son of Loki.

Loki The trickster.

Surt A fire giant.

Fenrir A wolf; son of Loki.

Vidar Son of Odin; god of
vengeance.

Thor The thunder god.

Time was cyclical in Norse mythology; nothing lasted forever, not even the gods. This universe would one day come to an end at Ragnarök (the doom of the gods), a final climactic battle between the gods and the giants that would destroy the world and annihilate the beings who lived in it. The cataclysm would not be final, however. A few survivors would be spared, emerging from sheltered refuges to repopulate a new, and better, world.

There were two detailed accounts of Ragnarök. The oldest made up the second half of the prophetic Eddic poem "Völuspá" ("The Seeress's Prophecy"), where a *völvur*, a seeress, raised from Hel told Odin the terrible series of events that would destroy the world.

The newer account of Ragnarök featured in "Gylfaginning" ("The Beguiling of Gylfi"), the first book of Snorri Sturluson's *Prose Edda*. Snorri's account – an equally awesome picture of the end of the world – was a synthesis that drew on (but often contradicted) "Völuspá" and many other Eddic poems, and probably other lost sources and traditions as well.

> Fate is heard in the note
> of the Gjallarhorn; loud
> blows Heimdall.
> *Poetic Edda*

It is unlikely that the Norse religion ever had a defined canon about Ragnarök and its aftermath. "Gylfaginning", despite being more complete than "Völuspá", still left many questions unanswered. But while neither version predicted when Ragnarök would happen, each warned its approach would be heralded by a varying series of catastrophic events.

Ragnarök in "Völuspá"

According to "Völuspá", a summer would come during which the sun would turn black. When this happened, Eggther, the giant who tended the wolf Fenrir, would sit on

Freyja, goddess of fertility,
searches for her gleaming necklace
stolen by Loki in the *Prose Edda* in a
1930 illustration by Katharine Pyle.

Prophecy in Norse religion

The inevitable fulfilment of prophecies played a central role in Norse mythology. Prophecy came through the practice of *seidr*, a shamanistic form of magic that was associated with the Vanir group of deities. This form of magic gave select individuals the ability to communicate with the dead and to see into the future.

Freyja, the Vanir goddess of fertility, taught Odin *seidr*: using it, he raised a seeress from the dead so that she could tell him about Ragnarök.

Seidr was practised by both humans and mythical beings, mostly by women who were known as *völvur* (wand-carriers). Following a ritual meal of the hearts of whatever animals were at hand, a *völva* would use chants and spells to invoke spirits, who could then be questioned about the future.

The term *seidr* survives to this day in the modern English word "seer" – this Anglo-Saxon term for a prophet derives from the Old Norse.

See also: Odin and the World Tree 134–39 ▪ War of the gods 140–41 ▪ Treasures of the gods 144–45 ▪ Death of Baldur 148–49

> ## Warning sounds heralded the end of the world in "Völuspá".

| The giant Eggther played his harp. | A cockerel woke the dead warriors of Valhalla. | A bird crowed at the gates of Hel; her dog bayed. | A third bird crowed in Gallows Wood. |

> ### The war of the gods began and the earth was annihilated by fire.

---

a mound and play his harp with delight at what was to come. Three birds would then crow to announce the beginning of Ragnarök. First, Gullinkambi ("Golden Comb"), who lived in Valhalla, would awaken the sleeping *einherjar* ("dead warriors") so they could prepare for their final battle. An unnamed rust-red bird would crow at the gates of Hel to rouse the underworld, and the third bird, Fjalar, would crow in the foreboding Gálvidur ("Gallows Wood"). The goddess-giant Hel's watchdog, Garm, would bay loudly, break the rope that tethered it to its cave, and run free.

Reigning chaos
Human society would then begin to break down as brother slayed brother and incest and adultery flourished. No man would spare another. Heimdall, the watchman of the gods, would blow the alarm on his horn, Gjallarhorn, while Odin would go to consult the preserved head of the wise god Mímir. The earth would start to shake, and the world tree Yggdrasil would shudder and groan, but it would not fall. Giants would go on the rampage

The Aesir god Heimdall blows his Gjallarhorn. The vigilant watchman was known for his acute vision and hearing. He was the first to know about the coming of Ragnarök.

and countless terrifed souls would descend to Hel. Hrym would lead the frost giants from the east; Jörmungand, the Midgard serpent, would churn up the sea in his rage; and eagles would shriek and feast on corpses. The sinister Naglfar would set sail with fire giants on board from Muspelheim, the home of the giants. Loki would be at the helm with his giant brother Byleist alongside him. Surt, the greatest of the fire giants, would advance from the south. Rocky cliffs would split open, spilling troll women from their crevices. The sky would crack as elves and dwarfs howled in terror.

According to the *Poetic Edda*, this would herald the start of battle. Loki's son, the monstrous wolf Fenrir, would kill Odin, only for Odin's son Vidar to avenge his death by thrusting his sword into the wolf's heart. Thor would slay Jörmungand, but stagger just nine steps before dropping dead himself.

Surt would slay the fertility god Freyr. As the battle raged, the sun would turn black and the stars would disappear from the sky. Steam and flames would shoot as high as the heavens as the ravaged land finally sank beneath the sea.

A return to tranquility
Soon, a new world would rise from the waves, eternally green and with crops that grew without sowing. »

The *Poetic Edda*

One summer, the sun turns black.

↓

Three birds announce the start of Ragnarök.

↓

Human society breaks down.

↓

Heimdall **sounds the alarm**.

↓

Loki and the giants **advance on Asgard**.

↓

The gods and giants **annihilate** each other in battle.

↓

The ravaged **earth sinks** below the sea.

↓

The *Prose Edda*

Three hard winters lead human society to fall.

↓

The **Great Winter** heralds the start of Ragnarök.

↓

Wolves swallow the sun, moon, and stars.

↓

Loki and the giants **advance on Asgard**.

↓

The gods and giants **annihilate** each other in battle.

↓

Surt spreads fire over the **ravaged earth**.

↓

The **earth sinks** below the waves.

↓

A new world rises from the sea.

The seeress saw an eagle fishing near a waterfall, and other bucolic images. Some of the Aesir gods (the poem didn't say how many) would meet again on the plain of Idavoll, where Asgard had once stood. They would talk about Ragnarök and remember their past. Baldur and his killer Hod would return from the dead, reconciled, and live in peace.

Omens and allusions

Some humans, the sons of two unnamed brothers, would also survive, and their kin would spread over the world. "Völuspá" went on to say that virtuous folk of the land would then live their days happily at a new, beautiful, gold-roofed hall called Gimlé. At this point, a "powerful mighty one, who rules over everything" would come from the heavens. "Völuspá" did not identify this mysterious figure, but many commentators have claimed that this was an allusion to the Christian Last Judgement.

"Völuspá" then ended with the reappearance of the serpent Nidhogg – before Ragnarök, this creature had gnawed endlessly at the roots of the eternal world tree Yggdrasil. Nidhogg would now fly over the new world carrying a cargo of corpses in its wings. "Völuspá" did not elaborate, but

There shall come that winter which is called The Great Winter.
The *Prose Edda*

Cyclical time

In Christian cosmology, time is seen as a linear process that begins with creation and ends on the Day of Judgement. Other religious traditions, including that of the Norsemen, see time as a cycle of repeated creation and destruction. However, the Norse did not have advanced calendrical knowledge, so descriptions of the timescale of this cycle were vague.

In Hindu cosmology, by contrast, time is precisely calibrated in cycles lasting from a few milliseconds to trillions of years. They believe that a complete cycle from creation to destruction lasts exactly 311.04 trillion years. Since Hindu cosmology also embraces the concept of multiverses, there are an infinite number of time cycles and an infinite number of universes being created and destroyed at any one time.

Modern physicists continue to ask whether time is indeed linear, cyclical, or simply illusory. The answer remains unresolved.

Nidhogg's survival was clearly a bad omen for the future. It may have implied that the new world, like the old, was also ultimately doomed to destruction.

Snorri's Ragnarök

The account of Ragnarök in Snorri Sturluson's "Gylfaginning" clearly displayed a debt to "Völuspá", and even quoted from it in places, but his work also differed from the earlier poem in a number of ways.

The first sign of Ragnarök's approach, according to Snorri, would be three hard winters followed by a complete breakdown of human society. As in "Völuspá", wars would break out everywhere and ties of kinship would count for nothing: adultery, incest, and fratricide would flourish during this time. Hard on the heels of this period would come Fimbulwinter ("The Great Winter"), during which the sun would dim and ice and snow would grip the world for

three years with no intervening summers. Then Sköll, the wolf who used to chase the sun, would finally catch his quarry and swallow it. Meanwhile, his brother Hati Hródvitnisson would catch and swallow the moon. The stars would disappear from the sky, swallowed by another monstrous wolf, Mánagarm.

As darkness engulfed the world, the earth would shake, uprooting trees and toppling mountains. The bonds and fetters of both Loki and his son, the wolf Fenrir – until now chained up by the gods – would shatter, setting them free to do their worst. As in "Völuspá", the rope that tethered the Hel hound Garm to his cave would snap, unleashing the animal.

Asgard under threat

The giants and their allies would now advance on Asgard. Huge ocean waves would surge over the land as raging Jörmungand, the Midgard serpent, twisted and thrashed his way ashore. The rising sea would loose the dreadful *Naglfar* (Nail Ship) from its moorings. The largest of all ships, *Naglfar* was made from the fingernails and toenails of dead people. It had been prophesied that Ragnarök could not happen until the ship was completed. Since both gods and humans would like to have seen Ragnarök delayed as long as possible, Snorri advised that no one should be allowed to die with untrimmed nails, as these would provide materials for the ship. *Naglfar* would be steered by Hrym, leader of the army of the frost giants.

The wolf Fenrir, Loki's son, would now advance, his mouth gaping so wide that his lower jaw touched the earth and his upper jaw was against the sky. Flames would burn from his eyes and nostrils. Alongside him, his brother Jörmungand would spew his »

Odin visited the head of Mímir
for advice and guidance during the gods' final battle with the giants during Ragnarök. Drinking from Mímir's Well bestowed knowledge.

venom across the sea and sky. To add to the turmoil, the sky would split apart and the fire giants of Muspelheim, led by Surt, would ride out surrounded by burning fire. Light would blaze more brightly from Surt's sword than from the sun. The giants' armies would cross Bifrost, the rainbow bridge spanning the gap between Asgard and Midgard, shattering it in the process. The troops would then gather on the field of Vígrid ("Battle Surge"), which stretched for a hundred leagues in all directions. Fenrir, Jörmungand, and Loki would be there, together with Hrym and his frost giants, while the fire giants of Muspelheim would form their own battle line.

The gods rally

Snorri wrote that Heimdall would then sound Gjallarhorn to awaken the gods to their danger, and Odin would ride to Mímir's Well to consult with the wise Mímir's head. Meanwhile, the branches of Yggdrasil would tremble, filling everything that lived in the nine worlds with fear. Then the Aesir and the *einherjar,* the dead warriors, would march out to do battle on the vast plain of Vígrid, led by Odin. Carrying his spear Gungnir and wearing a golden helmet and mail coat, Odin would take on Fenrir with Thor at his side.

Jörmungand would attack Thor before the god of thunder could help Odin. Freyr would fight Surt, who would defeat and kill him. The minor war god Tyr and the evil Hel hound Garm would fight each other to the death. Although Thor would kill Jörmungand, he would only step nine paces away from his foe before he, too, would fall down dead from the venom the serpent had spat at him. Without Thor's support, Odin would be swallowed by Fenrir.

Odin's son Vídar would immediately avenge his father's death, stepping down on Fenrir's lower jaw with one foot, grasping the wolf's upper jaw in one hand, and tearing him apart. Loki and Heimdall would battle together and kill one another. After this, mighty Surt would hurl fire, burning the whole world, after which it would

The sky splits and releases the fire giants of Muspelheim in an engraving of Ragnarök *(Downfall of the Aesir)* published in an 1882 book of Norse gods and heroes.

The Valkyries, Norse maidens who decided who lived or died in battle, head to war in Arthur Rackham's 1910 illustration *The Ride of the Valkyries*.

the waves, where crops would grow without having been sown. The surviving Aesir would begin to gather on Idavoll, where Asgard used to stand: all that would remain would be some golden gaming pieces lying in the grass. Odin's sons Vídar and Váli would arrive first, followed by Thor's sons Modi and Magni, having rescued Thor's hammer from the destruction of the old world. Last, Baldur and Hod would return from Hel, complete with the serpent Niddhogg. The heavens too would survive, and virtuous folk (who presumably died during Ragnarök) would feast in the halls of Gimlé and Brimir.

Two humans, a woman called Líf ("Life") and a man called Leifthrasir ("Thriving Remnant"), would survive Ragnarök and Surt's fire by hiding within the branches of Yggdrasil. They would sustain themselves on the morning dew and would go on to have so many descendants that the earth would be completely repopulated. The

sink beneath the sea, taking the gods, the battle dead, and all humankind with it. The inrushing waters would put out the flames. The fate of other beings – the frost giants, elves, and dwarfs – was not mentioned in Snorri's account of Ragnarök, but it is probably safe to assume that they too would perish.

A brighter future
Similar to "Völuspá", in Snorri's account a beautiful new world would soon shoot up from beneath

> Then the powerful, mighty one, he who rules over everything, will come from above.
> *Poetic Edda*

new world would be lit by a new sun, because the old sun would have given birth to a fiery daughter moments before being swallowed by Sköll the wolf.

This regeneration of the earth and sky contrasts with the foreboding at the end of "Völuspá". Snorri's optimistic vision of the future world, however, may well have been a result of his Christian beliefs. The "Völuspá" is likely a truer vision of the way the Norse traditionally saw the future – as an endless cycle of creation and destruction. ∎

Christ and Ragnarök

In the early stages of the conversion of the Norse to Christianity, monuments such as preaching crosses combined Christian symbols with scenes from old Norse myths, such as Ragnarök.

The Norse often accepted Christ as simply one more deity among many, but Christianity required a convert to believe that there was only one god. The monuments were created to aid the conversion process. For example, Denmark's Jelling rune stone, considered the country's earliest Christian monument, depicted Christ on the cross entwined by foliage. This was intended to draw a parallel between Christ and Odin, who hanged himself from the world tree Yggdrasil.

Other monuments reminded converts that the old gods were mere mortals, doomed to die, by juxtaposing the cross – the symbol of Christ's resurrection – with scenes of Ragnarök. The message: Christ alone was eternal and only he could offer his followers eternal life.

The Jelling rune stone, c.965 CE, sometimes referred to as "Denmark's birth certificate", combined both Christian and old Norse iconography.

WHEN THE WORM COMES TO THE WATER, SMITE HIM IN THE HEART

SIGURD THE DRAGON SLAYER

IN BRIEF

THEME
Hero versus monster

SOURCES
Völsunga Saga ("The Saga of the Völsungs"), Anonymous, c.1260 CE.

SETTING
Late Iron Age; Denmark or Germany.

KEY FIGURES
Sigurd Fafnisbane Son of the hero Sigmund.

Regin A dwarf smith.

Otter Regin's brother.

Andvari A dwarf, who can change into a fish.

Fafnir Regin's brother, who can turn into a dragon.

Brynhild A Valkyrie.

Grimhild A queen; mother of Gudrun, Gunnar, and Guttorm.

Gudrun Sigurd's wife.

Gunnar Gudrun's brother.

Sigurd Fafnisbane was one of the most popular legendary human heroes in Norse mythology, and the central character of the *Saga of the Völsungs*, which was written down in Iceland around 1260 CE.

Sigurd was the posthumous son of the hero Sigmund – the son of king Völsung, from whom the saga takes its name – and was fostered by Regin, a highly skilled dwarf smith. One day, Regin told Sigurd

the story of Otter's Ransom, a pile of gold the Aesir gods paid to Regin's father Hreidmar, king of the dwarves, as compensation for killing Regin's brother, Otter. (At the time, Otter had been in the form of the creature bearing that name.) The gold, however, had been cursed by its original owner, the dwarf Andvari, after the trickster Loki forced him to give up a gold ring to complete the ransom.

Otter's curse unfolds
Regin's brother Fafnir murdered his father to get the gold and turned into a dragon to guard it. Regin also wanted the treasure, so he urged Sigurd to kill Fafnir, plotting to murder the hero afterwards. To ensure Sigurd's success, Regin forged the magical sword Gram and gave it to him. After killing Fafnir, Sigurd accidentally drank some of the dragon's blood, gaining the ability to understand the speech of birds. From them he learned of Regin's treacherous

A carved portal from Hylestad stave church, Norway, depicts Sigurd slaying the dragon Fafnir. Such scenes were popular subjects for wood and stone carvers in the late Viking Age.

See also: The adventures of Thor and Loki in Jötunnheim 146–47 ▪ The death of Baldur 148–49 ▪
The twilight of the gods 150–57

intentions and beheaded him, taking the gold for himself. As the new owner of the cursed treasure, Sigurd was now doomed as well.

Having proved himself a great warrior, Sigurd became betrothed to the Valkyrie Brynhild. However, he forgot Brynhild after drinking a potion from queen Grimhild – who wanted the treasure for her family – and he married Grimhild's daughter Gudrun instead. Gunnar, Gudrun's brother, then sought Sigurd's help in winning the hand of Brynhild, whose hall was protected by a ring of magic fire through which only Sigurd could pass. Made to switch forms with Gunnar, Sigurd wooed the Valkyrie for his brother-in-law, but Brynhild was enraged to learn that she had been deceived and ordered Gunnar to kill Sigurd.

Gunnar's brother Guttorm agreed to do the deed and fatally wounded Sigurd, at the cost of his own life. Heartbroken, Brynhild threw herself on Sigurd's funeral pyre. Gunnar alone avoided the treasure's curse by abandoning the gold in a cave. ▪

Otter's ransom
passed hands many times after Loki forced Andvari to give it up. The gold cursed all who took possession of it, including the Aesir, who were doomed to die at Ragnarök.

Andvari, a fish dwarf, put a curse on the treasure as he gave it to the god **Loki**.

→

The Aesir gods paid the ransom to **Hreidmar** for the death of Otter.

↓

Hreidmar, king of the dwarves, was killed in battle by his son, **Fafnir**.

←

Fafnir, a shape-shifter, was killed by **Sigurd** for Fafnir's brother **Regin**.

←

Regin was beheaded by **Sigurd**, who he had plotted to murder.

↓

Sigurd was murdered by **Guttorm**, the brother of **Gunnar**.

→

Gunnar broke the curse by leaving the gold in a cave, where **Andvari** recovered it.

Dragon statues mark the boundary of the City of London, in reference to the story of England's patron saint St George and the dragon.

Dragons in myth

Common in many mythologies, dragons are serpent-like, often winged, reptilian creatures capable of breathing fire or venom. In Indo-European stories, dragons are usually malign creatures eventually killed by divine or human heroes. In Vedic Hinduism, for example, the dragon Vritra, a personification of drought, is slain by the god Indra. In Norse mythology, the god Thor kills the world-encircling Midgard serpent. A dragon-slaying hero appears in Near Eastern mythologies, including the story of the Babylonian god Marduk slaying the sea dragon Tiamat. The creature also features in early Christian stories, such as that of St George and the Dragon, where the dragon becomes a symbol of Satan.

In contrast, the dragons of Chinese mythology are revered beneficent creatures, associated with authority, power, and wisdom. They possess powers over natural forces, specifically those to do with water; they can control rain, tsunamis, and floods.

WONDERFUL THE MAGIC SAMPO, PLENTY DOES IT BRING TO NORTHLAND

THE KALEVALA

The poems of the *Kalevala*, land of heroes, were compiled by folklorist Elias Lönnrot in the mid-1800s. He wove together the numerous myths and legends of the Karelian and Finnish peoples, most of which had never before been written down. The poems, formalized in printed form, became the definitive Finnish epic at a time when Finland's culture and language were under threat, with the nation's declaration of independence from Russia still decades away.

The poems explore themes of creation, heroism, sorcery, violence, death, and concern, among other things the struggle of the heroes to

See also: The quest of Odysseus 66–71 ▪ The legend of King Arthur 172–77 ▪ The epic of Gilgamesh 190–97 ▪ The *Ramayana* 204–209

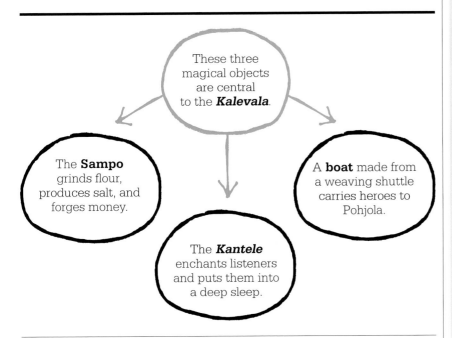

These three magical objects are central to the *Kalevala*.

The **Sampo** grinds flour, produces salt, and forges money.

A **boat** made from a weaving shuttle carries heroes to Pohjola.

The *Kantele* enchants listeners and puts them into a deep sleep.

Elias Lönnrot

Born in 1802, in Sammatti, Finland – at that time part of Sweden – Lönnrot studied medicine and worked as the district medical officer in Kajaani. A founding member of the Finnish Literature Society, he was passionate about his native tongue and developed an interest in the relationship between philology and folklore. He visited remote areas of Finland, Lapland, and Russian Karelia, listening to traditional songs and tales passed down orally through generations. He eventually compiled them into the epic which became the *Kalevala*.

There was controversy about how much editing Lönnrot undertook in order to fit these myths of varying origins and ages together. Still, he was celebrated for his final version, published in 1849, and appointed to the Chair of Finnish Literature at the University of Helsinki. The *Kalevala* comprises 50 poems in trochaic tetrameter, known as the "Kalevala meter". The emphasis on intonation is apt: almost every feat undertaken by characters in the epic is accomplished through incantation.

acquire the legendary Sampo, a mysterious talisman which gave its owner endless prosperity.

The *Kalevala* recounts the adventures of Väinämöinen, the first man; the blacksmith Ilmarinen; and the warrior Lemminkäinen. It begins with the story of creation, when the goddess Ilmatar lay down in the sea, heavily pregnant but bemoaning that she could not yet give birth. There, a bird laid seven eggs on her knees, and when she moved, the eggs fell and broke and the pieces formed the world. For »

Ilmatar on her bed of waves, as painted by romantic artist Robert Wilhelm Ekman (1860). A virginal spirit, she gave birth in the sea.

a time, Ilmatar was preoccupied with her creations, but after 700 years of pregnancy, she gave birth to the first man: the fully-formed Väinämöinen. Old and wise from birth, the hero is usually depicted with white hair and a beard.

The first challenge

Väinämöinen wove magic spells with his singing. Word of this skill traveled to Pohjola, far to the north, where a young minstrel named Joukahainen was consumed by envy. He challenged Väinämöinen to a singing match but when he lost, he sank into a swamp. Panicking, he offered Väinämöinen his sister Aino's hand in marriage in exchange for saving his life. But when Joukahainen returned home and told his sister, she drowned herself at the idea of marrying such an old man.

After this, Väinämöinen set out to woo another woman: the maiden of Pohjola, whose mother Louhi ruled the country. Joukahainen lay in wait with a poisoned crossbow, intent upon avenging his sister's death, and shot Väinämöinen into the sea. He was saved by Louhi, who promised to return him to Kalevala and give him her daughter's hand if he created the Sampo, a magical artifact. Väinämöinen offered to send the blacksmith Ilmarinen to forge the Sampo, and hurried home.

On his way, however, he met the maiden herself and proposed to her. She agreed, but said that first he must complete a list of seemingly impossible tasks. While carving a wooden boat from a spindle – the last of the tasks – Väinämöinen cut his knee with an axe and was unable to complete the task.

Ilmarinen's refusal

Returning home, Väinämöinen discovered that the smith Ilmarinen was unwilling to travel to Pohjola and forge the Sampo. As a result, he summoned a stormy wind to blow Ilmarinen there, and the smith

> Far away the news was carried, far abroad was spread the tidings of the songs of Väinämöinen, of the wisdom of the hero.
> *Kalevala*

made the Sampo out of white swan feathers, the milk of greatest virtue, a single grain of barley, and the finest lambswool. The epic never clearly defines the Sampo. However, based on the description of its purpose – to grind flour and produce salt and gold – it is thought to be a mill. When Louhi got the Sampo, she shut it inside a hill of rock and sent Ilmarinen home without the maiden.

Raised from the dead

Meanwhile, the warrior and adventurer Lemminkäinen set off for Pohjola, but not before leaving a magic comb with his mother. If he died, the comb would supposedly drip blood. When Lemminkäinen arrived, he also set his sights on the maiden of Pohjola. To win the maiden, Louhi set him three tasks: to catch the demon's elk, bridle the demon's horse, and kill the swan of Tuonela (the land of the dead). Alas,

Ilmarinen forges the Sampo, Berndt Abraham Godenhjelm (c.1860). The creation of the Sampo is just one of the tasks Väinämöinen is set in order to win the maiden's hand in marriage.

Väinämöinen fights Louhi, who is transformed into a bird, to defend the stolen Sampo. This battle is sometimes interpreted as a metaphorical fight for the soul of Finland.

Lemminkäinen was killed by a herdsman, who scattered his body parts in the river. At that moment, the comb he left behind dripped with blood. His mother rushed to Pohjola and brought him back to life by reassembling his body, anointing it with an ointment acquired from the gods, and chanting magic spells.

A second contest

Väinämöinen and Ilmarinen then competed for the hand of Louhi's daughter, who preferred the young blacksmith to the wise old man. Before he could marry the maiden, Ilmarinen had to perform three "impossible" tasks: ploughing a field of vipers, hunting the bear of Tuonela and the wolf of Manala, and fishing the great pike from the Tuonela River. He completed the tasks and a wedding feast ensued.

Only Lemminkäinen was not invited to the feast. Furious at the snub, he decided to settle the score. by challenging Louhi's husband to a duel. After a singing contest and

And he saw the Sampo forming, with its brightly coloured cover.
Kalevala

swordfight, Lemminkäinen killed the man and fled to an island full of beautiful women.

Stealing the Sampo

The three heroes were reunited much later, after Ilmarinen's wife was killed. Hearing of the wealth that the Sampo had brought to Pohjola, the men decided to sail there to steal it. On the way, their boat collided with a giant pike, which Väinämöinen killed. From its jaw, he created a *kantele* (a type of harp) which only he could play; the magic instrument had the power to enchant all living things. Using it, he charmed the people of Pohjola to sleep and his companions rowed away with the Sampo.

As the three men fled, Louhi awoke and used her powers to send obstacles to block their path. The

heroes survived but the *kantele* was lost in the water. Transformed into a giant bird of prey, Louhi gave chase to the heroes' boat, and during the battle, the Sampo, too, fell from the boat. It sank to the bottom of the sea, where it broke into pieces. Scattered in the depths of the sea, they produced salt, and Louhi was left with only the lid.

In retaliation, Louhi sent nine plagues to the people of Kalevala, but Väinämöinen cured them. She sent a bear to attack their cattle, but he defeated it. Louhi then hid the sun and the moon inside a hill, and took the gift of fire from man. Väinämöinen fought the people of Pohjola but eventually asked Ilmarinen to forge keys to the mountain of Pohjola to release the sun and moon. Relenting, Louhi finally set the sun and moon free. ∎

THE DAGDA WAS EIGHTY YEARS IN THE KINGSHIP OF IRELAND
A COMPLEX GOD

IN BRIEF

THEME
God, warrior, and king

SOURCE
Lebor Gabála Érenn ("The Book of the Taking of Ireland"), Anonymous, c.1150 CE.

SETTING
Ireland, 9th century BCE.

KEY FIGURES
The Dagda A "good god" with magical powers, also known as Eochaid Ollathair (Eochaid the All-father). Leader of the Tuatha Dé Danann: mythical figures who inhabited ancient Ireland.

The Morrigan The goddess of war and fertility; one of the Dagda's lovers.

Danu Ancestral goddess of the Tuatha Dé Danann.

Cethlenn Formorian queen and prophetess.

The Dagda acted as both father-god and provider for the Tuatha Dé Danann, a race of divine beings who were the mythical inhabitants of Ireland before the Celts. Children of the goddess Danu, they settled there in the 9th century BCE and brought talismans with them, including the Dagda's Cauldron – an enormous, endlessly replenishing source of food and drink.

A god with two sides

While the Dagda's name meant the "good god", his portrayal is more complex. He was celebrated for his wisdom, magical powers, and physical prowess, but also depicted as a crude comic figure whose tunic was too short. Along with his cauldron of plenty, he was known for carrying a magical club; one end killed people, and the other brought them back from the dead, emphasizing his life-giving powers.

The Dagda was a fearsome fighter all his life thanks to a hearty diet of porridge. He was also helped by one of his many lovers, the Morrigan, a goddess who could influence the outcomes of battle by her presence. However, the Dagda's 80-year reign ended after the Tuatha Dé Danann fought the Battle of Mag Tuired against the divine but monstrous Formorians. There, the Dagda "died of a dart of gore", a javelin thrown by a woman named Cethlenn, who was the wife of Balor, king of the Formorians, and also a prophetess. ∎

The Dagda's Cauldron drinking fountain in Tralee, County Kerry. The bronze sculpture shows the Dagda and other ancient Irish deities.

See also: The war of the gods and Titans 28–29 ∎ The treasures of the gods 144–45 ∎ Izanagi and Izanami 220–21 ∎ The night barque of Ra 272–75

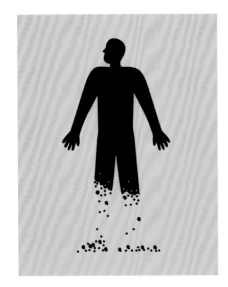

AS SOON AS HE TOUCHED THE EARTH, HE WAS A HEAP OF ASHES

THE VOYAGE OF BRAN

IN BRIEF

THEME
Journey to the otherworld

SOURCE
"Imram Brain" ("The Voyage of Bran"), *Lebar na Núachongbála* ("The Book of Leinster"), Anonymous, c.1160 CE.

SETTING
Ireland, 7th century CE.

KEY FIGURES
Bran Hero and son of Febal.

Woman An unnamed poet and seer, possibly one of the Sidhe, supernatural beings or goddesses.

Manannan A sea god, charioteer, and son of Lir.

Nechtan Son of Collbran, a member of the ship's crew on Bran's voyage.

Bran was a legendary Irish hero who went in search of an otherworldly paradise. He learned of this place from an unnamed woman in strange garb who appeared at his palace. She mesmerized Bran and his court by singing about a distant isle, a place where sorrow and evil were unknown, and where there was an abundance of beautiful maidens.

The Land of Women

The next day, Bran set off by sea with his men to search for this wonderful land. On the way, he met a figure in a chariot, who came towards him across the waves. Named Manannan, the mysterious charioteer sang to Bran, telling him about his journey and a future son, who was destined to be a hero. He also said that Bran would soon reach the Land of Women.

When they arrived at the Land of Women, Bran was pulled to shore by a strand of yarn, thrown to him by the leader of the women. He and his men were greeted with loving hospitality and a bed for every couple. One of the men, Nechtan, eventually grew homesick and encouraged the others to return to Ireland with him. The women's leader warned them, however, that if they did so, they should not land.

When their ship drew near to their homeland, no one recognized Bran and his men or knew who they were, as so many years had passed. Nechtan, not heeding the woman's warning, jumped ashore and turned to ash. Bran's ship sailed away, never to be heard of again. ∎

"There is nothing rough or harsh, but sweet music striking on the ear."
"The Voyage of Bran"
The Book of Leinster

See also: The quest of Odysseus 66–71 ▪ The labours of Herakles 72–75 ▪ Aeneas 96–101 ▪ The legend of King Arthur 172–77

ONE WILL BE LONG FORGETTING CÚCHULAINN
THE CATTLE RAID OF COOLEY

IN BRIEF

THEME
National hero

SOURCE
Táin Bó Cúailnge ("The Cattle Raid of Cooley"), Anonymous, 7th–8th century CE.

SETTING
1st century CE, the Kingdom of Ulster, Ireland.

KEY FIGURES
Cúchulainn A warrior.

Medb A goddess and queen of Connaught, an Irish province.

Ailill King of all Ireland, also known as King of Connaught.

Ferdiad An exiled friend of Cúchulainn.

Lugaid King of Munster and slayer of Cúchulainn.

Morrigan The war goddess.

The *Táin Bó Cúailnge* – in English, The Cattle Raid of Cooley – was the longest and most important tale from a group of texts known collectively as the Ulster Cycle. The story focused on the exploits of Cúchulainn, a young Ulster warrior and one of the greatest heroes of Celtic mythology.

The tale opened with a contest between a wife and her husband: the goddess Medb – queen of the province of Connaught – and Ailill, Ireland's king. Arguing about which of them was wealthier, Medb discovered that it was Ailill, for he owned a white-horned bull with

The first warp-spasm seized Cúchulainn, and made him into a monstrous thing, hideous and shapeless, unheard of.
Táin Bó Cúailnge

supernatural powers. Refusing to be beaten, Queen Medb decided to find the only other magical bull in the land – Dun, the Brown Bull of Cooley. Dun's owner would not surrender the bull, so Medb and Ailill invaded Ulster in order to steal the animal.

On the eve of battle, Medb learned that all the warriors of Ulster were mysteriously ill and unable to fight – except for a 17-year-old called Cúchulainn. Medb rejoiced that her victory would be easily accomplished, but a prophetess foretold, "I see very red, I see red". The next day, a bloody battle ensued.

Victory against the odds
Medb watched as Cúchulainn, transformed by a "warp-spasm" into a terrifying giant, slaughtered her troops one by one. The goddess continued to send the best soldiers in the land to fight him, but they were no match for the boy – his deadly spear could shoot 24 darts able to pierce every body part. At the height of the battle, Cúchulainn found himself locked in a three-day combat with a former friend – Ferdiad, an Ulster man in exile in Connaught. Cúchulainn emerged

See also: The quest of Odysseus 66–71 ▪ Aeneas, the founder of Rome 96–101 ▪ A complex god 164 ▪ King Arthur 172–77

victorious but exhausted. He was unable to go on. The Ulster warriors then woke from the spell that had laid them low and forced Medb and her troops to retreat.

The death of Cúchulainn

Despite losing in battle, Medb managed to capture Dun, the Brown Bull of Cooley. The two bulls were then set against each other and Ailill's white-horned bull was killed. Mortally wounded, Dun found his way back to Cooley but died when he got there. Medb's pursuit had caused carnage and death throughout the kingdom, yet she could not accept defeat. She convinced the sons of those slain by Cúchulainn to seek revenge. Among them was Lugaid, the king of Munster, whose father had

Morrigan signals Cúchulainn's death. The vibrant mosaic of the Tain Wall in Dublin by Desmond Kinney (1974) depicts scenes from the tale.

perished in the battle. The men conspired to kill Cúchulainn and Lugaid threw the fatal spear.

Cúchulainn washed his wound and drank water in a nearby lake. Barely able to stand, but refusing to die lying down like an animal, he tied himself to a standing stone and then died. His enemies feared him too much to get close enough to see if he was still alive. Three days later, the goddess Morrigan appeared as a raven – a Celtic symbol of death – on Cúchulainn's shoulder, confirming he was dead.

A hero's legacy

The fact that Cúchulainn's story is still widely told to this day is testimony to the Irish people's empathy with their hero. During the 20th century, he came to represent defiance in the face of British rule. Ulster unionists, however, prefer to focus on his defence of the province of Ulster from enemies to the south. ▪

The Hound of Chulainn

Originally named Sétanta, Cúchulainn was the nephew of King Conor of Ulster and, possibly, the son of the sky god Lugh. He earned his new name when, as a boy, he attended a banquet with his uncle at the house of the blacksmith Chulainn.

Having lagged behind on the way to the banquet, when he finally arrived at the house, Sétanta found himself facing Chulainn's ferocious guard dog. When it attacked him, Sétanta killed the hound in self-defence. To make amends to Chulainn, Sétanta promised to take the dog's place as protector of the Kingdom of Ulster. He then became known as the "Cú Chulainn" ("Hound of Chulainn").

Cúchulainn was a truly formidable foe, but his skills as a warrior eventually led to his undoing. Before he married, a Scottish woman, Aife, bore him a son in secret. Years later, a young man appeared and challenged Cúchulainn. Only after defeating the stranger did Cúchulainn realize he had killed his own son. Distraught, he was a broken man when he met his death at the hands of Lugaid, the king of Munster.

HE HAS THE NAME OF BEING THE STRONGEST AND BRAVEST MAN IN IRELAND

FINN MACCOOL AND THE GIANT'S CAUSEWAY

IN BRIEF

THEME
Warring giants

SOURCE
Tales and Sketches, William Carleton, 1845.

SETTING
Ancient Ireland.

KEY FIGURES
Finn MacCool A giant from Ireland.

Oonagh Finn's wife.

Benandonner A giant from Scotland.

In Celtic mythology, the creation of Northern Ireland's natural wonder, known as the Giant's Causeway, was the result of conflict between giants.

The rivalry in question was between the Irish giant Finn MacCool, who lived in Ulster with his wife, Oonagh, and a Scottish giant called Benandonner, who taunted him from across the sea. Finn, who was normally peaceable, grew so angry that he grabbed a huge clod from the ground to fling at Benandonner. He missed; the clump of earth landed in the Irish Sea, forming the Isle of Man, while the hole it left formed Lough Neagh. Finn then constructed a causeway

Just lie there snug, and say nothing, but be guided by me.
Tales and Sketches

of stones so he could cross the sea and fight Benandonner; but as he traversed the bridge, Finn caught sight of his would-be opponent.

The Scottish giant was truly enormous, and far larger than Finn. Fearing that he would be defeated, Finn fled back to Ireland and hid in his home. Such was his haste that he left one of his boots stuck in the ground – a boot-shaped rock can still be seen today. With Benandonner in hot pursuit, Finn's situation appeared dire. Fortunately, his wife devised a plan.

In plain sight

Oonagh baked iron griddles inside loaves of bread and made some cheese curds. She then constructed a giant cradle and told Finn to lie in it. Benandonner found their house, and Oonagh invited him in. When Benandonner demanded to see Finn, Oonagh replied that her husband was out – in fact, he was lying quietly in the cradle, disguised as a baby.

The Scottish giant settled down to wait. Oonagh offered him a loaf of bread. As he bit into it, the iron griddle inside broke two of his teeth. When he complained of its toughness, Oonagh replied that she

See also: A complex god 164 ▪ The voyage of Bran 165 ▪ The cattle raid of Cooley 166–67 ▪ Blodeuwedd 170–71

The Giant's Causeway is located in Antrim, Northern Ireland. Geologists trace its formation back to the rapid cooling of lava displaced by volcanic activity 50–60 milllion years ago.

was only serving him what Finn always ate. His pride insulted, Benandonner tried another loaf and shattered two more of his teeth, roaring with pain. Oonagh chided him for being weak, saying that her baby regularly ate the same loaves. She handed Finn one she had baked without a griddle inside. To Benandonner's surprise, Finn was able to eat it easily.

Running scared
Oonagh then challenged Benandonner to show his strength by squeezing water out of a white stone. Try as he might, it was impossible. The disguised Finn then took the stone, but secretly swapped it for the cheese curds Oonagh had made. When he squeezed them, clear whey ran down his hands. Stunned by this display of strength, Benandonner reached into the baby's mouth to test the sharpness of his teeth, and Finn savagely bit down on his little finger. Benandonner was now alarmed; if the baby was so large and strong, his father would surely be even more fearsome. Terrified, Benandonner fled the house before Finn could return and find him. Such was Benandonner's fear of Finn that he deliberately smashed the crossing between Ireland and Scotland, creating what is now known as the Giant's Causeway. ▪

Young Finn meets his father's old warriors, hiding in a forest, in an illustration from T. W. Rolleston's *The High Deeds of Finn* (1910).

The Fenian Cycle

In Irish and Welsh mythology, Finn MacCool is best known not as a giant, but as a hero who was said to have lived in the 4th century CE. Finn and his band of warriors, the Fianna, formed the subject of a series of stories called the Fenian Cycle, which was first documented in the 12th century CE.

As a boy, Finn's first great exploit was to catch the Salmon of Knowledge, which was full of the world's wisdom after eating hazelnuts from a holy tree by the River Boyne. When Finn then ate the fish, he acquired its powers and knowledge, becoming a great leader. As an adult, Finn won acclaim by killing Aillen, a fire-breathing being from the Underworld. He then assumed leadership of the Fianna, and guided them through many exploits and adventures. Finn's son, the poet Oisín, is the chief narrator of the Fenian Cycle.

In some myths, Finn never died but retreated to a hillside cave to sleep, ready to awaken at the hour of Ireland's greatest need. The Fenian Brotherhood, formed in the mid-19th century with the goal of independence for Ireland, took their name from the Fianna, as did the political party Fianna Fáil in 1926.

SO THEY TOOK THE BLOSSOMS AND PRODUCED FROM THEM A MAIDEN
BLODEUWEDD

IN BRIEF

THEME
Mythical woman

SOURCE
Math fab Mathonwy ("Math, son of Mathonwy"), *The Four Branches of the Mabinogi*, 12th-century Welsh folktales.

SETTING
Gwynedd, northwest Wales, c.1060–1200 CE.

KEY FIGURES
Blodeuwedd A woman made of flowers; wife of Llew Llaw Gyffes.

Llew Llaw Gyffes Son of Gwydion; Blodeuwedd's nearly immortal husband.

Math A magician; son of Mathonwy, Lord of Gwynedd.

Gwydion Nephew of Math; also a magician.

Gronw Pebyr Lord of Penllynn; lover of Blodeuwedd.

In ancient Welsh mythology, Blodeuwedd – meaning "flower-faced" – was the wife of the great hero Lleu Llaw Gyffes. She was not a real woman, but was instead made from the flowers of broom, meadowsweet, and oak by the magicians Math and Gwydion. Blodeuwedd was a key figure in the "Math fab Mathonwy", a book full of magic and invention, which was the last of the mythical *Four Branches of the Mabinogi*.

Llew Llaw Gyffes could only marry with the help of magic or divine intervention, due to a

The tree was a gift from a merciful god, its roots lapping up the blood to hold the spirits for blessed release into another, brighter age.
Math fab Mathonwy

tynged, or curse, applied to him by his own mother, Arianrhod. She was embittered at the loss of her virginity – of which the presence of her son was a constant reminder. Arianrhod was also angered by a series of tricks and humiliations she was subjected to by Math and his nephew Gwydion. As a result, she placed three curses upon Llew, the last of which stated that he would never have a wife from any race on the earth.

However, the cunning Math and Gwydion eventually managed to break this last curse by magic: they created Blodeuwedd and betrothed her to Llew Llaw Gyffes. The couple were married and given a palace to live in together.

Love at first sight
One day, while her husband was away on business, a man pursuing a stag arrived at Blodeuwedd's home. He was Gronw Pebyr, Lord of Penllynn. Being of a charming and hospitable disposition, Blodeuwedd welcomed the visitor. However, as soon as they looked into each other's eyes, the pair fell in love. After this, the couple commenced an affair and, determined to be together, they began to plot the

See also: The founding of Athens 58–59 ▪ Arachne and the spider 115 ▪ The voyage of Bran 165 ▪ Cúchulainn 166–67

> [Llew Llaw Gyffes] flew up in the form of an eagle, and gave a fearful scream.
> **Math fab Mathonwy**

death of Llew Llaw Gyffes. There was one major obstacle for the lovers: Llew's immortality.

Blodeuwedd's betrayal

There seemed to be no way in which Blodeuwedd's husband could be killed. He had previously told her that he could not be killed during the day or night, not indoors nor outdoors, neither riding nor walking, not clothed and not naked, nor by any lawfully made weapon. However, Blodeuwedd soon tricked Llew into giving away the secret,

Blodeuwedd met Gronw Pebyr as he hunted a stag near her home. They are depicted here by British artist Ernest Wallcousins for Charles Squire's 1920 book of *Celtic Myth & Legend.*

and he revealed to her that he could be killed at dusk, wrapped only in a net, with one foot on a trough and one on a goat, beside a river bank, and by a special spear forged for one year during the hours when everyone should be at Mass.

Armed with this information, Blodeuwedd arranged for Llew's demise. She and Gronw prepared an ambush, but things did not go to plan. When Gronw threw the spear, it hit Llew, wounding him but not killing him. In that split second, Llew turned himself into an eagle, and flew away. Gwydion, Llew's father, eventually discovered the severely wounded eagle perched high up on an oak tree. Realizing that the bird was Llew, he transfigured his son back into human form. Gwydion and Math then nursed Llew back to health, before mustering an army to take

back his lands from Gronw and Blodeuwedd. The latter fled, but Gwydion hunted her down and turned her into an owl. He told her that she would never see the light of day again and would be alone for eternity. Her name would forever be Blodeuwedd – which in the modern Welsh language now simply means "owl". ▪

The reverse side of an ancient Greek coin. This owl represented the goddess Athena, whose head was depicted on the other side.

Owls

Regarded as sacred in many cultures, the nocturnal owl is both a symbol of wisdom – because it can see in the dark – as well as of death and spiritual renewal.

In ancient Welsh mythology, these birds had a dark and foreboding significance. Gwydion turned Blodeuwedd into an owl because, due to her plot to kill her husband, he believed she should never see the light of day again. He knew that other birds – fearful of owls – would attack her if she appeared during daylight.

Owls are also found in Irish mythology. The heroine and dark goddess Echtach was a ghostly owl whose screeches were heard in midwinter, after sunset. She was reputed to haunt the region where her cannibal sister Echthge lived.

Athena, the ancient Greek goddess of wisdom and war, was often depicted with a little owl, which was regarded as a good omen. The Roman goddess of wisdom and arts, Minerva – Athena's counterpart – was depicted with an owl perched on her right hand.

WHO SO PULLETH OUT THIS SWORD IS THE RIGHTWISE KING BORN OF ALL ENGLAND

THE LEGEND OF KING ARTHUR

IN BRIEF

THEME
Kingship and heroic quest

SOURCES
Le Morte d'Arthur ("The Death of Arthur"), Sir Thomas Malory, 1485 CE.

SETTING
Southwest Britain, late 5th–early 6th century CE.

KEY FIGURES
Arthur King of Britain, a great warrior with a loyal following of knights. He became king after proving himself by drawing a sword from a stone.

Merlin A sorcerer and later advisor to King Arthur.

Mordred Arthur's illegitimate son by his half-sister; Mordred usurped the throne and later kills his father.

Guinevere Arthur's wife, who committed adultery with the knight Lancelot.

Lancelot du Lac A knight of the round table, who was in love with Guinevere.

Arthur himself was the military commander.
Historia Brittonum
Nennius, Welsh monk (c. 828 CE)

King Arthur has a semi-historical status as the warlord who ruled Britain during a period of chaos created by the departure of Roman forces from Britain. The Welsh Christian monk Nennius, who wrote the *Historia Brittonum* ("History of the Britons") in c.828 CE, was the first to mention Arthur, writing about him as the victorious leader of 12 battles that culminated in one at Mount Badon (c. 490 CE) against the invading Angles, Jutes, and Saxons. The cleric Geoffrey of Monmouth later included a wily warrior King Arthur in his *Historia Regum Britanniae* ("History of the Kings of Britain", 1136 CE), in which the king conquered Denmark, Iceland, Norway, Gaul, and more.

The Arthurian legend enjoyed a surge in popularity in the 12th century thanks to the Queen of England, Eleanor of Aquitaine, who was inspired by the romantic stories of knights and chivalry to bring troubadours into her court to tell Arthurian tales. One of the most famous contributions to the

The ruins of Tintagel Castle remain today. This castle was built in the 13th century CE, but archaeological findings suggest that there was an impressive fortress there in the time of Arthur.

legend came from Thomas Malory, who wrote his version from inside London's Newgate Prison. Malory based his 1485 work *Le Morte d'Arthur* ("The Death of Arthur") on such sources as *The Alliterative Morte Arthure* (a Middle English poem from c.1400 CE), the Vulgate Cycle (a series of 13th-century French romances), and the works of poet Chrétien de Troyes.

Fateful conception

Le Morte d'Arthur was split into 21 books by printer William Caxton in 1485. The first concerns the events that lead to Arthur becoming King of Britain. Fate dictated every aspect of Arthur's life – even his conception, which was aided by the dark arts of the wizard Merlin. Arthur's father, King Uther Pendragon, had been obsessed with Igraine, the wife of a Cornish

See also: The labours of Herakles 72–75 ▪ Aeneas 96–101 ▪ The *Kalevala* 160–63 ▪ The cattle raid of Cooley 166–67

duke named Gorlois. To avoid Uther's advances, Igraine hid in Tintagel Castle, on a precipice on the Cornish coast. Merlin struck a deal with Uther: he would make Uther look like Gorlois and spirit him into Igraine's chamber if Uther agreed to hand over the foretold child of the union to Merlin to raise as he saw fit. The deed was done, and according to Malory, Arthur was conceived three hours after Gorlois' death in battle. As the widowed Igraine then married Uther, this meant that Arthur could later claim legitimacy.

Just as Uther had agreeed, he gave the baby to Merlin, who took Arthur away to be raised by Sir Ector, a "true and faithful" knight with a son, Kay, about Arthur's own age. Arthur was raised ignorant of his parentage – which later proved his undoing. Arthur lusted after and eventually slept with King Lot's wife, Morgause, who was also the daughter of Igraine and Gorlois. With this affair, Arthur committed conscious adultery but also unconscious incest. Their union

led to the conception of a bastard son, Mordred, who Merlin had prophesied would destroy Arthur and all his knights.

The sword in the stone

Despite being Uther's son, Arthur did not become king through a simple process of succession. Instead, Arthur had to prove his worth. According to Malory, one day after the death of Uther, a great

The gallant Galahad, one of the three knights to hold the Holy Grail, pulls Excalibur from a stone to prove his worth – just as Arthur himself once did – as the king and his court look on.

stone of four square feet appeared in a London churchyard, with a steel anvil in the middle of it. A fine sword was stuck in the anvil, and the blade was inscribed with gold letters that read "Whoso pulleth out this sword of this stone and anvil, is rightwise king born of all England". It was destined to be taken from the stone only by the true king.

The Archbishop of Canterbury called for a tournament, hoping that this would shine some light on who the rightful king was. Even the strongest men could not withdraw the sword from the anvil. Many knights, including Ector's son, Sir Kay, went to London hoping to prove their worth. Upon arrival, however, Kay lost his sword, and sent Arthur to fetch another. Noticing the sword in the stone, but unaware of its significance, »

Thomas Malory

The author of *Le Morte d'Arthur* was born in 1416, the son of Sir John Malory of Newbold Revel, Warwickshire. Raised a country gentleman, Thomas Malory inherited the family title and estate in 1434. He was an educated man, yet by 1451 he was serving time in prison for an astonishing array of violent crimes, including robbery, extortion, and rape. It is likely that he used his time in prison – several stretches amounting to 10 years – to

write his work, sometimes described as the first English novel. Malory finished *Le Morte d'Arthur* in 1469, and had it printed by William Caxton in 1485.

The identity of Thomas Malory has long been the subject of debate. While most today believe that the Malory of *Le Morte d'Arthur* was the man from Warwickshire, the lack of information supplied by Malory himself led some 19th-century scholars suggest that he was actually a Welsh poet.

He shall be king and overcome all his enemies; and he shall be long king of all England, and have under his obeisance Wales, Ireland, and Scotland.
Le Morte d'Arthur

Lancelot and Guinevere are depicted by Herbert James Draper (c.1890). After Arthur's death, Guinevere became a nun, believing that their affair caused the destruction of the round table.

Arthur easily pulled the blade from the anvil. After proving several times that he could withdraw the sword, Arthur was hailed as the rightful king of Britain.

The sword in the stone was not the only famous blade in the tale of Arthur. The sword named Excalibur appears in many of the Arthurian legends, with some suggesting this is the very sword he pulled from the anvil. In Malory's tale, Arthur was given the sword by the "Lady of the Lake". After seeing the magical sword and scabbard in the middle of a lake, raised up by an ethereal hand, Arthur promised the Lady a future gift in exchange for them.

Grail quest

Books 13–17 of Malory's account contain the quest of Arthur and his knights for the "Sangreal", the "holy grail". This aspect of the Arthurian legend was a popular subject in medieval French accounts, such as the Vulgate Cycle. Malory based his information on the holy grail on a story from this cycle: *La Queste Del Saint Graal* ("the quest for the holy grail"). According to this account, the Grail appeared on the Round Table during the Christian feast of Pentecost, which celebrates Christ's disciples being endowed with the Holy Spirit. The grail brought forth food and drink

for all those assembled before it disappeared again. Arthur and his knights then dedicated themselves to searching for the Grail.

Tragic romances

The Round Table was a wedding gift from King Leodegrance to Arthur, who married the king's daughter Guinevere. This table is a key element of the legend – during Pentecost, King Arthur gathered his chosen knights in Camelot (his castle and court) and granted them seats at the Round Table in exchange for their fealty. Each knight swore an oath, promising never to take up arms in "wrongful quarrel" for the sake of love or worldly goods.

Despite this, many of the books of *Le Morte d'Arthur* contain tales of quarrels over love, which often ended in tragedy. This was the case for Sir Tristan, who loved the "belle Isolde", and was eventually killed by her husband, a king. The most famed romance in the

> Merlin warned the king covertly that Guinevere was not wholesome for him to take to wife, for he warned him that Lancelot should love her, and she him again.
> *Le Morte d'Arthur*

Excalibur is returned to the Lady of the Lake, by Bedivere. In Malory's tale, there were two women with that title: the maiden who held the sword, and Nimue, ruler of the Isle of Avalon.

legend is that between Guinevere, Arthur's wife, and his best knight, Sir Lancelot du Lac. The pair had an affair, but were so indiscreet that many schemed to expose their adultery to the king, including Arthur's bastard son, Mordred. Once the affair was exposed, the king was forced to declare war on Lancelot, thus dividing the Round Table as he pursued his own knight back to France. However, while Arthur fought in France, Mordred usurped his throne. This treason reunited Arthur and his knights.

The death of Arthur

As its title suggests, *Le Morte d'Arthur* ends with Arthur's death. Arthur and Mordred wounded each other fatally at the Battle of Camlann. As he lay dying, the wounded king ordered Sir Bedivere to throw Excalibur into the lake. When he did so, up rose the arm of the Lady of the Lake, who waved the weapon three times before she disappeared again. Bedivere carried Arthur to the lake, where he was met by women in black hoods, who took Arthur away in a boat. Malory left it open as to whether the "once and future king" might one day return. ∎

Twelve knights of the Round Table are named in all medieval tellings of the legend. Different sources suggest numbers ranging from 12 to 250 knights of the Round Table in total.

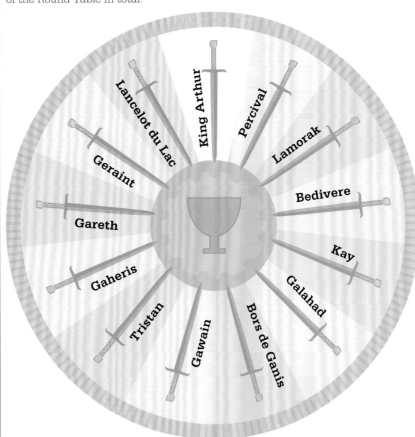

The Holy Grail

The Grail was supposedly the same vessel Jesus drank from at the Last Supper and that had caught blood from his wounds during the crucifixion. According to Malory, it had been taken to Britain by Joseph of Arimathea. The Holy Grail first appeared to Arthur's knights covered by a rich white cloth, accompanied by thunder and lightning.

Malory emphasized that the knights' quest was a journey of the soul as well as the body – spiritual effort was required to overcome sinfulness. Although Lancelot was a knight without peer, the sin he committed with Guinevere made him impure, and therefore unable to achieve true knowledge of the Grail.

In the early tales, the Grail was not explicitly called "holy", but it was associated with Christianity. Chrétien de Troyes described it as an elaborately decorated bowl that contained a single wafer for a Catholic Mass. Some scholars believe that the idea of the Grail can be traced back to the mystical cauldrons of Celtic mythology.

The Holy Grail is depicted in the middle of the Round Table. The Grail was variously imagined as a chalice, bowl, or stone.

ASIA

The earliest tablets containing the *Epic of Gilgamesh* are inscribed in ancient Mesopotamia.

The **fall of Babylon** marks the end of Babylonian and Akkadian rule in Assyria.

Greek writer Herodotus portrays the **ancient traditions of Persia** and other cultures in his *Histories*.

The **written Chinese script** is standardized under the Qin dynasty.

c.2100–1800 BCE   **539 BCE**   **440 BCE**   **221-206 BCE**

c.1595–1157 BCE   **c.450 BCE**   **c.400 BCE**   **c.140 BCE**

The *Enuma Elish*, an ancient Babylonian text, depicts the **creation of the universe** by the primeval gods.

Attributed to the sage Valmiki, the Hindu epic **Ramayana** expounds on the duties of mankind.

The oldest preserved parts of the anicent Hindu epic, the **Mahabharata**, are written down.

Prince Liu An discusses mythology and the ideal **social order** in a series of essays, the *Huainanzi*.

In around 4000 BCE, the first large cities emerged in Sumer, in southern Mesopotamia. Soon after, the peoples of the region developed cuneiform writing. This enabled them to record myths – such as that of the fertility goddess, Inanna – that had previously been passed down orally. This region was home to the *Epic of Gilgamesh*, one of the oldest of all surviving literary works, dating to 2100 BCE. The tale was recorded on clay tablets discovered in the Library of Ashurbanipal – named after the 7th-century BCE king – during an archaeological study of the ancient city of Nineveh. The *Enuma Elish*, a 16th-century Babylonian creation myth, was also recovered there.

Another civilization to emerge in the Middle East was that of the Persians. The first Persian Empire flourished from 550–c.330 BCE. Its myths revolved around the ideas of good and evil – also evident in Zoroastrianism, the imperial state religion from 600 BCE to 650 CE.

Myths from major faiths

The Hindu faith that developed on the Indian subcontinent from around 1900 BCE created much of the framework for Indian myths. Originally, these were passed on orally – including India's two greatest epic poems, the *Ramayana* and *Mahabharata*, which described the lives of the gods. However, Hinduism was not the only faith to influence mythology in India and across Asia. Siddhartha Gautama was born in modern-day Nepal around the sixth century BCE. Becoming the Buddha, he gained many followers and his teachings spread from India across the continent, influencing the myths of nations such as Japan, China, and Korea. From the 1st century BCE onwards, it became increasingly common for tales to be recorded in these parts of Asia. Myths were recorded in Sanskrit, which became the major written language of Hinduism, Buddhism, and other faiths that originated in this region.

Written narratives

The first royal dynasty in China emerged around 2200 BCE. Over the centuries, the political reach of these rulers extended from their power base in central China across Asia. During the second millennium BCE, Chinese script was developed. This allowed Chinese scholars to record myths and legends in works such as *The*

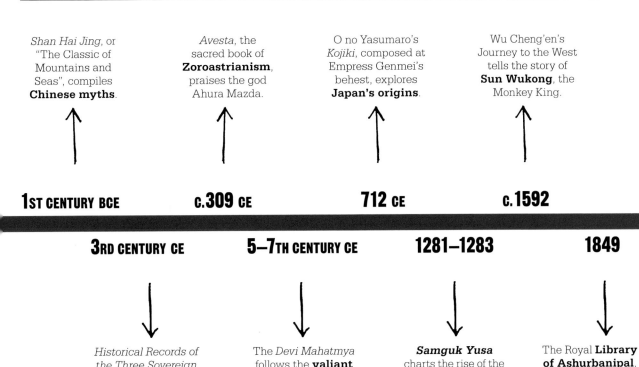

Shan Hai Jing, or "The Classic of Mountains and Seas", compiles **Chinese myths**.

Avesta, the sacred book of **Zoroastrianism**, praises the god Ahura Mazda.

O no Yasumaro's *Kojiki*, composed at Empress Genmei's behest, explores **Japan's origins**.

Wu Cheng'en's Journey to the West tells the story of **Sun Wukong**, the Monkey King.

1ST CENTURY BCE   **c.309 CE**   **712 CE**   **c.1592**

3RD CENTURY CE   **5–7TH CENTURY CE**   **1281–1283**   **1849**

Historical Records of the Three Sovereign Divinities tells the story of **Pangu's creation** of the world.

The *Devi Mahatmya* follows the **valiant goddess Durga** as she wages war on the forces of evil.

Samguk Yusa charts the rise of the Three Kingdoms of Korea through myth and history.

The Royal **Library of Ashurbanipal**, containing the *Epic of Gilgamesh*, is discovered in Nineveh.

Classic of Mountains and Seas and later Xu Zheng's *Historical Records of the Three Sovereign Divinities and the Five Gods*. The Japanese chronicle, *Kojiki*, was written in a form of Chinese, as was the Korean *Samguk Yusa*.

In some parts of Asia, myths were only written down in the 20th century, at the instigation of explorers from the West. The Ifugao of the Philippines, for example, continued to transmit their myths orally for more than 1,000 years, creating many different versions, which only began to be documented by anthropologists in the 1940s.

Order and chaos
A major theme in Asian mythology is the quest for balance, both in heaven and on earth. Marduk, the Babylonian god, helped to establish order by defeating the demonic forces of chaos and naming all things in the universe. This quest for balance appears in stories such as that of Pangu, who emerges from an egg – a theme that re-emerges in the Korean myth of Jumong – to bring order to a formless universe and ensure balance between the forces of Yin and Yang. The concept of *dharma* – living in balance with the cosmos and the world – is a major theme in the story of the Hindu god Rama. The Japanese myth of the rivalry between the gods Amaterasu and Susanoo also displays this clash between disorder and harmony.

Zoroastrian mythology is based on the idea of cosmic dualism. The god Ahura Mazda created a pure world, which the spirit Ahriman attacked with ageing, sickness, and death. Ahriman and Ahura Mazda are twin deities who are exact opposites: creator and destroyer.

Gods and founders
The idea of deities taking multiple identities or forms is common in many strands of mythology across the world, but especially in Asia. Vishnu, a principle Hindu god and the preserver in the Trimurti, has multiple avatars that he embodies to restore order to the world.

Legendary founding figures are another common theme in Asian mythology. Some are gods who created entire countries, such as Izanagi and Izanami in Japan. Others are mythical human figures, such as Dan'gun Wanggeom, who founded the first Korean Kingdom, or Yi, the fabled archer who saved the world from ten blazing suns. ∎

FROM THE GREAT HEAVEN THE GODDESS SET HER MIND ON THE GREAT BELOW

THE DESCENT OF INANNA

IN BRIEF

THEME
Fertility and the seasons

SOURCE
The Descent of Inanna, Anonymous, 3500–1900 BCE; *A Hymn to Inanna*, Enheduanna, 2285 and 2250 BCE; *Ishtar's Descent into the Underworld*, Anonymous, 7th century BCE; *Inanna: Queen of Heaven and Earth: Her Stories and Hymns from Sumer*, Diane Wolkstein and Samuel Noah Kramer, 1983.

SETTING
The Underworld.

KEY FIGURES
Inanna Goddess of fertility and war; Queen of Heaven.

Ereshkigal Queen of the Underworld; Inanna's sister.

Gilgamesh A demigod.

Anu The sky god; father of Inanna.

Gugalanna The Bull of Heaven; first husband of Ereshkigal.

Ninshubur Inanna's attendant.

Enlil Lord of the gods.

Nanna God of the moon.

Enki God of water.

Dumuzid Inanna's husband; a shepherd-god and god of fertility; later became the Babylonian god Tammuz.

Geshtinanna Dumuzid's sister, who takes his place.

Mesopotamian civilization was essentially urban, with people living in walled cities, yet it had an agrarian focus, too. Citizens had plots of land either within a city or outside its walls. If they had livestock, people would take the animals out to graze, but return them to the city at night, often keeping them in their own houses. In such a society, the fertility of humans, animals, and the land had great cultural significance. The people had shrines to fertility gods in their homes, sometimes decorated with figurines. Many myths, including *The Descent of Inanna*, featured the cycles of the seasons and fertility.

Revenge and death

Inanna was a great Mesopotamian deity, representing the realities around which life then revolved – fertility, procreation, sensuality, love, but also war. The goddess is mentioned in the earliest texts from the 4th millennium BCE, when she was the patroness of the important city of Uruk in Sumer (southern Iraq). Inanna was the subject of several ancient myths and a poem called *The Descent of Inanna*, which relates how she, the Queen of Heaven, determined to visit her widowed sister Ereshkigal, Queen of the Underworld.

Inanna hoped to attend the funeral rites of her sister's husband, knowing that her actions had led to his death. For Inanna had offered her hand in marriage to the heroic demigod Gilgamesh, only to be met with rejection and mockery. She had asked her father Anu, the sky god, to send the Bull of Heaven – the deity Gugalanna, Ereshkigal's husband – to seek revenge on Gilgamesh. Visible in the night sky as the constellation the Romans called Taurus, the bull had the power to consume crops, dry up rivers, and cause the earth to shake.

Anu agreed and sent the bull, but Gilgamesh, who possessed superhuman strength, killed and dismembered it. Because she felt responsible for his death, Inanna

The slaying of the Bull of Heaven is also recounted in *The Epic of Gilgamesh*. This illustration of it comes from *Myths of Babylonia and Assyria* by Donald A Mackenzie (1915).

See also: The abduction of Persephone 50–51 ▪ Orpheus and Eurydice 53 ▪ Osiris and the Underworld 276–83

Hymn to Inanna

The *Hymn to Inanna* was written in the 3rd millennium BCE by Enheduanna, high priestess of the city of Ur in Mesopotamia (now southern Iraq). She was the daughter of Sargon, the first king of the Akkadian Empire, and she was the first author in the world that we know by name. In her hymn to Inanna, the priestess described the Queen of Heaven as having powers greater than the highest of the gods – a powerful goddess of destruction who had the strength of a bull and soaked the weapons of her enemies in blood and gore. In the hymn, Inanna's battle cry shook the earth and the gods prostrated themselves at her feet. "Her wrath is a devastating flood which no one can withstand … she abases those whom she despises."

Edheduanna was a prolific writer, composing a set of temple hymns and dozens of poems on many themes. She was influential in politics, too, and at least once fled a rebellion but was restored to power.

Inanna is often depicted with wings and standing on two animals, as in this terracotta relief from the 2nd millennium BCE. She is also wearing her cone-shaped crown.

---

wanted to mourn with her sister in the Underworld. However, in some interpretations of the story, Inanna intended to conquer her sister's realm, so that she could extend her power into the Underworld.

An unwelcome guest

For the Mesopotamians, the Underworld was not unlike the real world, except that it was always dark, people were naked, and the bread and beer were stale. Named Kur, this realm was neither good nor bad but existed between heaven and earth, where the dead remained trapped between the two planes of existence.

Inanna knew that her descent into the Underworld could also lead to her death. As protection, she equipped herself with seven divine powers – symbolized in items that she wore and held. Inanna put on a turban, described as "headgear for the open country" and hung lapis lazuli beads around her neck. She wore twin egg-shaped beads on her breast, donned a fine *pala* dress, placed a pectoral over her chest named "Come, man, come", and adorned her hand with a golden ring. As Queen of Heaven, she also clasped the lapis lazuli rod and tape used for measuring the boundaries of her realm. Inanna's fine robes, attractive ornaments, and the mascara – called "Let a man come, let him come" – that she wore to make her irresistible, represented sexuality, beauty, and fertility. The rod and tape were instruments of her authority – acquired from Enlil, the

When she entered the seventh gate, the *pala* dress, the garment of ladyship, was removed from her body.
The Descent of Inanna

chief Mesopotamian deity, who had set down the decrees that established the foundations of civilized society. Before leaving heaven, Inanna told her attendant Ninshubur to seek the gods' help if she did not return.

When Inanna reached the entrance to the Underworld, the gatekeeper ran to tell Ereshkigal and was told to immediately lock the seven gates against the new arrival. To gain entry through each gate, Inanna had to relinquish her divine powers. Item by item, she was compelled to remove her turban and ornaments, and to give up the rod and measuring tape. Finally, at the last gate, she also had to take off her clothes, so that she was naked like everybody else.

In the Akkadian version of the story, something else happened when Inanna descended into »

The Mother Goddess Ishtar by Evelyn Paul (1916) portrays Inanna in all her finery before her descent into the Underworld. Ishtar is the Babylonian name for the same goddess.

c.5300–2335 BCE: The first records of **Inanna** are depictions of the goddess on vases from the **city of Uruk**.

c.3500–1900 BCE: A 415-line poem called **"The Descent of Inanna"** is written in **Sumeria**.

c.2285–2250 BCE: The priestess **Enheduanna** writes about Inanna after Sumeria became part of the **Akkadian Empire**.

c.2334–2218 BCE: The popularity of Inanna influences the cult of the Akkadian goddess **Ishtar**. The two are merged.

c.1300–1000 BCE: Inanna features in **"Gilgamesh, Enkidu, and the Netherworld"**, an episode in ***The Epic of Gilgamesh***.

c.700 BCE: A 145-line poem, **"Ishtar's Descent into the Underworld"**, is written in **Akkadian**.

the Underworld: the world above lost its ability to be fertile. Animals and humans would not reproduce and the land became barren. If the world descended into chaos, so too would the heavens. Mesopotamian religions created a hierarchy and structure of the heavens and earth in which the two must coexist.

Inanna's fate

When Inanna reached Ereshkigal's throne, she sat on it in her sister's place. The *Anuna*, the seven judges of the Underworld appeared and gave the goddess a "look of death", shouted at her, and proclaimed her guilty of arrogance. Inanna was transformed into a rotting corpse and hung on a hook.

The repeated use of the number seven is intentional as the number represented completion. The seven divine powers, the seven gates of the Underworld, and the seven

Underworld judges are thought to symbolize fundamental aspects of Nature as ordained by the gods and possibly relate to life, death, and the rule of divine law.

A soul for a soul

In the Sumerian version of the narrative, Inanna's loyal attendant, Ninshubur, went to the gods to ask for help freeing Inanna. Enlil, lord of the gods, and Nanna, the moon god, did not want to help her; only Enki, the wisest of the gods and god of water, agreed to help. He created two figures called the *gala-tura* and the *kur-jara* who could slip like phantoms into the

Underworld. There they recited the ritual words that Enki taught them, refusing the gifts of rivers of water and fields of grain in exchange for finding Inanna. They asked: "Give us the corpse hanging on the hook." *Gala-tura* scattered a life-giving plant over her body, and *kur-jara* sprinkled it with life-giving water, restoring Inanna to good health.

Just as Inanna was leaving the Underworld, the Anuna appeared again and declared, "If Inanna is to ascend from the Underworld, let her provide a substitute for herself." The goddess would not be allowed to escape scot-free. The Underworld demanded a soul for a soul.

> She does not return. She who goes to the Dark City stays there.
> **Inanna: Queen of Heaven and Earth**

Returning to earth, Inanna was accompanied by a band of demons anxious to seize someone to take her place. Inanna met members of her family and faithful servants, including Ninshubur, and did not want to let any of them go. Instead, she told the demons to follow her to a great apple tree on a plain.

Dumuzid's punishment

Under the apple tree sat Inanna's husband Dumuzid – a mortal king who had been deified and had become the god of fertility and shepherding. Dumuzid was "clothed in a magnificent garment and seated magnificently on a throne". Furious that her husband had not mourned her, Inanna handed him over to the demons. Dumuzid prayed to the sun god, his brother-in-law Utu, to turn him into a snake, but in spite of this transformation he was captured and taken to the Underworld.

Inanna, however, missed her husband and wept for him. His sister Geshtinanna agreed to take his place for half the year, so that Dumuzid could return to Inanna in spring and the land became fertile. When the crops had been gathered, Dumuzid returned to spend the barren winter in the Underworld, thus giving the world its seasons.

Humanity and mortality

The story of Inanna not only explained the seasonal cycle, but also gave an insight into what it meant to be human and how life was ordered. On earth, humans were the children of the gods; when they died, they became the children of Ereshkigal. This determined how they lived their lives. They believed it was good to be clothed, to have good food, and to be surrounded by loved ones. ∎

Cylinder seals provide important pictorial evidence of life and lore in Mesopotamia. This example from c.2250 BCE depicts the god Enki with life-giving water flowing from his body.

Priests of Inanna

Often identified as being neither male nor female, the role of the priests and priestesses of Inanna was to promote the fertility of the land. If they did not have sexual intercourse, it was thought that the land would no longer produce. They served at her temple in Uruk, the principal centre of worship, and at numerous other shrines and temples to the goddess throughout Mesopotamia.

As the goddess of fertility, Inanna was sometimes depicted as both male and female, and was said to have the ability to transform men into women and women into men. People who did not conform to Mesopotamian gender norms were often made into priests of Inanna. Such gender ambiguity also made Inanna an accessible deity as both men and women could identify with her.

In one ritual known as "sacred marriage", to ensure prosperity, a king would take the role of Dumuzid in an elaborate ceremony. This would include having intercourse with the high priestess of Inanna, herself impersonating the goddess.

COMMAND AND BRING ABOUT ANNIHILATION AND RE-CREATION

MARDUK AND TIAMAT

IN BRIEF

THEME
Order over chaos

SOURCES
Enuma Elish ("When on High"), Anonymous, 17th–11th century BCE; *Before the Muses: An Anthology of Akkadian Literature*, Ben Foster, 1993.

SETTING
The heavens and Babylon.

KEY FIGURES
Apsu Father of the gods.

Tiamat Mother of the gods; goddess of the sea.

Qingu Tiamat's warrior husband.

Ea Husband of Damkina and father of Marduk.

Marduk King of the gods in Babylonian religion; son of Ea and Damkina.

The *Enuma Elish* ("When on High") is a collection of seven tablets recovered in 1849 from King Ashurbanipal II's library in Nineveh, Iraq. The tablets shed light on Babylonian beliefs about creation. Their purpose, however, in charting the rise of Marduk as the chief god of Babylon was also to reinforce the power of the city's king as the god's representative on earth. The title

Enuma Elish comes from the opening line, which acted as a declaration of spatial location, expressing the belief that the gods were above everything that would exist. There are also frequent reminders that of all the things in heaven and on earth, "none bore a name". To the Babylonians, nothing in the world could exist unless the gods had named it.

Family of gods
According to the *Enuma Elish*, in the beginning there was nothing except sweet water and salt water. The sweet water was the god Apsu, and the salt water was the goddess Tiamat. When the two waters mixed together, they gave birth to the first generation of gods. Disturbed by the noisy chatter of the new gods, Apsu decided to kill what he and Tiamat had created.

When the most intelligent god, Ea, discovered his father's plot, he preempted it by killing Apsu and built a water temple out of his body.

Marduk kills Tiamat, the sea goddess in dragon form, in this illustration by Evelyn Paul from Lewis Spence's *Myths and Legends of Babylonia and Assyria* (1916).

See also: The war of gods and Titans 32–33 ▪ The epic of Gilgamesh 190–97 ▪ Ahura Mazda and Ahriman 198–99

If indeed I am to champion you, subdue Tiamat, and save your lives, convene the assembly, nominate me for supreme destiny!
Before the Muses

When Tiamat discovered that Apsu had been killed, she made terrible monsters and demons rise up and vowed to destroy every one of the gods. She created a warrior named Qingu, made him her husband, and gave him the Tablet of Destinies that held the fate of all living things. Fearing their mother's power, the gods needed someone to defeat Tiamat. Ea and his wife Damkina had a son, Marduk, who was filled with greater strength and wisdom than either of his parents. He was also said to have a divine radiance – called *melammu* in Akkadian, the language of Babylon.

A new leader

Marduk convinced the other gods that he could defeat Tiamat if they gave him their power and made him their king. After much debate, they agreed. Marduk attacked Tiamat, capturing her in his net and killing her. Marduk then ripped her body in two, and made the heavens from one half, and the earth from the other. Marduk used her eyes to form the Tigris and Euphrates rivers – hence the Greek name, "Mesopotamia", which means "between the rivers". After defeating Tiamat, Marduk attacked and destroyed her husband Qingu and made humankind from his blood. The gods were puzzled by this, but Marduk explained that humans would be useful servants. He then created Babylon to be the earthly home of the gods and their entrance to earth from the heavens; Babylon (or *Babilim* in Akkadian), means "gateway of the gods".

In contrast with its initial emphasis on the namelessness of everything, the myth ended by declaring Marduk king of all the gods and proclaiming all of his 50 names, many of which were related to gods whose power he had taken. Its dominant theme of Marduk's supremacy may mean that the work dates from the 17th century BCE when Babylon was the great capital of Mesopotamia or later, when the city was being rebuilt and seeking to re-establish its status. As a text, the *Enuma Elish* illustrates how the Babylonians viewed creation as a triumph of the gods over chaos. ▪

Akitu festival

The city of Babylon celebrated the Akitu festival at their New Year in the month of March or April. The word *Akitu* means "barley", which was harvested in spring. During this festival, which occurred over 12 days, an elaborate enactment of the *Enuma Elish* was performed. The statue of Marduk, the city's main deity, was paraded around the streets and taken to a "house" outside the city to the north. This was to signify the time in which chaos ruled. To re-establish order, Marduk was marched back into the city from the house to his throne in the *Esagila*, his temple in the centre of Babylon. The king would go to the temple to greet Marduk and kneel before his statue. The high priest would then strike the king on the cheek, hard enough to bring tears to his eyes – a sign of the king's humility and a reminder that the king ruled by Marduk's authority and was subject to the god.

Everyone in Babylon took part in the festival, regardless of their class. In doing so, people came together to reaffirm their beliefs. The Akitu rituals date back to the 2nd millennium CE or even earlier, and continued into the Common Era. The Roman emperor Elagabalus, a Syrian (r.218–222 BCE), is said to have introduced the festival into Italy.

Marduk-balatsu-ikbi, one of several Babylonian kings who bore the god's name, and his dagger bearer Adad-etir feature on a 9th-century BCE stone stela dedicated to the king by his eldest son.

WHO CAN RIVAL HIS KINGLY STANDING?

THE EPIC OF GILGAMESH

IN BRIEF

THEME
Mortality

SOURCES
Tablets found in the Library of Ashurbanipal, king of Assyria (c.668–627 BCE), at Nineveh; *The Epic of Gilgamesh*, Benjamin Foster, 2001.

SETTING
Uruk, a city in Sumer, southern Mesopotamia, after the Great Flood.

KEY FIGURES
Gilgamesh King of Mesopotamia.

Enkidu Close friend of Gilgamesh.

Shamash God of the sun and of justice.

Ishtar Goddess of fertility and war.

Utnapishtim An immensely wise, immortal man.

The goddess Aruru,
she washed her hands,
took a pinch of clay,
and threw it down …
in the wild, she
created Enkidu.
The Epic of Gilgamesh

Gilgamesh and Enkidu wrestle with lions to show their strength in an impression made by a third millenium BCE Sumerian cylinder seal.

The story of Gilgamesh follows the eponymous hero as he wrestles with the inevitability of death, discovers true friendship, and comes to understand the responsibilities of kingship. The long poem known as *The Epic of Gilgamesh* is among the world's earliest known works of great literature, and weaves together a series of tales thought to have been inspired by a king who ruled the Sumerian city of Uruk between 2800 and 2500 BCE.

Taming the tyrant

King Gilgamesh loved to walk the walls of Uruk, measuring the size of his kingdom. It was said that a king who knew the extent of his walls was noble and good. In reality, however, Gilgamesh was abusive towards his subjects and was a sexual predator who knew no bounds. When the people appealed to their gods for help in restraining their king, Anu, the sky god and supreme ruler of heaven, decided Gilgamesh needed a companion who could tame his wild nature.

Anu handed the task to Arura, the goddess of creation, who made Enkidu. At first, Enkidu was a savage man who ran with the animals, ate grass, and lived apart. In ancient Mesopotamia, if you lived outside the city walls or as a nomad, you were considered not only uncouth but dangerous. Until Enkidu was inducted into civilized society, he could not fulfil his role of taming and aiding Gilgamesh.

When Enkidu upset the traps of a local hunter, the man went to the king and urged him to provide Enkidu with a prostitute who would be able to subdue his wild temperament. Gilgamesh sent a temple prostitute called Samhat to have sex with Enkidu for seven days. After this, when Enkidu tried to run with the animals, they ignored him. Enkidu realized that something had changed – through his sexual awakening, he had started to become civilized. Samhat then took Enkidu to the city of Uruk, where she clothed him, fed him bread, and gave him beer to drink. Treated like a man for the very first time, Enkidu's transformation from animal to human was complete.

See also: The quest of Odysseus 66–71 ▪ The descent of Inanna 182–87 ▪ Marduk and Tiamat 188–89

Meanwhile, Gilgamesh had dreamed of a being whom he would love more than a woman – someone as strong as himself. Gilgamesh's mother, Ninsun, a minor goddess and a priestess in the temple, interpreted the dream and told him he would meet a man who would be an equal to him and a companion in his adventures.

Gilgamesh and Enkidu eventually met when Enkidu blocked Gilgamesh from entering the quarters of a new bride. The two men wrestled, and although Gilgamesh beat Enkidu, the king acknowledged Enkidu as an equal and as a brother.

Hunting Humbaba

Gilgamesh had long wanted to go on a quest to prove his strength. He set his sights on vanquishing Humbaba, the divinely appointed demon-protector of the cedar

Humbaba's mouth is fire; his roar is the floodwater; he breathes and there is death.
The Epic of Gilgamesh

forests, and stealing the tallest trees to take back as valuable timber for Uruk. Both man and beast, Humbaba was a formidable opponent: his strength was immense and he could breathe fire. Gilgamesh armed himself to the teeth and sought blessings from the temple priests. Alarmed, the city elders warned Gilgamesh that he »

Written in clay

The clay tablets from which the fullest version of the Gilgamesh epic have been pieced together were found in 1853 during excavations of the Library of Ashurbanipal II, in the ancient Assyrian city of Nineveh. Building on an oral tradition, and earlier written versions of the myth, the 12 tablets combine many different stories about Gilgamesh into a single epic poem. While some verses from the epic date to c.2100 BCE, the most recent version of the text, composed in Akkadian cuneiform, an ancient Semitic language of Mesopotamia, dates to the Neo-Assyrian period (9th–6th century BCE).

Gaps in the Ninevite version of the poem have been filled by text from the Middle Babylonian period (15th–11th century BCE) found in other locations. The discovery of the tablets changed the way scholars understood daily life in ancient Mesopotamia.

Part of *The Epic of Gilgamesh* is reproduced in this plaster cast dating from the 9th–7th century BCE. This tablet, the 11th of the famous 12, recounts the story of Utnapishtim and the Great Flood.

In myth	In history
Worshipped as a judge in the Underworld	Traditionally regarded as the fifth King of Uruk
Sometimes linked to Dumuzid the shepherd	Named in the Sumerian King List
In Sumerian sources, the brother of Ishtar (Inanna)	Supposed tomb discovered by archaeologists in 2003

King Gilgamesh

Clay masks of Humbaba, the demon giant slain by Gilgamesh, have been discovered in the ancient city of Sippur, on the river Euphrates in modern-day Iraq.

The dream has shown that misery at last comes to the healthy man, the end of his life is sorrow.
The Epic of Gilgamesh

was overestimating his abilities – for the king even to reach the forest, let alone fight Humbaba, he had to take Enkidu with him. Heeding the advice, Gilgamesh enlisted Enkidu's help, and the pair left for the forest. They were protected by Shamash, the god of the sun and of justice, invoked by Gilgamesh's mother.

Enkidu, whom I so loved, who went with me through every hardship, the fate of mankind has overtaken him.
The Epic of Gilgamesh

On reaching the forest, Gilgamesh and Enkidu were taunted by Humbaba, but before the demon could harm the pair, Shamash blew winds to trap Humbaba, and Gilgamesh and Enkidu gained the upper hand. Although Humbaba begged for his life, Gilgamesh killed him, cut down the cedars, made a raft, and sailed home to Uruk.

Ishtar's fury

Back in Uruk, Gilgamesh washed off the filth of battle and put on fresh robes. The Akkadian goddess Ishtar was watching and asked Gilgamesh to be her new husband. If he agreed, she said, he would gain riches beyond his dreams. Gilgamesh refused, referencing the fate of her previous husband, Dumuzid, whom she had sent to hell.

Angered by this insult, Ishtar went to her father, Anu, the god of the sky. She pleaded with him to give her the Bull of Heaven, so that she could send it to punish the people of Uruk for Gilgamesh's decision. Anu eventually relented, but warned his daughter that the beast would bring seven years of famine to Uruk. When the Bull of Heaven reached the city, the earth was torn open, and hundreds of people fell to their deaths through the cracks. The third time that the Bull attacked the city, Gilgamesh and Enkidu butchered the animal. After sacrificing its heart to Shamash, the two of them contemptuously threw a piece of the animal's hind leg at Ishtar, heedless of the disrespect this showed to the gods.

That night Enkidu had a dream in which Anu, Shamash, and Enlil (the god who granted kingship and had been Humbaba's master) discussed the deaths of Humbaba and the Bull of Heaven. In the dream, Anu and Enlil decided that either Enkidu or Gilgamesh should be killed. Shamash protested, saying that the pair had only gone to the cedar forest under his protection. Despite Shamash's best efforts, the gods decided that Enkidu must die.

Death and the quest

Coming to grips with his own mortality, as foretold in the dream, Enkidu desperately prayed to Shamash and cursed Samhat, the temple prostitute, for showing him the way to Uruk. Shamash rebuked him and told him to be glad of the adventures he had experienced. He assured Enkidu that Gilgamesh would give his body the finest resting place. Soon after, Enkidu fell ill and died 12 days later.

Lamenting his friend's death, Gilgamesh enlisted all of the people and animals to mourn with him. Calling together the finest

craftsmen in the land, Gilgamesh built a golden statue of Enkidu in his honour. He then abandoned civilization, put on animal skins, and wandered the wilderness in mourning. In doing so, Gilgamesh mirrored the early life of Enkidu. Enkidu had been a wild man who learned to become civilized; upon Enkidu's death, Gilgamesh, once civilized, became wild.

Gilgamesh then left Uruk on a quest for immortality, anxious not to die like his soulmate. When he followed the path that Shamash took through the sky at night, he found the tunnel to the heavens. By speaking to the guardians of the tunnels, he learned the story of Utnapishtim, a survivor of the Great Flood who, together with his wife, had achieved immortality and sat

What can I do, Utnapishtim? Where can I go? Death lives in the house where my bed is.
The Epic of Gilgamesh

at the assembly of the gods. Determined to discover the secret to eternal life, Gilgamesh set out to find Utnapishtim.

On his way to the Underworld, Gilgamesh met an innkeeper called Siduri, who tried to convince him to turn back. She told the king that the journey was not safe for mere mortals. When he insisted on continuing, she reluctantly gave him directions to Urshanabi, who ferried people across the River of the Dead. Gilgamesh found Urshanabi, who agreed to help him on his mission.

As they crossed the river, Urshanabi asked Gilgamesh why he had made the journey to the Underworld. Gilgamesh told him how his grief at the death of Enkidu had driven him to find immortality. His words convinced Urshanabi to take him to Utnapishtim.

When Gilgamesh eventually reached Utnapishtim, the man who had achieved immortality remarked on how worn out the king looked. Gilgamesh explained his pain at watching his friend die and said he was afraid of his own mortality. In response, Utnapishtim asked why Gilgamesh would go on a futile quest instead of enjoying what he had been given in life: "Why, O Gilgamesh, did you prolong woe?" »

Enkidu is created by the gods to subdue the oppressive ruler Gilgamesh.

Evenly matched in battle, the two develop a passionate bond.

Enkidu's love for Gilgamesh inspires him to empathize with his own people.

Enkidu's death sends the grieving Gilgamesh on a quest for immortality.

His mission a failure, Gilgamesh comes to terms with the inevitability of death.

Utnapishtim told Gilgamesh that humans could not be immortal. The gods, he said, decided the length of each human life, and did not reveal the time of death, so there was no point in searching for a way to avoid it.

The immortal man

Utnapishtim told Gilgamesh that he had earned immortality by saving humanity during the Great Flood. Such a thing could happen

Utnapishtim and his wife are believed to be the subjects of this devotional gypsum sculpture from 2600 BCE, excavated from beneath a shrine at Nippur, Iraq.

only once; Gilgamesh would never gain immortality that way. Seeking to prove this point to Gilgamesh, who still believed himself worthy of immortality, Utnapishtim challenged the king to stay awake for a total of six days and seven nights, instructing his wife to bake a loaf of bread for every night that Gilgamesh slept, so that he could not deny his failure.

Gilgamesh accepted the challenge, but immediately fell asleep. When he finally woke up, Utnapishtim rebuked the king for his arrogance, noting that while he wanted to overcome death, he was not even able to overcome his desire for sleep. So that no one

could find him again, Utnapishtim banished the ferryman Urshanabi, and sent Gilgamesh away.

A parting gift

Before Gilgamesh and Urshanabi left, Utnapishtim's wife, who was also immortal, convinced her husband to give Gilgamesh a present. He told the king that if he wanted youth, a flower at the bottom of the lake could provide it.

Hungry for this gift, Gilgamesh tied stone weights to his feet, dived into the lake, and retrieved the plant. Cutting the weights free, he resurfaced, found Urshanabi, and told him that he would test the plant on the oldest person in Uruk before using it on himself. On his way home, however, Gilgamesh stopped to bathe in a spring. Just at that moment, a snake stole the flower from his grasp, shed its skin, and was young again. Heartbroken, Gilgamesh realized that youth, like immortality, had escaped him. Now, he was fated to age and die. The king's story ended as it had begun, with Gilgamesh walking the walls of his city, surveying his domain. Although

The eternal life you are seeking you shall not find. When the gods created mankind, they established death for mankind, and withheld eternal life for themselves.
The Epic of Gilgamesh

> So someday you will depart, but till that day, sing and dance. Eat your fill of warm cooked food and cool jugs of beer. Cherish the children your love gave life. Bathe away life's dirt in warm drawn waters.
> **The Epic of Gilgamesh**

The boat built by Utnapishtim to survive the Great Flood is described as having six decks, equivalent to 55m (180ft) high, and being in the shape of a giant cube.

Gilgamesh could not become immortal, he had become a good king, who could describe not just the limits of his city, but the limits of human endeavour. His acceptance of mortality and of his own humanity left a lasting impression on the people of Uruk, who passed his story down through the generations.

Great Flood myths

The tale of how Utnapishtim and his wife survived the Great Flood is similar to other flood myths of the ancient Near East, such as the Sumerian flood myth of Ziusudra, the biblical tale of Noah, and the myth of Deucalion and Pyrrha in Greek mythology. Each of these revolves around a figure who rides out the flood in a large boat.

The story told in the *Epic of Gilgamesh* is remarkably similar to the biblical story of Noah and the ark. Utnapishtim tells how he had once been the king of a beautiful city called Shuruppak. Enlil argued for the destruction of humankind and, while his motives are unclear,

the gods consented to his plan – but Ea, the god of wisdom and water, enabled Utnapishtim and his wife to survive. Ea told Utnapishtim to fashion a boat, take aboard the seeds of all living things, and eventually repopulate the earth. When the boat was finished, Utnapishtim took animals, food, and beer onboard.

The flood raged for seven days and seven nights, and when the rains stopped, the boat drifted to a halt atop Mount Nimush, known today as Pir Omar Gudrun in Iraqi Kurdistan. There, Utnapishtim released a swallow, then a dove, and finally a raven to find dry ground. When none of the birds returned, Unapishtim knew it was safe to leave the boat. He made a sacrifice to the gods and to thank him for his deed, just like the story of Noah, they created a rainbow. ∎

The innkeeper's wisdom

Some scholars argue that the redemption of Gilgamesh was due to his encounter with the immortal Utnapishtim. Others cite Siduri, the innkeeper who lived on the edge of the sea. From her remote tavern, Siduri saw a man, Gilgamesh, dressed in animal skins approaching from the horizon. At first, she locked the door in fear, but then took pity on him. She offered him food, but he refused, saying he no longer had such needs, because he was in search of immortality.

Siduri told the king that death was part of being human. Instead of seeking immortality, he should take delight wherever he could. She said he should be proud of his children, delight in them holding his hand, and share his happiness with friends. These things, she said, were what it meant to be human.

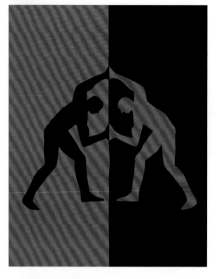

TWO SPIRITS, ONE GOOD, THE OTHER EVIL, IN THOUGHT, WORD, AND DEED
AHURA MAZDA AND AHRIMAN

IN BRIEF

THEME
Good versus evil

SOURCES
Avesta, Anonymous, collected c.3rd century CE; *Bundahishn* ("Primal Creation"), Anonymous, c.8th–9th centuries CE.

SETTING
The beginning and end of time.

KEY FIGURES
Zurvan The first being.

Ahura Mazda A god who lived in the light; creator of everything good.

Ahriman A dark god and Ahura Mazda's twin brother; the creator of everything bad.

Saoshyant The saviour of the world.

Zoroaster/Zarathustra Prophet of Ahura Mazda; author of Zoroastrian texts.

According to a particular branch of ancient Zoroastrianism, known as Zurvanism, Zurvan, the god of time, existed before anything else in the universe, and had the ability to create beings out of nothingness.

Zurvan longed to have children, so he created twin sons, Ahura Mazda and Ahriman. They were the fundamental and opposite aspects of nature – the light and the dark, the good and the evil – that were essential to the balance of the universe. Ahura Mazda was infinitely good and created light, the world, the moon, and stars, and finally, the "good mind" – the essential goodness of every being and thing in the world.

In reply, evil Ahriman resolved to make a world of his own. Hating all things good, he created the very opposite to the works of his brother, producing demons and dangerous creatures. Through his malicious work, disease, suffering, and death entered the world. Ahura Mazda was determined to thwart the works of his evil brother.

The first humans
Ahura Mazda fashioned humankind, designing them to be fundamentally good creatures. He first created Keyumars, or Gayomard, a human who some Zoroastrian sources call the first king to rule the earth. Ahriman tried his best to destroy his brother's creation, finally succeeding when he poisoned and killed him. Gayomard's death meant that humankind would always be mortal – yet his remains fertilized the ground, producing two rhubarb plants. Ahura Mazda took a soul and breathed it into the plants. They became Mashya and Mashyoi, a man and a woman considered the ancestors of all humanity. Ahura

This snarling beast may be a lion-gryphon symbolizing evil Ahriman. Made by metalworkers around the 2nd century CE, it was found near River Helmand in Afghanistan.

See also: The war of the gods 140–141 ▪ The twilight of the gods 150–157 ▪ Pangu and the creation of the world 214–215

[Ahura Mazda] is the most firm, the wisest, and the one … whose body is the most perfect, who attains his ends the most infallibly.
Avesta

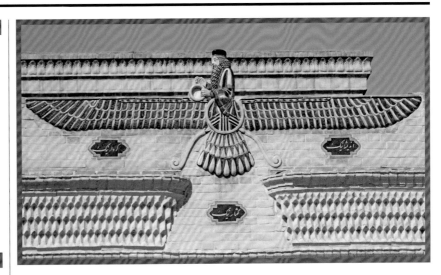

Ahura Mazda is depicted on a fire temple in Yazd, Iran. This c.6th-century BCE emblem incorporates and adapts the winged solar disc of Ashur, an ancient Assyrian deity.

Mazda told them that they were perfect, should obey the law, and must not worship demons – but they were given free will to choose between good and evil.

Before long, Mashya and Mashyoi began to question their obedience to Ahura Mazda's instructions and their reliance on his creation. Instead, they came up with their own innovations, such as fire, clothes, building, and war. They had originally lived off only plants, but now they began to hunt and eat meat. The demons' power over humanity was growing stronger. Eventually, Ahura Mazda gave Mashya and Mashyoi the ability to have children, and they in turn began to populate the earth.

End times

Neither Ahura Mazda nor Ahriman could totally defeat the other, so the brothers remained locked in an eternal struggle between good and evil. The war between Ahura Mazda and Ahriman will finally culminate at the end of time, with an apocalyptic battle in which the world will come to an end and the dead will be resurrected and judged. A saviour called Saoshyant ("one who brings benefit") will rise up and help Ahura Mazda in the fight for light against the many evil creations of Ahriman.

When Ahriman is finally defeated, Saoshyant will resurrect the dead, and humanity will begin again. The children of Ahura Mazda will be some of the first dead to be resurrected. This time, Ahriman will have no influence of any kind, and will have created nothing evil, not even death. Humanity will have the ability to live to its full potential – without any demons, disease, or destruction – and good will triumph over evil once and for all. ∎

Zoroastrian texts

The teachings of Zoroastrianism are based on ancient Persian literature, most specifically the *Avesta*, which was transmitted orally for centuries before being collected and written down during Persia's Achaemenid empire of 550–330 BCE.

Within the Avesta, the most critical section is the "Gathas", a collection of hymns attributed to the prophet Zarathustra (or Zoroaster in Greek). Said to have been given to the prophet by Ahura Mazda himself, the "Gathas" contains much of the mythology and cosmology of Zoroastrianism. Zarathustra was likely revising an existing polytheistic religion into what would become a dualist one.

Mostly compiled in the 8th and 9th centuries CE in Persia and India, the *Bundahishn* further developed the Avesta's stories on the origins and fate of the universe. While not considered scripture, the *Bundahishn* helped codify the Zoroastrian belief system.

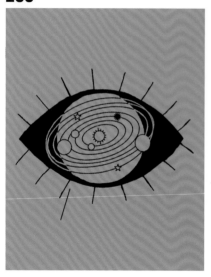

BRAHMA OPENED HIS EYES AND REALISED HE WAS ALONE

BRAHMA CREATES THE COSMOS

IN BRIEF

THEME
Creation

SOURCE
Brahmanda Purana,
Anonymous, 450–950 CE.

SETTING
The beginning of cosmic time.

KEY FIGURES
Narayana The supreme being.

Brahma The creator in the Hindu Trinity (Trimurti): Brahma (the creator), Vishnu (the preserver), and Shiva (the destroyer).

The Prajapatis 10 men created by Brahma to begin populating the earth.

Saraswati Brahma's daughter and consort; goddess of knowledge and the arts.

In Hindu mythology, there is no single creation myth or creator. Narayana, however, was the supreme being. When he first awoke from his cosmic sleep, he forged the creator god, Brahma, from his own body. Brahma, using the power of his mind, made the universe and produced four sons. These sons did not know how to have children, so Brahma then created 10 men, the Prajapatis, who did know how. They asked Brahma for a wife.

Daughter and consort
Brahma divided himself into two, and from the left half emerged a beautiful woman. Brahma's desire for his daughter was so powerful, that he sprouted three extra heads (one on each side and one behind) so that he could always look at her. Discomforted by his lustful stares, his daughter rose up to the sky, so Brahma grew a fifth head, which looked heavenwards.

The daughter fled, adopting various female animal forms as she ran – goose, mare, cow, doe – but

Brahma transformed into a deer, pursuing his own daughter metamorphosed into a doe, for the purpose of committing incest with her.
Brahmanda Purana

all of her disguises were in vain. Her father turned into the male counterpart of each animal she became and forced himself on her, creating all of the animal species across the earth.

The daughter became known as Shatarupa ("one with a thousand forms"). She was also revered as Saraswati, Brahma's consort and goddess of wisdom, who ruled over artistic and intellectual exploits and created the Sanskrit language. ∎

See also: The birth of Ganesha 201 ▪ The game of dice 202–03 ▪ The Ramayana 204–09 ▪ The fish eyed goddess finds a husband 211

SIVA PLACED THE ELEPHANT'S HEAD ON THE TORSO AND REVIVED THE BOY
THE BIRTH OF GANESHA

IN BRIEF

THEME
A god reborn

SOURCE
Shiva Purana, Anonymous, 750–1350 CE.

SETTING
Mount Kailash, in the Himalayas.

KEY FIGURES
Parvati Consort of Shiva and goddess of fertility; a form of Shakti, the divine creative force.

Shiva The destroyer in the Hindu Trinity (Trimurti): Brahma (the creator), Vishnu (the preserver), and Shiva (the destroyer).

Ganesha The elephant-headed god; remover of obstacles and patron of scribes; wrote down the epic *Mahabharata* from the sage Vyasa's dictation.

Shiva, the destroyer god, was married to the goddess Parvati, who balanced out his warlike tendencies. Parvati desperately wanted a child, but her husband did not. When he told her this yet again, Parvati decided to

The elephant-headed god, Ganesha, is often pictured riding on a rat. In this 19th-century watercolour by an unknown Indian artist, he is also playing the dhola (double drum).

have a bath, and told the guards to prevent anyone from entering. As Parvati washed, she formed the dirt on her skin into a child, which came to life. Still bathing, Parvati told her new son to guard the door.

When Shiva tried to access his wife's chamber, he was blocked by a young man, who refused to let him pass. "Do you know who I am?" Shiva asked. The boy said that did not matter – his job was to guard his mother's door. "Your mother? That makes me your father", bellowed the angry Shiva. Parvati's son still wouldn't let him past, so Shiva lost his temper and chopped off the boy's head.

Parvati's heart was broken. She demanded her son be brought back to life, or she would transform from Gauri (the creative goddess) into Kali (the destructive goddess). Shiva ordered his goblin attendants, the *ganas*, to bring back the head of the first creature they could find, which was an elephant. Shiva placed the animal's head on the boy's shoulders, and his son was reborn. Shiva named him Ganesha. ∎

See also: Brahma creates the cosmos 200 ▪ The game of dice 202–03 ▪ The Ramayana 204–09 ▪ Durga slays the buffalo demon 210

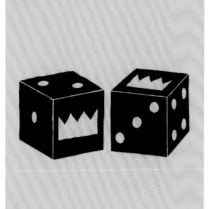

O KING. IT IS WRONG TO GAMBLE ONESELF!

THE GAME OF DICE

The Game of Dice is a pivotal moment in India's epic, the *Mahabharata*. Thought to be the longest poem ever composed, the *Mahabharata* is a collection of stories that reflect the history and culture of Hindu civilization and tell the stories of families feuding for power.

The Game of Dice tells of the legendary conflict between two branches of an Indian ruling family, the Pandavas and the Kauravas. Gambling with dice was a sacred ritual: kings could not refuse a game of dice any more than they could a battle. It was linked to the concept of *daiva* (fate) and the

Dushasana tries to unravel Draupadi's sari, but Krishna protects her modesty. She is standing on the cross-shaped board of the dice game, *chaupar*, still played in India today.

See also: Ahura Mazda and Ahriman 198–99 ▪ Brahma creates the cosmos 200 ▪ The birth of Ganesha 201 ▪ The *Ramayana* 204–09

The Bhagavad Gita

The *Mahabharata* details the power struggle between the Kauravan and Pandavan families, as well as the role of Krishna, the eighth incarnation of Vishnu, in these events. The Gita, often seen as a spiritual treatise, is an episode in the *Mahabharata*, and details a conversation between Krishna and Prince Arjuna – leader of the Pandavas – on the eve of battle during the Kurukshetra War. Krishna appeared to the prince as his friend and charioteer. When Arjuna said that he did not want to fight, and believed killing to be wrong, Krishna questioned his logic, and argued that he must fulfil his duty as dharmic protector of his kingdom.

In awe of such philosophical knowledge, Arjuna asked his friend who he really was. Krishna revealed his universal form with multiple heads and limbs, and Arjuna saw the universe existing in him. Arjuna then realized his own infinitesimal place in the cosmos, picked up his weapon, and fought the battle.

Mounted on Arjuna's horse, Krishna encourages the prince to fight in this 17th-century illustration from the *Mahabharata*.

balance between human and divine action. The story of the Game of Dice illustrates *dharma* (the moral order of the universe) and the chaos that ensues when *dharma* breaks down.

Draupadi's humiliation

Duryodhana, the Kauravan prince and eldest son of a blind king, was envious of the Pandavan palace. Although he had inherited the control of much of his father's kingdom at Hastinapura, he was jealous of his Pandavan cousins. During a tour of their palace, Duryodhana embarrassed himself on several occasions, culminating in his slipping and falling into a pond. Draupadi, the wife of the Pandavan brothers, mocked him.

Duryodhana then invited his cousins to a game of dice. One of them, Yudhishthira, played and recklessly gambled away his kingdom, his brothers, and his wife. His loss condemned some of his family to servitude, and others to 12 years' exile. When a servant was sent to take Draupadi to the slave quarters, the menstruating Draupadi was in the royal bath. She refused to leave, but was dragged by her hair into the court.

Draupadi wore only a single layer of fabric – a sari with no underlayers – and was streaked with blood. No one came to her aid to preserve her modesty. To justify this outrage, the men claimed that Draupadi deserved no respect as she had been married to five brothers from a single family. Their

A huge mass of cloth wound from Draupadi's body lay in a heap on one side. But the original sari was still on her.
Mahabharata

mother had decreed that what one brother had won should be shared by them all.

The Kauravan brothers ordered the five Pandavas and their wife to be disrobed. Draupadi prayed to Krishna, and as Duryodhana's brother Dushasana pulled at the fabric on her body, each yard was divinely reproduced. Try as he might, he could not unravel Draupadi's never-ending sari. Finally, exhausted, Dushasana admitted defeat, and Bhima, one of the Pandava brothers, vowed to kill him one day in revenge.

Exile and war

Sent into exile for 12 years, the Pandavas used this time to prepare for war. When Krishna discovered their plot, however, they were forbidden from returning to their kingdom. Krishna attempted to mediate, but war was inevitable, and when it came, Bhima killed Dushasana, and all other Kauravan brothers were killed in the battle. With this, the Pandavas were the rulers of Hastinapura. ▪

RAMA
IS VIRTUOUS AND THE FOREMOST AMONG ALL RIGHTEOUS MEN

THE RAMAYANA

IN BRIEF

THEME
Moral conduct

SOURCE
The Ramayana, Valmiki,
c.5th century BCE.

SETTING
Ayodhya, India; Lanka, an
island fortress.

KEY FIGURES
Rama Seventh incarnation of
Vishnu; prince of Ayodhya.

Sita Wife of Rama.

Ravana A ten-headed demon.

Brahma Creator of the
Universe.

Dasharatha King of Ayodhya.

Lakshmana Rama's half-
brother.

Bharata Rama's half-brother.

Kaikeyi One of Dasharatha's
wives; mother of Bharata.

Hanuman A divine monkey.

[Rama], you are
famed throughout
the three worlds for
your glory, for your prowess,
your devotion to
your father; integrity and
virtue abound in you.
The Ramayana

The Incarnations (Avatars) of Vishnu

1. Matsya Fish Vishnu

2. Kurma Turtle Vishnu

3. Varaha Wild Boar Vishnu

4. Narasimha Lion-headed Vishnu

5. Vamana Dwarf Vishnu

6. Parashurama Axe-wielding Vishnu

7. Rama King of Ayodhya

8. Krishna The Dark One

9. Buddha The Enlightened One

10. Kalki Harbinger of the End

The epic poem *Ramayana*, written in Sanskrit and one of the major works of Hindu literature, tells the story of Prince Rama of Ayodhya and his quest to save his wife, Sita, from her ten-headed captor, Ravana, who is the king of the *Asuras*, or demons.

When Brahma granted a boon – a sacred wish – to Ravana, as a reward for his 10,000-year fast, Ravana asked Brahma to make him invincible to any god. His wish granted, Ravana began causing havoc across the three worlds – earth, air, and heaven – and the gods asked Brahma to intervene.

Meanwhile, on earth, King Dasharatha of Ayodhya, despite taking three wives, still had no son. Anxious for an heir, he arranged a great fire sacrifice (*yajna*) as an offering to Brahma.

The birth of Rama
When Brahma looked down from heaven at the flames of the king's ritual sacrifice, it occurred to him that while Ravana had asked for protection from gods and demons, he had forgotten to ask for protection from man. So Brahma decided that he would bring Lord Vishnu to earth in human form to

See also: Brahma creates the cosmos 200 ■ The game of dice 202–03 ■ The birth of Ganesha 201

The marriages of Prince Rama and his brothers are depicted in this miniature (c.1700-1750). This Pahari (meaning "from the mountains") art is from India's Himachal Pradesh region.

defeat Ravana. King Dasharatha's prayers were granted, and sons were born to each of his three wives: Rama to Kausalya; the twins Lakshmana and Shatrughna to Sumitra; and Bharata to Kaikeyi.

The princes all grew up learning the arts of warfare and reading sacred texts. One day, the sage Vishvamitra came seeking help to defeat the demons that were disturbing sacrificial rites in the forest. Rama and his half-brother Lakshmana accompanied the sage, and learned how to use divine weaponry. Vishvamitra praised Rama's skill, telling him he had been born to rid the world of evil.

The prince is banished

Twelve years later, the ageing Dasharatha prepared to have Rama crowned as king. Rama was the bravest and most virtuous son, and his father's favourite. But on the eve of the great event, Dasharatha's third wife, Kaikeyi, reminded her husband of two boons he had granted her many years earlier. She demanded that Rama be banished to the wilderness for 14 years and that her son, Bharata, be crowned king instead. Duty bound, the king ordered his beloved son Rama into the wilderness. Rama's wife, Sita, demanded she join her husband in banishment, as did his loyal half-brother Lakshmana. As the three left the palace for exile, King Dasharatha died of a broken heart.

Bharata discovered his mother's plot and followed Rama into the forest, begging him to return and »

Rama battles the superhuman Asura (sometimes referred to as "titans") on an illustrated *Ramayana* folio from about 1700.

The worship of Rama

Rama is the seventh incarnation of Vishnu and a major Hindu deity in his own right. From the first millennium BCE, Rama was widely recognized as an avatar of Vishnu and considered "the ideal man". By around the 12th century CE, he came to be revered as a god.

Rama worship strengthened significantly in the late 16th century when Tulsidas, a poet-saint and devotee of Rama, wrote the epic poem *Ramcharitmanas*, which equated Rama with Brahman, the Supreme Being.

Characterized by duty, integrity, and devotion, Rama's rule over the perfect, utopian society at Ayodhya extended to the whole world and became known as *ramraj*. Mahatma Gandhi used this ideal to visualize a new age of democracy, religious tolerance, and equal justice for all during India's independence movement against British rule, which finally ended in 1947.

Each year, Rama's birthday is marked by the spring festival, Rama Navami, and his life is celebrated during the Hindu autumn festival of Navratri.

claim his rightful throne. But Rama was steadfast in his duty to carry out his father's orders, and so Bharata reluctantly ruled in his half-brother's absence, keeping Rama's golden sandals on the throne, ready for his return.

Sita's abduction

Thirteen years later, in the forest by the sparkling Godavari River, the demoness Shurpanakha appeared and fell in love with the beautiful Rama. Failing to seduce him, she then pursued Lakshmana. Spurned again, Shurpanakha became incensed and flew towards Sita in a rage. The brothers caught the demoness and cut off her nose and ears. The following day, when Shurpanakha's brothers came to avenge her, Rama and Lakshmana showered them with arrows. Little did they know that Shurpanaka had another brother, Ravana, who would also seek revenge.

One day, Sita spotted a golden deer by their forest settlement and became bewitched by it. Rama, intent on pleasing his wife, tried to capture it for her. The deer fled, leading Rama farther into the forest. Lakshmana heard Rama's voice calling out for help; he drew a protective circle around Sita and left her to follow the voice. Now that Sita was alone, a hermit appeared asking for food. Wanting to uphold her people's generosity, Sita stepped outside of the circle. The hermit shed his disguise, revealing himself as the demon, Ravana, with 10 heads and 20 arms. He threw Sita over his shoulder, and summoned his flying chariot. The old vulture Jatayu, who had been keeping watch over the three exiles, tried to block the chariot, but Ravana chopped off one of its wings.

Ravana's chariot flew across the seas onwards to the island of Lanka, where the demon was king. Piece by piece, Sita dropped her jewellery from the chariot, leaving a trail behind her. When they landed, Sita refused to live in Ravana's palace, so he left her in a garden of ashoka trees. Determined to woo her, he sang to her, told her stories, and showered her with compliments, sweet-smelling flowers, and fine jewels – but Sita remained faithful

> He [Rama] may be poor, he may have been turned out of his kingdom, but my husband must retain my respect.
> *The Ramayana*

to Rama, who was travelling with Lakshmana in search of Sita. When they passed through the land of the apes, they met the monkey hero Hanuman. The monkeys showed them the fallen jewellery, which formed a trail towards Lanka. The only missing piece, Rama realized, was his wife's hairpin.

Rescue and war

Hanuman assumed a gargantuan form and leapt across the sea to Lanka. He crisscrossed the island looking everywhere for Sita, but was unable to find her until he saw a beautiful, solitary woman in a garden, wearing a single hairpin. Hanuman approached Sita, reassuring her of his good character and divine lineage, and gave her Rama's signet ring as proof he came from Rama. Hanuman told Sita to jump onto his back so he could safely deliver her back across the sea, but she

The vulture Jatayu lies wounded amidst the wreckage of Ravana's cart, after trying to stop him abducting Sita, in this 18th-century manuscript illustration made in the Kangra style.

refused, insisting that only her husband should liberate her. Hanuman asked her for a token he could show Rama to help comfort him, and so she gave him her hairpin, which she had kept as a symbol of her status as a married woman.

Hanuman then created chaos in Lanka, killing many of Ravana's warriors before allowing himself to be caught and delivered to the demon. Now face-to-face with Ravana, he urged him to let Sita go, but Ravana set his tail on fire. Hanuman escaped and used his blazing tail to set the citadel aflame. Over the next five days, his army of monkeys built a long bridge to Lanka, made of stones inscribed with Rama's name. A bloody war ensued between the armies of Ravana and Rama, ending with Rama's slaying of the demon and reuniting at last with his beloved wife, Sita. On Ravana's death, his noble brother Vibhishana was crowned the new king of Lanka.

Rama tests Sita

Now together again, Rama asked Sita to perform a test of fire to prove her chastity after living at the house of another man. Sita plunged into the flames and Agni, Lord of Fire, returned her unscathed, proving her innocence. Now back in Ayodhya after 14 long years in exile, Rama was at last crowned king.

In a final book of the *Ramayana*, likely added later, Sita's chastity was questioned further. Following town gossip, Rama banished his beloved to the forest. She was watched over by the sage Valmiki, who was, at the time, composing the *Ramayana*. Sita gave birth to twin boys, who learnt to recite the

The hero Rama and ten-headed Ravana take aim at each other on a late-18th-century ceremonial hanging that is a fine example of *kalamkari* textile painting from south India.

sage's poem. When the story was performed to King Rama, he was overwhelmed with grief. Valmiki then brought Sita to him, but she called upon the earth mother, who had once given birth to her, to free her from this unjust world. With this, the earth opened, and Sita vanished into the ground forever. ▪

A living text

The *Ramayana* is one of the world's longest epic poems and in Hindu tradition is considered the first example of poetry. Attributed to the revered poet Valmiki, the core material is dated to c.500 BCE, but the story is thought not to have been fixed in its current form until a millennium later.

The *Ramayana*'s story is known throughout the Indian subcontinent to Hindus, Jains, and Buddhists. Muslim scholars and poets have a long history of interpreting the text and of painting its various scenes as miniatures. During the 16th century, the Mughal emperor Akbar had the poem translated into Persian and painted on the walls at his court.

Locations featured in the *Ramayana* are still revered as religious and pilgrimage sites, and the story continues to be told in various media – from poetry, drama, song, and dance to puppet shows, films, cartoons, and comics. A 1980s television version was watched by more than 100 million viewers.

I AM THE LADY, RULER OF THE WORLDS

DURGA SLAYS THE BUFFALO DEMON

IN BRIEF

THEME
Triumph of good over evil

SOURCE
"Devi Mahatmya" ("Glory of the Goddess"), *Markandeya Purana*, Anonymous, 5th–7th century CE.

SETTING
Heaven.

KEY FIGURES
Mahishasura Buffalo Demon.

Brahma The Creator in the Hindu Trinity (Trimurti).

Vishnu The Preserver in the Hindu Trinity (Trimurti).

Shiva The Destroyer in the Hindu Trinity (Trimurti).

Indra King of the gods.

Durga Warrior goddess and pre-existing cosmic force, also known as Devi and Shakti.

In Hindu mythology, the buffalo demon Mahishasura sought immortality to secure a victory for his fellow Asuras over the benevolent deities, the Devas. He undertook a long penance to the god Brahma, but the creator god rejected his request. Mahishasura then asked that he should not be killed by any man, nor by the Trimurti – the Hindu Trinity of Brahma, Vishnu, and Shiva. Brahma agreed, knowing what was to be.

Mahishasura amassed his troops, first devastating the earth, then defeating the Devas in the heavens, forcing them to flee. Indra, king of the gods, begged the Trimurti to find a solution. Brahma, Vishnu, and Shiva focused their power into a great flame, from which emerged the goddess Durga, who pre-existed as a cosmic force and was celebrated as a creator of the universe. Clutching an array of weapons given to her by the gods, the many-armed goddess rode her lion into battle and destroyed the army of the Asuras. Mahishasura attacked her repeatedly, sometimes

Durga slays Mahishasura in his horned male form as she sits astride her lion amid deities in this 19th-century image by Indian painter Raji Ravi Rama.

shape-shifting into different forms, until finally the goddess cut off his head, ending his terrible reign.

Durga's victory is celebrated during her annual 10-day festival, called Durga Puja in northeastern India and Dashain in Nepal. ∎

See also: ▪ Brahma creates the cosmos 200 ▪ The *Mahabharata* 202–03 ▪ The *Ramayana* 204–09

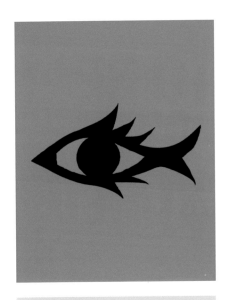

O! MEENAKSHI! FISH-EYED GODDESS! GRANT ME BLISS!
THE FISH-EYED GODDESS FINDS A HUSBAND

IN BRIEF

THEME
Marriage

SOURCE
Tiruvilayaadal Puranam
("The Sacred Sports of
Shiva"), Paranjothi Munivar,
17th century CE.

SETTING
Madurai, Tamil Nadu,
South India.

KEY FIGURES
Meenakshi Divine ruler of the
Pandyan Kingdom; avatar
(incarnation) of Parvati.

Malayadwaja Pandya
Second Pandyan king; father
of Meenakshi.

Brahma The Creator in the
Hindu Trinity (Trimurti).

Vishnu The Preserver in the
Hindu Trinity (Trimurti).

Shiva The Destroyer in the
Hindu Trinity (Trimurti).

Parvati Goddess of fertility;
consort of Shiva the Destroyer.

Meenakshi is known as the Fish-Eyed Goddess, having been blessed with beautiful fish-shaped eyes. She was regarded as the divine ruler of the city of Madurai by the Pandyan Dynasty – sea traders and sailors who adopted the symbol of the fish on their coins and flags.

The legend of the Fish-Eyed Goddess, who has inspired hymns and rituals, tells of a Pandyan king of Madurai named Malayadwaja

You shine with the
green emerald splendour!
You are the spouse of Siva.
Your eyes resemble fish!
Sacred Songs of India
V. K. Subramanian (1998)

Pandya, who prayed for a child. The gods brought forth a daughter with three breasts from a pit of fire. A divine voice told the king that the third breast would vanish when his daughter met the husband of her destiny. The king named her Meenakshi, and taught her *shastras* (traditional sciences) to prepare her for the throne.

Holy matrimony
Following the death of her father, Meenakshi, now a powerful warrior, travelled north to wage war on his enemies. She conquered the abodes of Brahma, Vishnu, and the Devas, travelling further to the abode of Shiva. She triumphed over Shiva's attendants and his bull guardian, Nandi. Next in her line of attack was the hermit Shiva himself, but the moment they looked at each other, she realized she must be an incarnation of his consort Parvati, goddess of fertility, love, and devotion. That instant, Meenakshi lost her third breast. Shiva and Meenakshi travelled to Madurai and were married. ∎

See also: The *Mahabharata* 202–03 ▪ The *Ramayana* 204–09 ▪ Durga slays the buffalo demon 210

YOU ARE TO BE THE KING OVER ALL THE WORLD

THE ORIGINS OF THE BAIGA

IN BRIEF

THEME
Protecting Mother Earth

SOURCE
The Baiga, Verrier Elwin, 1939.

SETTING
Soon after the creation of the world, the state of Madhya Pradesh, central India.

KEY FIGURES
Nanga Baiga Male ancestor of the Baiga people.

Nanga Baigin Female ancestor of the Baiga people.

Dharti Mata The Baiga people's Mother Earth.

Thakur Deo The Baiga people's Lord of the Village.

Bhagavan The Creator.

The Baiga people from the area around the Mandla hills in central India believe that their male ancestor, Nanga Baiga, was a great magician. According to legend, he was the first man and Nanga Baigin was the first woman.

The Baiga people believe that their early ancestors were born beneath a cluster of bamboo trees, having emerged from the womb of the earth mother Dharti Mata. She is the consort of Thakur Deo, the Lord of the Village and the oldest and most venerated of the Baiga gods. Dharti Mata is worshipped in

All the kingdoms of the world may fall to pieces, but he who is made of earth and is lord of the earth, shall never forsake it.
The Baiga

the month of Jeth (May), just before the rainy season, when she is said to lie ready to be impregnated.

Keepers of the world
Bhagavan the Creator spread the earth out flat, but could not stop it from moving around. He invited Nanga Baiga and Nanga Baigin to help him secure the four corners of the world. Nanga Baiga sacrificed a sow to Dharti Mata, and a white cock to Thakur Deo.

Dharti Mata, who had been rocking back and forth, stood perfectly still when drops of the sow's blood fell on her. She was pleased with the sacrifice and told Nanga Baiga that from now on she would listen to him when she became angry and started to rock.

Nanga Baiga and Nanga Baigin found four large nails and drove them into the corners of the earth to keep it steady. Bhagavan told the Baiga pair that they must guard the world and keep its nails in place. And with that, they became the keepers of the world.

When Bhagavan had finished creating the world, he asked all of the tribes to assemble, for he wanted to assign them a king. Once everyone had come together,

See also: Brahma creates the cosmos 200 ▪ The birth of Ganesha 201 ▪ The game of dice 202–03 ▪ The *Ramayana* 204–09

Members of the Baiga take part in the three-day *Dharohar* festival hosted in Indore, India. The event is a celebration of World Tribal Day, held annually on 9th August, and is a showcase of tribal culture.

Bhagavan saw that many were dressed in their finery, while Nanga (meaning nude) Baiga wore nothing but leaves. He took Nanga Baiga and positioned him on his throne, making him king over all the world.

Nanga Baiga was pleased, but because a member of the Gond people had once shown great kindness to him, he replied: "Make the Gond king, for he is my brother". The Creator honoured the request and rewarded Nanga Baiga with his blessing.

Serving Mother Earth

Bhagavan told Nanga Baiga that, as long as they did not forsake the earth, the Baiga people would survive. Then he told him how to cultivate the land. He said that the Baiga could dig roots and eat them, or pick leaves and sell them, but that they must never plough the earth for she was their mother. Instead, he told them to cut down the undergrowth, burn it, and sow seeds in the ashes. They would not gain riches, but they would grow enough to survive.

Bhagavan then showed Nanga Baiga how to follow this slash-and-burn method of farming, and told him that the seeds are best sown when rainfall is expected. Once the Creator had taught Nanga Baiga everything he needed to know for his people to survive, it was time for the Baiga to receive the seeds. As Nanga Baiga took them from Bhagavan, some fell from his hand. The Creator told him: "It is good, it should be so, for only the poor will ever be content to be servants of Dharti Mata". ▪

Women collect leaves in the forest. Like other Baiga farmers, they continue to follow the agricultural practices set out by Bhagavan.

Baiga farming today

An Adivasi (tribal) group, most of whom live in and around the state of Madhya Pradesh, central India, the Baiga farmers often live in hilly terrain and avoid the plough. Instead, they practise a traditional form of slash-and-burn cultivation called *bewar* as described in the Baiga foundation myth above.

It is out of the same respect for Mother Earth that the Baiga remain semi-nomadic. The practice of shifting, or rotating, cultivation means that they move to a new plot of ground every few years, rather than stay put and exhaust the ground by continually cultivating it.

During the 19th century, colonial forest officials forced many Baiga people to adopt the plough. One Baiga is reported to have said, "When … we first touched the plough, a man died in every village."

The Baiga people coexist with the Gond people – another Adivasi group – and have done for many centuries. The Gond favour the same agricultural practices, which are sustainable in the face of climate change.

YANG BECAME THE HEAVENS YIN BECAME THE EARTH
PANGU AND THE CREATION OF THE WORLD

IN BRIEF

THEME
The creation of the universe from chaos

SOURCE
Historical Records of the Three Sovereign Divinities and the Five Gods, Xu Zheng, 3rd century CE; *The Master Who Embraces Simplicity: Inner Chapters*, Ge Hong, 4th century CE.

SETTING
The beginning of time.

KEY FIGURE
Pangu The first living being; creator of the Earth; a semi-divine human portrayed with animal qualities.

According to the most commonly accepted (Daoist) Chinese creation story, before the creation of the universe there was only formless chaos. Eventually, a cosmic egg emerged from the chaos, and coalesced over the course of 18,000 years. Inside the egg was the first living entity, Pangu: a semi-divine human who, according to Xu Zheng's account of his myth, took the form of a horned, furry giant. Other descriptions of Pangu portrayed him with the head of a cat, the trunk of a serpent, and the paws of a tiger. His name, "Pangu", literally translates to "coiled antiquity" in Chinese, because

prior to his hatching from the egg, his body had been twisted around to fit inside its confines.

Rising heavens
Pangu could not stand to be constrained inside the egg so he smashed his way out. The whites became heaven and the yolk, the earth, while the larger pieces of the shell became the sun and moon, and the smaller pieces, the stars.

In one version of the myth, after Pangu hatched, he split dark Yin from light Yang – the oppositional principles of nature, which were born from chaos. Over the next 18,000 years, Pangu transformed nine times each day. Every day the ethereal Yang rose three metres (10 ft) higher, forming heaven, while the heavy Yin sank three metres (10 ft) deeper and became the earth. Pangu, who stood between the two to keep them apart, grew three metres (10 ft) taller each day, becoming a giant. He grew to be 45,000 km (28,000 miles) tall – the

Pangu is often portrayed as a dwarf clothed with leaves, as he is in this illustration from an anonymous Chinese text (c. 1800) which depicted important figures in Chinese history.

See also: Creation 18–23 ▪ Creation of the universe 130–33 ▪
Yi shoots the sun 216–17 ▪ Jumong 230–31 ▪ Cherokee creation 236–39

Pangu's body became the five sacred mountains. Each corresponded to one of the five Chinese cardinal points: north, east, south, west, and centre.

Left arm: (Mount Heng, Shanxi Province)
"Permanent Mountain"
Element: Water

Feet: (Mount Hua, Shanxi Province)
"Splendid Mountain"
Element: Metal

Head: (Mount Tai, Shandong Province)
"Tranquil Mountain"
Element: Wood

Belly: (Mount Song, Henan Province)
"Lofty Mountain"
Element: Earth

Right arm: (Mount Heng, Hunan Province)
"Balancing Mountain"
Element: Fire

His breath became the wind and clouds; his voice became peals of thunder. His left eye became the sun; his right eye became the moon.
Historical Records of the Three Sovereign Divinities and the Five Gods

Yin and Yang

The maintenance of the correct balance of the universe is a key theme of Daoist thinking. This is expressed through the concept of Yin and Yang – a phrase generally familiar in the Western world as representing the dual or opposing characteristics of one entity.

The words "Yin" and "Yang" translate as the "dark side" and "sunny side" of a hill respectively. More broadly, though, they stand for the dual features that make up the cosmos, such as woman and man, death and birth, and heaven and earth. Although these forces might appear to be opposites, they are, in fact, complementary. Neither Yin nor Yang is regarded as being superior or able to exist without the other. According to the *I Ching*, the ancient Chinese book of divination, natural catastrophes, such as famine and flood, are caused by a loss of equilibrium between Yin and Yang.

distance between Yin and Yang. Pangu was more divine than heaven and more sacred than the earth, but some accounts suggest that he had divine assistance in his creation of the universe. He was aided by cosmic beings: a unicorn, a tortoise, a phoenix, and a dragon.

Shaping the earth

Once the heavens and earth had formed, Pangu began to die. His body divided up to create the most important features of the universe. His breath became the wind and the clouds, and his voice, the thunder. His right eye became the moon and his left, the sun. His hair became the stars, while his sweat and bodily fluids became the rain. Pangu's blood and semen gave rise to the seas and rivers, while his muscles and veins acted as tunnels in the earth. His teeth and bones became metal and rock, and his bone marrow, pearls and jade. Pangu's body hair became the plants and trees. Some accounts say that the small fleas that lived on his body became people after being touched by the wind; others suggest that Pangu formed the human race from clay.

Pangu's arms, head, belly, and feet became China's five sacred mountains – sites of religious ceremony connected to one of the five elements and the five cardinal points. Mount Tai was believed to have been formed from Pangu's head, because of its location in the east, where the sun rises. ▪

THE TEN SUNS ALL ROSE AT ONCE, SCORCHING THE SHEAVES OF GRAIN
YI SHOOTS THE SUN

IN BRIEF

THEME
Saving humanity

SOURCES
The *Huainanzi* ("Writings of the Masters of Huainan"), Anonymous, 2nd century BCE; *Shan Hai Jing* ("The Classic of Mountains and Seas"), Anonymous, 1st century BCE.

SETTING
Ancient China

KEY FIGURES
Xihe A solar deity.

Di Jun Xihe's husband, god of the eastern sky, and an agricultural deity.

Yao A legendary Chinese emperor (c.24th century BCE) who served as a model of wisdom and virtue.

Yi A skilled bowman.

Xiwangmu A Chinese goddess.

Chang'e Yi's wife.

Originally there were ten suns. Xihe, a solar deity, had given birth to them by her husband Di Jun, a god of agriculture. The spirits of the suns were three-legged crows. Every day Xihe harnessed one of the divine sun birds to her carriage and travelled around the world, bringing light and heat to its people. One day, disaster struck when all ten sun birds flew into the sky at once.

This caused the temperature on earth to rise to dangerous levels, scorching the lands and preventing plants from growing. The people were too hot to breathe and came close to starvation. To make matters worse, terrible monsters emerged and roamed the land. They included a man-eating boa constrictor, a giant bird, and a huge wild boar with sharp tusks. Xihe and Di Jun could not persuade the suns to depart the heavens.

Yao saves the day
At this time, Yao, the ruler of China, urged Di Jun to send help, which arrived in the form of Yi the archer. Yi came down to earth carrying the red bow and white arrows that Di Jun had given to him. Yi hunted down the deadly beasts, and saved humanity from their attacks. He then turned to the problem of the ten suns. Drawing his bow, Yi shot an arrow at one of the suns. The sun exploded, and its three-legged crow spirit fell to earth. One by one,

Yi shoots at the suns in an image from the *Shan Hai Jing*. One version of the myth relates that the suns fell into the sea, forming a rock that evaporated water to stop the sea flooding the land.

See also: Pangu and the creation of the world 214–15 ▪ The adventures of the Monkey King 218–19 ▪ The legend of the five suns 248–55

> So Yi was the first to bring merciful relief to the world below from all its hardships.
> **Shan Hai Jing**

Yi shot down the suns until just one remained. Yao told Yi to spare this last sun, as the people still needed its heat and light. For this action, which saved humanity and restored order to the world, Yao was given the title "Son of Heaven". He is revered in Chinese legends as a wise and judicious sovereign.

Tragic existence

Yi had arrived on earth with his wife Chang'e and apprentice Fengmeng. As a reward for shooting the sun birds, the Chinese goddess Xiwangmu gave Yi an elixir of immortality, but it proved to be his undoing. Yi, who was a mortal, did not want to imbibe the elixir because he could not bear to be separated from his wife.

One day Fengmeng, who was jealous of his master's skill and fame, broke into Yi's house while the archer was out hunting. Fengmeng demanded the elixir from Chang'e. Rather than give it to him, she drank it herself. Now immortal, she flew to the nearest celestial body, the moon, so she could remain close to her husband. When Yi found that his wife was gone, he set up an altar to her and laid out her favourite foods as an offering to her; he did this every year to mark the day she had left.

Yi's life came to an end when treacherous Fengmeng beat him to death with a branch from a peach tree so that he himself could be the greatest archer on Earth. After his death, Yi was worshipped as Zongbu, a god who prevents disaster. His wife is now venerated as the spirit of the moon. ▪

Xiwangmu gives the elixir of **immortality** to Yi.

Yi does **not drink** it.

Fengmeng tries to **steal** it.

Chang'e drinks the elixir instead.

Immortal, Chang'e flies to the moon.

An actress dressed as Chang'e flies up to a model moon during the Mid-Autumn Festival in Jinhua, Zhejiang Province of China.

The Mid-Autumn festival

On the 15th day of the eighth lunar month, when the moon is full, the Mid-Autumn Festival is celebrated in China and Vietnam and by people of Chinese and Vietnamese origin worldwide. The event, which dates back to around 1600 BCE, is traditionally a thanksgiving for the annual rice or wheat harvest, marked by social gatherings and offerings for a bountiful year to come.

A central feature of the festival is the veneration of the moon goddess Chang'e, one of many Chinese deities who are still revered. Gathering at night with friends and family, people burn incense, pray, and offer food to the lunar deity, just as Yi did, when Chang'e had departed the earth. The best known of the foods is mooncake, a circular pastry commonly filled with a sweet bean paste. The round shape of the cakes is symbolic of togetherness and unity. As well as being offered to the moon goddess, these cakes are often given to friends and family at this time, usually in elaborate, beautiful packaging.

I'LL ROAM THE CORNERS OF THE OCEANS AND GO TO THE EDGE OF THE SKY

THE ADVENTURES OF THE MONKEY KING

IN BRIEF

THEME
The path to enlightenment

SOURCE
Journey to the West, Wu Cheng'en, c.1500–82.

SETTING
Ancient China and India.

KEY FIGURES
Sun Wukong The Monkey King.

The Jade Emperor The mythical ruler of heaven.

The Buddha The founder of Buddhism, who lived and taught in India from the 6th–4th century BCE.

Xuanzang A Buddhist monk.

Guanyin The Buddhist goddess of mercy.

Zhu Bajie A half-pig, half-man; Xuanzang's disciple.

Sha Wujing A river monster; Xuanzang's disciple.

The classical Chinese story of Sun Wukong begins with the union of heaven and Earth. From this union, a stone egg was created which emerged from the Mountain of Flowers and Fruit. From the egg, a monkey was born named Sun Wukong. At first, Sun Wukong played with the other animals who lived on the mountain. Eventually he grew in ambition, and, declaring himself the Monkey King, became a demon. With his new status, Sun Wukong became an immensely powerful and skilled fighter, able to transform into 72 different animals and objects and leap halfway around the world in a single jump. He armed himself with a gold-banded staff, which could magically change size according to his needs.

Immortal and imprisoned

Despite his status as the Monkey King, when it came time for Sun Wukong to die, he was dragged to the Underworld. Instead of submitting to his fate, however, he erased his name from the Register of Life and Death, making himself immortal. Hearing of Sun Wukong's activities, the Jade Emperor, ruler of heaven, summoned him and gave him a position at court, hoping it would end his exploits. Sun Wukong expected a senior office, but was given the lowly post of superintendent of stables. When he realized how unimportant his position was, he flew into a rage. He declared himself the Great Sage and equal to the Jade Emperor.

At first, the Jade Emperor tried to placate Sun Wukong by making him the guardian of the Heavenly Peach Orchard. The entente ended, however, when Sun Wukong was not invited to a banquet with the other deities. He rebelled against the Jade Emperor, stole and ate the peaches of immortality from the

How dare they treat me [Sun Wukong] with such contempt? On the Mountain of Flowers and Fruit I am a king.
Journey to the West

See also: The war of the gods and titans 32–33 ▪ Pangu and the creation of the world 214–15 ▪ Yi shoots the sun 216–17

garden, and defeated all of the forces the Emperor sent to kill him. With all other hopes lost, the Jade Emperor appealed to the Buddha to control Sun Wukong. The Buddha seized him in his hand, which he transformed into an enchanted mountain – the rebellious Monkey King was now trapped indefinitely.

Dutiful disciples

Several centuries later, a Chinese monk called Xuanzang made a pilgrimage west to India to gather more complete versions of Buddhist texts there were in China. Xuanzang was helped by Guanyin, the goddess of mercy, who arranged for several disciples to protect him in his journey, in order to atone for their past misdeeds. The first was Sun

Xuanzang is aided by Sun Wukong and Zhu Baiji, pictured here crossing a river as they approach the Great Buddha Temple, in Zhangye, in the Gansu Province of China.

Wukong, who was freed from his mountain prison. To keep him under control, Guanyin placed a band around his head that would tighten if Xuanzang chanted a particular mantra. The next disciple was Zhu Bajie, a former immortal banished from heaven for drunkenness and reborn on earth as a pig monster. Lastly was Sha Wujing, also a former immortal, exiled from heaven for smashing a crystal goblet – he was now a grotesque river monster.

Xuanzang's 17-year ordeal was beset with hazards engineered by the Buddha in order to cultivate his spiritual growth. Finally, Xuanzang returned the sacred writings to China and was given Buddhahood. Sun Wukong had proved a loyal and effective bodyguard, protecting Xuanzang from many demons. As a reward, Sun Wukong was also elevated to the status of Buddha ("awakened one"), and was subsequently awarded the title of "Victorious Fighting Buddha". ∎

Xuanzang

The figure of Xuanzang in literature was based on a historical figure. Born in c. 602 CE, in Luoyang, central China, he was ordained as a novice monk at 13, and as a full monk seven years later.

Buddhism had arrived in China from India in the 3rd century BCE. Xuanzang's concern was that the texts being used to study Buddhism were often incomplete and inaccurate. He decided to journey to India himself to study and to collect the texts. Despite an imperial ban on foreign travel at the time, Xuanzang set out in 629 CE, returning 17 years later with hundreds of Buddhist texts in Sanskrit.

At the request of Emperor Taizong of the Tang dynasty, Xuanzang also compiled an account of his journey entitled *Great Tang Records on the Western Regions*. This work would go on to inspire Wu Cheng'en's *Journey to the West*, now viewed as one of the most influential Chinese novels of all time. Xuanzang studied for the rest of his life in Chang'an, now Xi'an, where Indian Buddhist texts were translated into Chinese.

HAVING FINISHED MAKING THE LANDS, THEY WENT ON TO MAKE ITS SPIRITS

IZANAGI AND IZANAMI

IN BRIEF

THEME
The creation of Japan and its spirits

SOURCE
Kojiki ("Records of Ancient Matters"), O no Yasumaro, 712 CE.

SETTING
Japan in the Age of Spirits.

KEY FIGURES
Izanagi Creator god.

Izanami Izanagi's younger sister and wife.

Kagutsuchi A fire spirit.

Yomotsu-shikome
A hideous hag.

Tsukuyomi God of the moon and night.

Amaterasu Goddess of the sun and universe.

Susanoo God of the sea and storms.

The first heavenly deities gave Izanagi ("He who beckoned") and Izanami ("She who beckoned") the task of making Japan – known as the *kuniumi* ("creation of the land"). From their union, they were to produce Oyashima, comprising the eight largest Japanese islands, and also six smaller islands. To do this, the couple made an earthly home. From the bridge between heaven and earth, Izanagi used a jewelled spear to stir up the sea below. As he withdrew the spear, clumps of salt fell from it to form an isle where Izanagi and Izanami were married. During the ceremony, Izanami spoke first, admiring her husband, "What a fine young man!"

Birth and death
Izanami soon gave birth to two islands, but they were misshapen. The couple asked the spirits why and were told that it was because Izanami had spoken first at their wedding. Repeating the ceremony, they took care that Izanagi was the first to speak. The next births were the beautiful islands of Japan.

Izanagi and Izanami then created many spirits to represent Japan's natural features. All was

The eight islands of ancient Japan

IKI

SADO

OKI

TSUSHIMA

YAMATO

IYO

TSUKUSHI

AWAJI

well until Izanami gave birth to Kagutsuchi ("Flickering Flame Elder"), a fire spirit who burned her so severely during labour that she died. Izanagi took his sword and beheaded Kagutsuchi, whose corpse produced eight warrior gods and eight mountain gods.

Izanagi then journeyed to the underworld to retrieve Izanami. Standing outside the hall where she was staying, he asked her to come back to earth. Izanami replied that she had to seek permission to leave because she had eaten food cooked at the hearth of the Underworld, an act that bound her there.

When Izanagi grew impatient for a response, he looked into the hall. There he beheld Izanami's

See also: Creation 18–23 ▪ Creation of the universe 130–33 ▪ Brahma creates the cosmos 200–01 ▪ Cherokee creation 236–38

decayed body, crawling with maggots. Angered that Izanagi should see her like this, Izanami sent the hag Yomotsu-shikome ("Ugly woman of the Underworld") to chase him away, along with eight thunder spirits that had emerged from her corpse and 1,500 warriors.

Izanagi fled back to earth and rolled a boulder across the portal to the Underworld. Izanami and Izanagi stood on either side of the boulder, and he declared they were divorced. Utterly bereft, Izanami swore to strangle 1,000 people every day, but Izanagi vowed to counter this with 1,500 births.

Feeling unclean after his contact with the dead, Izanagi disrobed and bathed. His discarded

Izanagi brandishes the spear to whip up brine to create Onogoro, the island home of Japan's creator deities, in an illustration by 19th-century Japanese artist Kawanabe Kyosai.

clothing became 12 spirits, and when he washed his body, he created 14 more. The last three were the most mighty gods: from his right eye came Tsukuyomi, spirit of the moon; from his left eye sprang Amaterasu, spirit of the sun; from his nose came Susanoo, who ruled the sea and storms. The conflict between Amaterasu, also a goddess of fertility, and Susannoo, whose forces destroyed crops, would soon rival the epic enmity between Izanagi and Izanami. ▪

Shintoism

Japan's main religion, Shinto ("way of the gods") draws on the nation's indigenous beliefs. Its practices were first recorded in two early 8th-century texts, the *Kojiki* ("Records of Ancient Matters") and *Nihon Shoki* ("Chronicles of Japan"), both of which include the creation myth of Izanagi and Izanami. With no particular founder and no strict dogma, Shintoism encompasses many different traditions and influences. Its most important feature is the worship of *kami* (spirits), which are often forces of nature that reside in features of the landscape such as rocks and rivers. *Kami* also include venerated ancestors who perform the role of guardians for their descendants.

Kami are revered through prayer and ritual, which can take place at small household altars called *kamidana* ("god shelves"), where the family *kami* are enshrined and offerings are laid. There are also larger public shrines that house national *kami* and the sacred objects associated with them.

The union of Izanami and Izanagi is represented by the sacred Meoto Iwa ("Wedded Rocks"), linked by a rope bridge, near the Ise Grand Shrine in southern Japan.

ALL MANNER OF CALAMITIES AROSE EVERYWHERE

SUSANOO AND AMATERASU

Amaterasu, goddess of the sun, and her younger brother Susanoo, god of the sea, quarrelled constantly, and Susanoo often played tricks on his sister. Tired of his mischief, their father Izanagi ordered Susanoo to go into exile in the Underworld. Before he left, however, Susanoo journeyed to the heavens in order to see his sister.

Believing he had come to steal her realm, Amaterasu was alarmed at her brother's arrival. She parted her hair and strung it with precious pendants, which she also hung from her arms. She then armed herself with a bow and 1,500 arrows, and when Susanoo arrived, she

See also: Ahura Mazda and Ahriman 198–99 ▪ Pangu and the creation of the world 214–15 ▪ Izanagi and Izanami 220–21

> When he went up to
> heaven, all the mountains
> and rivers boomed and
> the land shook.
> *Kojiki*

stamped on the ground and
demanded to know the reason
for his visit. Saying that he had
only come to say farewell, Susanoo
suggested that they give each
other a personal possession and
use them to produce spirit-offspring
as a sign of good faith.

To show that his intentions
were good, Susanoo handed
Amaterasu his sword. She broke it
in three and rinsed the pieces in
the well of the heavens. She then
put them in her mouth, chewed

Susanoo, armed with his sword,
sets about killing the dragon who had
slain seven sisters. The god's previous
behaviour would be forgiven when he
saved the final sister from the dragon.

them, and spat them out, producing
three female sea spirits. Susanoo
then asked Amaterasu for her
pendants. He bit them into small
pieces and spat them out, creating
five male spirits.

Sibling conflict

After this exchange, relations
between Amaterasu and Susanoo
were initially peaceful. However,
Susanoo quickly resumed his
former bad behaviour. He declared
that the children born from his
sword were "weak-limbed women"
and ran amok through his sister's
heavenly realm in a destructive
rampage. He devastated her rice
paddies and threw excrement
about the hall where she had
celebrated the harvest feast.

Susanoo then went to the hall
where Amaterasu and other spirits
were weaving cloth. He broke a »

Kojiki

The *Kojiki* ("Records of Ancient
Matters") is Japan's oldest
surviving written work. Based
on oral tradition, it is a mixture
of dialogue, song, narration, and
commentary, and provides a
long and wide-ranging history
of the four islands of Japan.

The first book, set in the Age
of Spirits, recounts the story of
how Japan and its spirits were
created and developed. The
second and third books are set
in the Age of Mortals and detail
the deeds of legendary human

heroes and the imperial lineages
of the rulers of Japan, all the
way to the death of Empress
Suiko in 628 CE.

The compiler of the *Kojiki*
was a nobleman and chronicler
called O no Yasumaro. He
carried out the task on the
orders of Empress Genmei,
who reigned from 707 to 715 CE,
and wanted Japan's myths and
legends to be recorded more
accurately. Once completed, the
Kojiki, became highly influential
in the development of beliefs,
practices, and customs in the
Shinto religion.

hole through its ceiling and dropped a sacred colt that he had skinned into their midst, causing chaos. The shock made one of the spirits inside slam her weaving shuttle into herself, causing a fatal injury. Amaterasu was so appalled and frightened she hid in a cave deep in the centre of the earth called Ama-no-Iwato ("Heaven's Boulder Cavern") and refused to leave. This plunged the world into darkness.

The spirits gathered together outside the cavern to persuade Amaterasu to come out of hiding. Omoikane, the god of wisdom and adviser to the spirits of heaven, devised a cunning plan. He gathered hard stone from the upper reaches of the Milky Way and iron from the mountains of heaven. Using these materials, he then instructed other spirits to fashion small curved

Amaterasu hides in a cave but the spirits trick her into leaving. Here, in Utagawa Kunisada's 19th-century woodblock print, she emerges from the darkness radiating divine light.

> So the high plains of heaven were cast into utter darkness … endless night came to cover the world.
> *Kojiki*

pendants (known as the Yasakani-no-Magatama) and an eight-sided mirror (called the Yata-no-Kagami).

Uprooting a tree, Omoikane planted it outside the entrance to the cavern. He strung the upper branches with the pendants, and the lower branches with prayer strips made of white mulberry paper and blue hemp. In the middle of the tree, he hung the eight-sided mirror. The dawn goddess Ame-no-Uzume then overturned a bucket near the

entrance of the cavern and began to dance on it. As she danced, she bared her breasts and pulled her girdle down past her waist. The other spirits laughed uproariously.

Hearing the commotion, Amaterasu curiously peered out of the cavern. As she emerged, she caught sight of her reflection in the mirror. As she was momentarily transfixed, Ame-no-Tajikarao, a strong god hiding close by, pulled her out into the open. A sacred rope was flung over the cavern's entrance to stop her going back into the cave. The other spirits told Amaterasu she could no longer withhold her radiance. She agreed never to hide herself again and once more the world was bathed in her light.

Death and rebirth

With Amaterasu out of hiding, the gods had to decide what to do with Susanoo who, in acting erratically, selfishly, and destructively, had committed a serious breach of traditional Japanese moral values. First, in punishment for his actions,

he had his fingernails, toenails, and facial hair torn off. He was then to be exiled from heaven to earth.

When the spirits also imposed a fine of 1,000 tables laden with food, Susanoo asked the female food spirit O-ge-tsu-hime for help in finding food. She agreed, but pulled the food from her nose, mouth, and backside. Susanoo found this so offensive that he slew her, but O-ge-tsu-hime's corpse flourished again, mirroring the harvest cycle of death and rebirth. Silkworms emerged from her head. Rice came from her eyes, millet from her ears, red beans from her nose, barley from her reproductive organs, and soya beans from her rear. These grains and beans were transformed into seeds, and Susanoo sowed and harvested them to pay his fine.

After being banished from heaven, Susanoo went to Mount Torikami, on the Spirit River. As he walked through the countryside, he saw a chopstick floating down the river and, following the direction from which it had come, he found an elderly couple with a beautiful daughter. All three were weeping. The old man, Ashi-nazu-chi, said

---

The Imperial Regalia of Japan, also known as the three sacred treasures, were passed from Amaterasu's grandson to the Emperor and were used as part of the enthronement ceremony. They represent wisdom, benevolence, and valour.

Yata-no-Kagami (Eight-Hand Mirror)
Used by the gods to lure Ame-no-Uzume-no-Mikoto from her cave.

Yasakani-no-Magatama (Pendant)
Decorated the tree around which Ame-no-Uzume danced.

Kusanagi-no-Tsurugi (Grass-Cutting Sword)
Given to Amaterasu by Susanoo.

---

that the couple had once had eight daughters, but each year one had been devoured by a dragon called Yamata-no-Orochi. Now only their youngest daughter, Kushi-nada-hime, was left.

Killing the dragon

Susanoo was told that the dragon had eight heads and eight tails, and was so huge that it spanned eight valleys and eight peaks. He agreed to kill the dragon in return for Kushi-nada-hime's hand in marriage. Susanoo ordered the elderly couple to make a batch of extra strong sake, and to make a fence with eight doors – at each one, they were to place a cask of the sake. When the dragon arrived, it drank from each of the casks. The sake was so strong that the beast quickly fell asleep. Susanoo then used his sword to hack it into pieces. Inside the corpse, he found a mighty blade that came to be called Kusanagi-no-Tsurugi, which he later gave to Amaterasu to atone for his bad behaviour. With the dragon slain, Susanoo and Kushi-nada-hime married, and had six generations of offspring. ∎

Emperor Hirohito (1901–89)
is dressed for his coronation in 1928. At this time, Hirohito was revered as a direct descendant of the gods.

Kami and the Japanese emperors

After her dispute with Susanoo was resolved, Amaterasu turned to bringing order to the earth. Her two sons were unable to accomplish this task but eventually her grandson Ninigi was sent down. Amaterasu gave him three powerful treasures: the pendants, the mirror, and the sword that Susanoo had given her.

Ninigi brought order to Japan. He married Kono-hana-sakuya-hime, the granddaughter of the original creators Izanagi and Izanami. Ninigi's great-grandson was Jimmu, the legendary first emperor of Japan, who was said to have reigned in 660–585 BCE. Jimmu's chief wife was a descendent of Susanoo and Kushi-nada-hime. As such, the emperors were regarded as being the direct descendants of many of the most important *kami* (spirits worshipped in the Shinto religion). The emperor's traditional title is Tenno ("heavenly sovereign"). In 1945, however, as part of Japan's surrender after World War II, Emperor Hirohito renounced his divine status.

YOUR RICE OF THE SKYWORLD IS GOOD

FIRE AND RICE

IN BRIEF

THEME
The origins of agriculture

SOURCES
The Religion of the Ifugaos,
Roy Franklin Barton, 1946; *The Mythology of the Ifugaos*, Roy
Franklin Barton, 1955.

SETTING
Kayang, in Luzon, the
Philippines.

KEY FIGURES
Wigan Ifugao hunter; brother
of Kabigat.

Kabigat Ifugao hunter; brother
of Wigan.

Bugan Wigan's wife.

Lidum "The Giver"; a male
god of the Skyworld.

Hinumbían A male god of
the Skyworld; shared a home
with Lidum.

Dinipaan The blacksmith
god of the Upstream Region.

The story of Wigan and
his brother Kabigat is
a founding myth of the
Ifaguo, a tribe originating in the
highlands of the Philippines. It
explores the symbiotic relationship
between humanity's Earthworld
and the Skyworld of the gods,
and how they negotiated their
mutual sustenance.

In Kayang, Wigan and Kabigat
wanted to go hunting. To see if
their hunt would prove successful,
Wigan chose his fattest chicken
and sacrificed it to several lesser
gods, such as the Tired-Ones, who

lived in the Upstream region and
the Downstream region, and the
Alabat gods, who lived in the
moutains and owned the game.
The omen was good, so Wigan and
Kabigat took their spears and dogs
into the hills in search of a wild pig.

To the heavens

The brothers entered the forest
and, sighting a pig, sent their dogs
running, yelling encouragement.
They drove their quarry ever
upwards until it eventually climbed
up into the Skyworld. Wigan and
Kabigat followed the pig all the way
up to the Skyworld. They found it
by the house of the gods Lidum and
Hinumbían, and Wigan speared it.

When Hinumbían rebuked
Wigan for killing one of the pigs of
the Skyworld, Wigan replied, "This
is no pig of yours. We followed it all
the way from Kayang." Then Wigan
and Kabigat carried the dead pig to
Lidum and Hinumbían's granary
and, cutting it up, shared it with
the gods. Both gods took small

A seated Bulul (rice god) holds
a basket used for harvesting." This
15th-century wooden carving, made for
an Ifugao home or granary, comes from
the island of Luzon, in the Philippines.

See also: Prometheus helps mankind 36–39 ▪ Nanga Baiga 212–13 ▪ The killing of Luma-Luma 308–09

pieces of the flesh, mixed them with blood and rice, and ate them raw. They asked Wigan and Kabigat why they were not eating, and Wigan told them that they would not eat raw meat.

Mutual gifts

Wigan and Kabigat took their share down to the Earthworld, where they made fire with a bamboo drill, and cooked both meat and rice. They summoned the spirits of the place, children of either Lidum or Hinumbían, and gave them food to eat. These spirits took the food back to the Skyworld to share with their fathers. Delighted with the tasty offerings, Lidum and Hinumbían summoned Wigan and Kabigat and asked them for the precious gift of fire. In exchange, they offered jewels, but Wigan held out for the Skyworld rice, which was so much better than the bearded rice that grew in the Earthworld.

The gods opened up their granary, and gave Wigan two bundles of seed rice. In return, Wigan made them a fire. The gods excitedly carried the fire into the house, but set the house ablaze.

> Thou, Rice, here!
> Multiply like sands …
> ***The Religion***
> ***of the Ifugaos***

The Ifugao rice terraces in the mountains of Luzon were built 2,000 years ago. Watered by intricate irrigation systems, they were handed down from one generation to another.

They called for Wigan to come and take back the fire – instead, he quenched it with water, then built the gods a fireplace to contain the flames. In return, the grateful gods told Wigan and Kabigat exactly how to cultivate and store the rice, and how to make the rice fields.

Feeding humanity

Back in Kayang, Wigan told his wife Bugan that in order to create the rice fields, she must wrap herself in a blanket and remain absolutely still while he stabbed the earth repeatedly with a digging stick. After he had created eight fields, Bugan moved – from then on, when Wigan stabbed the ground, he turned over just a small amount of soil. Wigan reprimanded her, but Bugan said, "We have enough. Our children can increase the fields." Appeased by this, Wigan stabbed his stick into the bank above the

fields, causing water to gush out and irrigate the fields. With this, Wigan knew that he would soon become the first human to harvest the rice of the gods.

When the rice was ripe, the blacksmith god made knives for the harvest and exchanged them for Wigan's chickens. Wigan stored the rice in the granary with rituals and sacrifices to the gods of the Skyworld, the Underworld, and the Upstream region, and to the Bulul granary-gods. Wigan invoked the gods again, so that in Kayang the rice should always increase and flourish and, in doing so, would mirror the seasonal cycle of birth, death, and renewal. ▪

THERE WAS A MAN CALLED DAN'GUN WANGGEOM WHO CREATED A CITY AND FOUNDED A NATION
THE LEGENDARY FOUNDATION OF KOREA

IN BRIEF

THEME
Origin of the nation

SOURCE
Samguk Yusa ("Memorabilia of the Three Kingdoms"), Iryon, 1281–1283 CE.

SETTING
Mount T'aebaek-san, and the ancient kingdom of Choson.

KEY FIGURES
Hwanin King of heaven.

Hwanung Son of the king of heaven; first ruler of earth.

Ungnyeo A bear who was transformed into a woman.

Dan'gun Wanggeom Son of Hwanung and Ungnyeo; founder of the first Korean kingdom.

One of the oldest foundation myths of Korea, the story of Hwanung and his son cemented in Korean culture the belief that its people are composed of a single homogeneous group. According to this myth, all Koreans descend from the legendary founder of the ancient kingdom of Choson in 2333 BCE.

The descent
Hwanung was the son of Hwanin, the king of heaven and supreme deity. One day, Hwanung asked his father if he could descend to earth and govern his own land. Although he was sad to see his son go, Hwanin realized that Hwanung would be a good ruler for mankind. Hwanin then opened the gates of heaven and commanded his son to make his way to Mount T'aebaek-san (somewhere in or close to what is now Korea).

Accompanied by 3,000 spirits Hwanung descended from heaven onto the summit of the mountain.

Mount T'aebaek-san was the legendary home of Hwanung's sacred city. The mythical mountain's location is unknown, but this peak in Korea's Gangwon region now bears its name.

See also: The founding of Athens 56–57 ▪ The founding of Rome 102–05 ▪ Izanagi and Izanami 220–21 ▪ Jumong 230–31

The *Samguk Yusa*

The oldest record of the myth of Dan'gun is to be found in the *Samguk Yusa* ("Memorabilia of the Three Kingdoms"), compiled in 1281–1283 by the Buddhist monk Iryon. This is a collection of Korean folkloric tales that was written in the era of the Mongol empire (1206–1368).

The Dan'gun myth affirms the primordial origins of the Korean people and is seen as proof of their divine right to rule over their homeland. The Korean peninsula has been invaded by the Mongols, China, and Japan through the centuries. The story received renewed attention in the 20th century when it was used to justify state nationalism, territorial claims, and Korean unification. This arose in 1948 amidst Cold War international tensions that were unfolding on Korean soil, with the north, supported by China and the Soviet Union, fighting the south, backed by the US and other Western countries. This division remains today.

He arrived under a sandalwood tree, where he established a sacred city, Shinsi ("City of God") and appointed the noble spirits of the wind, rain, and clouds as ministers of a government composed of 360 departments. Hwanung himself took on the title of divine ruler of the human realm.

This enabled him to supervise agriculture, the preservation of life, the curing of disease, the meting out of punishments, and the establishment of a moral order that reflected the values of the heavenly society he was bringing to earth.

Heir to the throne

One day, a bear and a tiger came to Hwanung and begged him to transform them into human beings. He agreed, and gave them each a piece of sacred mugwort plant and 20 bulbs of garlic. He told them to eat it all and to stay in the dark for 100 days in order to become human. They accepted the bargain, and went to a cave where they would be out of the sunlight. But the tiger, driven by hunger, soon gave up and left. The bear patiently remained and was transformed into a beautiful woman at the end of the 100 days.

The bear-woman, Ungnyeo, was deeply grateful to Hwanung and made daily offerings for him on the summit of the T'aebaek mountain. Although she had no husband, she prayed for a son. Moved by her heartfelt prayers, Hwanung transformed himself into a human and had a child with her, whom she named Dan'gun

> If you eat this and do not see daylight for one hundred days, you will receive a human form.
> **Hwanung**

Dan'gun with mountain peaks behind him. This was painted by Chae Yong-sin, around 1850. Yong-sin was a prominent and successful 19th-century portrait painter.

Wanggeom. Dan'gun grew to become a wise and powerful leader, and eventually took over the land that his father Hwanung had governed. Dan'gun founded the first Korean kingdom, and called it Choson. He established its capital near the city which is known today as Pyongyang.

Later, Dan'gun moved the capital to another city – Asadal on Mount Paegak. He ruled the nation for 1,500 years. At the age of 1,908, Dan'gun returned to the sacred city of Shinsi on T'aebaek-san, and was immortalized, becoming a mountain god. ▪

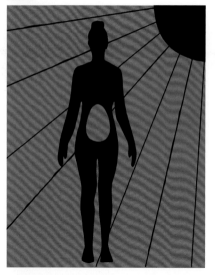

HAE MOSU MADE THE SUN SHINE AND ITS RAYS CARESSED YUHWA'S BODY
JUMONG

The myth of Jumong, the Holy King of the East, can be traced back to the foundation of the kingdom of Koguryo, one of the Three Kingdoms of Korea that succeeded Choson and dominated the Korean peninsula for much of the first millennium CE. The story charts the creation of this new state and the founding of an enduring dynasty.

One day, Celestial Emperor Cheonje sent his son Hae Mosu down to earth, where he came across Yuhwa bathing by the Ungsim Pond with her two sisters.

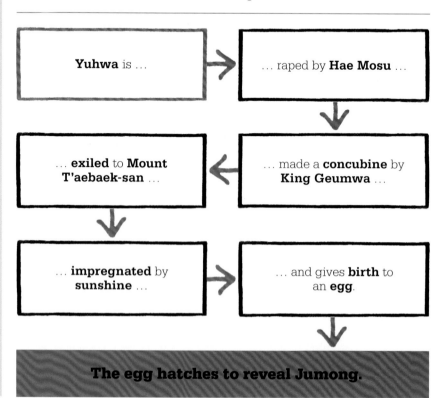

Yuhwa is ... → **... raped by Hae Mosu ...**

... exiled to Mount T'aebaek-san ... ← **... made a concubine by King Geumwa ...**

... impregnated by sunshine ... → **... and gives birth to an egg.**

The egg hatches to reveal Jumong.

See also: Origin of the universe 18–23 ▪ The Kalevala 160–61 ▪ The legendary foundation of Korea 228–29

Captivated by her beauty, he took all three women to his palace on the Yalu River, just beneath Unginsan (Bear Spirit Mountain) where he trapped them. Her two sisters managed to escape, but Yuhwa was left alone with Hae Mosu, who raped her.

When Habaek, Yuhwa's father, found out, he was outraged and confronted Hae Mosu. He told Habaek that he had been sent from the heavens and he intended to marry Yuhwa. To test if the man did have the power of the heavens, Habaek challenged him to a duel. When he realized Hae Mosu had the strength of a god, he tried to trap him in an enormous leather pocket after getting him drunk. Hae Mosu burst through the pocket and fled, never to see Habaek or Yuhwa again.

The young archer

Now alone, Yuhwa was sent into exile by her father to the southern side of Mount T'aebaeksan. Yuhwa was discovered there by King Geumwa of Dongbuyeo,

Hae Mosu descends from heaven in a golden carriage pulled by five dragons. Hae Mosu died before he was able to see his son, Jumong, found a new dynasty.

who was touched by her beauty and sorrow, and decided to make her his concubine.

When Hae Mosu – who bitterly resented his defeat by Yuhwa's father – made the rays of the sun caress her body, she became pregnant and gave birth to an egg five days later. The king quickly realized the egg was not his but that of the celestial prince. Unable to smash its unbreakable shell, he returned the egg to Yuhwa, who wrapped it in a cloth and placed it in a warm spot. When the egg finally hatched, a child was born. By the age of seven, he was able to make his own bows and arrows, and was then named Jumong ("Excellent Archer").

Narrow escape

When Jumong was 12, King Geumwa's sons, bitterly jealous of his abilities, conspired to have him killed. Learning that his life was in danger, Jumong fled to the River Om, where he cried out that he was the grandson of the Ruler of Heaven. Rising up from the fast-flowing waters of the river, terrapins and fish formed a bridge over which he could cross. As soon as he was safely on the other side, the bridge dissolved and left his pursuers stranded on the other side.

Jumong travelled on, reaching Cholbon-ju in 37 BCE and founding his capital there. He named the new state Koguryo and took "Ko" as his surname, beginning the longest dynasty in Korean history. ■

The egg

The powerful, primordial motif of the egg features at the heart of creation myths around the world. In several traditions, such as the tale of Pangu in Chinese mythology, the universe begins as an egg, from which all life hatches and develops. In other myths, such as the story of Jumong, the birth of a human from the primordial egg in miraculous circumstances defies nature, and signals the cosmically ordained role of the hero in shaping future events.

In producing a heroic protagonist, the egg is not only a potent symbol of new life, but a gift from the universe that enables the foundation of an entire nation and – in Jumong's case – a new era for Korea under his leadership. Similar national origin myths can be found in the ancient folktales of many nations, including Finland, Egypt, Angola, and India.

The Orphic egg, in Greece, was believed to hatch the hermaphroditic deity Phanes, also known as Protogenus, from whom all other gods were descended.

THE AME

RICAS

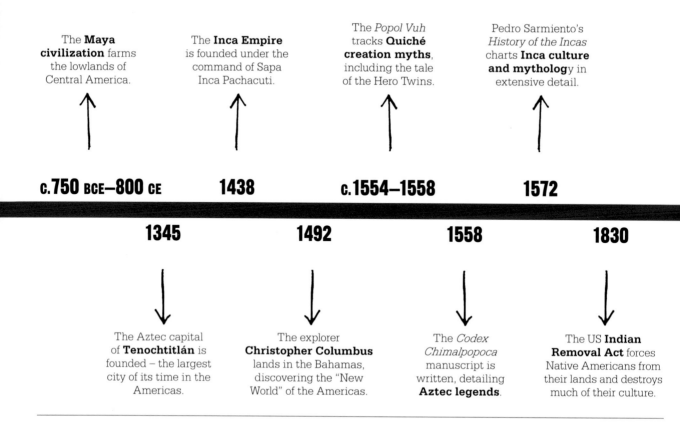

The **Maya civilization** farms the lowlands of Central America.

The **Inca Empire** is founded under the command of Sapa Inca Pachacuti.

The *Popol Vuh* tracks **Quiché creation myths**, including the tale of the Hero Twins.

Pedro Sarmiento's *History of the Incas* charts **Inca culture and mythology** in extensive detail.

c.750 BCE–800 CE   **1438**   **c.1554–1558**   **1572**

1345   **1492**   **1558**   **1830**

The Aztec capital of **Tenochtitlán** is founded – the largest city of its time in the Americas.

The explorer **Christopher Columbus** lands in the Bahamas, discovering the "New World" of the Americas.

The *Codex Chimalpopoca* manuscript is written, detailing **Aztec legends**.

The US **Indian Removal Act** forces Native Americans from their lands and destroys much of their culture.

The first humans to settle in the Americas were the Palaeo-Indians, who crossed into North America from Asia about 22,000 years ago. Over subsequent millennia, they migrated south and by 16500 BCE, Patagonia at the southern tip of South America had been settled by peoples such as the Tehuelche.

From about 3500 BCE onwards, Mesoamerican civilization emerged in Central America, establishing the first cities in around 1800 BCE. The myths and legends of these early peoples were highly influential on later civilizations, such as the Maya, who flourished from 750 BCE to the 9th century CE, and the Aztec Empire, which developed in the 13th–16th centuries CE. In South America, the Inca rose to prominence and developed its

mythology from the 12th–16th centuries CE. The indigenous peoples of North America also developed highly diverse cultures and legends – from the Inuit of the Arctic, who emerged in the 11th century CE, to the Navajo nation, who migrated to the southwest in around 1400 CE.

Old World vs. New
The arrival of Europeans in the late 15th century transformed the New World; the diseases they carried killed millions and conversion to Christianity and Westernization erased many indigenous myths. While the damage caused to the Americas by the arrival of European settlers is incalculable, subsequent first-hand interactions with the indigenous peoples meant that, from the 16th century onwards,

many myths were preserved in writing for the first time. They were documented by European writers such as Johannes Wilbert, exploring remote areas which lay undiscovered by the Old World. However, many Native American and First Nations Canadian myths were lost by the end of the 18th century as settlers and new colonies attacked the native cultures and forced them to assimilate to the settlers' way of life.

Methods of storytelling
Native Americans did not generally use written languages until their first contact with white settlers. All branches of American mythology were once preserved by oral tradition, but some Mesoamerican peoples, such as the Maya and Aztecs, developed systems of

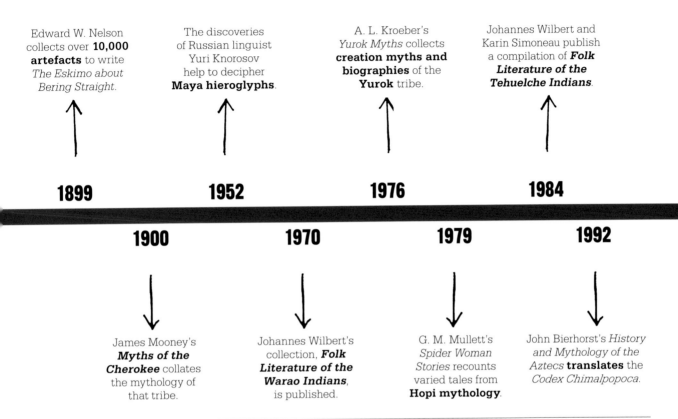

Edward W. Nelson collects over **10,000 artefacts** to write *The Eskimo about Bering Straight*.

The discoveries of Russian linguist Yuri Knorosov help to decipher **Maya hieroglyphs**.

A. L. Kroeber's *Yurok Myths* collects **creation myths and biographies** of the **Yurok** tribe.

Johannes Wilbert and Karin Simoneau publish a compilation of *Folk Literature of the Tehuelche Indians*.

1899 **1952** **1976** **1984**

1900 **1970** **1979** **1992**

James Mooney's **Myths of the Cherokee** collates the mythology of that tribe.

Johannes Wilbert's collection, *Folk Literature of the Warao Indians*, is published.

G. M. Mullett's *Spider Woman Stories* recounts varied tales from **Hopi mythology**.

John Bierhorst's *History and Mythology of the Aztecs* **translates** the *Codex Chimalpopoca*.

hieroglyphs that allowed them to record their myths in collections such as the *Popol Vuh* and the *Codex Chimalpopoca*. Other peoples used different systems to document their tales. The Inca, for example, may have used knotted cords.

Common beginnings

In general, most American peoples believed in a creator deity. Many of the most central myths of the Americas detail how heaven, earth, and all living beings were created. For the Inca, this was Viracocha, who made the cosmos. Kóoch, the Tehuelche sky father, had a similar role. The Aztecs believed the universe was initially brought into being by a dual male-female god called Ometeotl, who also created the first four gods. Another key creator figure was the Earth Mother,

who appeared as a spider in many Native American mythologies and was humanity's teacher.

The hero who helped or taught humanity was a recurring theme in American myths. The Warao people of South America honoured a figure called Haburi who invented the dugout canoe. The Maya "Hero Twins" helped humans by defeating the Lords of the Underworld, saving humans from sacrifice. The Hero Twins also share characteristics with trickster gods. These cunning deities are also popular in North American myths, such as the Raven tales of the Inuit and First Nations peoples.

Understanding the universe

The mythology of the Americas is deeply bound with their indigenous peoples' views on spirituality and

religion. In particular, it shows the deep links between humanity, the natural world, and the cosmos. American myths conceptualize the cosmos in unique ways. The Cherokee creation myth, for example, portrays the world as an island afloat on the sea, held up by cords, while the Warao envisage their world as a land mass entirely encircled by the ocean.

American myths often included the celestial bodies. The rivalry between the sun and moon is a common theme, occurring in several Aztec, Inca, and Tehuelche myths. For the Aztecs in particular, existence was based on a cycle of five suns and eras, each ending in destruction, and human sacrifice was essential to preventing the fall of the fifth and final sun – and with it, the end of the world. ∎

THE EARTH IS A GIANT ISLAND FLOATING IN A SEA OF WATER
CHEROKEE CREATION

IN BRIEF

THEME
Creation of the world

SOURCE
Oral tradition, recorded in
Myths of the Cherokee,
James Mooney, 1900.

SETTING
The beginning of time.

KEY FIGURES
Water Beetle Dâyuni'sï
("Beaver's Grandchild"); the
first creature to create the land
that became the earth.

Buzzard The animal
responsible for the earth's
mountains and valleys.

Tsiska'gïlï The red crawfish.

Brother and Sister The first
humans.

Native American creation myths typically entwine the natural and spiritual worlds, often endowing godlike attributes to animals, the sky, and the earth. Many involve a Great Spirit who creates the world and everything in it. Within these broad similarities, however, tribal myths vary greatly. For the Inuit, living on the edge of the Arctic Ocean, the goddess, Sedna, is a key figure, responsible for creating all marine life. In Iroquois mythology, coming from the northeastern Woodlands, the earth comes into being on the back of a giant sea turtle.

The island

The Cherokee live in the southeast Woodlands. Like the Iroquois tale, the Cherokee creation myth begins with a watery world. Some versions suggest that animals existed before the earth did, when everything was water. They lived high above this, in a spirit realm called Gälûñ'lätï.

The animals looked down on the water and wondered what lay beneath the surface. One of the creatures, Water Beetle, offered to explore, but there was no place to land, so he dove deep under the water. He found some muddy clay and swam up with it, placing it on the water's surface.

The clay spread, forming a large island. Long cords at each of the four cardinal points fastened the earth to the spirit realm in the sky. At some point in the future, when the earth grows too old, the cords will break and the earth will sink back into the water.

From the sky, the animals watched as the island grew. The birds flew down to inspect the new land. It was still soft and muddy, so after waiting a while longer, Buzzard swooped down and flew

The water beetle Dâyuni'sï ("Beaver's Grandchild") carved by the sculptor John Julius Wilnoty (1940–2016), a member of the Eastern Band of Cherokee Indians.

See also: Creation 18–23 ▪ Creation of the world by Pangu 214–15 ▪ San creation myth 284 ▪ The Dreaming 302–07

The Creation Story

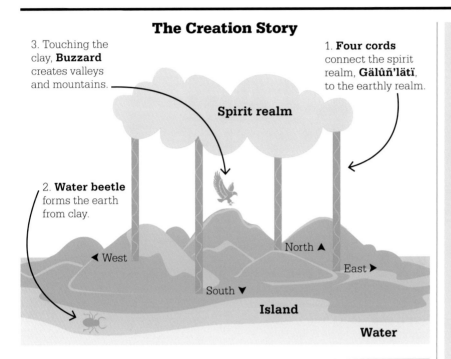

3. Touching the clay, **Buzzard** creates valleys and mountains.

1. **Four cords** connect the spirit realm, **Gälûñ'lätï**, to the earthly realm.

Spirit realm

2. **Water beetle** forms the earth from clay.

◀ West

North ▲

East ▶

South ▼

Island

Water

over the island. Wherever his tired wings brushed the ground, they carved out deep valleys; wherever he flew up again, mountains sprung up. This explains why the Cherokee's traditional homelands contain so many mountains.

Night and day

When the soil was completely dry, the animals descended to earth and found it was very dark. So they took the sun and made it move across the sky from east to west each day. At first, the sun was too close to the earth, and so hot that it burned the crawfish Tsiska'gïlï', turning it red. The Cherokee believe that this spoiled the crawfish's meat, and will not eat it.

The animals moved the sun up, until it was seven handbreadths high, sitting just under the sky arch. After this, the animals and plants tried to stay awake for seven

days and seven nights to keep watch. They had been told to do this by their creator, long before the earth was even made. Those that managed to stay awake were rewarded. This explains why animals such as owls and panthers can see and hunt at night. The cedar, the pine, and other plants also stayed awake, and they were rewarded with the ability to remain green in every season.

Human beings

Man eventually came to live upon the island. The first people were a brother and sister. The brother struck the sister with a fish and told her to bear children. Every seven days after this, the woman gave birth to a child. However, the population grew so rapidly that the world started to become too crowded – from then on, women could only give birth once a year. ■

Anetso

In Cherokee mythology, during the time before the brother and sister came to live on earth, there was a competition between birds and the other animals. The birds turned some small creatures into bats and flying squirrels so they could join the birds in playing against the other animals.

This myth is reflected in the ball game of anetso, which is at the heart of Cherokee tribal identity. The Cherokee have played the game, a precursor of lacrosse, for hundreds of years. Even today, elders retell the story of the mythical first competition to players before a game.

Anetso is a fiercely physical game, where rough tackles are encouraged, but it is also deeply spiritual. A tribal member known as a "conjurer" helps to prepare the athletes with cleansing rituals before and after matches, while other tribal members perform dances and ceremonies.

Because you [deciduous trees] have not endured to the end, you shall lose your hair every winter.
Myths of the Cherokee

WEAVER OF LIFE I AM

SPIDER WOMAN

Many of the southwestern tribes of the United States, such as the Hopi, the Keres, the Choctaw, and the Navajo all share similar creation myths explaining how the first humans came to be. The Hopi creation myth states that in the beginning, all that existed was water. It hung between the realm above – the skies – and the realm below, which would become the earth. Tawa, the Sun Father, controlled everything above, and Spider Woman, the Earth Mother, ruled below.

Creating nature

Spider Woman, also known as "Thinking Woman", or "Spider Grandmother", was a creator goddess, said to be as old as time, yet as young as eternity. To the Navajo, Spider Woman is also a teacher who gave the sacred art of weaving to humanity. The Hopi refer to the creator goddess as *Kokyangwuti* in their language, but

Spider Rock is a 250-metre (830-ft) stone spire formed 230 million years ago in Canyon de Chelly, Arizona. It is traditionally regarded as the lair of Spider Woman.

also revere the Spider Grandmother as *Gogyeng Sowuhti*, a spirit of wisdom and medicine. She dwells in the Underworld, which the Hopi see as a place from which all life is born and must emerge.

Creating nature

According to the Hopi, Tawa and the Earth Mother worked together to create the world. Gazing at the

See also: Cherokee creation 236–37 ▪ The Woge settle a dispute 240–41 ▪ The raven and the whale 242–43

Spider Woman carries a cross, symbolizing fire, on this Mississipian shell disc (c.1000 CE). The Choctaw believe fire was gifted to humans by Spider Woman after animals refused it.

empty sky, Spider Woman spun a huge web, laced it with dew, and threw it out into the sky, creating stars above. Then Tawa and Spider Woman decided to populate the earth with animals.

Tawa dreamed of birds flying and fish swimming in the waters, and Spider Woman formed these animals one by one out of clay.

They lay still until she covered them in a blanket she had woven. As she murmured over them, the creatures stirred, and Spider Woman gave each a spirit.

Tawa and Spider Woman then decided to create humans to care for the animals. Again, Spider Woman fashioned these new beings from clay, and she and Tawa laid the blanket over them. This time, however, they did not move, so, gathering them in her arms, she and Tawa sang until the humans came to life. Tawa would bring light to shine upon them each day and rain would fall. The Sun Father and the Earth Mother now decided that they had fulfilled their roles and would not create any more beings, instead allowing them to multiply.

Parting guidance

Spider Woman divided the growing people into tribes, giving them their names and languages. The Hopi, Zuni, Ute, Comanche, and Pueblo people were led from the Underworld by Spider Woman.

Together the first gods placed a sacred blanket over the new beings and chanted the song of life. The beings stirred into life.
A Dictionary of Creation Myths

When they reached the surface, Spider Woman showed her people the power of the soil, running it through her hands and teaching them about growing food. She said that crops would flourish in their lands because Tawa would shine his light and rain would fall. Spider Woman then returned to the Underworld, promising the people that she and Tawa would always watch over their creations. ▪

Navajo weaving

While many historians believe that the Navajo learned the art of weaving from the Pueblos, Navajo mythology teaches that Spider Woman brought spinning and weaving to the tribe, sharing her knowledge with the people. According to the Navajo, Spider Woman's son made the first spindles from lightning and the first loom from the sun, sky, and earth.

Weaving blankets and rugs remains a valuable source of income for the Navajo, but it is also central to their holistic spirituality, which makes no distinction between art and daily life. Through example and their stories, elders still teach this worldview today.

Young weavers hear the myth of the art's origins at the same time as they begin to learn the process. Before they start, elders instruct them to find a spider web in the early morning, still sparkling with dew, and to place their palm on the web without destroying it. In this way, their spirits can receive Spider Woman's sacred gift of weaving.

BEGIN A DEERSKIN DANCE FOR IT BECAUSE EVERYTHING WILL COME OUT WELL FROM THAT
THE WOGE SETTLE A DISPUTE

IN BRIEF

THEME
Bringing balance to the world

SOURCES
Oral tradition transcribed in *World Renewal: A Cult System of Native Northwest California*, A L Kroeber and E W Gifford, 1949.

SETTING
Northwestern California in the time of the Woge.

KEY FIGURES
Woge The first people of the Yurok tribe; ancient beings who lived along the Klamath River.

Kepel Ancestors of the Yurok tribe; upstream from the Turip villagers.

Turip A tribe living downstream from the Kepel.

Central to the culture of the Yurok and other Native Americans are traditional ceremonies that feature sacred dances. Among the most important is the Deerskin Dance (deer were a crucial food source), which is still performed during World Renewal rituals to safeguard the earth. In Yurok mythology, the dance is also specifically associated with the building of a salmon dam. The account of the dance's origins was told to the US anthropologist Alfred L. Kroeber in the early 1900s by Jim, a Yurok from Pekwan in present-day Humboldt County.

In the time of the Woge – the ancient spirit beings that the Yurok considered to be the First People –

A Hupa man stands spear in hand ready to fish in an image from 1923 by Edward S. Curtis. At this time salmon were important for survival in the areas where tribes had rights to fish.

See also: Cherokee creation 236–37 ▪ Spider Woman 238–39 ▪ Raven and the whale 242–43 ▪ The first canoe 258–59

Spiritual leaders

Men and women who take on the role of spiritual leader in Native American communities, still command great respect. Although many tribes no longer use the word "shaman", such leaders are said to receive power and knowledge, primarily through dreams, from ancestral prehuman spirits who departed or transformed themselves into animals, trees, rocks, and plants when humans arrived. Many of today's leaders are healers, using their spiritual powers and natural medicine to treat sickness. In the past, they were often called upon to predict the future, or to bring good fishing or hunting.

Traditionally, spiritual leaders of northwestern California play a key role in the annual World Renewal ceremonies. To prepare, the leaders go to nearby hills to fast and pray, and call upon the healing powers of their ancestral spirits. During the ritual, wearing masks and regalia, they perform healing rites and take part in the sacred dances.

Traditionally, Yurok and Hupa shamans were women who received their calling in dreams. This Hupa shaman was photographed in 1923.

large salmon no longer swam up River Klamath to where the Kepel people lived. They could only catch small fish and became upset as the salmon were their staple food. The cause was a dam erected near the mouth of the river by the people of Turip; the mature fish coming from the ocean to spawn upriver could not swim beyond that point.

One Kepel man decided they should remove the dam and take it to their village. With help from his people, he pulled it from the river and carried it off. The people of Turip were angered by the loss of their dam. They wanted it back and set off towards Kepel to try and regain it.

A peaceful settlement

As the Turip people approached, their chief saw the many Kepel villagers at work installing their new dam. Fearing that his people might be killed if they attacked, he decided not to fight the Kepel people. As they stood on the hillside overlooking the dam, he told his men, "We had better give it up and let them keep it. We will take care of this dam also; we shall visit now and then to see it."

The Kepel man who had taken the Turip dam then announced that it would stay at his village and declared that a Deerskin Dance should begin "because everything will come out well from that". He called on the people to dance and to rebuild the dam every year, warning that "much sickness" would result if they failed to do so.

Watchful spirits

Then the Woge, who approved of the dam, began to leave the Kepel villagers to find places from where they could watch over all of the people. At each place they vowed to create a Deerskin Dance to bring good fortune, and the people at each of these new sites were happy; upriver at Olar, for instance, they said: "When it is bad in the world, it will become well again when they dance here."

Some Woge stayed close to Kepel, going up into 10 small hills overlooking the village to watch out for the smoke from villagers' fires indicating that, as promised, they had come together at Klamath River to remake the salmon dam.

Every year, the Yurok re-enacted the dam-building in autumn at the peak of the salmon season. This ritual culminated in the Deerskin Dance, performed by men bearing poles hung with deerskins, followed by a Jump Dance. The event, which Kroeber saw and described, continued into the 20th century. ▪

Very well, keep it well. Hold to it as long as they make the Deerskin Dance, because it will be good for the people.
World Renewal

SHE WAS THE SHADE OF THE WHALE

THE RAVEN AND THE WHALE

For the Inuit in Alaska and other parts of the western Arctic region, Raven was a powerful creator god. He created the world, bringing light, man, and animals into being. At the same time, Raven was a trickster and a shape-shifter, concealing his human form inside a bird's body. This is a common characteristic of other animal heroes in Native American myth.

Inuit stories involving Raven and the whale explored the dual nature of Raven's transformation: he changed his shape, but also learned from the disasters that befell him. In many retellings of the story, the trickster hero was entirely manipulative and self-serving, while other adaptations allowed Raven to redeem himself through healing dances and songs. Central to each story, however, was the sacred sacrifice of the whale, and the honouring of its *inua*, or soul.

Raven sees the whale

According to one Inuit myth, Raven gazed out at sea from the shore, admiring the world he had created. In the wide expanse of blue, he spied a large, graceful shape moving through the water. Curious, Raven flew closer and realized it was a whale. He had never seen the inside of this mammoth creature and commanded the great beast to open its mouth. When the whale obeyed, Raven flew inside, carrying his fire drill as he always did.

He found himself in a room, beautifully lit by a lamp at one end and guarded by a young woman.

The Inuit carved masks, such as this 19th-century stylized raven, to wear at ritual dances. Animal masks were popular, but masks could also represent people or characteristics.

See also: Cherokee creation 236–37 ▪ Spider Woman 238–39 ▪ The Woge settle a dispute 240–41 ▪ The Hero Twins 244–47

> The raven raised one of its wings, pushed up its beak, like a mask, to the top of its head, and changed at once into a man.
> **The Eskimo about Bering Strait**

Raven recognized the woman as the whale's *inua*, its heart and soul. The woman told Raven to stand back from the lamp. He did as she asked but noticed that oil dripped into the lamp from a tube running along the whale's backbone.

Tempted by the oil

The *inua* offered to fetch berries and oil for her guest. Before she left the room, she warned Raven not to

Carved from wood, this mask takes the form of a whale, but also resembles a canoe with oars. It may have been worn during Inuit ceremonies to ensure a successful hunt.

touch the tube from which the oil was dripping while she was out of the room. The same thing happened the next day, and the day after that. Each time the woman fetched food for Raven, she warned him not to touch the oil.

For three days, Raven was patient, but on the fourth day, he could not contain his greed. As soon as the woman had left the room, Raven clawed at the tube and licked the oil as fast as he could. When he ripped the tube from the ceiling to make the oil flow faster the oil gushed out, flooded the whale's belly, and extinguished the lamp, plunging the room into total darkness.

The *inua* never returned. Raven rolled around inside the whale as it thrashed about in the ocean. The great animal only became still as the waves washed its dead body

to the shore. As soon as the people heard about the whale, they ran to the shore to cut away the meat, and Raven escaped unnoticed. He returned as a man and warned the people that if they found a fire drill inside the whale they would die.

The people ran away in fright while Raven, who transformed back into a bird once more, gave thanks to the whale's *inua* for the feast he was about to enjoy. ▪

The sacred whale hunt

The whale hunt is an ancient Inuit practice, central to the Artic people's survival and beliefs, a version of which continues today. Whaling communities prepared for the annual hunt by making new clothes and boat covers. Hunters performed cleansing ceremonies, and armed themselves with specially carved amulets and

Inuit people traditionally hunted narwhals and other whales, sea otters and seals. They also fished for salmon through holes in the ice.

weapons. These rituals showed great respect to the whale and its spirit, and represented deeply held beliefs that the hunters' success depended on securing the spirit's cooperation.

After the hunt, the Inuit welcomed the dead whale with a gift of fresh water presented in a ceremonial bucket. They sang songs to celebrate the whale's sacrifice. Honouring the whale in this way ensured success the following year, for the whale's spirit would return to the sea to tell other whales that it had been well treated.

AND THE SUN BELONGS TO ONE AND THE MOON TO THE OTHER

THE HERO TWINS

IN BRIEF

THEME
Sacrifice and rebirth

SOURCES
Popol Vuh, Anonymous, mid-16th century.

SETTING
Earth; Xibalba (The Maya Underworld), at the beginning of time.

KEY FIGURES
Hun-Hunahpu Father of the Hero Twins.

Xquic Moon goddess; mother of the Hero Twins.

Hunahpu and Xbalanque The Hero Twins; sons of Hun-Hunahpu and Xquic.

Vucub-Caquix Macaw god; father of Zipacana and Cabrakan.

Hun-Came and Vucub-Came The two highest death gods of the Underworld.

un-Hunahpu and Vucub-Hunahpu were the twin sons of the divine matchmaker Xpiacoc and the midwife goddess Xmucane. Hun-Hunahpu's wife was a deity called Xbaquiyalo, and together they had twins: Hun-Chowen and Hun-Batz. The twins' boisterous ball-playing attracted the ire of the Lords of Xibalba; a deadly Underworld of disease and decay.

The Lords lured the twins to the Underworld to play the ball game against them. Before the game could take place, however, the twins were subjected to a series of challenges. When they failed, they were sacrificed and buried

See also: The adventures of Thor and Loki in Jötunheim 146–47 ▪ The epic of Gilgamesh 190–97 ▪ The legend of the five suns 248–55

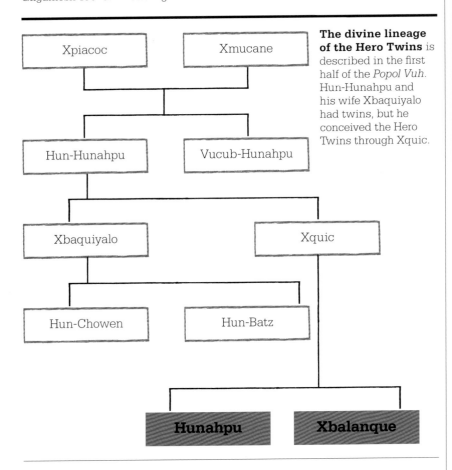

The divine lineage of the Hero Twins is described in the first half of the *Popol Vuh*. Hun-Hunahpu and his wife Xbaquiyalo had twins, but he conceived the Hero Twins through Xquic.

beneath the ball court in the Underworld. Hun-Hunahpu was decapitated and his head hung from a calabash tree as a warning to those who might cross them. Even after death, he retained his potency. His spittle dripped into the hand of a moon goddess Xquic and impregnated her.

Xquic, fleeing her angry father in the Underworld, sought refuge with Hun-Hunahpu's mother on earth. Xmucane accepted her »

Xquic picks Hun-Hunahpu's head from the forbidden tree, mistaking it for a gourd, in this illustration by Gilbert James for *The Myths of Mexico and Peru* by Lewis Spence (1913).

The Popol Vuh

The *Popol Vuh* provides the fullest account of many key Maya myths, and is perhaps the most important sacred Mesoamerican document still in existence. It is divided into three parts: the first concerns the world's creation, the second focuses on the tale of Hunahpu and Xblanque, and the third depicts the founding of the Quiché dynasty.

Drawing on centuries of oral tradition, the *Popol Vuh* was originally written in Maya hieroglyphs from 1554–58. It was consulted whenever the Lords of the Quiché gathered in council (*Popol Vuh* means "Book of Counsel"). After the Spanish arrived in the early 16th century, they burned Maya hieroglyphic books, but the *Popol Vuh* survived, and was secretly transcribed into Quiché, a Maya language, using the Roman alphabet.

A copy of the transcribed document found its way to Chichicastenango, a town in the Guatemalan highlands. From 1701 to 1703, the parish priest, Francisco Ximénez, translated the text in parallel Quiché and Spanish columns. His manuscript remains the oldest surviving written account of the *Popol Vuh*.

Wall hieroglyphics from Quiché appear as illustrations in Ximénez's *Popol Vuh* manuscript. Extracts are kept in the Rossbach Archaeological Museum in Guatemala.

The Hero Twins play against the lords of the Underworld, in a stone relief from the South Ballcourt in the ancient city of El Tajin, Mexico.

into her household. Xquic gave birth to Hunahpu and Xbalanque, who grew up to be the Hero Twins.

Young cunning

The Hero Twins' older half brothers, Hun-Chowen and Hun-Batz, worried that the new arrivals would overshadow them, and tried to kill them. They forced Hunahpu and Xbalanque to hunt for them, but the twins used this slight to get the better of them. They told Hun-Chowen and Hun-Batz that some birds they had shot were caught in high branches and had not fallen down. When Hun-Chowen and Hun-Batz climbed up to get them, the tree grew so tall that they were unable to descend. Marooned there, they turned into monkeys, but were

so embarrassed by their new appearance that they ran away from home.

Taming unruly gods

The storm god Huracan asked the Hero Twins to defeat the boastful macaw god Vucub-Caquix, who claimed that his metal nose was the moon and his shiny nest, the sun. The Hero Twins approached him while he was feeding in a tree and shot him with a blowgun. He got away, so the Hero Twins turned to trickery. They persuaded two elderly gods, Great White Peccary and Great White Coati, to approach Vucub-Caquix posing as healers. The macaw god accepted their help, but they pulled out his ornaments and replaced his eyes with corn kernels. Robbed of his splendour, he perished.

Huracan then requested that the Hero Twins dispatch Vucub-Caquix's equally boastful sons:

Zipacna, a demon crocodile monster, and Cabrakan, the earthquake god. Zipacna had earlier killed the Four Hundred Boys, who were the gods of alcohol. Hunahpu and Xbalanque made a fake crab out of flowers and a rock and placed it in a narrow space

Afterwards you will come back to life again … did you not bring us here in order that we should entertain you, the lords, your sons, and your vassals?
Popol Vuh

beneath an over-hanging mountain. Zipacana crawled into the crevice. When he tried to grab it, the Twins brought the mountain down on him, turning him into stone.

Zipacna's brother Cabrakan, the earthquake god, prided himself on bringing down mountains. The Hero Twins told him that they knew of a perpetually growing mountain. Cabrakan demanded to be shown it so he could destroy it. As he followed the Hero Twins, he grew hungry. They fed him a roasted bird they had enchanted. When he ate it, he grew weak, and the Hero Twins tied him up and buried him. Now, he held up mountains rather than destroying them.

Final match

One day, as the Hero Twins played ball, their noisy playing once again disturbed the lords of the Underworld, who summoned Hunahpu and Xbalanque to another game in the Underworld.

The lords of the Underworld won the first match, and the Hero Twins had to spend a night in Razor House, which was full of sharp stone knives that moved of their own accord. The Hero Twins survived by persuading the blades to stop moving. They survived the drafts and hail of the Cold House, the beasts of Jaguar House, and the flames of Fire House. Their final trial was Bat House. Disaster struck when a bat swooped down and beheaded Hunahpu. Xbalanque made a new head for his brother using a squash, or gourd, and the Hero Twins resumed playing, using Hunahpu's head as a ball. The Hero Twins distracted their opponents, reattached Hunahpu's head, and won the match.

Furious at their defeat, the lords of the Underworld plotted to kill Hunahpu and Xbalanque by burning them in a stone pit. The Hero Twins had been informed of this plan, and willingly jumped into the flames. Their bones were ground down into powder and dumped into a river. After five days, they were reborn as catfish and then took human form. The Hero Twins wandered the Underworld as anonymous vagabonds and won great fame as wizards. The lords of the Underworld summoned them to perform, not knowing they were the Hero Twins.

In their show, Xbalanque seemed to sacrifice Hunahpu, rolling his decapitated head along the floor, removing his heart, and then bringing him back to life. When Hun-Came and Vucub-Came demanded the trick be done on them, Xbalanque and Hunahpu promptly sacrificed them. Revealing their true identity as the Hero Twins, they refused to resurrect their victims. From then on, they declared, there would be no more human sacrifices to the Lords of the Underworld. The Hero Twins then ascended into the heavens; Xbalanque became the sun and Hunahpu the moon. This brought the cosmos to its present order. ∎

The Mesoamerican ballgame was a ritual sport dating back to the 2nd millennium BCE. Sculptural reliefs at ballcourts after c. 800 CE indicate the sport may have included human sacrifice. The courts, which were around 60 meters (197 ft) long, and included two goal rings that players strove to get a heavy rubber ball through.

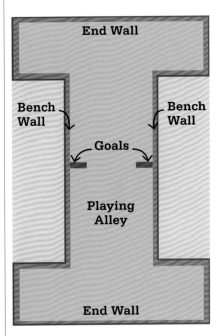

Goal sideview

End Wall

Bench Wall

Bench Wall

Goals

Playing Alley

End Wall

Interpreting the Hero Twins

Some scholars have challenged the interpretation of Hunahpu becoming the moon. This is because the Maya generally view the moon as feminine. As such, it is suggested that Hunahpu actually became Venus, the morning star.

Another tradition sees the Hero Twins as representing different phases of the sun; Hunahpu symbolizing the day and Xbalanque, the night. There is even a theory that proposes that Hunahpu only represents the full moon, and that his mother Xquic accounts for its other phases. Other interpretations paint the myth as an exploration of the possibility of rebirth through the rite of sacrifice.

Many of these uncertainties stem from the *Popol Vuh* itself. Even though it draws on an ancient myth, the original Mayan text was composed decades after the arrival of the Spanish, which may have led to inconsistencies in its content.

SO THEN THE SUN WENT INTO THE SKY

THE LEGEND OF THE FIVE SUNS

IN BRIEF

THEME
The cycles of creation

SOURCE
"The Legend of the Suns",
Codex Chimalpopoca,
Anonymous, 1558; *History and
Mythology of the Aztecs*, John
Bierhorst, 1992.

SETTING
The beginning of time.

KEY FIGURES
Ometeotl Creator deity.

**Tezcatlipoca, Quetzalcoatl,
Xipetotec, Huitzilopochtli**
First-generation gods.

Tlaloc God of fertility and rain.

Chalchiuhtlicue Second wife
of Tlaloc.

Tlaltecuhtli Sea monster.

Mictlantecuhtli Lord of
the dead in the Underworld.

Tonatiuh, Fifth Sun Sickly
god Nanahuatzin, transformed.

I n Aztec mythology the present
world was not the first to exist;
it was preceded by four others.
Each world began with the creation
of a new sun and ended with its
destruction. Our world, therefore,
is the Fifth Sun.

Before the creation there was
Ometeotl, who resided on the
highest level of heaven. The deity,
whose name means "dual cosmic
energy", was both male and female.
Ometeotl gave birth to the first
generation of gods: Tezcatlipoca,
Quetzalcoatl, Xipetotec, and
Huitzilopochtli. These four gods
created all of the other deities, then
made the world and its flora and
fauna. To give light to this world,
Tezcatlipoca ("smoking mirror")
was chosen to be the First Sun. At
this time, a primitive race of giants,
who subsisted only on roots and
acorns, peopled the Earth.

The relationship between
Quetzalcoatl (the "feathered
serpent") and Tezcatlipoca became
the driving force of creation. The
two gods had markedly different
characteristics. Quetzalcoatl was
associated with harmony, balance,
and learning. Tezcatlipoca was a
force of destruction, conflict, and

> Here are wisdom tales made
> long ago, of how the earth was
> established, how everything
> was established … how all the
> suns that there were began.
> **History and Mythology
> of the Aztecs**

change. Yet Quetzalcoatl, jealous
that Tezcatlipoca had been chosen
to be the First Sun, knocked him
down from the heavens into the
sea. Tezcatlipoca rose from the
water in the form of a giant jaguar.
In his fury he ordered the jaguars of
the world to devour the race of
giants. The earth was plunged into
darkness. After 676 years, the age
of the First Sun was over.

Another race of people was
created. Quetzalcoatl became the
Second Sun. This world lasted only
364 years. Tezcatlipoca ended it

The Aztec Empire

The Aztecs arrived in central
Mexico from the north around
1250 CE and settled in marshy
swampland. According to
legend, they chose the site of
their capital – an island in Lake
Texcoco where Mexico City now
stands – after seeing an eagle
eating a snake on a cactus. They
founded the city in 1325 and
named it Tenochtitlán ("Place
of the cactus fruit"). To protect
themselves, Aztec rulers made
marriage alliances with other
city-states. Acamapichtli, the

product of one such union,
founded the Aztec imperial
dynasty in 1376. In 1428, the
emperor Itzcoatl allied with two
other city-states in the Aztec
Triple Alliance and led the
conquest of other neighbouring
city-states. Tenochtitlán became
the capital of a vast Aztec
Empire and was one of the
world's largest cities when the
Spanish conquistadors arrived
in 1519. However, the Aztecs
could not withstand European
weapons and the diseases the
Spanish brought, and the empire
was overthrown in 1521.

See also: The epic of Gilgamesh 190–97 ▪ Cherokee creation 236–37 ▪ Spider Woman 238–39

by avenging his earlier slight, striking down Quetzalcoatl, and creating a great hurricane that swept all the people away.

Drought and floods

As Quetzalcoatl and Tezcatlipoca had selfishly brought disorder to creation through their rivalry, the other gods decided that someone else should have the honour of being the new sun. The Third Sun was the rain god Tlaloc. He was married to Xochiquetzal, goddess of beauty. Their union ended when Tezcatlipoca kidnapped and seduced Xochiquetzal. Mourning his beloved wife, the grief-stricken god refused to send down rain to nourish the earth and the world became parched. The people continuously beseeched him to end the drought but to no avail. Tired of their appeals, Tlaloc instead sent down torrents of fire that turned the

Quetzalcoatl and Tezcatlipoca lock in combat in an image from the *Codex Borbonicus* (c.16th century). Aztec scribes painted with pigments derived from plants, trees, rocks, and insects.

Five Suns

Tezcatlipoca – 676 years

↓

Quetzalcoatl – 364 years

↓

Tlaloc – 312 years

↓

Chalchiuhtlicue – 676 years

↓

Tonatiuh – Aztec era

world to ash. The Third Sun was the shortest lived of all, existing only for 312 years.

When Tlaloc remarried, taking Chalchiuhtlicue, the goddess of streams and still waters, as his wife, Quetzalcoatl allied himself with her, and she became the Fourth Sun. Tezcatlipoca, however, again helped to bring an end to this world. He told Chalchiuhtlicue she did not sincerely love the people of this fourth world, but was only benevolent because she wanted their praise.

Chalchiuhtlicue cried so hard that her tears created a great deluge that flooded the world and lasted for 52 years. All but two people were turned to fish. The couple who survived were called Tata and Nene. They floated on a hollow log and subsisted on just a single ear of maize each, which

was supplied by Tezcatlipoca on the condition that they ate nothing else. As the flood waters subsided, Tata and Nene caught a fish and roasted it, defying Tezcatlipoca's instructions. When the god found out, he turned them into dogs. The Fourth Sun had lasted 676 years.

United against the enemy

Realizing now that their disputes had caused only destruction, Quetzalcoatl and Tezcatlipoca began to work together. A vicious sea monster called Tlaltecuhtli had taken up residence in the oceans. Its body was covered with multiple mouths to satisfy its relentless »

The Aztecs used a dual calendar – a solar calendar of 365 days for agriculture and a sacred ritual calendar of 260 days. The latter is grouped into 20 equal periods for 20 deities, each lord of its own domain, encircling the sun god, Tonatiuh.

the Earth. First he had to seek permission from Mictlantecuhtli, lord of the Underworld. When Quetzalcoatl requested the bones, Mictlantecuhtli said he would hand them over if Quetzalcoatl walked around him four times while blowing a conch-shell trumpet. It was a trick. The conch Quetzalcoatl was given had no holes to blow through. Undeterred, the god accomplished the task by using worms to eat holes in the side of the shell and placing bees inside it to make it hum. Quetzalcoatl is often depicted with a conch shell on his chest.

His plot foiled, Mictlantecuhtli handed over the bones, but then sent servants ahead of Quetzalcoatl to dig a hole to trap him. On his way back to earth with the bones, the god stumbled into the pit. He clambered out, but in the fall the bones broke into pieces.

Quetzalcoatl sought the help of the fertility goddess Cihuacoatl, who ground down the bones and poured the dust into her cauldron. The gods then gathered round and pierced their bodies, letting their blood flow into the bonemeal. From this mixture, they created the

appetite. To defeat this formidable foe, Quetzalcoatl and Tezcatlipoca took the form of serpents, and Tezcatlipoca used part of his body as bait to try to catch Tlaltecuhtli. When the monster surfaced, Quetzalcoatl and Tezcatlipoca seized it and ripped it in two. Half was thrown upwards to create the sky and stars; the other half floated in the ocean and became the earth. In the fight, Tezcatlipoca lost his right foot; he is often depicted with a piece of obsidian in its place.

Taking the earthly body of Tlaltecuhtli – still living even after its violent division – Xipetotec

and Huitzilopochtli transformed it into elements that could sustain human beings in the future. The monster's hair became trees and grasses, its skin was turned into plants, its nose into hills and valleys, its eyes and sockets into wells and caves, and its shoulders into mountains. Tlaltecuhtli's voraciousness still remained, and he demanded human blood as a form of sacrifice.

Recreating humans

Quetzalcoatl decided to journey to the Underworld to gather the bones of previous generations of humans and create a new race to repopulate

"Gods, what will [the human race] eat? Let food be looked for." Then the ant went and got a kernal of corn …
History and Mythology of the Aztecs

present race of humans, whose first woman and man were called Oxomoco and Cipactonal.

Feeding the new world

The newly created human race needed food. Quetzalcoatl spotted a red ant carrying a maize kernel. He followed it until it disappeared into a crack in a mountain – Mount Popocatépetl, the mountain of sustenance. Quetzalcoatl was so curious about what lay within that he transformed himself into a black ant and crawled through the narrow opening. There he found a chamber filled with seeds and grain.

It was clear to Quetzalcoatl that this mountain had the potential to feed humans if they could only get inside it. The god tried to lift it with ropes but was unable to break it open. He asked Oxomoco and Cipactonal, who had the ability to divine the future, what to do. They told him that Nanahuatzin – a humble and sickly god, whose name meant "full of sores" – was destined to help him. Nanahuatzin was duly called forth to the food mountain. There, with the help of rain and lightning gods, he split it open. The contents were then

Mictlantecuhtli, the god of the dead and ruler of the Underworld, was often depicted as a skeleton. To placate him, the Aztecs are said to have practised both human sacrifice and cannibalism.

scattered across the world, providing nourishment for the human race.

The quest for happiness

The gods were happy that the humans had food, which gave them the strength to work, but Quetzalcoatl noticed that their lives were joyless. He decided that humans needed something that would bring them excitement and happiness, and make them dance and sing. He went on a journey across the heavens to find a solution and met a beautiful goddess called Mayahuel. They fell madly in love. To show their deep affection for each other, they came down to earth and transformed themselves into a single tree, each becoming one of its two branches.

Mayahuel's grandmother was one of the Tzitzimimeh, a nocturnal group of skeletal fertility goddesses. Furious that her granddaughter had run off with Quetzalcoatl, the

goddess descended with the other Tzitzimimeh from their celestial home to earth to find Mayahuel. When they discovered the tree »

Women and children, as well as conquered warriors, were among the victims sacrificed by the Aztecs to propitiate the gods.

Blood and sacrifice

Sacrifice was the central feature of Aztec religion, as it was how man repaid the gods for their actions. The letting of blood was an important act that Aztec priests often carried out on themselves. They drew blood by stabbing themselves with thorns or stingray spines in the cheeks, arms, legs, and even penis.

The Aztecs also practiced human sacrifice in order to appease the gods – both of their own people, and enemy prisoners of war. The most common method of sacrifice was to pull out the victim's heart. The process was carried out on an altar at the top of a temple, where the victim was held down by four men while a specially trained priest plunged a flint knife into the ribs, allowing the heart to be extracted. In each 18-month "cycle", Aztec priests would sacrifice one person in this manner each month, killing thousands of people each year. The Aztecs also sacrificed people through gladiatorial combat, drowning, decapitation, burning, and burying alive.

they swept down on it and split it asunder. The Tzitzimimeh fell on Mayahuel, tearing her apart. Quetzalcoatl, who survived the attack, was heartbroken. He gathered together Mayahuel's scattered remains and buried them, weeping on the ground. From this grief sprang forth the maguey plant – the source of the joyous drink Quetzalcoatl had set out to find. Its sap could be used to make *pulque*, a thick, milk-coloured, alcoholic drink. The Aztecs and other Mesoamerican people considered pulque to be a sacred beverage, and it was drunk ritually during sacred ceremonies.

The Fifth Sun

The world was still in darkness. A council of gods gathered in the city of Teotihuacán to determine who would become the Fifth Sun and provide light for humanity. Whoever was chosen would have to sacrifice themselves by jumping into a huge fire from a high platform constructed above it. The first contender was the haughty and rich god Tecciztecatl, a son of Tlaloc and Chalchiuhtlicue. The poor and sickly Nanahuatzin also volunteered for the honour, albeit reluctantly. Before the gods chose, the two contenders had to

But [the Fifth Sun] spent four days without moving, just staying in place.
History and Mythology of the Aztecs

Tonatiuh, the last sun god, receives blood from a bird in a painting from the *Codex Borgia* (c.1450). The image also depicts the 13 holy birds, Quecholli, representing the 13 divine Aztec lords.

fast and purify themselves by ritually shedding blood. Tecciztecatl ostentatiously burned costly incense. When the time came to let his own blood, he lay down on feathers instead of the customary branches of the fir tree and pulled jade spines from a gold ball to prick his skin. In contrast, Nanahuatzin used the thorns of the maguey plant to draw out his blood, and because he could not afford incense he burned scabs from his own body.

The other gods built up the fire as Nanahuatzin and Tecciztecatl made their preparations. After four days of rituals, the decisive moment arrived. First to prove himself was Tecciztecatl. The arrogant god mounted the platform but, gripped by fear, could not bring himself to leap into the flames. Nanahuatzin, however, showed no hesitation. He

jumped off the platform and plunged into the fire and was incinerated. Shamed, Tecciztecatl quickly followed suit.

The flames died down. Suddenly, Nanahuatzin burst into the skies and became the Fifth Sun, which brought light to the world again. His new name was Tonatiuh. Soon afterwards, Tecciztecatl also soared into the skies. There were now two suns at the same time. This was not what the gods had envisaged – the cowardice of Tecciztecatl had shown that he was not worthy of being a new sun. Papaztac, the god of the sacred drink pulque, threw a rabbit at Tecciztecatl's face. It dimmed his light, ensuring he would never shine as brightly as a sun. He became Metztli the Moon, which still bears the imprint of a rabbit.

Sacrifice of the gods

Tonatiuh, the Fifth Sun, hung motionless in the sky for four days. The gods begged him to move, but he refused to do so until he had received a blood sacrifice. At this, Tlahuizcalpantecuhtli, god of the planet Venus, grew angry and launched a dart at the Sun using an *atlatl* (an Aztec tool that increased the velocity of projectiles). The dart missed. Tonatiuh threw a dart back at Tlahuizcalpantecuhtli and it pierced his head, turning him into the god Itztlacoliuhqui, who spread frost with the dawn. The gods realized they had to make an offering to persuade Tonatiuh to move. Numerous gods offered themselves to Quetzalcoatl, and he removed their hearts with a sacred knife. Their blood ensured that the Fifth Sun moved through the heavens. The gods had sacrificed themselves to help mankind.

The Aztecs believed this sacrifice by the gods was key to the survival of all humanity. Aztec warriors had a responsibility to capture enemies to sacrifice to Tonatiuh; they thought that if they ceased to replicate the gods' blood offerings, the world would end with a series of earthquakes. Only acts of sacrifice could ensure that the Fifth Sun kept moving across the sky and that the world continued to exist. ∎

Teotihuacán

The city of Teotihuacán was a place of pilgrimage for the Aztecs, who admired its magnificent ruins and thought it the cradle of civilization. Teotihuacán ("the place where gods are created") is the Aztec word for the city; its original name is lost to us. The city lay 48 km (30 miles) northeast of their capital Tenochtitlán and had been built between the 1st and 7th centuries CE. At its peak in the mid-5th century, it was probably the largest city in pre-Columbian America. Its major thoroughfare – the Avenue of the Dead – was flanked with civic buildings, temples, and tombs.

The city's most impressive feature was its immense Pyramid of the Sun, and there was also a slightly smaller Pyramid of the Moon. Both structures are mentioned in the Fifth Sun myth, as the "hills" raised by the gods where, before their ordeal, Tecciztecatl and Nanahuatzin purified themselves.

At the heart of Teotihuacán is the citadel, a large courtyard where a third pyramid was built c.200 CE. When the great seven-tiered Temple of Quetzalcoatl was completed, more than 200 people from outside the city were then sacrificed there, including 36 young warriors.

Leaders of Aztec Religion

The Aztec Emperor was the gods' representative and the high priest of Tenochtitlán.

The High Priest of the god Huitzilopochtli served as joint head of all priests in the capital Tenochtitlán.

The High Priest of Tlaloc shared the leadership, directing lower orders serving in the community.

Priestesses served in the temples. Priestesses, who cut their hair to signify chastity, often cleaned or lit the fires.

Every temple and every god had its own priestly order.

Priests took charge of rituals and ceremonies. They also taught novice priests.

IN THE BEGINNING, AND BEFORE THIS WORLD WAS CREATED, THERE WAS A BEING CALLED VIRACOCHA
VIRACOCHA THE CREATOR

IN BRIEF

THEME
Creation of the world

SOURCE
The History of the Incas, Pedro
Sarmiento de Gamboa, 1572;
*An Account of the Fables and
Rites of the Incas*, Cristóbal de
Molina, c.1575.

SETTING
The Andes, the beginning
of time.

KEY FIGURE
Viracocha The creator god;
god of the sun, and storms.

Ymaymana Servant of
Viracocha.

Tocapo Servant of Viracocha.

Lying over 3,800m (12,500ft) above sea level in the Andes mountains, Lake Titicaca straddles the border between Bolivia and Peru. It is the largest lake in South America, and the Inca people viewed its vast waters as the font of all life.

The lake existed in the darkness before all things, and from it the creator god Viracocha emerged. In the darkness, Viracocha made a race of giants to populate the void. Realizing they were too large, he destroyed them, and created the human race instead. Viracocha demanded that people should live without pride or greed, but they disobeyed him. Angered, he sent a great flood, which swept his creations away.

Teaching humanity
After the land had dried, Viracocha started again from scratch. First he brought light to a dark world. In the southern part of Lake Titicaca lies the Island of the Sun. Sleeping on this island were the sun, the moon, and the stars. Viracocha roused them from their slumbers and gave them their places in the heavens. The sun was jealous of the moon's brightness, so Viracocha threw ashes over the moon's face to make it cloudy and dull.

He then enlisted the help of two servants whom he had saved from the flood – Ymaymana and Tocapo – who, in other versions of the story, were his sons. Aided by them, Viracocha gathered clay

Viracocha the creator god is depicted with his signature white hair and beard in this pottery from the Moche people, who lived in northern Peru from the 1st–7th century CE.

See also: Izanagi and Izanami 220–21 ▪ The legend of the five suns 248–55 ▪ Makemake and Haua 324–25

Lake Titicaca is home to dozens of populated islands, including Isla del Sol, where Viracocha is believed to have commanded the sun to rise.

from the shores of Lake Titicaca and used it to make mankind and all of the animals. He assigned each animal its place, and gave the birds their songs.

Viracocha and his servants fanned out from Lake Titicaca, walking northwest while calling out and telling people to go forth and settle the world. They named all of the different trees and plants, and informed mankind which fruits were safe to eat or use as medicine. So that he would not overwhelm or frighten any of his human subjects, Viracocha travelled disguised as an old man in a white robe with a long beard, carrying a staff and book. Walking from town to town, he observed the people's behaviour, punishing all who treated him unfairly, and rewarding all who treated him kindly.

Merciful god
All was peaceful until Viracocha arrived at Cacha. There he was attacked by its inhabitants who did not realize who he was. The disguised god brought down flames from the heavens, burning the countryside. The awestruck people pleaded the god for forgiveness, and Viracocha complied, using his staff to make the flames die down. The grateful people of Cacha built a shrine to Viracocha and made him offerings, and later, the Incas would erect the largest of Viracocha's temples on the site of this miracle.

Viracocha moved on to Urcos, where the people treated him well. As an act of gratitude, he created a monument – or huaca – there. Then, in Cuzco, which would eventually became the capital of the Inca Empire, he declared that a great empire would form there. The last stop in Viracocha's journey was Manta, in modern-day Ecuador. From there, he walked west across the water, until he finally disappeared over the horizon.

The Incas believed that, in crossing the water, Virococha relinquished his spirit and control of humans to the Inca pantheon and to nature. From this moment on, Virococha no longer took part in the affairs of humanity. ▪

Some were swallowed up by the earth, others by the sea, and over all there came a general flood.
The History of the Incas

Huacas

Huacas are structures, objects, or landscape features believed by the Incas to be charged with spiritual forces. Almost anything can have this sacred property, from an oddly shaped ear of corn to a natural spring. At the most significant huacas are shrines where priests performed rituals. The word "huaca" comes from the Quechua word *huacay*, which means "to wail". This is because people prayed to the gods by crying out to them. This allowed the worshipper to interact with the supernatural world, and lobby the gods for favours such as a good harvest, victory in battle, or protection from illness.

The most important huacas were in Coricancha, a temple in Cuzco dedicated to the sun god Inti, and Wanakawri, a mountain nearby. After conquering the Inca Empire in 1572, Spain tried to eradicate the huacas and convert the region to Catholicism. However, many huacas survive to this day.

THE CANOE WAS A WONDER
THE FIRST CANOE

IN BRIEF

THEME
Escape from the supernatural

SOURCE
Folk Literature of the Warao Indians, collected by Johannes Wilbert, 1992.

SETTING
The Orinoco Delta in northeastern Venezuela, the homeland of the Warao.

KEY FIGURES
Mayakoto A hunter, also known as "The Roaster".

Haburi One of Mayakoto's two children.

Hahuba A double-headed snake god.

Wauta An elderly frog-woman.

Dauarani A goddess known as the Mother of the Forest.

Warao Indians in a dugout canoe, in the Orinoco River Delta, Venezuela. The Warao (boat people) live by fishing, hunting, and gathering berries, and still use canoes for transportation.

Mayakoto, a hunter in the Orinoco Delta, lived with his two wives who had each given him a baby son. The younger baby's name was Haburi. Mayakoto carried a flute that he played when he was returning home from fishing as a signal for his wives to light the cooking fire.

One day Mayakoto was swallowed by the snake god Hahuba, who assumed Mayakoto's form and went home to his wives. The wives, however, knew that something was amiss because their husband had not played his flute as he returned. So they gathered their children and fled into the jungle. Hahuba chased after them, but they managed to escape. One of them scattered locks of her hair on the ground, and it turned into a fence of thorns.

The wives came to the house of Wauta, an old frog-woman. At first, Wauta would not let them in,

See also: Fire and rice 226–27 ▪ Viracocha the creator 256–57 ▪ The sky makes the sun and earth 260–61

but once she heard the cries of the babies she relented. Hahuba, who had caught up with the group, banged on Wauta's door. The frog-woman opened it a crack and, when Hahuba peeped through, she decapitated the snake god with an axe. Its headless body ran off into the jungle.

Wauta's greed

Mayakoto's wives settled in Wauta's household, but one day while they were out gathering food, Wauta turned the babies into men. When the wives returned to find the babies gone, Wauta pretended not to know what had happened. The men did not recognize their mothers, and the women did not recognize their sons. Wauta made the men hunt birds for her, and took the best of their haul for herself. Their mothers were given only small birds to eat, and Wauta urinated on those before handing them over.

Matters became worse after Haburi unwittingly committed incest with his mother. One day

> The head fell on the floor, bouncing up and down.
> **Folk Literature of the Warao Indians**

while the men were out hunting, some otter people told them about their mothers' true identity. When the men returned to Wauta's house and told their mothers the truth about their parentage; they decided they should all flee.

Haburi attempted to fashion canoes so that they could escape. He tried to do so with clay, and then wax, but neither held. Finally, he made a perfect canoe with the bark of the cachicamo tree – the world's first canoe. The men and

their mothers paddled away. Wauta splashed after them, and managed to clamber aboard. It appeared they were stuck with her, but then Wauta spied a beehive. The greedy woman jumped off and threw herself on the tree to suck off the honey. The quick-thinking Haburi threw a tree trunk on Wauta, trapping her, and she later transformed into a frog for good.

At world's end

The men and their mothers paddled to the mountains at the world's end, where the Warao believe the gods reside. When their journey ended, the canoe changed into a giant female serpent and the paddle turned into a man. The couple became lovers and returned to the Orinoco Delta, where the woman became the goddess Dauarani, the "Mother of the Forest".

Dauarani, who did not like the damp swamps, left her lover for the mountains at the edge of the earth. Her soul lived in the east where the sun rises, and her body in the west where the sun sets. ∎

Hahuba

The Warao see their world as being totally surrounded by the sea. In the centre, beneath the landmass that is the Warao's home, lies a double-headed snake god known as the "Snake of Being", or Hahuba. He encircles the Warao's land, and the gap between his two heads is the mouth of the Orinoco River, where it flows into the Atlantic Ocean.

Hahuba's movements are what cause the movement of the tides, and the sandbanks

are parts of Hahuba that have emerged above the water. The Warao live on the highest ground and build their houses on stilts from protection from the annual floods.

When a baby is born, the Warao believe that Hahuba sends a warm breeze to welcome the child. In day-to-day life, babies and small children often hang on to their mothers' necks in order to get around. Living in the swampy environment of the Orinoco River Delta, in Venezuela, many Warao learn to swim and paddle before they can even walk.

The extensive network of inlets and tributaries, shown in this satellite image of the Orinoco Delta, is home to around 20,000 Warao.

THE CREATOR OF THE WORLD HAS ALWAYS EXISTED

THE SKY MAKES THE SUN AND EARTH

IN BRIEF

THEME
Creation of the world

SOURCE
Folk literature of the Tehuelche Indians, Johannes Wilbert and Karin Simoneau, 1984.

SETTING
The beginning of the world in the mythology of the Tehuelche hunter-gatherers of Patagonia.

KEY FIGURES
Kóoch The creator, a being who brought about the ocean, the sun and the moon, and the stars.

Nóshtex A monstrous giant created by the night; father of Elal.

Cloud-woman Raped by Nóshtex, mother of Elal.

Elal A friend of animals, and creator of the Tehuelche people.

K óoch, whose name means "sky", was the Tehuelche creator, believed to have always existed. For a long time, he lived alone among the dark clouds in the east because there was no sun. Realizing how solitary he was, the creator wept. He cried for so long and so hard that he created the ocean, the first element of the natural world. He then sighed deeply; his breath became the winds that dissipated the dark clouds and created twilight.

Surrounded by the dimly lit ocean, Kóoch wanted to see the world. He rose up into space, but could not see any more clearly. He reached out a finger to scratch at the shadows. As he did so, a bright spark leaped from his hand, and became the sun, lighting up the ocean and the sky.

After Kóoch had created the wind, the clouds, and the light, he pulled an island up from the bottom of the ocean. He populated it with all kinds of animal-people, made

Tehuelche paintings of animals, hunters, and human hands, in the Cueva de las Manos or "Cave of the Hands", in Patagonia, Argentina, date back to c.7,000 BCE.

See also: Cherokee creation 236–37 ▪ The legend of the five suns 248–55 ▪ Viracocha the creator 256–57 ▪ The first canoe 258–59

Tehuelche youths dance wearing feather "horns", to celebrate a girl's reaching puberty. Depicted by English explorer George Chaworth Musters in *At home with the Patagonians* (1871).

birds and insects that flew through the air, and filled the ocean with fish. The sun sent light and heat, and the clouds brought rain.

Sun and moon

Seeing how dark the island was after the sun had gone to sleep, Kóoch put the moon into the sky. At first, the sun and moon were unaware of each other, but the clouds soon spread the word and carried messages between them. They longed to meet, but when they did, they wrestled for three days, arguing over who should travel the sky by day. As they fought, they became lovers, and the sun scratched the moon's face.

Night was displeased by the light and incensed by their lovemaking, so he brought forth monstrous giants. One was Nóshtex, who raped a cloud-woman and fathered Elal, whom Kóoch declared would be greater than his father. Nóshtex then killed the cloud-woman, whose blood can still be seen at sunrise, believing that she had brought a curse on him. Nóshtex wanted to eat the baby he had ripped from her womb, but Elal was saved by his grandmother, the field mouse, who arranged for him to be taken away from the island to safety on the mainland.

Creating the Tehuelche

Elal inherited the supernatural powers of Kóoch, and made a new home in Patagonia, where he took all the animal-people from the island where he had been living. They were pursued by the giants, but Elal defeated them all, including his father Nóshtex, just as Kóoch had foretold. Elal created the Tehuelche people from sea lions, gave them the gift of fire, and taught them how to survive. Then he left them, to live in the sky forever. ▪

Elal and Karro

The evening star, Karro, was the daughter of the sun and moon. She was also sometimes portrayed as a siren. The mythical hero Elal fell in love with her and flew up to the stars on the back of a swan to ask Karro to marry him. After Elal passed many tests, Karro's parents agreed to the union and the two were married. Elal later turned Karro into a mermaid; she lived in the sea and created the tides for her mother the moon. Her songs played an important part in religious rites. After that, Elal lived in the stars, waiting for the souls of the Tehuelche when they died. They were guided to him by the good spirit, Wendeuk, who kept account of people's deeds, and told Elal all the things they had done in life. The dead were transformed into stars, and they looked down from the sky on those they had left behind.

It was when the moon wrestled the sun, and when this world was made.
Folk literature of the Tehuelche Indians

ANCIENT
AND AFR

EGYPT
ICA

The *Pyramid Texts* are **etched into the tombs** of 10 Egyptian rulers by unknown scribes.

Spells and advice to **guide people through the Underworld** are collected in the *Book of the Dead*.

Greek philosopher **Plutarch** revisits the Egyptian myth of *Isis and Osiris*.

In the **"Scramble for Africa"**, European powers divide the African continent into colonies.

2494–2181 BCE   **c. 1550–50 BCE**   **1ST CENTURY CE**   **1881–1914**

c. 2181–1650 BCE   **30 BCE**   **17TH CENTURY CE**   **1906**

Hundreds of funerary spells are inscribed on the tombs of ordinary Egyptians and are later collected as the **Coffin Texts**.

With the defeat of Mark Anthony and the death of Cleopatra, **Rome conquers Egypt**.

European traders begin to **enslave Africans** and ship them overseas, ultimately creating a global diaspora.

E. A. Wallis Budge researches the **realm of the dead** (*Duat*) in *The Egyptian Heaven and Hell*.

The continent of Africa is rich in myth, which divides into two categories: the mythology of ancient Egypt, which we know from ancient inscriptions and manuscripts; and the varied and vigorous mythologies of sub-Saharan Africa, which we know from robust oral traditions that began to be recorded in the 19th century by anthropologists.

Egyptian mythology

The development of ancient Egypt can be broadly arranged into three main periods: the Old Kingdom (2686–2181 BCE), the Middle Kingdom (2055–1650 BCE) and the New Kingdom (1550–1069 BCE). Yet its roots date back to the Early Dynastic Period starting in 3100 BCE, and its history stretches forward into the period of Roman rule and the Common Era. Such a long time period – with separate eras defined by cultural development – would suggest that Egyptian mythology might also have evolved, but in fact there is remarkable consistency throughout Egyptian history. This is partly because the mythology was always very supple and flexible, able to absorb ambiguities and downright contradictions.

Egyptian texts speak of "tens of thousands and thousands of gods", but all these gods are, in essence, aspects of the original creator, the "lord without limit". Therefore, gods could split into two, or coalesce with other gods, as required. The pharaoh Akhenaten (1352–1336 BCE) tried to rationalize the overlapping muddle of Egyptian deities and focus all worship on the Aten, represented by the visible disc of the sun, regarded as the sole creator and sustainer of the world. This radical move threw Egypt into turmoil. An inscription in the name of Akhenaten's successor, the boy king Tutankhamun, tells how, "The temples of the gods and goddesses fell to pieces. ... The land was turned topsy-turvy, and the gods turned their backs on it. ... If anyone prayed to a god or goddess for help, they would not come. Their hearts were broken."

Over the course of 3,000 years, aspects of Egyptian myth that at first applied only to the kings were extended, until all Egyptians could hope for new life after death, in the Field of Reeds. This idealized vision of Egyptian life in the Nile Delta was located in the east where the sun rises. Inscriptions of spells and prayers that first appear in the Old

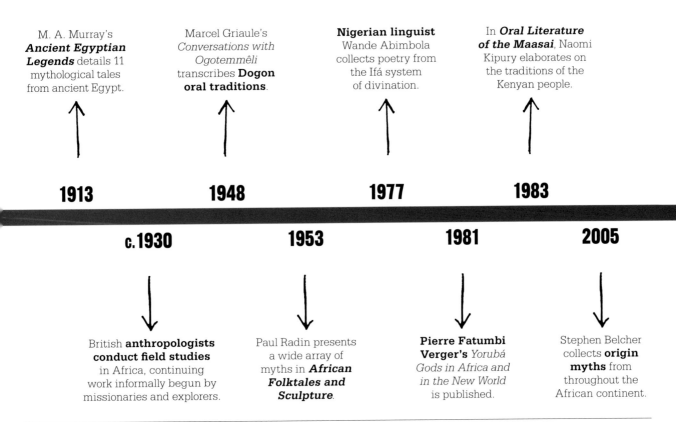

M. A. Murray's **Ancient Egyptian Legends** details 11 mythological tales from ancient Egypt.

Marcel Griaule's *Conversations with Ogotemmêli* transcribes **Dogon oral traditions**.

Nigerian linguist Wande Abimbola collects poetry from the Ifá system of divination.

In *Oral Literature of the Maasai*, Naomi Kipury elaborates on the traditions of the Kenyan people.

1913

1948

1977

1983

c. 1930

1953

1981

2005

British **anthropologists conduct field studies** in Africa, continuing work informally begun by missionaries and explorers.

Paul Radin presents a wide array of myths in **African Folktales and Sculpture**.

Pierre Fatumbi **Verger's** *Yorùbá Gods in Africa and in the New World* is published.

Stephen Belcher collects **origin myths** from throughout the African continent.

Kingdom pyramids of the pharaohs (*Pyramid Texts*) were adapted for private use in the Middle Kingdom (*Coffin Texts*), and by the New Kingdom they had been codified in the most famous Egyptian text of all, the *Book of the Dead*. Most Egyptian myths have to be pieced together from mentions in such spells, but a few were written down in narrative form, notably *The Contendings of Horus and Seth* – a violent and comic tale of trickery and rivalry between two gods.

Sub-Saharan tales

The Akan-Ashanti trickster Ananse, who is both a man and a spider, is a fountainhead of comic and violent storytelling, and Ananse stories have spread across West Africa, to the Caribbean and the USA. Oral storytelling is fluid and adaptable, and can easily transfer across boundaries in this way. Gods and traditions of West African peoples such as the Yorùbá and the Fon travelled with enslaved Africans to the New World, where they formed the basis of new "voodoo" religions. Legba, the Fon equivalent of the Yoruba god Eshu, became the Vodou god Legba.

If the system of Ifá divination presided over by Eshu – a god who can assume 256 different forms – seems complicated, it is nothing when compared to the convoluted metaphysics of the myths of the Dogon in Mali. Their highly complex belief system embodies the fundamental idea that humanity is the "seed" of the universe, and the human form echoes both the first moment of creation and the entire created universe. Each Dogon village is laid out in the shape of a human body, and is regarded as a living being.

Living religions

The impact of Sub-Saharan mythologies on people's daily lives is still evident. The East African myth of En-kai creating cattle and giving them to the Maasai laid the cultural foundations for that people's way of life. The poetic myths of the San Bushmen of the Kalahari desert in southern Africa tell of the doings of the Early Race of beings who are both human and animal, such as the creator Kaang. Both man and mantis, Kaang dreamed the world into being. Today, San shamans still enter a similar dream state to exercise powers such as rainmaking, healing, or hunting magic. ∎

I WAS ALONE WITH THE PRIMEVAL OCEAN

THE CREATION AND THE FIRST GODS

IN BRIEF

THEME
Creation

SOURCES
Pyramid Texts, Anonymous, 2700–2200 BCE; *Coffin Texts*, Anonymous c.2050–1800 BCE; *Book of the Dead,* Anonymous, c.1550–50 BCE; *Book of Smiting Down Apophis*, Anonymous, c.312 BCE; *Memphite Theology*, Pharaoh Shabaqo, c.710 BCE; *The Destruction of Mankind*, Anonymous, c.1279 BCE; transcribed in *Legends of the Gods*, E.A. Wallis Budge, 1912.

SETTING
Ancient Egypt.

KEY FIGURES
Atum The creator god; also the sun god Ra, or Atum-Ra.

Shu God of air.

Tefnut Goddess of moisture.

Hathor The eye of Ra; also (in lioness form) called Sekhmet.

Geb The land.

Nut The sky.

Thoth God of reckoning.

Osiris King on earth; ruler of the Underworld.

Horus God of the sky.

Seth God of the desert and disorder.

Isis Goddess of marriage, fertility, and magic.

Nephthys Goddess of death and the night.

I n the beginning there was nothing but the primal ocean, called Nun – "non-being" – according to the ancient creation myths described in images and hieroglyphic inscriptions on tomb walls in Egypt. At Heliopolis, one of Egypt's most ancient cities, now part of Cairo, people worshipped Ra, the sun god. In his function as creator, Ra was worshipped as Atum, meaning "the all".

The first gods

Atum emerged from the chaos of Nun in whose waters he had dwelt inert. From his own body, he created other gods. From his nostrils Atum sneezed out Shu, the god of air, and from his mouth he spat out Tefnut, the goddess of moisture, sending both far across the water. Later, Atum sent his right eye, the sun, to look for Shu and Tefnut. This eye was the goddess Hathor, a devouring flame full of wild and unpredictable force. When she returned with Shu and Tefnut, she was angry with Atum, for another eye had grown in her place. She wept bitter tears, which became the first human beings.

Atum took the eye that was both Hathor and the sun and set it on his brow in the form of an angry cobra, to rule over the world until

The god Khepri – who later merged with Atum – was depicted in scarab form. Because the beetle appeared to hatch from nowhere, the Egyptians likened its birth to the world's creation.

the end of time (when all creation would pass away, and once more the world would be covered by the infinite flood). Then Atum caused the primal waters to recede, so that he had an island on which to stand.

Resting on this hillock, called the "benben" mound, Atum brought the world into being. He used three

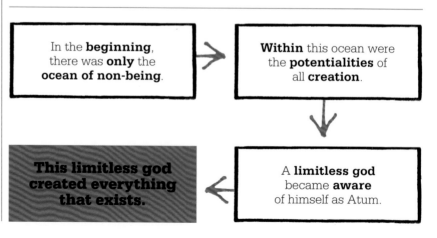

In the **beginning**, there was **only** the **ocean of non-being**. → **Within** this ocean were the **potentialities** of all **creation**.

↓

This limitless god created everything that exists. ← A **limitless god** became **aware** of himself as Atum.

See also: Prometheus helps mankind 36–39 ▪ The night barque of Ra 272–73 ▪ Ra's secret name 274–75 ▪ Osiris and the Underworld 276–83

innate forces to call forth all the elements of creation. They were: Heka, creative power or magic; Sia, the gift of perception; and Hu, for pronouncement. The forces became gods in their own right and were his companions in the solar barque – the vessel that Atum sailed across the sky as Ra, the sun god. All was regulated by a fourth power – the goddess Maat – who represented cosmic harmony.

The gods multiply

Atum's firstborn, Shu, the dry air of calmness and preservation, and Tefnut, the moist air of change, together created Geb, the dry male land, and Nut, the moist female sky. Nut lay on top of Geb, and the sky mated with the earth.

The children of Nut and Geb were the numberless stars. Such fecundity angered Shu, who then

Ra sails beneath the arched form of Nut above the reclining earth god Geb, in a scene from the *Book of the Dead*, compiled in the 16th century BCE.

cursed his daughter to never again give birth in any month of the year. However, Thoth, a god of reckoning and learning, gambled with the moon god Khonsu and won Nut five extra days, to be added to the 12 lunar months of 30 days each. On these days she gave birth to Osiris, Horus, Seth, Isis, and Nephthys.

To prevent further offspring – or, according to another source, to leave Atum some space to create and populate the world – Shu decided to separate the couple. He wrenched his sky daughter Nut away and held her aloft with his hands, then pinned down his son Geb, the earth, with his feet. This story is thought possibly to have inspired the later Greek legend of Atlas – the Titan condemned to bear the sky on his shoulders.

The nine greatest gods

Nut, Geb, and their five children, together with Shu and Tefnut, were known as the Ennead and were the nine greatest gods under Atum. Like him, they contained the forces

of both order and chaos. Osiris – first king on earth, then ruler of the Underworld – embodied order. Seth, who lived in the desert and tried to usurp Osiris's power, embodied chaos. Each took one of their sisters as a wife; Osiris married Isis and Seth married Nephthys. Seth also lusted after Isis, and Osiris had a child, the god Anubis, by Nephthys.

Horus, the other child of Geb and Nut, was a god of the sky, whose name means "he who is »

The Nile

The Egyptian creation myth is influenced by the flooding of the Nile Delta, an annual event that ancient Egypt's rich civilization depended upon. The inundation deposited new fertile silt along the banks of the river, enabling the ancient Egyptians to farm on a grand scale. The flooding of the Nile was worshipped as the work of Hapi, god of fertility, who lived in a cavern at the first cataract at Aswan. "He floods all the fields the sun god [Ra] has made, giving life to all creatures", one hymn related. Hapi, half male and half female, was a chid of Horus.

The regenerating Nile flood almost certainly inspired the creation concept of the waters of Nun, the primeval ocean that the Egyptians believed had covered the world at the beginning of time. It is also no coincidence that Atum-Ra, sun god and creator, was symbolically born from this ocean in their mythology, just as the fields of the Nile Delta appeared each autumn when the floodwaters receded.

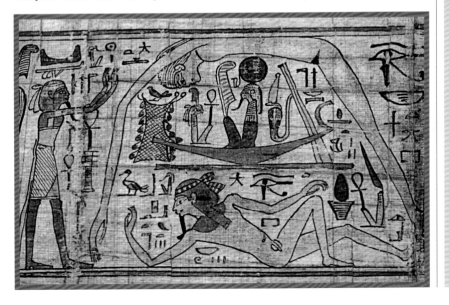

The Eye of Horus, personified as the goddess Wedjat, was often used to protect against danger in the afterlife. This bracelet is from the tomb of the pharaoh Shoshenq (9th century BCE).

far above". Horus was depicted as a falcon with outstretched wings, whose eyes were the sun and moon. Thanks to his inability to see on dark, moonless nights, the god was also sometimes known as Blind Horus.

Quelling a rebellion

After Atum had created the world, he faced a revolt from his children or, according to some sources, from the henchmen of Seth. As Atum was growing old and was too frail to fight the rebellious gods himself, on the advice of Thoth, he named Horus as his champion. Taking on the form of a great winged disc, Horus faced them in single combat. His opponents turned themselves into birds, fish, hippopotamuses, and crocodiles, but Horus soon caught and defeated them all.

A second battle followed. Seth plucked out Horus's left eye, the moon, and Horus tore off Seth's testicles. In his battle rage – and

Horus, the Youthful One, cometh in peace, and he hath made manifest on his journey deeds of very great might.
Thoth
Anonymous inscription on the walls of the Temple of Horus at Edfu

temporarily blinded without the moon's light – Horus not only defeated the rebels, but also cut off the heads of many gods loyal to Atum. The other gods fled, and in the chaos the solar barque came to a halt as one of the four pillars that held up the sky fell into the sea. The universe was about to collapse.

Horus dies and is reborn

Osiris stepped into the breach to restore order, and the humiliated Seth was forced to carry him on his back. Osiris then brought Seth's testicles back to him and restored the eye of Horus, which became a powerful symbol of wholeness, protection, strength, and perfection. Horus, however, was too weakened by his wounds, and after giving his eye to Osiris, he died. Osiris used the eye to rebalance the universe and give the gods back their heads.

After their defeat at the hands of Horus, Atum called the rebels before him and swallowed them. Inside his stomach, the gods quarrelled and killed one another.

This "death" of the gods did not cause their extinction; instead, they carried on much as before. Horus was the only god who died during the revolt, and his divine essence was incorporated in Osiris as "Horus who is in Osiris". This enabled him to be reborn as Horus, the child of Isis and Osiris. For this reason, the first Horus is sometimes known as the Elder Horus, but his miraculous rebirth means that the two gods are, in fact, one and the same deity. Horus, son of Isis and Osiris, later died when stung by a scorpion, but was resurrected by his mother's magic.

Hathor terrorizes humans

Just as the gods had earlier rebelled against the authority of Atum, so too did humankind. To punish these new insurgents, Atum sent down his right eye, the goddess Hathor, in her form as a lioness, in which she was called Sekhmet.

His intention was to alarm and punish the ungrateful humans and reduce their numbers, but once

> I [Amun] created every man identical with his neighbour; I did not order them to commit perversion; it is their hearts that violated what I said.
> **Coffin Texts**

Sekhmet had tasted blood, she lost control. Lusting for more, she killed everyone she found, wading through their gory remains.

At nightfall, in a bid to placate Sekhmet, Ra mixed red ochre into barley beer so that it looked like blood. He then poured 7,000 jugs of the liquid over the land where she was intent on her killing spree. At dawn, Sekhmet saw the "blood" and voraciously lapped it all up. She became so drunk that she fell asleep for three days; when she awoke, her bloodlust had passed,

A sistrum, a sacred rattle in the shape of an ankh – the symbol of life – was played to worship Hathor. This sistrum handle (c.664–525 BCE) depicts the horned head of the cow goddess.

and the remaining humans were spared. From then on, Hathor – in her lioness form as Sekhmet – became associated with an annual festival that celebrated the survival of humanity. During the festivities, people drank beer mixed with pomegranate juice.

A complex goddess
Atum valued the strength of Hathor's fiery nature and wanted her close by him to protect him. When she returned to him, the creator god is said to have welcomed her back as "Beautiful One", which was one of the goddess's many names.

A highly popular deity and worshipped throughout Egyptian society, Hathor was accorded multiple roles. She was sometimes worshipped as the wife of Horus and mother of Ihy, a child god of music. She was the goddess of love, beauty, dance, pleasure, and, most significantly, procreation and

motherhood. Women visited her shrine to pray for children. In contrast to her lioness aspect, Hathor was usually represented as a cow. Her cult, probably rooted in early fertility rites, was said to predate the dynastic period. People also believed that Hathor could help souls to be reborn in the afterlife. ∎

Egyptian trinity

Differing creation myths evolved in ancient Egypt's major cities – Heliopolis, Memphis, Hermopolis, and Thebes. A black stone tablet from Memphis, ground down almost to illegibility by its use as a millstone, names the creator as Ptah, a limitless almighty divinity. Called the "giver of life at will", he conceived all creation in his

Ptah, the patron god of craftsmen, was worshipped in Memphis, one of Egypt's great cities. Ptah was said to have shaped the physical world.

heart, and gave it form by naming it. At Thebes, the "hidden god" Amun was the creator god, in the form of the serpent Kematef. Elsewhere, it was Atum, "the all", who was also Ra, the sun god.

A hymn from the reign of Ramesses II (1279–1213 BCE) declares that "God is three gods above all – Amun, Ra, and Ptah. His nature as Amun is hidden; he cannot be known. He is Ra in his features, and Ptah in his body". The words suggest that all three were viewed as aspects of the same creator god.

HAIL TO YOU, RA, PERFECT EACH DAY!

THE NIGHT BARQUE OF RA

IN BRIEF

THEME
Rebirth and renewal

SOURCES
Book of Amduat, Anonymous,
c.1425 BCE; *Coffin Texts*,
Anonymous, c.2050–1800 BCE;
Book of the Dead, Anonymous,
c.1550–50 BCE; *Book of
Smiting Down Apophis*,
Anonymous, c.312 BCE.

SETTING
Ancient Egypt and Duat, the
Underworld.

KEY FIGURES
Ra The sun god.

Heka, Sia, Hu, and Maat
Ra's companions in the
night barque.

Thoth Moon god and
steersman.

Isis Goddess of magic.

Seth Ra's protector.

Khepri God of rebirth.

Seth spears the serpent Apophi,
from a detail on an Egyptian scribe's
coffin (c. 984 BCE), representing the
victory over the forces of darkness
that allowed the sun god to rise again.

Ra was god of the sun and
also a creator god, who
rose from chaos to create
himself. Every day he crossed the
heavens in a barque, the "Boat of
Millions of Years", bringing sun to
the land. When Ra rose in the east
each morning, the barque was
called *Manzet* ("becoming strong").
By sunset, the boat was known as
the *Mesektet* ("becoming weak").

Every night, Ra undertook a
deadly journey as he sailed through
the Underworld, Duat, in his night
barque. With him in the boat were
divine personifications of his
powers: Heka (creative power), Sia
(perception), Hu (the word of god),
and Maat (cosmic harmony). All
night, Maat held up the *ankh*, the
hieroglyphic sign for "life", so that
Ra, although now dead, could later
nurture new life inside himself.
Also with him in the night barque

See also: The creation and the first gods 266–71 ▪ Ra's secret name 272–73 ▪ Osiris and the Underworld 276–83

> Over the body of Ra, the serpent Mehen casts his protecting coils, for now is the time of danger.
> **Ancient Egyptian Legends**

were other gods, including the steersman Thoth; Isis, whose spells made the boat move; and Seth, who guarded and protected Ra's lifeless body as he journeyed through the 12 gates that marked the passage of the hours of darkness and the 12 countries of Duat.

Into the underworld

Beyond the first gate, a great company of gods greeted Ra. They prepared the barque for its journey through the night and took hold of the tow ropes running through the 12 countries of the Underworld to pull the boat along the river.

In the seventh and most perilous country of Duat, Isis summoned up the serpent god Mehen to form a sacred protective canopy over Ra. However, another serpent lay in wait for the sun god – the chaos serpent Apophis (or Apep), Ra's eternal enemy. Stretched along a sandbank in the middle of the river to conceal his monstrous form, Apophis fixed the gods with his hypnotizing gaze and opened his mouth wide to swallow the river and the night

barque. The goddess Isis disabled Apophis with her words of power, Seth speared the serpent, and Ra, in the form of the Cat of Heliopolis ("Sun City"), cut off its head. Chaos was held at bay for another day, although a revived Apophis lay in wait again the next night, hoping to swallow Ra and so extinguish the sun forever.

The sun rises again

As Ra passed through the eighth land of Duat, called Sarcophagus of the Gods, embalmed and mummified deities cried out in praise of Ra. In the tenth country, the god of rebirth – Khepri, in the form of a scarab beetle – united his soul with the soul of Ra to accompany him through the remaining stages of the journey.

The twelfth and final country took the form of another monstrous serpent, named Life of the Gods. But the barque was towed safely through the serpent's mouth, Ra was fully transformed into Khepri, and his old body was thrown overboard. The *Manzet*, the sunrise barque, then emerged into the glorious dawn. ▪

> Hail to thee, Ra, at thy rising; the night and the darkness are past.
> **Ancient Egyptian Legends**

The sun god

Ra was not the oldest of the ancient Egyptian gods, but he became revered above all others as the creator of everything. From the Second Dynasty (c.3000 BCE), his chief centre of worship was the city of Heliopolis (now part of Cairo). By the Fifth Dynasty (c.2500 BCE), the pharaohs of Egypt were identifying themselves with Ra and building temples to the god. Later pharaohs referred to themselves as "sons of Ra" and added his name to their own. Ra himself took three main forms. As the sun rising in the east, he was Khepri, the scarab beetle. As the midday sun, he was Ra, usually shown with the body of a man and the head of a falcon, surmounted by a golden disc encircled by the sacred cobra Uraeus. As the sun set in the west, he was Atum, the god of creation, sometimes protrayed as an old man leaning on a stick. This daily cycle of death and rebirth came to symbolize the life cycle of humankind, with the hope of finding, like Ra, a new birth at the end of life.

A chest ornament, or pectoral, found on a mummy of the 1st millennium BCE, shows a scarab beetle, whose form Ra took at the end of his journey through Duat.

ISIS LIVED IN THE FORM OF A WOMAN, WHO HAD THE KNOWLEDGE OF WORDS OF POWER
RA'S SECRET NAME

IN BRIEF

THEME
Rivalry between gods

SOURCES
Papyrus Turin 1993,
Anonymous, c.1295–1186 BCE;
Papyrus Chester Beatty 11
Anonymous, c.1295–1186 BCE.

SETTING
Ancient Egypt.

KEY FIGURES
Ra The sun god; tricked into
revealing his secret name.

Isis Goddess of magic;
Ra's sister and wife; her
Egyptian name was Aset
("Queen of the Throne").

For the Egyptians, a name was essential to a person's being. To erase someone's name after death was to destroy that person in the afterlife. Ra, king of gods and men, had so many names that even the gods did not know them all. Isis, the mistress of magic, had power over words and learned the names of all things, so that she would become as great as Ra. Eventually, the only name Isis did not know was Ra's secret name.

Ra sailed across the sky each day, and each day he grew old. His mouth went slack, and his spittle dribbled to the ground. Isis caught up Ra's spittle and shaped it with some dust into a snake, which she left in Ra's path. When he stumbled over it, the snake bit him, and Ra fell down with a terrible cry. The other gods heard him and asked, "What is wrong?" But Ra could not reply. The snake's bite had taken the fire of life from him, and his limbs trembled as the poison surged through his body.

Isis stands behind Ra as he receives an offering on this carved stele from Egypt's Third Intermediate Period (c.1069–664 BCE). Ra is identifiable by the sun disk over his head.

When Ra regained his voice, he summoned the other gods to him, and asked for their help. Then Isis, radiant with power, whose words could make a man choked to death live again, offered to cure the sun god but said that to do so he would have to tell her his name. Finally, in fear of death, Ra released his secret name from his heart. Using the name, Isis chanted a spell, the poison left Ra's body, and he was made strong again. ∎

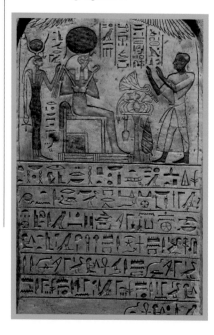

See also: The creation and the first gods 266–71 ▪ The night barque of Ra 272–73 ▪ Osiris and the Underworld 276–83

Ra	Isis

Ra: Ra cries out in pain.

Isis: What's wrong?

Ra: I have been wounded by some deadly thing – some thing that I did not make.

Isis: Has a serpent dared to lift its head against you? I will drive it away with my words of power.

Ra: Be quick, for my eyes are blurring. I am shaking all over, and covered in sweat.

Isis: Tell me your name. That is the word of power that will make you live.

Ra: I am he who made heaven and earth. I knitted together the mountains, and made the waters. When I open my eyes, it becomes light, and when I close my eyes, it becomes dark.

Isis: Tell me your name so that I can heal you.

Ra: My name will pass from my body into yours – the name that I have kept secret since the dawn of time.

Isis: Flow out, poison, and spill to the ground! By the power of his name, which has passed from his heart to mine, Ra shall live!

Isis saves Ra from death by snake poison, but only as a ploy to learn his name and so assume some of the sun god's power, which she then passes to her son, Horus.

Amun-Ra

Ra the sun god was visible to the naked eye (especially in his form as Aten, the disc of the sun), but the creator god was also worshipped by the Egyptians as an unknowable mystery in the form of Amun, the hidden god. Amun was often fused with Ra as Amun-Ra. His cult centre was at the great temple of Karnak at Thebes (now Luxor). Although the temple's rituals were the exclusive preserve of its priests, who acted in the king's name, there is some evidence that Amun was regarded as a god to whom the poor and dispossessed could plead for help. He is described in an ancient Egyptian hymn as "the great god who listens to prayers, who comes at the voice of the poor and distressed, who gives breath to the wretched". Under the merged identity of Amun-Ra, Amun became the chief god of the Egyptians, worshipped as the creator of all things, who brought himself into being by saying, "I am!" – the source and sustainer of all existence.

NUT, THE GREAT, SAYS: "THIS IS MY SON, MY FIRST-BORN, OSIRIS"

OSIRIS AND THE UNDERWORLD

IN BRIEF

THEME
Death and the afterlife

SOURCES
Book of the Dead, Anonymous, c.1550–50 BCE; *The Book of Am-Duat*, Anonymous, c.1425 BCE; *The Contendings of Horus and Seth*, Anonymous, c.1147–1143 BCE; *De Iside et Osiride* ("Isis and Osiris"), Plutarch, lst century CE.

SETTING
Ancient Egypt, Phoenicia, and the Underworld.

KEY FIGURES
Osiris Wise ruler and later king of the Underworld.

Isis Sister and wife of Osiris.

Seth Jealous brother of Osiris.

Ra The sun god.

Nephthys Sister of Isis.

Horus Son of Osiris and Isis.

Anubis Jackal god associated with mummification.

Isis, when the tidings reached her, at once cut off one of her tresses and put on a garment of mourning.
De Iside et Osiride

O siris – son of the earth god Geb and the sky goddess Nut – originally ruled as a king of mortals. It was he who taught the Egyptians how to survive, how to make and use tools, and how to cultivate and harvest wheat and barley. His sister and wife, the goddess Isis, taught the women how to spin and weave, and how to make bread and beer from grain. Isis herself was worshipped throughout Egypt as the goddess of mothers, fertility, magic, healing, and funerary rites. Her cult later spread to Greece and across the Roman Empire.

Leaving Isis as his regent, Osiris then travelled around the world teaching his skills to the rest of mankind, for which he earned the title Wennefer, meaning "the eternally good". Osiris's brother Seth was jealous of his gifts and acclaim, and was enraged that Osiris had left Isis, rather than him, to act as regent.

Seth's cunning plan

When Osiris returned from his travels, Seth plotted to kill him, take his throne, and marry Isis himself. He invited Osiris to a great banquet, where he produced a wonderful casket that was made of cedarwood and inlaid with ebony and ivory. Seth promised to give this chest to whoever fitted exactly into it. His guests all tried the chest for size, but it fitted none of them. At last Osiris took his turn, and he fitted perfectly – Seth had carefully constructed the chest to Osiris's precise measurements.

Before Osiris could get out of the chest, Seth and his 72 accomplices slammed down the lid and nailed it shut. They sealed the chest with molten lead and threw it into the Nile. The chest – now Osiris's coffin – was washed down the river to

The Medjed fish, depicted here in bronze, was said to have eaten Osiris's phallus when his body parts were scattered. It was sacred to the city of Per-Medjed, later called Oxyrhynchus.

the coast and across the sea to Phoenicia. A tamarisk tree grew up around it, enclosing the chest in its trunk, with the dead king inside.

The search for Osiris

The king of the city of Byblos saw the tamarisk tree and admired its size. He ordered it to be cut down for use in his palace. The trunk, with the chest still concealed in it, was made into a pillar to support the palace roof.

Meanwhile, Isis grieved for Osiris and set out to find him. After a long search, she arrived in Byblos and sat weeping by a spring. When the maidservants of the queen of Byblos came to the spring, Isis plaited their hair and gave it a lovely fragrance. The queen sent for Isis, befriended her, and made her nursemaid of her baby. Isis nursed the child by giving it her finger to suck and resolved to make the infant immortal. At night, she enveloped the child in flames to burn away its mortal parts. In the form of a swallow she also searched for her husband. The bird called plaintively as she flew about the wooden pillar where the chest was concealed, knowing that Osiris was nearby.

See also: The creation and the first gods 266–71 ▪ The night barque of Ra 272–73 ▪ Ra's secret name 274–75

Isis and Nephthys are depicted lamenting over the murdered Osiris. The scene decorates a gilt coffin from the Roman period of ancient Egypt, c.1st century BCE.

When the queen of Byblos saw her baby on fire, she screamed in terror and broke the magic, preventing the child from becoming immortal. Isis now revealed her true self and pleaded with the queen for the pillar with the chest inside to be taken down. Isis then removed the wood that had grown around the chest containing the body of her beloved Osiris. Throwing herself upon his coffin, she uttered such terrible cries that the queen's youngest son died of the shock.

Seth finds the body

Isis put the coffin on a boat and sailed away across the sea back to Egypt. When she landed and came to a quiet spot, she opened up the coffin and laid her face on the face of Osiris, weeping. The goddess then concealed the coffin, with the corpse inside it, in a thicket of papyrus reeds. Seth was out hunting that night and found the coffin. Wrenching it open, he cut Osiris's body into 14 pieces, which he scattered across Egypt.

Isis and her sister Nepthys, however, gathered up the parts of Osiris's body. Wherever they found a piece, Isis magically made a wax model of it and left the model in the care of local priests, thereby establishing shrines to Osiris across the whole of Egypt.

When the sisters had gathered together the god's dismembered body, they sat beside it and wept. Ra, the sun god, took pity on them, and sent the jackal god Anubis »

Colourful stone reliefs dating from the 12th-century BCE adorn the walls of the impressive temple to Osiris at Abydos, Egypt.

Abydos

The cult centre of Osiris was at Abydos in Upper Egypt, about six miles (10 km) from the Nile River. Here, for more than 2,000 years the mysteries of the god were celebrated annually in the last month of the inundation, as the flood waters receded. Although little is known about the rituals of the temple, their objective was to ensure eternal life for the souls of the dead when they entered the Underworld where Osiris reigned. In a public ceremony, priests would also carry an image of the god from the temple to a tomb believed to be the god's, attended by a great procession of Osiris's worshippers.

At the same time, a public festival would re-enact the story of Osiris's murder, the grief of Isis and Nepthys, the trial of Seth, and the battle between the supporters of Seth and Osiris. At the end of the drama, the actor playing Osiris would reappear in triumph in the sacred barque, and the *djed*-pillar, a stylized sheaf of corn which symbolized his rebirth, would be erected.

The murder of Osiris and its aftermath

Seth envies his brother, King Osiris. With an evil trick, he traps Osiris in a casket and throws it into the River Nile.

The coffin drifts down the Nile and is swept over the sea to Phoenicia where a tamarisk tree grows around it.

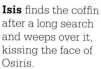

Isis sails away with the coffin but Seth finds it, cuts Osiris's body into 14 pieces, and scatters them across the whole of Egypt.

Isis finds the coffin after a long search and weeps over it, kissing the face of Osiris.

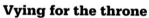

and the ibis god Thoth to help them. Together they pieced Osiris's body back together into its true shape. Then Anubis embalmed the body with fragrant ointments and wrapped it in linen bandages, before laying it on a lion-headed bier. The wrapped and embalmed body of Osiris became the first mummy, setting a pattern for all of the kings that followed.

His divine force, however, was not quite spent: Isis changed herself into a kite and, hovering over the mummified body, fanned the breath of life back into Osiris for long enough to conceive a child, Horus, who would avenge his father. Then Osiris descended to the Underworld and became its ruler. Isis devoted herself to caring for the shrines of her dead husband.

In time, Horus sought to challenge Seth and establish his right to the throne of his father Osiris. Horus and Seth appeared before the Ennead. This council of the nine major gods met for 80 years without reaching a decision as to which of the two had the better claim.

Vying for the throne

Thoth wrote to Neith – creator of the universe, mother of the sun god Ra, and goddess of war – to ask for a judgement. Neith awarded the throne to Horus. Ra favoured Seth, however, because Seth protected him every night from the chaos serpent Apophis. Outraged by Neith's decision, Ra became neglectful of his duties and only cheered up when the goddess Hathor exposed herself to him and made him laugh.Despite Neith's judgement, the gods continued to dispute the question of who should rule, until Isis tricked Seth into

The jackal god Anubis attends to the dead in a wall painting from the tomb that an artisan named Sennedjem built for himself in Set Maat near Thebes in the 12th century BCE.

The child, Horus, challenges Seth and asserts his right to his father's throne at a council of the gods.

Seth and Horus turn into hippopotamuses in a contest which neither wins.

Finally, Osiris, Lord of the Dead intercedes for his son and Horus is crowned king.

Anubis mummifies Osiris's body after Isis and Nepthys recover the pieces.

Isis turns herself into a kite and fans life into Osiris so that she can conceive a child to avenge him.

speaking against his own case. Furious, Seth challenged Horus to a battle. Both gods transformed themselves into hippopotamuses and stayed underwater to see who could remain submerged for longer.

Isis fashioned a harpoon with a copper barb and flung it into the water. First it hit Horus; he cried out to his mother, who quickly recalled the harpoon. She hurled it back into the water, and this time it pierced Seth. He, in turn, asked Isis how she could so mistreat her brother, and again she recalled the

It is no good, this cheating me in the presence of the Ennead and depriving me of the office of my father Osiris.
The Contendings of Horus and Seth

Falcon-headed Horus stands with his father Osiris and his mother Isis on this funerary stele dedicated to the gods of Abydos in the reign of Seti I (1290–1279 BCE).

harpoon. This so infuriated Horus that he leapt out of the water and cut off his mother's head. Then the goddess transformed herself into a headless statue of flint so that the Ennead could see what her son Horus had done to her.

Quarrelling continues

The gods searched for Horus to punish him. Seth found him asleep beneath a tree and gouged out both his eyes, burying them in the ground where they grew into two lotuses. When the goddess Hathor found Horus weeping in the desert, she captured a gazelle and milked it. Then she knelt beside the young god and poured the milk into his eye sockets to restore his sight.

Hathor told the gods what Seth had done, but they had wearied of the quarrelling and declared a truce. Appearing conciliatory, Seth invited Horus to come to his house, and Horus accepted. That night

when Horus was asleep, Seth lay between his thighs, and spilled his semen into Horus's hand. When Horus revealed to Isis what Seth had done, she cut off her son's hands and threw them into the water, replacing them with new hands. Then Isis took semen from Horus and smeared it on the lettuce that was Seth's staple food. Seth » duly consumed the lettuce, unaware that it contained his rival's potent semen.

Still pursuing his quest for the throne, Seth dragged Horus before the Ennead and claimed that he – Seth – must be made ruler, because he had taken the male role in his intercourse with Horus. The horrified gods spat in Horus's face. Horus categorically denied the charge and demanded that his semen and that of Seth should be called before the Ennead as witnesses. When summoned, the semen of Seth cried out from the water where Isis had thrown it, but the semen of Horus called out from the body of Seth. The judgement was clear. The gods declared in favour of Horus, which infuriated Seth. He demanded a further contest with Horus, calling for them to race each other down the

The Weighing of the Heart, illustrated here in the Book of the Dead, was one of a series of trials the deceased were thought to undergo in the immediate afterlife.

Nile in stone boats. Seth built a huge boat from the solid stone of a mountain peak. Horus's boat was of cedarwood, which he disguised to look like stone by coating it with gypsum. His boat floated, but Seth's sank. In fury, Seth turned himself back into a hippopotamus and scuttled Horus's boat.

The gods were no nearer a final decision, so they asked Thoth to write to Osiris in the Underworld. Osiris asked why his son should be cheated of his rightful inheritance, and Horus was at last installed as king of Egypt. Seth went with Ra to thunder in the skies, as the god of storms, violence, and the desert.

A fearsome Underworld

Osiris now ruled as the Lord of the Dead. The Egyptians thought of Duat, the Underworld, as a narrow valley with a river running through it. It was separated from the land of the living by a mountain range; the sun rose from the eastern end each morning and sank into the western end at night. The path to the Underworld was fraught with

> O my heart of my different forms! Do not stand up as a witness against me … do not be hostile to me in the presence of the Keeper of the Balance
> **Book of the Dead**

dangers. There were occasional respites, such as when the goddess Hathor met the deceased at the end of the desert kingdom of the falcon god Seker and offered rest in the shade of her sacred sycamore tree, and fruit and water for refreshment. In the main, however, the path from this world to the next was beset with terrifying creatures, such as a nameless dog-headed beast; it tore out hearts, swallowed shadows, and dwelt by the Lake of Fire.

The deceased used spells, many of which appear in the Egyptian *Book of the Dead*, to negotiate this terrifying obstacle course. They had to pass through as many as seven gates, each with its own grotesque guardian. Then they were led by Anubis into the Hall of the Two Truths, where their heart was weighed in a balance against the feather of Maat, the goddess of truth and justice. Anubis checked the balance, and Thoth, the scribe of the gods, recorded the result on leaves from the tree of life.

If the heart was so weighed down with the guilt of evil thoughts and acts that it outweighed the feather of truth, it would be cast down to be gobbled up by the

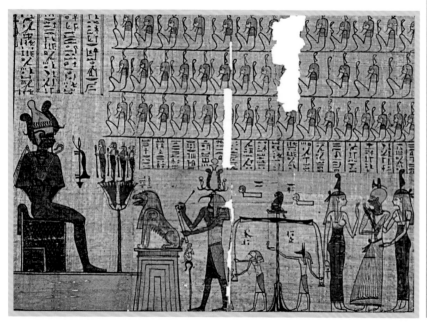

The passage from death to new life in the Underworld

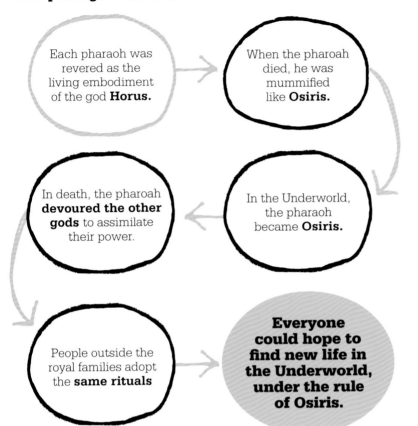

Each pharaoh was revered as the living embodiment of the god **Horus.**

→

When the pharoah died, he was mummified like **Osiris.**

In death, the pharoah **devoured the other gods** to assimilate their power.

←

In the Underworld, the pharaoh became **Osiris.**

People outside the royal families adopt the **same rituals**

→

Everyone could hope to find new life in the Underworld, under the rule of Osiris.

Books of the dead

In the era of the Old Kingdom, only Egyptian kings could secure for themselves or others a new existence in the afterlife. During the Middle Kingdom years, non-royal individuals started to make funerary arrangements, in imitation of the king. The Old Kingdom prayers and spells – the *Pyramid Texts* from the royal pyramids – were adapted in the Middle Kingdom for use by private individuals as the *Coffin Texts*, and codified in the New Kingdom into the *Book of the Dead* (sometimes translated as "Spells for Coming Forth by Day"). The *Pyramid Texts* show that the pharaoh believed that in death he would be embodied as Osiris; Nut and Geb would claim him as their son, and he would become a ruler in the Underworld. In one spell, the king hunts and eats the other gods, "feeds on the lungs of the wise ones, and is satisfied with living on hearts and their magic." Once he has absorbed the power of every god, "the king's lifetime is eternity."

---

she-monster Ammut. This devourer of the dead had the head of a crocodile, the foreparts of a lion, and the rear of a hippopotamus.

Final judgment

If the heart did not outweigh the feather of truth, the deceased could continue on their journey. Horus – now in the Underworld with his father and the other gods – took the deceased by the hand and led them into the presence of Osiris. The Lord of the Dead was seated in his shrine with Isis and Nepthys standing behind him, and the four sons of Horus before him on a lotus flower. Forty-two judges of the Underworld assisted Osiris in his deliberations. Those who pleased

Osiris might hope for eternal life in the Field of Reeds (a perfect version of Egypt); to sail as stars across the night sky; or to join the throng in the great barque of Ra to be reborn anew each morning with the sun.

When he put Osiris in charge of the Underworld, Ra promised that his reign would last for millions of years, but would end. Ra said, "I will destroy all creation. The land will fold into endless water … I will remain there with Osiris, after I have changed myself back into a serpent." This serpent, the original true form of Ra, contained the forces of creation and chaos. The serpent would sleep in the cosmic ocean, its tail in its mouth, until it awoke to re-create the world. ■

A depiction of Ammut from the *Book of the Dead of Nebqed* (c.1400 BCE), reveals the she-monster waiting under a lake of fire for those who fail the feather of truth test.

IF THEY BUILT FIRES, EVIL WOULD COME

SAN CREATION MYTH

IN BRIEF

THEME
Man's relationship with animals

SOURCE
African Myths of Origin, Stephen Belcher, 2005.

SETTING
The beginning of time in present-day Botswana and South Africa.

KEY FIGURES
The San Bushmen; the indigenous hunter-gatherer people of southern Africa.

Kaang The supreme and creator god of the San people.

The San believe that in the beginning people lived beneath the ground, where everything was light and warm, even though there was no sun. However, the creator god, Kaang, decided that he wanted to make another world above ground, and so he produced a tall and expansive tree. Proud of his creation, he called a man up from the earth to take a look at this tree. The man was followed by a woman, and then all the other creatures followed.

The people and the animals soon made their home in Kaang's new world. He told them all to talk to one another and live in peace. He also forbad them to light a fire, as it had great destructive force.

However, this new world had a disadvantage: the sun was warm, but the nights were cold and dark, and people realized that, unlike the birds and other animals, they had no fur or feathers to keep them warm. Contrary to Kaang's instruction, the people decided to light a fire. Although this warmed them and gave them some light, the fire also terrified the other animals.

Kaang punished the humans for their disobedience by rendering them and animals unintelligible to one another. Instead of words, the animals now heard shouts and cries and fled in fear – destroying the harmonious relationship that had previously existed between humans and other creatures. ■

San hunters shoot antelope with poison-tipped arrows, then track their dying prey over several days – depicted here in rock art from Game Pass shelter, in the Drakensberg Mountains.

See also: The creation and the first gods 266–71 ▪ En-kai and the cattle 285 ▪ Ananse the spider 286–87 ▪ The Dogon cosmos 288–93

I WILL GIVE YOU SOMETHING CALLED CATTLE
EN-KAI AND THE CATTLE

IN BRIEF

THEME
Beloved creatures

SOURCE
Oral Literature of the Maasai,
Naomi Kipury, 1983.

SETTING
The East African savanna.

KEY FIGURES
En-kai The supreme god of
the Maasai.

The Maasai A nomadic
community that graze their
cattle on the grasslands of
East Africa.

The Doroba A clan within
the Maasai community, who
were formerly hunter-gatherers
and blacksmiths.

The Maasai – a nomadic cattle-raising community, historically with a fierce warrior-like reputation – are thought to have orginated in the lower Nile valley, migrating to the savanna of East Africa in the 15th century. Their one supreme god, En-kai, is often associated with the thunder clouds that bring the rains, causing the grass to sprout and provide fresh grazing for their herds.

In the beginning, En-kai told Maasinta, the first Maasai, to build an enclosure using thorn bushes. En-kai then lowered a leather rope from a black storm cloud, and down this rope descended a multitude of cattle – creatures that the world had never seen before.

Dorobo, who lived with Maasinta and was the first of the Doroba clan, was upset, complaining that he had not got any of the cattle. In some versions of the tale, Dorobo shouted so loudly that En-kai took back the rope; in others, Dorobo used his metal-working skills to make a knife, then cut the rope. Either way, no more cattle descended from the

May the milk
of my cattle be poison
if you ever taste it.
**Maasinta, *Oral Literature
of the Maasai***

sky. Maasinta was angry with Dorobo and cursed him and his people to be forever poor and without cattle, living by hunting wild animals. This explained why the Doroba clan were hunters and blacksmiths, not pastoralists.

The Maasai people believe that En-kai granted all of the cattle on earth to their community. When the Maasai take cattle from others, they believe that it is not theft: they are simply reclaiming what En-kai had declared was rightfully theirs. ∎

See also: Spider woman 238–39 ▪ The Woge settle a dispute 240–41 ▪
San creation myth 284 ▪ The Dogon cosmos 288–93

TIE THE CALABASH BEHIND YOU AND THEN YOU WILL BE ABLE TO CLIMB THE TREE

ANANSE THE SPIDER

IN BRIEF

THEME
How wisdom was spread

SOURCE
Oral tradition, recorded in *African Folktales and Sculpture*, edited by Paul Radin, 1953; *African Folktales in the New World*, William Bascom, 1992; *Anansi: The Trickster Spider*, Lynne Garner, 2014.

SETTING
West Africa at the beginning of time.

KEY FIGURES
Nyame The high god and creator; also known as Nyankupon.

Ananse A trickster hero; took the form of a spider.

Ntikuma The son of Ananse.

In the beginning, Nyame, the sky god of the Asante people, was the repository of all stories and knowledge. Ananse, a trickster hero in spider form, went to Nyame and brazenly asked how much all this wisdom would cost. Surprised by the spider's audacity, Nyame set him a seemingly impossible task. To win the knowledge of the sky god, Ananse had to bring back four items: a python, a leopard, a swarm of hornets, and a fairy.

Ananse set off and, standing outside the hole where the python lived, he wondered aloud whether the snake was longer than a palm branch above him. When the

The spider wanted to own all the stories known in the world.
African Folktales in the New World

python heard this, he slithered out of his hole and offered to stretch out on the branch and be measured. As he lay there, however, his body began to twitch. The spider offered to tie him to the branch so that he could determine his precise length. When the python consented to this plan, Ananse trussed him up and carried him off to Nyame.

A spider's deceit

Ananse continued to use tricks for the remaining tasks. To catch the leopard, Ananse dug a deep hole and covered the opening with leaves. The leopard fell in and, seeing Ananse at the rim, begged him for help. Ananse offered to weave a dense web around the leopard to lift him out. The leopard agreed, but then found himself stuck in Ananse's web, and the spider had a second prisoner.

To catch the hornets, Ananse trickled water into their nest and began to drum on the ground with little sticks to create the sound of falling rain. He then called out and offered the hornets a dry refuge in his calabash (gourd). The grateful hornets flew in, and immediately Ananse inserted a plug and took the captive insects to Nyame.

See also: San creation myth 284 ▪ En-kai and the cattle 285 ▪ The Dogon cosmos 288–293 ▪ Eshu the trickster 294–297

> Very great kings were not able to buy the sky god's stories, but Kwaku Ananse has been able to pay the price.
> **African Folktales and Sculpture**

Lastly, Ananse trapped the fairy by putting out a doll covered with sticky gum – a tar baby – beside a bowl of yams. The fairy thanked the doll and, when it did not reply, touched it and became stuck. Ananse then carried her off to Nyame, who was amazed that the spider had managed to complete the tasks he had set. True to his word, he made Ananse the god of all stories and fables.

Clever but unwise

When Ananse had received all the wisdom in the world, he stored it in his calabash, a hollowed-out gourd, and then set out to look for a safe place where he could hide it. Going into the forest, he found a tall tree with spiky bark and decided to climb it and deposit the calabash high up near its crown. However, the calabash was large and, when he tied it in front of him and tried to climb the tree, he could not reach out far enough to grip the trunk, and kept falling down. Unknown to Ananse, his young son Ntikuma had followed him into the forest, and was laughing at his father.

"Why don't you tie the calabash behind you?" suggested Ntikuma, "and then you will be able to climb the tree." Ananse was angry that his son had watched his failed attempts but he followed Ntikuma's advice. As he was rearranging the calabash, however, it fell to the ground and shattered. At that very moment, a fierce storm hit the forest, and torrential rain washed the contents of the calabash into the river and out to the sea. The wisdom of Nyame spread all over the world, allowing all people to inherit a share.

As Ananse went home with Ntikuma, he consoled himself with the thought that the wisdom had proved of little value; it had taken a small child to set him right. ▪

Ananse the Spider is depicted at the centre of the finial of a decorative wood and gold leaf staff, dating from around 1900, that was carried by a linguist (storyteller) of the Asante people.

Ananse and Br'er Rabbit

When Africans were taken as slaves to the New World, their stories went with them. Ananse's trickster exploits travelled to the United States and the Caribbean with the Asante people from the Gold Coast (now Ghana), West Africa. Another well-known African-American trickster figure, however, is Br'er Rabbit, a figure from the folklore of south and central Africa, who became well known through the Uncle Remus stories. Narrated by a fictitious former slave in the American south, the stories were adapted and compiled by Joel Chandler Harris and were first published in 1881

The tales of Ananse and Br'er Rabbit share similar themes. Br'er Rabbit gets stuck to a tar baby that Br'er Fox has left out to trap him. Ananse, too, is trapped by a tar-baby as he steals his wife's peas, and he himself uses a tar baby to catch a fairy and complete Nyame's challenges.

ALL THAT WAS IMPURE WAS CAST OUT WITH THE WATER

THE DOGON COSMOS

IN BRIEF

THEME
The duality of mankind

SOURCES
Conversations with Ogotemmêli, Marcel Griaule 1948; "Dogon Restudied: A Field Evaluation of the Work of Marcel Griaule", W E A van Beek, 1991, *Current Anthropology*; *Dogon: Africa's People of the Cliffs*, Stephenie Hollyman and W E A van Beek, 2001.

SETTING
West Africa; the beginning of time.

KEY FIGURES
Amma The creator god; foremost deity of the Dogon.

Nommo The first pair of twin spirits created by Amma; also the name for the eight ancestors of the Dogon.

Lébé The oldest human ancestor; a priest.

This flat earth was a female body, with an ant's nest as its sexual organ.
"Dogon Restudied: A Field Evaluation of the Work of Marcel Griaule"

The Dogon are a reclusive people who live in an isolated part of West Africa that extends from Mali in the southeast to Burkina Faso in the northwest. Dogon mythology is highly complex, relies on oral tradition rather than texts, and has many variations. The central myth concerns the creation of the universe by the Dogon high god Amma, the birth of the twin Nommo spirits, and the death of Lébé, all of whom are key figures across the Dogon tales that have been recorded by anthropologists.

Birth of the Nommo

The Dogon creator deity, Amma, shaped the cosmos out of clay. First he flung clay pellets into the sky to make the stars, and then he made the sun and moon as two clay bowls, inventing the art of pottery. The sun was encircled with red copper, and the moon with white. With the celestial bodies in place, Amma turned to terrestrial matters. He took the clay, squeezed it between his hands, and spread it north to south and east to west to form a flat earth, which was female.

Amma was lonely. Filled with sexual desire, he longed to have intercourse with the earth, but when he tried to penetrate an ants' nest (the earth's vagina), a termite mound rose up. After he cut the mound out of the way, Amma was able to couple with the earth. However, his assault upset the balance of the cosmos, and so his seed produced only a jackal – a creature the Dogon associate with deformity and disorder. The next time Amma planted his seed in the earth it produced twin beings "born perfect and complete". Called the Nommo (or Nummo), their twin nature represents the perfect balance of creation.

Large figures of a male-female pair are common representatives of the mythical progenitors of the Dogon. The statues receive sacrifices intended to protect a community from hardships.

The Nommo were hermaphrodites, green in colour, and half-human, half-serpent. They had red eyes, forked tongues, and flexible arms without joints. The Nommo were present in all water, and without them the beginning of life on earth would have been impossible.

The Nommo ascended to the heavens to be with Amma. From their lofty position the twins saw that their mother, Earth, was naked. To remedy this, they descended with plants from heaven to clothe her. The fibres of these plants helped to carry the watery essence of the Nommo across the land and bring fertility to it.

Male and female

The Nommo (or Amma, in some versions of the myth) drew two outlines on the ground, one on top of the other. One of them was male, and the other was female; from these two outlines, the first man and the first woman emerged. Whereas the first jackal had only a

See also: Ananse the spider 282–83 ▪ San creation myth 284 ▪ En-kai and the cattle 285 ▪ Eshu the trickster 294–97

> Each human being was endowed with two souls of different sex.
> *Conversations with Ogotemmêli*

single soul, these first humans and their descendants had two souls of opposite genders; one inhabited the body, while the other dwelled in the sky or in the water, connecting humanity to nature. This dual nature manifests itself physically; the Dogon believe males and females are born with physical aspects of the opposite gender and that there is still some feminine essence inside of every man and some male essence inside of every woman. The Dogon tradition of

male and female circumcision severs the spiritual link between a person's soul of the opposite gender, and is an important coming-of-age rite in Dogon society.

Twin connections

The first two people had eight children: two pairs of male twins and two pairs of female twins. This set of eight twins were also called the Nommo. They are the ancestors of the Dogon. These Nommo are represented by eight animals – the snake, tortoise, scorpion, crocodile, frog, lizard, rabbit, and hyena – because, according to Griaule, these animals were born in the sky at the same time as the Nommo, and shared a soul connection with them. Each individual Nommo had both a human twin and an animal twin, and although the eight were different species, the animals »

Cave paintings from the Bandiagara Escarpment in Mali depict figures and symbols which are most likely of the Dogon. Some, however, believe they are examples of Sangha or Songo art.

Diverse ideas

The first study of the Dogon came from Marcel Griaule, whose *Conversations with Ogotemmêli: An Introduction to Dogon Religious Ideas* was published in 1948. Over 32 successive days, Ogotemmêli, a blind Dogon elder, had met with Griaule and spoken about Dogon mythology.

Scholars today view the study as the ruminations of one member of the community, rather than a detailed exposé of Dogon thought in general. African religions place greater emphasis on doing the right thing (orthopraxis) than believing the right thing (orthodoxy). As a result, within any one group there can be a range of varying individual beliefs and ways of describing the world and its creation. Later studies of the Dogon have therefore given rise to many different myths and interpretations.

were also paired together. This set off a chain of links, extending beyond animals to plants to create a vast network. The Dogon believe that each individual has a soul connection to one-eighth of the living things in the world.

According to some versions of the myth, the eight ancestors were created when one of the first two Nommo rebelled against Amma and tried to create a separate world

The Nommo are often depicted with upraised arms, as in this small sculpture. This is thought to represent a reaching towards the heavens in prayer for rain.

of his own. He procreated through sexual intercourse with the placenta that held him inside the womb of his mother, Earth, but the fruits of this incestuous union were solitary and impure. Contaminated by this abominable act, the world faced the prospect of descending into a state of utter chaos, but Amma regained control of the cosmos by murdering the other Nommo. He was torn apart and his body was scattered across the earth, then the eight Nommo ancestors were created from his body parts. The Dogon later created ancestral shrines (called *binu*) at places where the parts had landed.

Early humans

The eight Nommo procreated and began to populate the earth. At this stage, humans were primitive beings who lived in holes in the ground like animals and could only use basic sounds to communicate. When the Nommo had produced many children, the eight ascended to heaven.

However, when the Nommo realized that the human world was in chaos, they returned to earth one by one, in order of age, each bringing a valuable skill. First the eldest Nommo, a blacksmith, introduced humans to fire and metalworking by stealing a piece of the sun in the form of a live ember and a white-hot iron rod. Another Nommo taught the art of weaving to mankind, and another the art of constructing clay granaries. These were topped with a thatch to prevent rain washing away the clay, and were modelled on the anthill

In order to purify the universe and restore order to it, Amma sacrificed another Nommo.
Art of the Dogon
Kate Ezra, art historian (1988)

Amma filled with his seed when he impregnated the earth. Their bases were square to represent the four cardinal points – north, south, east, and west.

Chaos and sacrifice

The eighth Nommo was impatient and descended to earth before her sister, the seventh Nommo. This angered the seventh Nommo so much that she turned into a giant serpent, but humans feared the snake and made weapons to kill her, using the skills taught by the first Nommo, the blacksmith.

The death of the seventh Nommo brought more chaos. The other ancestors decided that they must sacrifice Lébé, who was the first *Hogon* (spiritual leader of the community) and the oldest man in the family of the eighth Nommo. Lébé was the first human to die, and thereby brought mortality to mankind. His body was buried in a primordial field with the head of the seventh Nommo, under the anvil of the blacksmith Nommo. The blacksmith struck the anvil with his tools, awakening the spirit of the seventh ancestor. The serpent then devoured Lébé – combining the spirits of the seventh and eighth Nommo forever. These two

Dogon dancers don masks for *dama* funerary rites in Tireli, Mali. These are enacted to lead spirits of the deceased out of the village and towards their final resting place with the ancestors.

Nommo represented language, which was considered the essence of all things: the seventh Nommo was the master of the Word and the eighth was the Word itself.

Cleansing gifts

When the serpent vomited Lébé's remains out in a series of stones, they made the shape of a body. First came eight *dugé* stones, which are formed when lightning strikes the ground. These stones marked the joints at the pelvis, shoulders, elbows, and knees. Then came the smaller stones, forming the long bones, vertebrae, and ribs. The stones were a gift from the

Nommo to humanity. They held Lébé's life force, and were a physical manifestation of speech. The stones also absorbed all that was good from the ancestors and cleansed the people of their impurities with the water that was the Nommo's essence and life force. When Lébé's remains were being ejected, torrents of purifying water also came forth. It brought fertility to the land, and enabled humanity to plant crops and farm.

The Dogon view Lébé as the manifestation of the regenerative forces of nature. To this day, *Hogon* wear stones that symbolize Lébé's remains, and remind them of their link to their ancestors. Although Amma is the supreme deity in Dogon religion, and prayers and sacrifices are made to him, the chief focus for most of the Dogon's rituals is ancestor worship. ∎

Water and the Dogon

Water is crucial in the myths and lives of the Dogon people. Mali, the Dogon homeland, sits on the edge of the Sahara Desert, where water can be scarce and the amount of rainfall dangerously variable. The water cycle in the area is variable. Both droughts and monsoons afflict the region, and rivers and lakes appear and disappear again.

Rejecting the pressure to convert to Islam, the Dogon first set up their villages at the base of Mali's Bandiagara Escarpment 1,000 years ago, attracted by its defensibility and its springs; they later spread to the nearby plateau, where they built deep wells.

THE QUEEN WANTS TO KILL YOU

ESHU THE TRICKSTER

IN BRIEF

THEME
Chaos and balance

SOURCE
Ifá Divination Poetry, Wande
Abimbola, 1977; *Orixás:
Deuses Iorubas Na África e No
Novo Mundo* ("Yorùbá Gods of
Africa and The New World"),
Pierre Fatumbi Verger, 1981.

SETTING
Yorùbáland, western Africa.

KEY FIGURES
Eshu The trickster.

The king A selfish ruler who
was punished by Eshu.

A queen One of the king's
many wives.

The heir The king's eldest son.

Two women Best friends
who were blessed by Eshu.

A Babalawo A priest and
diviner of the Ifá religion.

I n Ifá, the religion of the Yorùbá
people of western Africa,
individuals interact on a daily
basis with spiritual entities known
as *orisha*. These include nature
spirits – Shango, for example, is
associated with lightning, and
Ogun with iron and metalwork – as
well as heroes from the past who
have become deified. One of the
figures often found in myths about
the *orisha* is Eshu the trickster, also
known as Èsù-Elegba.

Sometimes Eshu's activities are
funny or harmless but at other times
his behaviour is actively destructive
to humans. Many Yorùbá-influenced
religious traditions have been
influenced by Christianity, and

See also: San creation myth 284 ▪ En-kai and the cattle 285 ▪ Ananse the spider 286-87 ▪ The Dogon cosmos 288-93

Eshu has been likened to the devil. However, scholars have concluded that the "devil" featured in these religions owes his character more to traditional conceptions of Eshu the trickster than the Christian model of Satan. Eshu is a being of chaos, but is also essential to meting out justice, keeping the universe in balance, and ensuring that no individual becomes too powerful.

The selfish king

Eshu often acts to punish others, especially those who have not shown him sufficient respect. There was a king who, despite his wealth and the large tracts of land he owned, never sacrificed anything to Eshu, not even a chicken or some kola nuts. Eshu decided to teach him a lesson.

The king had many wives but he was negligent towards them – one in particular felt aggrieved by her husband's lack of attention. Eshu visited her in the form of a wizard and said that if she could cut off a few whiskers from the king's beard, he would use them to make an amulet with magical power that would reignite the king's affection for her.

Next, Eshu visited the king's eldest son and heir. The son was not trusted by the king, who feared the young man wanted to usurp his authority and seize power. Taking the form of one of the king's servants, Eshu told the son to prepare his warriors and meet at the royal palace that very night, because the king was intent on going to war.

Finally, Eshu took the form of a trusted page and visited the king himself. "Your Majesty", the trickster whispered, "one of your wives is jealous of your power and she plans to kill you this night »

Eshu is depicted with a headdress of gourds in this wooden figure from Nigeria (c.1880–1920). While Eshu is usually considered to be male, the trickster is portrayed here as a woman with protruding breasts.

Eshu's punishments could be harsh, with consequences extending beyond those who had done wrong.

Eshu decides to **teach** the selfish **king** a **lesson**.

⬇

Eshu **tells** the king that his **wife and son** will **steal** the **throne**.

His **wife cuts his beard** to make a love charm.

His **son brings an army to the palace,** with disasterous results.

The king and his family are killed in punishment for their lack of respect.

Spread of religion

The Yorùbá community in southwest Nigeria and parts of Benin number more than 40 million people, but its influence has been far wider as a consequence of the Atlantic slave trade from the 16th to 19th centuries. Large numbers of men, women, and children suffered appalling conditions on a journey to an often short and brutish life in the New World. Yorùbá religious thought and practice travelled with the slaves, and their influence can be seen in religions such as Candomblé in Brazil, Vodou (often misnamed "voodoo") in Haiti, and Santería in Cuba.

This c.1900 Nigerian *Adjella-Ifa* depicts a woman, with a baby on her back, carrying a divination bowl topped with a hen. A *Babalawo* will cast nuts into the bowl for divine insight.

and place her son on the throne." Eshu warned the king: "You had better take care and keep vigil."

That night, as the king pretended to sleep, his aggrieved wife stole into his chamber with a knife intent on cutting a few whiskers from his beard so as to

Eshu turns right into wrong, and wrong into right.
Yorùbá Poetry
Bakare Gbadamosi
and Ulli Beier, 1979.

have the wizard make the charm. Thinking that she wished to kill him, the king jumped up and pried the knife from her hand. The commotion alerted the king's son, who was outside with his warriors, and they now rushed into the bedroom. Seeing his distraught mother and the king with a knife in his hand, he thought that his father wished to harm his mother. Meanwhile, the king, seeing the warriors, assumed that his son had come to seize power. A massacre ensued, in which the king and his family all lost their lives.

The two friends

While Eshu punished those who did not know their place, he also rewarded those who behaved well. There were once two young women who were the best of friends. They

did everything together: when they planted yams in the field they did so side by side; they wore the same dresses; and had even taken a pair of brothers as their husbands.

The women promised each other that they would remain friends for the rest of their days. To secure this pact they visited a *Babalawo* (diviner), who cast his sacred palm nuts and discerned that to have their friendship blessed they needed to offer a sacrifice to Eshu. However, they neglected to carry out these instructions and Eshu, in turn, decided to teach them a lesson.

The hat trick

One day the two friends were working in the fields, singing together as they worked the soil with their hoes. Eshu appeared wearing a flamboyant hat, one half red and the other half white, and as he walked between the two women they both greeted him. After he had gone on his way, one of the women turned to the other and commented on his appearance. "What a wonderful red hat he was wearing!" she exclaimed. "Are you blind?" asked her companion. "Surely you saw that the hat was white!" When Eshu returned later that day, he passed between the women again as they rested on their hoes. This time, he rubbed their tired backs.

"I am so sorry", said one woman to the other, "you were indeed right and his hat was red". "Are you mocking me?" replied her friend. "I could see it was clearly white!" Offended by each other's contrariness, the two friends came to blows, but rather than jeopardize their friendship, they decided to follow the *Babalawo's* advice. They prepared a sacrifice to Eshu, who accepted their offering and blessed their relationship such that they remained the best of friends to the end of their lives.

Eshu and divination

While Eshu is a figure of both chaos and order, this is not his only role in the Ifá religion. He is also a messenger, a being of multiple faces and personas who links everyday people with Olodumare, Ifá's supreme god. The Yorùbá believe that Eshu plays an important and dual role in divination; first, the spirit constantly monitors the transaction between the human world and the divine. Then, when a human makes a sacrifice, Eshu acts as an active conduit for divine energy – he lends the diviner *ashe* (power) and transports this power to the gods. In return, he brings divine gifts, such as knowledge or healing, back to the human world.

Duality plays an important role in Yorùbá mythology, not just in the dual nature of Eshu, but in the

Eshu wore a **hat** with a different **colour on each side** facing north, south, east, and west.

Eshu **assaulted** the king's wife in daylight in front of **witnesses**.

The goat said that the culprit was wearing a **red hat**.

Others saw different colours, depending on **where they stood** when they saw the attack.

Eshu got away with murder because nobody could agree on what they saw.

Eshu's hat of many colours featured in more than one myth. He wore it to best King Metolonfin, who boasted that his amazing four-eyed goat (actually the sun) allowed him to be all-seeing.

concepts of *ori and ese*, meaning "head" and "legs", respectively. *Ori* is essentially a person's potential and destiny, while *ese* is their hard work. The Yorùbá believe that both are necessary to succeed in life – one cannot be effective without

the other. A Yorùbá divination poem gives this warning: "All *ori* gathered to deliberate but they did not invite *ese*. Eshu said, "You do not invite *ese*; we will see if you are able to achieve success." ∎

Gods of the Yorùbá

Yorùbá cosmology does not take a single coherent form. This is largely due to the fact that many ethnic groups were, over the years, absorbed and assimilated into the community that we now know as the "Yorùbá". The diverse groups brought their own religious knowledge and insights and these were often incorporated into the evolving Yorùbá religious system.

As in many African religions, the Yorùbá believe in a high god, called Olodumare. Although

Olodumare is the creator and supreme being, it (the Yorùbá do not assign a gender to the deity) is remote from the people.

The Yorùbá have not erected any monuments to Olodumare, instead interacting with and appealing to minor spirits, the *orisha,* who control various aspects of everyday life. The *orisha* are either associated with the colour white (for calm and gentle spirits) or black and red, denoting a more aggressive or mercurial nature. Eshu is traditionally depicted in a black and red hat.

The *orisha* Yemoja is the mother of all other *orisha* and the goddess of the ocean and water. Accordingly, she is typically depicted in blue.

OCEANIA

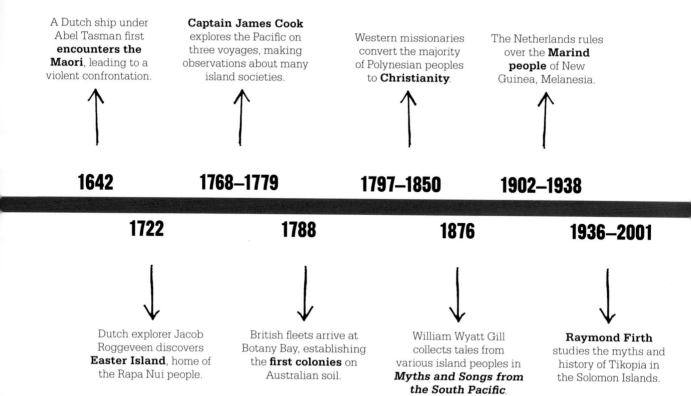

A Dutch ship under Abel Tasman first **encounters the Maori**, leading to a violent confrontation.

Captain James Cook explores the Pacific on three voyages, making observations about many island societies.

Western missionaries convert the majority of Polynesian peoples to **Christianity**.

The Netherlands rules over the **Marind people** of New Guinea, Melanesia.

1642　　**1768–1779**　　**1797–1850**　　**1902–1938**

1722　　**1788**　　**1876**　　**1936–2001**

Dutch explorer Jacob Roggeveen discovers **Easter Island**, home of the Rapa Nui people.

British fleets arrive at Botany Bay, establishing the **first colonies** on Australian soil.

William Wyatt Gill collects tales from various island peoples in *Myths and Songs from the South Pacific*.

Raymond Firth studies the myths and history of Tikopia in the Solomon Islands.

Apart from the landmass of Australia, Oceania is comprised of islands flung across more than 8.5 million square kilometres (3 million square miles) of the Pacific Ocean. The myths of the peoples of Oceania often differ greatly due to the vast geographical distances between them. The Aboriginal Australians in particular have traditions highly distinct from the rest of Oceania. The indigenous peoples of Australia were the first people to settle in Oceania, and probably came from South Asia around 65,000 years ago.

The next major group to arrive in Oceania were the Papuans, who arrived in New Guinea more than 40,000 years ago. The origins of many Oceanian tales can be traced back to this period. While Australia was relatively culturally isolated until the arrival of Europeans in the late 18th century, the Papuans interacted more with other peoples who came to these lands. Between 5,000 and 3,000 years ago, new sea-borne migrants from Southeast Asia arrived in Melanesia, northeast of Australia, settling on islands such as Fiji and the Solomon Islands. By 1000 BCE, settlers had established themselves in the islands of Micronesia in the west Pacific, north of Melanesia.

The next wave of migration, around 2,000 years ago, was eastwards to Polynesia. Over the centuries, Samoa, Tonga, Tahiti, Easter Island (Rapa Nui) and the Hawaiian Islands were settled. New Zealand was the last major area in Oceania to be inhabited by humans; the Maori arrived there around the 13th century CE.

The peoples of Polynesia were descended from a Melanesian group called the Lapita, who were skilled navigators and explorers. Splitting into many tribes, the Lapita had settled in the Bismarck Archipelago northeast of New Guinea by 2000 BCE, and populated the west Pacific from c.1600 CE onwards.

Key themes

A major theme in the mythologies of Oceania is the creation of the world. In many Aboriginal myths, creation occurred during "The Dreamtime", a period when spirits and supernatural beings wandered across the world, forming the landscape. While the Aboriginal creation is described as a gradual process, in Polynesian lore it is far more dynamic – typified by the widespread figure of Ta'aroa, a god

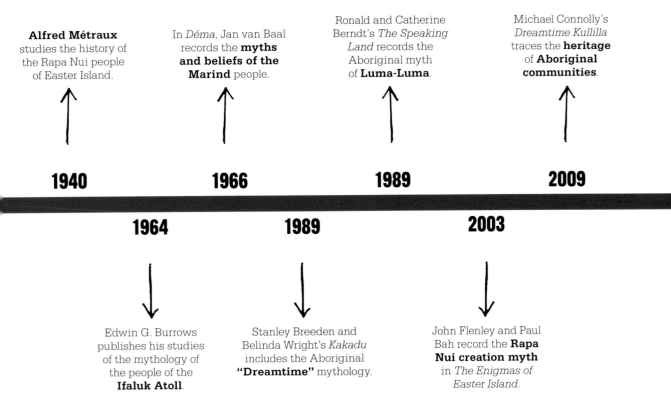

Alfred Métraux studies the history of the Rapa Nui people of Easter Island.

In *Déma*, Jan van Baal records the **myths and beliefs of the Marind** people.

Ronald and Catherine Berndt's *The Speaking Land* records the Aboriginal myth of **Luma-Luma**.

Michael Connolly's *Dreamtime Kullilla* traces the **heritage of Aboriginal communities**.

1940

1966

1989

2009

1964

1989

2003

Edwin G. Burrows publishes his studies of the mythology of the people of the **Ifaluk Atoll**.

Stanley Breeden and Belinda Wright's *Kakadu* includes the Aboriginal **"Dreamtime"** mythology.

John Flenley and Paul Bah record the **Rapa Nui creation myth** in *The Enigmas of Easter Island*.

who broke out of his shell to bring everything into being. Creation myths also explore the birth of humanity. In the Maori tradition, Tane – a forest god who appears across many Polynesian cultures – made mankind by breathing life into sand and mud. In Easter Island myths, Makemake, the god of sea birds, created life by ejaculating into clay, while Papuan myths say that humans were originally featureless fish that were shaped into people by ancestral deities called the *déma*.

Myths of the islanders

The island geography of Oceania has a big influence on its stories. The Micronesian myth of Aluluei, for example, emphasises the importance of navigation and exploration. The trickster god Maui appears in many Polynesian myths; as a mighty fisherman who hauled whole islands up from the ocean floor, he is credited with the mythical origin of Hawaii and New Zealand, where fishing was central to island life. In Maori lore, New Zealand's North Island is the fish Maui caught, and the South Island is his canoe.

Oral tradition

The myths of Oceania are based on ancient oral poetic tradition. This was often closely bound up with indigenous religion, as priests were frequently the repository of myths. Their stories were preserved down the generations through prodigious feats of memorization.

Remembering these tales was essential because many of them established the genealogy of a family or clan. The Maori trace their ancestry back to the canoe that brought their first ancestors to New Zealand, and Papuan tribes link themselves to their ancestral deities, the *déma*. Myth also helped to establish the *mana* – an important concept in Oceania, meaning "power" or "prestige" – of individuals or places, as well as recording what was taboo.

Oceania's myths were also central to the preservation of ritual. In the story of Luma-Luma, for example, the giant taught sacred rites to the Gunwinggu people of northern Australia before they killed him. Tales such as this began to be transcribed by European anthropologists during the 19th century, but were originally recited to audiences, learned and passed on as a sacred ceremonial duty. ∎

COME AND HEAR OUR STORIES, SEE OUR LAND

THE DREAMING

IN BRIEF

THEME
Living landscape

SOURCES
Oral tradition, recorded in
*Kakadu, Looking After the
Country the Gagudju way,*
S. Breeden and B. Wright,
1989; and in *Dreamtime
Kullila dreaming stories:*
Michael J. Connolly
(Munda-gutta Kulliwari), 2009.

SETTING
Dreamtime, Australia.

KEY FIGURES
Warramurrungundjui The
creator; fertility mother.

Rainbow Serpent A feared
creator; also known as Almudj
and Ngalyod.

Biami A creator spirit.

Gumuk Winga An old
woman.

Dating back to between
50,000 and 65,000 years,
Aboriginal Australian
have the longest continuous
cultural history of any peoples
on earth. Prior to the European
invasion of Australia in 1788,
around 600 different groups of
Aboriginal peoples existed, each
with its own language. Common to
these groups is the Dreaming or
Dreamtime, a term anthropologists
gave to the Aboriginal concept of a
formative period or state in which
ancestral creator spirits emerged
and landscapes, animals, and
people were formed. The creator
spirits gave each group its tools,
language, and culture, and laid
down the laws by which the people
were to live.

The Dreaming can be expressed
through song, dance, painting, and
storytelling, creating a tapestry of
knowledge, cultural values, and
belief system that are passed down
the generations. Each Aboriginal
group has its own creation stories,
although some are shared. They
explain the close relationship
between the land and the

*Our spirituality is a oneness
and an interconnectedness
with all that lives and
breathes, even with what
does not live or breathe.*
Mudrooroo
Australian novelist and poet (b. 1938)

Aboriginal people and why caring
for nature and wildlife is so
important to Aboriginal culture.

Fertility mother
One of the most important
Dreaming stories for the Gagudju
people of the Kakadu area in the
Northern Territory is that of the
creator spirit Warramurrungundjui.
The story tells how life began when
Warramurrungundjui emerged from
the sea and gave birth to the first
people, equipping them with
various languages. She created
mountains and creeks, and used
her digging stick to create water
holes – still important not only as
a life source but also as a place
to meet and honour the creator
beings. She also carried a bag
filled with yams and other plants
to scatter on her wanderings.
Warramurrungundji controlled the
weather, too, and could summon
rain, wind, and drought.

Dancers perform at the Laura
Aboriginal Dance Festival, in Laura,
a sacred meeting ground for Aboriginal
peoples in Cape York, a remote area
in Far North Queensland. The area is
known for its spectacular rock art.

See also: Creation 18–23 ▪ Creation of the universe 130–33 ▪ Creation of the world by Pan Gu 214–15 ▪ Cherokee creation 236–37 ▪ Creation of the world by Kóoch 260–61 ▪ The creation 266–71

After creating the whole landscape, Warramurrungundji turned herself into a rock, so that she would be ingrained in the landscape forever. Today, the Gagudju people honour her in sacred fertility ceremonies.

Rainbow serpent

Like most Aboriginal tribes, the Gagudju people revere the Rainbow Serpent. Dreaming stories tell how the serpent, whom the Gagudju call Almudj or Ngalyod, forged passages through rocks, created waterholes, and split rock faces to make hills. Unlike many Dreamtime figures who could shapeshift into humans or animals and back again, Almudj never changed her form.

Almudj created the wet season, enabling all forms of life to multiply. She is a creative force, but she is also feared and does not like to be disturbed. If angered, she can flood the land and drown anyone who breaks her laws. She lives in a deep, dark pool beneath the waterfall at Djuwarr Rock, southeast of Darwin. At times, Almudj can be seen standing on her tail, creating a rainbow in the sky.

The image of the Rainbow Serpent is common in rock art, especially in paintings dating from the end of the pre-estuarine period (c.60,000–6,000 BCE), and often appears alongside images of yams. Archaeologists believe that rising sea levels caused changes in the physical environment that brought about a reliance on wild yams during this period. Yams needed water, and Almudj provided it.

Creator and lawgiver

According to the Dreaming stories of the Kullilli people of southwest Queensland, the Rainbow Serpent

The rock paintings of fish at Nanguluwur Rock Art Site at Kakadu National Park, Northern Territory, were made during the estuarine period (6000 BCE–500 CE), when sea waters rose and valleys flooded.

lay dormant underground until she awoke in the Dreaming and pushed her way to the surface. She travelled the land, leaving behind the imprint of her body wherever she slept. After covering the whole earth, she called to the frogs, but they were sluggish, their bellies full of water after the long sleep of the Dreaming. The Rainbow Serpent tickled their stomachs and when the frogs laughed, water flowed out of their mouths and filled the hollow tracks left by the serpent on her travels. This created rivers and lakes, which, in turn, woke all the animals and plants of the land.

The Rainbow Serpent then created laws that would govern all living beings. When some of the creatures began to cause trouble, »

Dreamtime

The origin of the term "Dreamtime" can be traced back to Francis Gillen, a late 19th-century stationmaster and ethnologist who worked in Alice Springs and spoke Arrernte, the language of Aboriginal people in central Australia. He coined the term Dreamtime to represent the belief system of *Altyerrenge*, a word that means "to see and understand the law".

Gillen met and worked with Walter Baldwin Spencer, a Lancashire-born biologist and anthropologist studying Arrernte, who used Gillen's term in his 1896 account of an expedition to Cape Horn. Without this endorsement, the term might never have left Alice Springs. Today, the term "Dreamtime" is applied to all Australian Aboriginal belief systems.

she pledged to turn those who obeyed her into humans and those who did not into stone. The serpent kept her word and gave those she transformed into humans a totem of the creature they had previously been, such as kangaroo, emu, and carpet snake. The human tribes then began to distinguish themselves by their totems.

To ensure there was enough food for everyone, the Rainbow Snake forbade the people from

The joyful cries of Australian magpies at daybreak are a celebration of their success in creating the first dawn, according to the Wathaurong people of southwest Victoria.

eating the creatures that their totems symbolized. This belief partly explains why totems are such a significant part of Aboriginal cultural identity.

First dawn

Many Dreamtime stories describe the origin of natural phenomena and the formation of particular landmarks. The Wathaurong people of southwest Victoria, for example, have a Dreaming story that explains the origin of the sunrise. They say that the sky once covered the earth like a blanket, blocking out the sun's light and making everyone crawl around in the dark. The clever magpies decided to do something about the situation. They collected long sticks in their beaks and, working together, pushed them against the sky until they had lifted it up. However, the sticks were not strong and the sky was in danger of collapsing. Acting quickly, the magpies grabbed even

> We are all visitors to this time, this place. We are just passing through. Our purpose here is to observe, to learn, to grow, to love ... and then we return home.
> **Aboriginal saying**

longer sticks and pushed them up until the sky locked into place. The sun then appeared in the first ever dawn, prompting the birds to burst into joyful song.

Creating a river

The Yorta Yorta people, who have traditionally occupied an area in northeastern Victoria and southern New South Wales, recount a story that explains the formation of the River Murray, Australia's longest watercourse. At the time of creation, Baiame, a creator spirit,

The Rainbow Serpent

One of the most important characters in the Dreaming stories of many mainland Aboriginal groups, the Rainbow Serpent is often connected with watercourses, such as billabongs (a pond left behind after a river changes course), rivers, creeks, and waterholes. It is considered to be the source of all life and the protector of the land and its people.

Stories vary among the tribes, depending on local climatic conditions. Those of

the monsoon areas, for example, link the Rainbow Serpent to the rain and wind. Its connection to climate can make the serpent a destructive force.

The Rainbow Serpents's mythology is further linked to social relationships and fertility. It is often featured in ceremonies marking young men's transition from adolescence to adulthood.

A fearsome Rainbow Serpent bristling with sharp teeth decorates the roof of a cavern in a sandstone overhang at Mount Borradaile, Arnhem Land, Northern Territory.

Mount Elephant, a landmark in the Goldfields region of Victoria, is said by the Tyakoort Wooroong people to be the body of a man turned into stone after a bloody fight

in exchange for the axe, Elephant accepted. The two men met at present-day Pitfield Diggings (a former mining site southwest of Ballarat) and made the swap. Later, however, Buninyong decided that he no longer needed the axe and wanted to get back his gold. When Elephant refused to return it, Buninyong invited him to a duel at the same spot where they had met.

No sooner had the fight got underway than Elephant put his spear through Buninyong's side. Moments later, however, Buninyong struck Elephant's head with his stone axe. The two wounded men staggered off in opposite directions and soon both died. Their bodies turned into mountains. On the side of Mount Buninyong, a hole symbolizes the cut made with Elephant's spear, while another hole on the top of Mount Elephant represents Buninyong's deadly blow to Elephant's head. ■

saw an old woman, Gumuk Winga, with an empty *coolamon* (carrying vessel). The old woman appeared hungry, so Baiame suggested that she should go and search for yams. Picking up her digging stick, the old woman set out on her mission, accompanied by her dog. Gumuk Winga walked and walked, but could not find any yams. As time went on, she became weary and slowed down, dragging her digging stick through the earth. Day had turned to night, but still there was no sign of any yams.

Baiame waited for Gumuk Winga but she did not return. Eventually the spirit summoned the Rainbow Serpent, who was sleeping beneath the earth, and asked him to search for the old woman and bring her back safely. Almudj set off, following the marks left by the old woman's digging stick. The snake's body moved gracefully across the land, leaving deep crevices in the hills

and valleys. The rainbow colours from his body covered the trees, plants, birds, butterflies, and all other creatures.

All of a sudden, Baiame called out loudly. Thunder cracked, lightning flashed across the sky, and rain fell. It rained for days, and the crevices left by Almudj filled up with water. When the rain stopped and the mist cleared, the Murray River – called *Dungala* by the Yorta Yorta people – was formed.

Battle of the mountains

The Tyakoort Woorrong people of southwestern Victoria have another story about how the landscape around them was created. They relate that the area's two most prominent mountains, Mount Elephant and Mount Buninyong, were once men. Elephant had a stone axe, which Buninyong coveted. When Buninyong offered some gold

The elders guard the Law and the Law guards the people. This is the Law that comes from the mountain. The mountain teaches the Dreaming.
Guboo Ted Thomas
Aboriginal leader (1909–2002)

SPEAR ME SLOWLY. I STILL HAVE MORE TO TEACH YOU

THE KILLING OF LUMA-LUMA

Luma-Luma is one of many devious monsters that fill Aboriginal folklore. This version of his story, as told by Mangurug, a senior member of the Gunwinggu tribe of Arnhem Land, in northern Australia, is often used in local rituals conducted to initiate boys into manhood.

The story shows the origin and importance of vital rituals he gave to humanity, at a terrible cost to all: he would wreak havoc across the land, and die for it, but he still wanted to pass these rituals on.

Luma-Luma was a giant who had two wives, although in some versions of the story he began life as a whale, swimming to Arnhem Land from the east, and crossing the sea from Indonesia. Landing at Cape Stewart, Luma-Luma and his two wives then set off westwards, bringing with them sacred rituals and totems, known as *mareein*, which were gifts for mankind. Luma-Luma kept the ritual objects in a basket, or dilly bag, and also carried long spears to be used for fighting.

Greed takes over
Wherever they went, Luma-Luma declared that the food gathered and cooked by the people they encountered was taboo, and so sacred that only he could eat it. Terrified, the people abandoned their food – wild honey, large yams, freshly speared kangaroos, and fish – leaving it for him to consume.

His wives scolded him for making the people go hungry, but it was no use. Luma-Luma kept on eating, using the *mareein* he carried in his basket to justify his

An Arnhem Land aboriginal hunter spears a kangaroo in a 20,000-year-old rock painting at Nourlangie Rock, Kakadu National Park, in Australia's Northern Territory.

See also: The Dreaming 302–07 ▪ Ta'aroa gives birth to the gods 316–17 ▪ Tane and Hine-titama 318–19

He's eating our children.
What are we going to
do to him?
The Speaking Land

The full-breasted woman, shown
with two dilly bags and a digging
stick, is probably associated with
a fertility ritual.

too many spears, so he had time
to show them the rituals he knew.
They included *ubar* (which
reminded women they should
obey their husbands); *lorgun*
(an initiation ritual); and *gunabibi*
(a string of songs and dances to
win the favour of totemic spirits).
According to some versions of the
story, he also gave them the sacred
criss-cross designs they painted on
their faces during these ceremonies
and the dances that were part of
the rituals.

Once Luma-Luma was satisfied
that the people had received the
rituals, and after giving them his
basket of totems, he finally died.
The people did not bury him but
instead propped him up against
a tree on the beach, tied ropes
around him, and built a canopy
to shade him.

In time, his body was swept
into the sea and disappeared under
the water. There, he came back to
life as a sea creature; some claimed
he became a whale once more. ■

behaviour. In the evenings, he wore
the basket full of *mareein* around
his neck and beat his special
clapping sticks together,
while his wives danced, all to
demonstrate sacred rituals.

One day, Luma-Luma and his
wives arrived at a place where the
corpses of children were laid out
on platforms. Luma-Luma started
to eat these corpses. When the

people saw the empty platforms
and Luma-Luma's giant tracks,
they were horrified. Sick of him
eating their food – and now their
children – they plotted to kill him.

Imparted knowledge
Armed with sticks and spears,
the people attacked Luma-Luma
and his wives. The giant told them
to spear him slowly and not use

THE WORLD OF
MYTH
IS NEVER FAR OFF

THE DÉMA

IN BRIEF

THEME
Foundation and fertility

SOURCE
*Déma: Description and
Analysis of Marind-Anim
Culture (South New Guinea)*,
Jan van Baal, 1966.

SETTING
Papua New Guinea.

KEY FIGURES
Nubog The earth.

Dinadin The sky.

Geb and Mahu (Sami) The
déma forefathers.

Girui A déma dog.

Aramemb The déma of
medicine men.

Piakor Wife of Mahu and Geb.

Uaba Son of Geb and Piakor.

Rugarug-évai A déma hostile
to Uaba.

Often when listening
to a myth being told,
I had the impression that
it all happened only a
few months ago.
Father Jan Verschueren
Missionary and ethnographer

In the beginning there were two déma, or spirt beings: Nubog, the female earth, and Dinadin, the male sky. Their children Geb and Sami (also called Mahu) are the mythical ancestors of the Marind-Anim people of Western New Guinea, who all regard themselves as descended from one or the other. Traditionally, the ritual re-enactment of the myths about these déma, and the many other déma they engendered, was central to Marind-Anim identity and culture. A yearly cycle of re-enactments began with the ritual of the Mayo (a cult initiation) in the dry season and concluded with a headhunting expedition and a celebratory feast after the Imo ritual in the wet season.

Humans take form

The story of how the first humans originated begins with a great feast that the déma were holding underground in the far west of

Marind-Anim wear elaborate
costumes representing their déma
totems in a photograph taken at a
ritual re-enactment of myth in Dutch
New Guinea in the 1920s.

Marind territory. As they ate and drank, the déma gradually burrowed eastwards. Up on the surface of the earth, a déma dog named Girui heard the commotion. Wondering what was going on, he tracked the underground journey of the déma.

Girui followed the noise until he reached Kondo, where the sun rises. There the noise became very loud and he scratched away at the bank of a creek to discover its source. As he dug, water poured out of the earth, bringing with it strange beings like catfish, with no facial features and with arms, legs, fingers, and toes that formed part of their torsos. These were the Marind-Anim people. A stork déma then began to peck away at the creatures, but they were so hard that the bird's beak bent, giving it the slight curve that it has today.

Aramemb, the déma of medicine men, warned off the dog and the stork and made a big fire of bamboo to dry out the fish people. Each time the bamboo stems cracked in the heat, their bodies erupted and ears, eyes, noses, and mouths sprang out. Aramemb then took his bamboo

See also: The night barque of Ra 272–73 ▪ Ta'aroa gives birth to the gods 316–17 ▪ Tane and Hinetitama 318–19

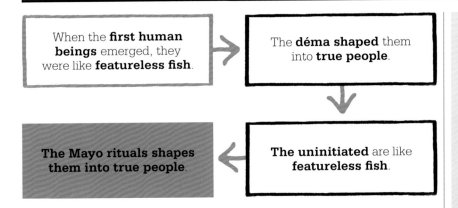

When the **first human beings** emerged, they were like **featureless fish**.

The **déma shaped** them into **true people**.

The **uninitiated** are like **featureless fish**.

The Mayo rituals shapes them into true people.

Kinship groups

In many ways, the invisible world of the déma was once more important to the Marind-Anim than the world in which they lived. Jan van Baal, an anthropologist and governor of Dutch New Guinea during the 1950s, observed that everything comes from the déma. Marind-Anim society is divided into two strands (moieties), each of which comprises two kinship groups (phratries), with their own déma totems, such as dog, stork, coconut, banana, sago, and many more. In a cohesive and relatively peaceful society, the different groups went headhunting together, repelling outsiders that could pose a threat.

While all Marind-Anim share the same myth world, each phratry has its own specific myths, versions of myths, or cycles of myths that inform its particular rituals. Some myths are shared across the phratries, such as the story of Uaba and Ualiwamb (see p.314), and the tale of the origin of man. It was common for phratries to visit one another to view re-enactments of déma stories.

knife and cut the arms, legs, fingers, and toes free. The trimmings that he threw away became leeches, which are abundant in the Marind-Anim lands to this day.

In fact, the dog had dug two holes. From the second hole came all the other tribes, or the *Ikom-anim* (outsiders), who quickly dispersed. Geb and Mahu then arrived in their canoes and took the new Marind-Anim humans aboard. Geb and Aramemb took the people who made up the Geb-zé and Aramemb "phratries" (kinship groups), and Mahu took charge of the Mahu-zé people.

A bamboo wife
The myths of the Geb-zé phratry say that Geb is a self-created being, whose face was pecked out of a stone by a stork. In the west, he grew into a red-skinned man trapped in an anthill where he suffered unbearable heat from the setting sun. Unable to find a wife, he mated instead with a stem of bamboo into which a stone axe could be fitted. The stem bore him several children.

After a while, Mahu, who lived in a beehive nearby, brought his two wives to visit Geb, who became

so excited at the sight of the women that Mahu took pity on him, and gave him one of his wives, Piakor, as a gift. As the wife of Geb, Piakor gave birth first to birds, then to fish, and after that to two boys and a girl. When the girl, Baléwil, was in the final stage of pregnancy herself, she went to the beach to give birth. She was in labour so long that the tide carried her out to sea, where she became a bank of hardened loam.

Geb was a headhunter. He kidnapped children, especially red-skinned boys, took them back to the anthill, and cut off their heads in his fiery lair. Eventually, the people decided that something must be done about Geb, but the men were reluctant to approach the anthill. To encourage them, the women brought water to quench its heat. When they poured it onto the anthill, Geb emerged, and the people cut off his head.

Sun, moon, and first fruits
Terrified by this assault, Geb's head fled underground and eastwards to Kondo, the place of the sunrise, where it climbed up a yam tendril into the sky to become the sun. It then travelled through the sky

to the western horizon before returning underground to Kondo, a journey it has repeated every day since. Meanwhile, Geb's headless body was divided up among the different clans and became the land.

There are also myths of Geb as the white-skinned moon. As a boy, Geb lived on the beach near »

Skulls decorate the tomb of a headhunter warrior in a Long House in New Guinea. Headhunters believed the skulls contained a sacred force that would enable their déma to multiply.

> Everything comes from the déma. That is the way the Marind see it when they refer to the déma as the originators of all things.
> **Jan van Baal**

Kondo and spent all his time fishing. He stayed so long in the sea that his body became covered with barnacles. One day, two women of marriageable age came along the beach. Geb was so ashamed of his body that he hid in the sand. When the women saw him, they told some men, who dug Geb out and cleaned off the barnacles with digging sticks and stone axes. The men then sexually assaulted Geb and treated his wounds with their seed. That night the first banana grew from Geb's neck. People came from all around to try the new fruit, which had the secret name of Kandéwa. A banana déma has lived near a deep pool at Kondo ever since.

A myth of the Mahu-zé phratry goes on to relate how the banana déma Wangai and Warungai attended a feast at Sangar. It had been organized by the déma Wokabu to celebrate the first pig hunt. It was customary on such occasions for guests to take gifts of the new fruit. At this pig feast, Wokabu's wife Sangon ate so much she repeatedly had to defecate. Her faeces formed the first sago palm, which became a staple foodstuff and a totem of the Geb-ze phratry.

Meanwhile, Geb was still a prisoner. After being assaulted for the second time, he decided to escape. He climbed up to the sky on a yam tendril and became the moon – the spots on the moon are his wounds, and the other marks ringworm. As both a red-skinned man imprisoned in the west, and a white-skinned boy trapped in the east, Geb unites the opposite powers of sun and moon in the figure of one dualistic déma.

Uaba and Ualiwamb

Geb and Piakor's son, the fire-déma, Uaba, is also the sun incarnate. When Uaba was to be initiated into the Mayo cult at Kondo, he brought with him a young woman, Ualiwamb (also called Kanis-iwag, Betel Woman), to take part in the *otiv-bombari*, a

Controversial rituals

Marind-Anim girls and boys were indoctrinated in the way of the déma from an early age. The sexual assault of Geb, the prolonged copulation of Uaba and Ualiwamb, and other myths were re-enacted in six-month-long cycles of initiation rituals. Elaborate costumes were worn and the performers temporarily embodied the spirit of the déma.

These ceremonies were intended to promote the fertility of humans, livestock, and crops. They were held, among other reasons, to facilitate marriage and to mark a woman's return to menstruation after giving birth. Ceremonies such as the *otiv-bombari*, intended to make a woman fertile, were viewed as a duty by the Marind-Anim. Yet the sexual behaviour in these rituals shocked outsiders, who saw it as cruel and immoral.

The Marind-Anim lived under Dutch rule from 1902 to 1938. By the 1920s, the Dutch authorities had outright banned *otiv-bombari*, as well as orther Marind-Anim rites, such as headhunting and cannibalism.

sexually promiscuous ritual that formed part of the Mayo ritual. However, before the ceremony got underway, Ualiwamb ran away. Pursuing her westwards, Uaba eventually reached the coast, where he saw her enter a hut with a large amount of sago. He waited until nightfall and then followed her.

The next morning, groans were heard coming from the hut, and Uaba and Ualiwamb were found locked in sexual intercourse, unable to separate. The people put them on a stretcher and carried them back to Kondo, preceded by the déma Rugarug-évai, who laughed and scoffed at them all the way. When they arrived at Kondo, Uaba managed to kill Rugarug-évai, but he still could not free himself from Ualiwamb.

Meanwhile, Aramemb had been searching for Uaba ever since he had set off to find Ualiwamb. When he came to Kondo, he entered the hut where Uaba and Ualiwamb lay entangled, and seized Uaba in an attempt to shake or twist him free. The friction sparked the first fire (*rapa*), which shot out of Ualiwamb. As the flames erupted around her, she gave birth to the first cassowary and the first stork, whose feathers were singed black by the flames.

Fanned by the monsoon winds, the primal fire spread, creating a broad beach on the coast, valleys that became riverbeds inland, and many natural features in the landscape. The fire also caused animals to flee into the sea, but the lobster was scorched by the flames and turned red.

In some versions of the myth, the cassowary déma, Dawi, tried to beat out the fire with its hunting club, an attempt that led to a piece of land covered in coconuts breaking away and being caught in an iguana's jaws. This story helped to explain the origins of the nearby island of Habee, and its appearance, which resembled an animal's head.

The story of Sosom

In the Aramemb phratry, Uaba's brother is a giant called Sosom, who wears a string of enemy heads.

Kar-a-kar, déma of sweet potato, is evoked during funeral rites. This oil painting of Kar-a-kar is by Pater P Vertenten, a Belgian missionary in New Guinea in the early 1900s.

The story of Sosom is the root of the ritualized homosexuality that was practised among the Aramemb. Castrated by the people for his unruly behaviour – or in some versions of the story, by the mother of a girl with whom he had become locked in sexual intercourse – Sosom then chased the women away with his growling and initiated the men in homosexual rites. The Marind-Anim believed that it was through such rites that boys became strong and learned to be men.

Grand celebration

Traditionally, the Marind-Anim's annual cycle of ritual re-enactments of the déma stories ended in an intervillage feast, and a *déma-wir*: in this grand retelling of the myths, the protagonists competed to put on the best show. The characters performed dramatic dances in elaborate costumes while *déma-nakari* ("little sisters") represented their déma's minor attributes and acted out the many subplots. ∎

MASTER OF EVERYTHING THAT IS

TA'AROA GIVES BIRTH TO THE GODS

IN BRIEF

THEME
The cosmos is made from a shell

SOURCE
Oral tradition, transcribed in *The World of the Polynesians: Seen through their myths and legends, poetry and art*, Antony Alpers, 1987.

SETTING
The beginning of time in Tahitian mythology.

KEY FIGURES
Ta'aroa The creator god, originator of the entire cosmos.

Tane Ta'aroa's son, the god of light and forests. In some places, Tane is a woman rather than a man.

Tu Ta'aroa's son, the god of war and craftsmen.

Before the cosmos was created there was just a blank void. Amidst this expanse of nothingness floated a huge egg-shaped shell. Inside was the feathered creator god Ta'aroa, who had no mother or father.

Eventually, Ta'aroa grew tired of this confined existence. He forced open his egg, cleaving it in two, and crawled out to the edge of the broken shell. When he called out to the darkness, there was no reply – the only sound was Ta'aroa's voice. Growing up alone on the shell from which he had emerged, Ta'aroa became frustrated at having no-one to do his bidding, so he resolved to bring creation and life to the void.

Ta'aroa's first action was to push up one half of the broken shell, which formed the dome of the sky. He then used the other half of the shell to make the rocks that formed the earth's foundation. To create a habitat for life, Ta'aroa used his own flesh to make soil and his innards to make the clouds. Ta'aroa's tears then formed the waters of the earth, filling up the oceans, lakes, and rivers. His backbone became the mountain ranges and his ribs their ridges.

Ta'aroa creates other gods and human beings in this wooden statue (c.17th–18th century) from Rurutu, one of the Austral Islands in what is now French Polynesia.

See also: Pan Gu and the creation of the world 214–15 ▪ Viracocha the creator 256–57 ▪ Tane and Hine-titama 318–19

Ta'aroa's feathers made vegetation and his guts became lobsters, shrimps, and eels. He used his toe- and fingernails to give sealife its shells and scales.

Finally, his blood became the glowing colours in the sky and in rainbows. Great Ta'aroa had used his entire body except for his head; that part remained sacred to himself.

The god's children

Ta'aroa then summoned forth a multitude of other gods from his body (which is why he is often depicted with them crawling over him). One of his children, Tane, illuminated creation by hanging the sun, moon, and stars in the sky. Tane became the god of peace and beauty, and sometimes the god of forests and birds.

Of all Ta'aroa's children the most able craftsman was Tu, who had helped his father create more species of plants and animals to fill the world. Ta'aroa then made the first man and woman and persuaded them to procreate.

Ta'aroa in Polynesian cultures		
Name	**Place**	**Role**
Ta'aroa	Society Islands (including Tahiti)	The creator deity.
Kanaloa	Hawaii	A sea deity, and a god of death.
Tagaloa	Samoa	Creator of the universe.
Tangaloa	Tonga	Ancestor of a long-running dynasty.
Tangaroa	New Zealand	God of the sea.

Ta'aroa had created the world with seven levels, placing humanity on the bottom one. Much to his delight, people multiplied more and more quickly. As they shared their space with plants and animals, they soon occupied all the levels of the earth.

Inside the shell

When Ta'aroa had finished the task of creation, he had a revelation: everything that existed in the cosmos was contained in a shell. He had been contained within a shell, the sky was the shell of heavenly bodies, and earth the shell of everything that lived there. The shell of all humanity was the womb of the woman from whom they had emerged.

Despite this awareness, Ta'aroa knew that everything still belonged to him. Although he had come out of a shell, he was still the supreme creator of all. ▪

Tiki: Polynesian wood carvings

Polynesia encompasses over 1,000 islands that form a triangle in the southern Pacific, from Hawaii at the peak to New Zealand in the southwest and Rapa Nui (Easter Island) in the southeast. The indigenous peoples of these islands generally share the belief that gods are all-pervasive and can take many other forms, such as humans, animals, or features of the landscape. People present offerings to the carvings that depict these forms. These carvings are known as *tiki* and are made across Polynesia. In some parts of Polynesia, *Tiki* was also the name of the first man to be created. *Tiki* can be made in a range of sizes, from large human-shaped statues to pendants worn as necklaces.

When Europeans began colonizing Polynesia they tried to suppress traditional culture and religious practices, destroying many *tiki* in the process. However, *tiki* statues are still made today throughout Polynesia.

Carved wooden *tiki* keep watch as a Russian sailor explores a *morai* (cemetery) on the island of Nuku Hiva, in this engraving from c.1807.

DEATH OBTAINED POWER OVER MANKIND

TANE AND HINE-TITAMA

IN BRIEF

THEME
Mortality

SOURCE
Oral tradition, transcribed in *Polynesian Mythology and Ancient Traditional History of the New Zealand Race, as Furnished by their Priests and Chiefs*, Sir George Grey, 1855.

SETTING
The beginning of time.

KEY FIGURES
Rangi The sky father.

Papa The earth mother.

Tu God of war and hunting.

Tawhirimatea God of storms.

Tane God of forests.

Tangaroa God of the sea.

Hine-hau-one The first woman; mother of Hine-titama.

Hine-titama Daughter and wife of Tane.

Maui A demigod and trickster.

In Maori mythology, before the world was created, there was only Rangi, the sky father, and his wife Papa, the earth mother, who lay in an embrace so tight their sons lived in total darkness in the narrow space between their bodies.

Tired of these conditions, their sons discussed how to force apart their mother and father. The warlike Tu wanted to kill them both, but the forest god Tane persuaded his brothers that their parents should just be separated. After each of his brothers had failed to prize the couple apart, Tane did so by placing his shoulders on Papa and pushing Rangi up with his legs.

With this, Tane began to fill the world with forests, but his work was disrupted by his brother Tawhirimatea, who had grown angry that their parents were forced to live apart. Tawhirimatea sought revenge by raising a great storm across the earth. It was Tu, the god of war, who withstood him, bringing peace to the earth.

World of darkness

Over time Tane grew lonely. Woman had not yet been created, so he coupled with non-humans, fathering insects, stones, streams, and plants. Finally, Tane, longing for a partner, went to a beach and shaped the first woman out of sand and mud, which led to her being named Hine-hau-one, meaning "earth-formed maiden". She and Tane conceived a daughter, and named her Hine-titama, meaning "maiden of the dawn".

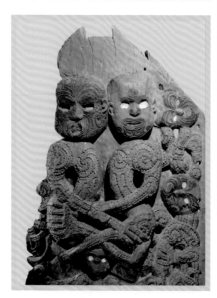

Rangi and Papa copulate in an 18th-century Maori carving. In Maori culture, *whakairo* (carving) is both an artistic and a spiritual practice.

See also: Creation of the universe 130–33 ▪ Ahura Mazda and Ahriman 198–99 ▪ Brahma creates the cosmos 200 ▪ Izanagi and Izanami 220–21

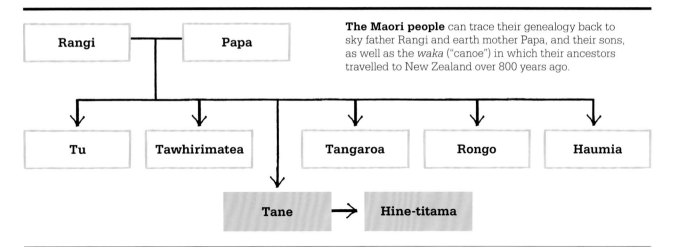

The Maori people can trace their genealogy back to sky father Rangi and earth mother Papa, and their sons, as well as the *waka* ("canoe") in which their ancestors travelled to New Zealand over 800 years ago.

War canoes, or *waka tua*, are still used in Maori ceremonies. At the annual IRONMAN race in New Zealand, *waka* escort competitors to the start of the swimming leg.

Hine-titama was raised not knowing who her father was. When she grew up, Tane married her. Hine-titama lived happily as Tane's wife, and had children with him, until she found out that he was actually her father. Appalled, she fled to the underworld. Her father followed her and begged her to return, but Hine-titama refused. She told him that he should stay where he was to look after his children in the world of light.

Hine-titama chose to remain in the underworld to care for those who entered the world of darkness. There she took on a new name, Hine-nui-te-po, meaning "great maiden of the darkness".

No humans had entered the underworld until the actions of the trickster Maui, who had been told that anyone who crawled through Hine-nui-te-po's body would banish death from humanity. While the goddess slept, Maui assumed the form of a worm and tried to enter her body through her vagina. When Hine-nui-te-po realised, she quickly shut her legs, crushing Maui to death: from then on, humanity was forever doomed to be mortal. ▪

The war god Tu

Of all the sons of Rangi and Papa, only Tu withstood the attack from the storm god Tawhirimatea: Tane could do nothing to stop his trees being destroyed, Tangaroa fled to the ocean, and Haumia and Rongo hid themselves in their mother's body, the earth.

After the winds had died down, Tu blamed his brothers for not supporting him and attacked them. He cut down trees in Tane's forests, caught fish from Tangaroa's water, and dug up the plants from the soil where Haumia and Rongo had hidden.

Tu's actions supplied humans with a template for making use of the resources of the natural world through ritual and farming. Tu also set a precedent for war between humans by fighting with his brothers. The Maori name for New Zealand's armed forces is *Ngati Tumatauenga*, meaning "Tribe of the God of War", in honour of Tu.

BUT THE REDOUBTABLE MAUI WAS NOT TO BE DISCOURAGED

MAUI OF A THOUSAND TRICKS

IN BRIEF

THEME
The gift of fire

SOURCE
Myths and Songs from the South Pacific, William Wyatt Gill, 1896.

SETTING
Polynesia at the beginning of time; the Underworld.

KEY FIGURES
Maui A trickster god.

Buataranga Maui's mother; a goddess.

Tane The forest god.

Akaotu Tane's favourite red pigeon.

Mauike The fire god.

Ru Maui's father and a god.

Tama-nui-te-ra The "great god of the sun", called Ra.

When he was a youth, Maui, the great hero of Polynesian mythology, was given the task of guarding the path to the Underworld. Maui lived in the upper world, where humanity resides. Buataranga, Maui's mother, spent most of her time in the Underworld but sometimes visited her son in the upper world. The food she gave him was always cold, whereas the meals she brought for herself were always hot, thanks to the (closely guarded) secret of fire that was kept in the Underworld and unknown to the upper world.

One day Maui stole some of his mother's meal while she was sleeping. Maui preferred the cooked

See also: Prometheus helps mankind 36–39 ▪ Fire and rice 226–27 ▪ Ta'aroa gives birth to the gods 316–17 ▪ Tane and Hine-titama 318–19

Tane is known as Tane Mahuta ("King of the Forest") in Maori legend. The largest Kauri tree in Waipoua Forest, New Zealand, over 1,000 years old, bears this name in honour of the god.

Maui then put himself inside the bird and flew into the Underworld. As he darted past the demons, they could only grab at Akaotu's tail, pulling off a few of his feathers.

Buataranga's warning

Maui flew to where his mother Buataranga lived whenever she was in the Underworld. Because there were no red pigeons living in the lower realm, Buataranga knew that something was amiss and quickly deduced that her son was involved. Maui resumed his human form, and the red pigeon settled on a breadfruit tree.

Maui told his mother that he had come to find out how to kindle fire. She told him that she did not know the secret herself and that whenever she needed to cook she went to the

The fire god, confident in his own prodigious strength, resolved to destroy this insolent intruder.
Myths and Songs from the South Pacific

fire god Mauike, who gave her lighted sticks. Buataranga warned her son, however, not to approach Mauike because of his violent temper and great strength.

Playing with fire

Undeterred, Maui went straight to Mauike's house and asked him for a firebrand. When he was given »

food and resolved to discover how she heated it. For that, he knew he had to gain access to the Underworld. Following his mother as she returned to her home, Maui saw her speaking to a black rock, which opened up when she recited a poem.

So that he, too, could visit the Underworld, Maui committed the poem's words to memory. He knew that getting in unnoticed would require trickery, so Maui visited his friend Tane, the forest god, who owned many pigeons. Maui demanded Tane's most prized bird, a red pigeon called Akaotu who was tame and well-trained. Tane lent Maui the bird but made him promise to return it unharmed. Taking the pigeon with him, Maui returned to the rock where his mother had entered the Underworld. He recited the poem and the portal opened. Using his trickster powers,

Maui in Polynesian mythology

Tales of the trickster god appear throughout Polynesian mythology, although the god's name may vary; Maui's Samoan equivalent is called Ti'iti'i. In Maori mythology, Maui is said to be a human, miraculously saved from death by ocean spirits when he was very young after his mother threw him into the sea. The exact details of his exploits tend to vary with location. Common elements include the stories of Maui pushing up the sky, snaring the sun, and gaining the secret of fire, but accounts of Maui's end

differ. In the Cook Islands, he is believed to have ascended to the heavens. In some Hawaiian myths, he has his brains dashed out. The other gods tire of his tricks and dash him against the rocks after he tries to steal a banana they are roasting. In Maori mythology, Maui is a mortal killed by the goddess of death as he tries to win eternal life. Maui's most recent incarnation is in the 2016 Disney animation *Moana*, where the eponymous heroine, a chief's daughter, searches for Maui in a bid to save her people.

Maui fishes for the islands

One of Maui's greatest feats was pulling up land from the ocean floor using his magic fish hook, thereby creating the islands of the South Pacific. The magic hook was fashioned from the jaw of one of Maui's ancestors, according to Maori mythology, and helped the god to create New Zealand. While out fishing with his two brothers in a canoe, Maui baited the hook with blood from his nose and hauled up a fish that became the land mass that formed North Island, known in Maori as *Te Ika-a-Maui* ("The Fish of Maui"). The South Island was formed from Maui's canoe, it is known as *Te Waka-a-Maui* ('The Canoe of Maui'). In Hawaiian myth, Maui is credited with hauling up the Hawaiian Islands, while in the Cook Islands, he is said to have brought up Manihiki from the briny depths.

Maui hooks the fish that became New Zealand's North Island. Maori legend has it that Maui's brothers squabbled over parts of the fish, creating mountains and fjords.

it, he immediately threw it into a stream. Maui repeated his request and again threw the firebrand away. When Maui asked for fire a third time, Mauike gave him live coals on a piece of dry wood, which Maui also threw into a stream. His insolent behaviour was calculated to provoke Mauike, who snapped when Maui asked for flame a fourth time. He ordered Maui to leave, threatening to toss him in the air.

Maui stood his ground, and cheekily replied that he would relish a trial of strength. Mauike went inside his house to don his war *maro* (loincloth). When he returned he was shocked to find that Maui had magically grown larger. Mauike seized Maui and tossed him to the height of a coconut tree but in mid-air Maui made himself so light that the fall did not hurt him at all. Mauike threw Maui even higher. Once more, Maui used magic to ensure he would be unharmed. Exhausted from his efforts, Mauike panted for breath. Maui then threw the fire god high into the air twice, causing him grave injuries.

As Maui prepared for a third throw, Mauike begged him to stop, fearing another fall could be fatal. Maui relented on condition that he be taught the secret of fire. Mauike agreed, and led Maui into his house. He showed Maui some bundles of dry coconut fibre and dry sticks. Mauike gathered some of them together and rubbed two smaller sticks over the pile. This started a fire that quickly became a mighty blaze. Maui, still angry at having been tossed in the air, spitefully allowed it to burn down Mauike's house. The flames then spread

Clouds cannot stay over Hawaiian islands for long. Legend says that if they do, Maui will hurl them away so far that they never return.

across the Underworld. Maui grabbed the two fire sticks and ran back to his mother's house, where Akaotu was still waiting for him, lacking some of his beautiful feathers. Repairing his tail, Maui hid inside the bird again, grasped a fire stick in each claw, and flew back to the upper world before returning the pigeon to Tane.

Meanwhile, flames from the great fire in the Underworld had now spread to the upper world and people began using them to cook their food. Like Maui, they found they preferred hot meals. Once the fire had been put out, however, there was no one in the upper world who knew how to make flames – no one except Maui, who kept a fire in his house. The people went to Maui and asked him to share his secret, which he did.

Maui raises the sky

At this time the sky, which was made of solid blue stone, was about 2m (6½ft) above the ground. This did not leave much space for humans. Maui's father Ru planted stakes in the ground, which raised the sky just enough for all humans to walk unimpeded. Maui, however, was unimpressed and impudently asked his father what he was doing.

> From that memorable day all the dwellers in this upper world used fire-sticks with success, and enjoyed the luxuries of light and cooked food.
>
> ***Myths and Songs from the South Pacific***

Maui's greatest battle was with the sun, called *Tama-nui-te-ra* in Maori mythology. Here, his brothers hold the ropes tight and Maui forces the sun to give his people longer days.

Ru was in no mood for Maui's insolence and threatened to throw him into oblivion. Maui persisted in annoying his father, who angrily flung him up into the sky.

Maui transformed himself into a bird and flew to safety. He then returned to Ru in the form of a giant human. Placing his head between his father's legs, he raised himself to his full height, thrusting Ru up above him. He did this with such force that the sky moved far from the earth, creating the present great distance between them. Ru became stuck – his head and shoulders got caught up in the stars. Unable to move, Ru eventually died, and his bones fell to earth as the pumice stones that litter the volcanic landscapes across Polynesia.

A last battle with the sun

Maui still had one great task to achieve. The sun god Ra (short for Tama-nui-te-ra, "great god of the sun") was unreliable, appearing at erratic times during the day and night and making it difficult to get work done. No one had been able to persuade him to appear regularly.

Maui resolved to remedy this. He made six ropes of strong coconut fibre, and fashioned them into nooses. He went to where Ra rose from the Underworld and placed a noose there. Maui then positioned the other five nooses along Ra's customary path.

When Ra rose up, the first noose tightened around his feet. As he moved, the other nooses trapped his knees, hips, waist, underarms, and neck. Maui then tied the sun god to a rock, pulling the ropes so tight that Ra could barely breathe. Fearing death, Ra agreed to help the people by appearing more regularly. Maui then released him, but kept the ropes attached, so the sun could be raised up and down in the sky.

Maui's bold feats became well known and admired across all Polynesian cultures. Through his masterful cunning, he was able to outwit all other gods, to the great benefit of humanity. ∎

WHAT WOULD YOU SAY TO OUR DRIVING THE BIRDS TO EASTER ISLAND?

MAKEMAKE AND HAUA

IN BRIEF

THEME
Creation and worship

SOURCES
Ethnology of Easter Island, Albert Métraux, 1940; *The Enigmas of Easter Island*, John Flenley and Paul Bahn, 2003.

SETTING
Easter Island; the beginning of time.

KEY FIGURES
Makemake God of seabirds.

Haua Goddess; wife of Makemake.

Priestess A local preacher.

In the mythology of the Rapa Nui people, who are indigenous to Easter Island, the world was created by a god named Makemake. The chief god of the birdman cult, he was often depicted in art as a skull with goggle eyes, or as a sooty tern.

Makemake created the first human beings. Trying to procreate, the god first masturbated into a calabash full of water, but this produced no offspring. Then, he copulated with stones – which still bear the holes he created in them –

Prehistoric carvings line the coast of Easter Island, and overlook Moto Nui Island, the destination of a dangerous annual race competition, which would often claim lives.

but that did not work either. Lastly, he masturbated into clay, and as a result, four gods were born – Tive, Rorai, Hova, and Arangi-kote-kote.

One day, these gods gave a priestess the task of guarding a skull in the bay of Tongariki, on Easter Island. When the skull was swept away by a huge wave, the

See also: Viracocha the creator 256–57 ▪ Tane and Hine-titama 314–15 ▪ Ta'aroa gives birth to the gods 316–17 ▪

>
> We shall have no peace until we find a place where men cannot find us.
> *Easter Island*
>

priestess swam after it for three days, until she eventually came ashore on the island of Matiro-hiva.

The goddess Haua, wife of Makemake, appeared, and asked the priestess what she was doing. She replied that she was looking for a skull. "That is not a skull," Haua told her, "it is the god Makemake".

New gods
The priestess stayed on the island with Haua and Makemake, and the gods fed her the fish they caught. Then Makemake suggested that they should drive all the seabirds to Rapa Nui, as this was what he had come to the island to do. Haua agreed, and said that the priestess should join them and teach people how to worship their new gods.

The three of them set out, driving the birds in front of them, in search of a place where they could leave them to nest. First they tried the island of Hauhanga, where they stayed for three years, but men found the nests and took the eggs to eat. Then they went to Vai Atare, but once again men stole the eggs and used them as food. Makemake and Haua agreed that they needed to find a place that man could not reach. So they settled on the rocky islets of Motu Nui and Motu Iti, just off the coast of Rapa Nui.

Egg hunt
All this time the priestess travelled around Rapa Nui, teaching people how to worship their new gods, and to set aside a portion for them before each meal, and say "Makemake and Haua, this is for you".

At the sacred site of Orongo, the skull-mask of Makemake and the vulva of Haua were carved all over the rocks, along with depictions of a bird-headed man clutching an egg. From this spot, competitors representing the Easter Island chiefs set off and vied to collect the first egg of the season from the islets. When a chief was victorious, he was declared the birdman, the living representative of Makemake on earth for the coming year. ▪

Makemake as depicted in a Easter Island petroglyph carved from red scoria, c.1960. Scoria was also used to build the red hatlike structures of Easter Island's famous moai statues.

Rongorongo boards
Some of the most intriguing artefacts to survive the collapse of Easter Island culture are rongorongo boards. Since their discovery in 1864, these pieces of wood, carved with hieroglyphs, have been a source of much debate over whether or not they actually represent a consistent written language. While the glyphs remain undeciphered to this day, oral history means that the rongorongo boards are believed to have been viewed as sacred objects, probably used by trained chanters or bards for telling myths. On one board, out of a total of 960 symbols, 183 are representations of a sooty tern, symbolizing the god Makemake. The "Santiago Staff" has the longest of any inscription, with 2,320 glyphs.

In 1995, independent linguist Steven Fischer stated that he had deciphered 85 per cent of the rongorongo boards. He proposed that the significant rongorongo texts, including the Santiago staff, documented, through a triad structure of images, the creation of the world and everything in it through a series of copulations. His claims, however, have attracted several objections from scholars who note that, amongst other discrepancies, only half of the inscriptions on the Santiago staff fully obey Fischer's triad structure.

WHEN I UTTER HIS NAME, HE HEARS IN THE HEAVENS

MAPUSIA AND THE WORK OF THE GODS

IN BRIEF

THEME
Gods and society

SOURCE
Oral tradition, transcribed by Raymond Firth in *The Work of the Gods in Tikopia*, 1940; *History and Traditions of Tikopia*, 1961; *Tikopia Ritual and Belief*, 1967; *Rank and Religion in Tikopia*, 1970; and *Tikopia Songs,* with Mervyn McLean, 1990.

SETTING
Tikopia, Solomon Islands.

KEY FIGURES
Saku Hero and, as Mapusia, supreme god.

Te Samoa Companion and rival of Saku.

Te Seme Saku's killer.

Atua Fafine Ancestral goddess of Tikopia.

Atua i Raropuka Ancestral god of Tikopia.

Communal rites known as the Work of the Gods bound Tikopian society together at every level – mythology, religion, community values, social status, economics, and simple survival. The rites were said to have been instituted by Saku, the hero of the people of Tikopia, a tiny Pacific island. Saku (whose name was a sacred taboo, so never uttered) was the son of Asoaso, a Kafika chief, and a woman from neighbouring Faea. Born some generations after the first creator gods brought the island into being and at a time when their successors exercised dangerous supernatural powers, Saku established order and consolidated the power of the Kafika, one of Tikopia's four clans.

Saku clothed the island people, and by doing so awoke their human consciousness, giving them minds with which to acquire knowledge. He also made the sacred adzes (axelike tools) whose blades were traditionally fashioned from the shell of the giant clam. At that time, everything in the world had a voice, even the trees and the rocks, but Saku ordered them to be silent. He then commanded the rocks to form

> Kafika as a habitation and a name, was the prize for which the aspirants for leadership strove.
> **History and Traditions of Tikopia**

a pile, and the earth to cover it, creating a platform on which the Kafika temple could be raised.

Asserting his authority
Saku had a friend and rival whose powers were similar to his own. The man – Te Samoa –was said to have come to Tikopia from Samoa, more than 2,000 km (1,243 miles) away. In friendly contests, the two men pitted their skill and speed in planting and harvesting crops, for example, but Saku was usually the winner. The rivalry grew more intense, however, when they began

Tikopia

A mere 5 sq km (1.9 sq miles), Tikopia is part of the Solomon Islands of Melanesia, but its culture is essentially Polynesian. Although the first Europeans arrived here more than 400 years ago, until the 1980s there were no shops, electricity, or motor vehicles. A strong belief in the gods flourished in this remote place, whose inhabitants always felt they were at the mercy of the elements. When New Zealand anthropologist Raymond Firth first went there

in 1928, the island's population was about 1,200. Firth became fascinated by the culture of Tikopian society – at that time quite untouched by Western ideas – and wrote 10 books and numerous articles about the island people.

When Firth died in 2002, the president of the Polynesian Society, Sir Hugh Kawharu, paid tribute to him with a lament, which included the promise: "Your spirit is still alive among us, we who have become separated from you in New Zealand, Tikopia, and elsewhere."

See also: Fire and rice 226–27 ▪ The killing of Luma-Luma 308–09 ▪ Maui of a thousand tricks 320–23

Chiefs of Tikopia meet with officers from the French ship *Astrolabe*. The explorer Jules Dumont d'Urville and his men visited the islands of Polynesia in an expedition from 1826 to 1829.

to build the Kafika temple. Saku felled a great tree to create the temple's supporting post and dug a deep pit to set it in. He jumped in and asked Te Samoa to lower the base of the tree into the pit. Saku had worked out how to escape between its roots to avoid being crushed, and was able to climb out. Now it was Te Samoa's turn to jump in and dig, but Saku promptly moved the trunk so that his rival was trapped. Te Samoa begged to be released, but Saku rammed in earth around the post, burying him.

Saku's strength was legendary. When his mother's relatives in the village of Faea asked him to cut palm fronds for thatching their roofs, he uprooted a whole sago palm – a tree that stands around 25 m (82 ft) tall. Another time he asked the people of Faea if he could take some seedlings of taro, a root crop, to plant on his own land. They agreed, but instead of seedlings, he seized the entire plantation of taro.

Rising to the heavens
When Saku tried to appropriate his neighbour's land and plant crops there, however, the neighbour's family joined forces against him. Saku was killed by the youngest son – Te Sema – whose name means "the left-handed one".

According to the myth, Saku's death was divinely ordained. His spiritual mother, the goddess Atua Fafine, had advised Saku to leave the earth rather than use his great strength to kill Te Sema. She and

the deity Atua i Raropuka were the ancestral gods of Tikopia. In the earliest times, when the island was pulled up from the sea, the two deities were already sitting on the ground. Atua Fafine was weaving a mat of pandanus leaf, while Atua i Raropuka plaited a mat of coconut fibre – both traditional island crafts.

Just as Atua Fafine had planned, Saku's acceptance of death meant that he arrived among the gods unpolluted. As a result, he could say to each god, "Give me your *mana*", that is, their supernatural powers. After this, he was renamed Mapusia and became the most powerful of the gods, feared and appeased by the people of Tikopia.

Supreme power
The name Mapusia was taboo except in certain rituals invoking the god's help. "When I utter his name he hears in the heavens and bends over to listen to what is being said," runs one traditional Tikopian song. He was called Te Atua i Kafika ("the Deity of Kafika") by the clan as a whole, or Toku

Ariki Tapu "My Sacred Chief" by the Ariki Kafika (head of the clan). He was also Te Atua Fakamataku, "the Fear-Causing Chief", who created thunder by clattering his staff from side to side in the sky.

Mapusia was regarded as the god above all others by the people of Tikopia. As the anthropologist Raymond Firth was told, "No god can come and supplant him; he is high because he is strong." The »

Because [Saku] had power below here, when he died he went to the gods and was lofty among the gods.
History and Traditions of Tikopia

Mapusia! Fly in your paths.
Stroll about in the Heavens
and enter the Surumanga.
The Heavens shall obey.
Tikopia Songs

all-seeing god had four eyes, two in front and two behind, and his anger was terrible. An individual who offended Mapusia might be struck down with illness or death. If the whole society failed to appease him, he might send pestilence, a tropical cyclone, or drought.

Such events are realities in Tikopian life. The remote island is particularly vulnerable to tropical storms and subsequent famines, as was demonstrated in December 2003, when it was devastated by Cyclone Zoë. Whole villages were swept away, and their land was soaked with seawater, taking three years to recover.

To appease the gods

The rituals known as the Work of the Gods were considered essential for mollifying the gods and earning their protection. Because Mapusia was the principal *atua*, or god, of the Kafika clan, the Ariki Kafika (clan chief) acted as the high priest. It was the Ariki Kafika who decided when to "throw the firestick" – the laying of a ceremonial brand across the fire – to formally start the ritual. Charcoal from the brand would then be placed on the chief's brow.

The Work of the Gods was divided into two six-week ritual cycles, the Work of the Trade Wind and the Work of the Monsoon; both natural forces were crucial to the success of crops and the prevention of famine. The whole of Tikopian society devoted itself to performing the necessary sacred tasks. These included the rededication of the sacred canoes, the reconsecration of temples, harvest and planting ceremonies, and a sacred dance festival. Turmeric, extracted in the trade wind season and said to be the perfume of Mapusia, also had a special preparation ritual, as it was used in an edible form, in a sacred dye for bark cloth, and in a ritual body paint. The priest would chant: "I eat ten times your excrement, My Sacred Chief," using a conventional Tikopian expression to indicate his subservience to the god. "Your turmeric-making will be prepared." The priest then offered Mapusia food and kava. The drink was made from the root of the kava plant, which grows throughout Southeast Asia and the Pacific islands, and has psychoactive, anaesthetic, and sedative properties.

Remembering the sequence of rituals and accompanying dances, and ensuring that all were carried

Tikopia islanders integrate dance and songs, calling such recreational performances *mako*. Serious songs are termed *fuatango*. Firth described their urge to dance as "almost obsessional".

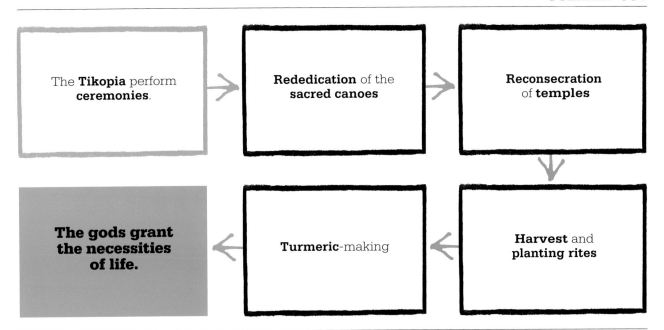

The **Tikopia** perform **ceremonies**. → **Rededication** of the **sacred canoes** → **Reconsecration** of **temples**

The gods grant the necessities of life. ← **Turmeric**-making ← **Harvest** and **planting rites**

out correctly, was an impressive collective act of memory and commitment. The purpose was to maintain contact with the *atua*, the gods whose favour was required to feed and protect the Tikopia.

A practical exchange
The food and kava offered to the gods were believed to be the most effective way of ensuring a plentiful harvest of staple crops, such as

breadfruit or yams. They were not simply acts of worship, but part of a logical system of trade between the Tikopia and the *atua*. The people performed the rituals for the gods, and in return the gods granted the Tikopia the necessities of life.

It was a system in which ritual performance and economic activity, such as food production, were inextricably combined. Although the ostensible sacrifice to the gods

was of food and kava, as the *atua* consumed only the essence of the food and kava offered, the rest was available for human consumption.

The real sacrifice was of time and energy, but it was not wasted, as many of the activities – such as plaiting mats, making thatch, or fixing canoes – were economically valuable. The rites ceased in the 1950s when there were too few *atua* believers to perform them. ■

In most types of dance there is vigorous bodily movement of rhythmic kind, often with highly structured gestures of hands and arms in progressive style.
Tikopia Songs

Atua

The word *atua* is translated as "god" or "spirit", but *atua* were thought to be as real as human beings. One of the ceremonial dances of the monsoon season was the Taomatangi, the dance to quell the wind. The *atua* were believed to be present, sitting with their backs against sacred stones, the male *atua* cross-legged, the female *atua* with legs stretched out in front of them. When Raymond Firth photographed this dance, the Tikopia were amazed that

the *atua*, whom they could collectively see, were not visible to the camera. Throughout the 20th century, Christianity eroded traditional Tikopian beliefs. After an epidemic in 1955 in which 200 people died, including the Ariki Kafika, there were not enough believers left to carry out the Work of the Gods. The remaining chiefs performed a final ceremony, a "kava of parting", to inform the *atua* that their rites were being abandoned and that they should drink their kava and retire to rest forever in their spirit homes.

I DO NOT FORGET THE GUIDING STARS

ALULUEI AND THE ART OF NAVIGATION

IN BRIEF

THEME
Knowledge of the seas

SOURCES
Oral tradition transcribed in
An Atoll Culture, Edwin
G Burrows and Melford
E Spiro, 1953; *A Flower in My
Ear*, Edwin G Burrows, 1963.

SETTING
Ifaluk Atoll, Micronesia,
northwest Pacific islands.

KEY FIGURES
Aluluei The god of
seamanship.

Aluluei's daughter One
of the god's three children.

Segur The god of navigators.

Valur The god of fish; son
of Aluluei.

Werieng The god of seabirds;
son of Aluluei.

Paluelap The great navigator;
another son of Aluluei.

A luluei is one of the oldest gods of navigation in the world. He was the son of the canoe captain Pälülop, but was killed by his older brothers Big Rong and Little Rong. His father then brought him back to Earth as a spirit with many eyes, which the people of Micronesia believe then became the stars, which they use for navigation.

Aluluei was not an ordinary man; according to the Ifaluk people of Micronesia, he had two faces, so that he could see all around him,

and although his upper body was human, his bottom half was that of a stingray. The Ifaluk, based on the Ifaluk atoll (in the Caroline Islands, in Micronesia) believe that Aluluei did not initially know all the lore of the sea – until he acquired it with his daughter's help.

Visiting gods
Long ago, Aluluei was living on the island of Bwennap – a sandy island with just one tree growing on it. There he took a wife, and had several sons and a daughter.

Early one morning, Aluluei's daughter was bathing in the sea when she saw a canoe approaching. Three gods were paddling the canoe: Segur, god of navigators; Valur, the god of fish; and Werieng, the god of birds. Valur and Werieng were two of Aluluei's sons. Aluluei's daughter ran to her father and asked him to prepare food for their visitors, and then she went back to the shore to welcome them. But the gods kept paddling, and it seemed

Coconuts are abundant and important to the people of the Pacific islands, who called the coconut palm the "Tree of Life" because all of its parts can be used in their communities.

See also: Viracocha the creator 256–57 ▪ The first canoe 258–59 ▪ Ta'aroa gives birth to the gods 316–17 ▪ Maui of a thousand tricks 320–23

Islanders spot a coral reef as they sail by Puynipet in the Caroline Islands. These long boats, also used in Hawaii, Samoa, Tahiti, and New Zealand, are fast and stable in choppy waters.

they were going to pass by without stopping. So Aluluei's daughter picked up a tiny coconut, no bigger than her fist, and held it up, calling for them to come to her. When they asked her why, she explained she had a coconut for them to drink. They instructed her to bring it out to their canoe.

Neverending sustenance

Aluluei's daughter waded out into the sea with her coconut. When the gods saw how small it was, they scoffed, saying it would not be enough to quench the thirst of three men, but Aluluei's daughter told them to drink it anyway.

Valur took the coconut and began to drink. He drank and drank until he could drink no more, but still the coconut held plenty of water. He passed it to Werieng, and Werieng passed it to Segur, and after both gods had drunk their fill, there was still plenty of water left in the little nut. The gods laughed

> See all the islands?
> See all the birds?
> See all the fish?
> ***An Atoll Culture***

with delight that one tiny coconut could hold so much water. They asked Aluluei's daughter to climb into their canoe, and when she had done so, they spread out their sea chart for her, marked with all the islands, birds, and fish. They told her they were so grateful to her for bringing them the coconut that they would give her the chart, and advised her to take it to her father.

Shared wisdom

When Aluluei's daughter took the chart to her father, he understood its value at once. It contained all the lore of seamanship: everything a man would need to know to become a great captain. Aluluei sent for his son Paluelap, the great navigator, and showed him the chart. Aluluei instructed his son to teach the people everything that was on the map, so that they could learn how to sail safely from island to island. Not everyone understood, but some did, and they became the first captains. Aluluei's decision to share the knowledge is typical of the Ifaluk people, who do not believe there is a set boundary between the self and others. ▪

Ifaluk canoes

The making and sailing of outrigger canoes is crucial to the islanders of Ifaluk, a coral atoll in the Caroline Islands, who use them for fishing and as a means of transport. Ifaluk canoes all have the same traditional design, and are always painted red, black, and white. Every Ifaluk canoe carries a wooden image of Aluluei, god of navigation.

Ifaluk society is ordered by social rank, and each person is assigned to one of eight clans at birth. The only way a person can increase their social status is by becoming a master navigator, canoemaker, or the oracular mouthpiece of a god. The master navigator has the highest status in Ifaluk society. Many of the songs passed down in the Ifaluk oral tradition discuss the making and sailing of canoes; navigating using the wind, currents, fish and birds, and stars; and issuing laments for those who were lost at sea.

DIRECTO

RY

DIRECTORY

The all-pervasive nature of myth across the world illustrates its centrality to the human experience. Since the beginning of time, people have told stories in order to make sense of their world. While many of these myths carry a seemingly explicit purpose – for example, those that centre on the founding of a city and, in doing so, help validate its origins – others, with their cast of heroes and monsters, speak more generally to latent fears inherent to the human condition. Myths often share archetypal figures – such as the trickster god, and the noble warrior – yet vary greatly across national and cultural boundaries. The stories below all belong to their respective cultures, and yet share characteristics with those explored earlier in the book.

BLUE MEN OF THE MINCH
Scottish, 9th century CE

The Minch is a strait off the north-west coast of Scotland, said to be inhabited by aquatic blue creatures known as "storm kelpies". These mermaid-like beings were half human, half fish, and were accused of luring children into the water and devouring them. They had the power to control the waves and raise storms that could sink ships. When the blue men approached a ship, they shouted the beginning of a rhyme that the captain needed to complete in order to save his vessel from being capsized.
See also: The quest of Odysseus 66–71 ▪ Numa outwits Jupiter 106–07 ▪ Finn MacCool and the Giant's Causeway 168–69

BEOWULF
Anglo-Saxon, 10th century CE

King Hrothgar of Denmark often hosted his warriors in Heorot, a huge mead-hall, to celebrate their victories. Angered by the noise of these celebrations, for many years the demon Grendel came from the swamplands and killed the Danes. Beowulf, the young warrior, came to Denmark's aid and killed Grendel. All seemed well until Grendel's mother emerged from her lair to avenge him. Beowulf destroyed her, and returned to Geatland, where he became king. When a thief awoke a local dragon, Beowulf defeated it in battle, but was mortally wounded. Dying, his body was burned on a giant funeral pyre, and placed in a burial mound overlooking the sea. As the oldest extant poem written in (Old) English, *Beowulf* is now regarded as a foundational epic.
See also: Sigurd the dragon slayer 158–59 ▪ The legend of King Arthur 172–77 ▪ The epic of Gilgamesh 190–97

RAGNAR LODBROK
Norse, 9th century CE

Ragnar Sigurdsson was a semi-mythical Viking warrior who featured prominently in several Norse sagas (stories). The first of his three wives was the legendary shield-maiden Lagertha. Ragnar was said to have led the siege of Paris in 845 CE. His final campaign was in northern England, where he was captured by a local king and thrown into a pit of snakes.
See also: War of the gods 140–41 ▪ Sigurd the dragon slayer 158–59 ▪ The legend of King Arthur 172–77

ROLAND
French, 8th century CE

Roland was a courageous Frankish soldier based on a historical figure – a regional governor under King Charlemagne who died fighting the Basques at the Battle of Roncevaux Pass (778 CE). One of Charlemagne's bravest generals, Roland was a popular subject for medieval minstrels, with many epic poems (such as *La Chanson de Roland*) describing Roland's honourable deeds. Other stories describe Roland's victory over Ferragut, a Saracen giant who was vulnerable only in the stomach.
See also: The quest of Odysseus 66–71 ▪ The voyage of Bran 165 ▪ The legend of King Arthur 172–77

BAYARD THE MAGICAL HORSE
French, 12th century CE

Bayard, the horse of Renaud, a knight of Charlemagne, was said to have understood human speech and grown in size magically in order to carry Renaud and his three brothers into battle on his back. Renaud had fallen into dispute with Charlemagne after killing the king's nephew. After a series of battles, Renaud was pardoned on the condition that he go on crusade and give up Bayard. When Renaud agreed to this, Charlemagne tried to kill the horse by chaining him to a stone and throwing him into a river – but Bayard smashed the stone and fled to live in the forest.
See also: The labours of Herakles 72–75 ▪ Perseus and Medusa 82–83 ▪ The legend of King Arthur 172–77

REYNARD THE TRICKSTER-FOX
French/Dutch/German, mid-12th century CE

The red fox Reynard was a central figure in the mid-12th-century epic *Ysengrimus*. This series of fables described how Reynard was able to consistently defeat his larger and stronger foe, the wolf Isengrin, through his wits and cunning. In one episode, Reynard used quick thinking to persuade Isengrin to catch fish using his tail, so that the wolf became stuck in the ice when the water quickly froze over again.
See also: Numa outwits Jupiter 106–07 ▪ The adventures of Loki and Thor in Jötunheim 146–47 ▪ Finn MacCool and the Giant's Causeway 168–69

LORELEI THE SIREN
German, 19th century CE

Lorelei is a rock on the bank of the Rhine in Germany. It is associated with a legendary maiden called Lore Lay who was found guilty of enchanting men and causing their deaths. She was sentenced to confinement in a nunnery. En route she persuaded her guards to allow her to climb the rock so she could view the Rhine one more time. When she got to the top, she thought she saw one of her lovers in the waters and jumped off, falling to her death. Her spirit became a siren that lured passing fishermen seductively to their deaths.
See also: The quest of Odysseus 66–71 ▪ Jason and Medea 84 ▪ Pyramus and Thisbe 124

THE RETURN OF KING SEBASTIAN
Portuguese, 16-17th century CE

Sebastian of Portugal was born in 1554, succeeding his grandfather John III as king in 1557. When he came of age in 1578, King Sebastian launched a crusade against the Muslim Sultanate of Morocco. A devout and pious Catholic, he disregarded his advisers, and quickly advanced inland. The Portuguese army was completely encircled and defeated, and the 24-year-old king was killed in the battle, although his body was never recovered. As a result, a myth arose that Sebastian would one day return to save Portugal. This belief became known as "Sebastianism".
See also: The quest of Odysseus 66–71 ▪ Aeneas, founder of Rome 96–101 ▪ The legend of King Arthur 172–77

MARI AND SUGAAR
Basque, pre-4th century CE

In the mythology of the Basque people of northern Spain and southern France, nymphlike beings called "lamiak" inhabited the countryside. One of the best-known was Mari, who lived in mountain caves and was served by a group of witches called "sorginak". Her husband was a serpentlike being called Sugaar. Every Friday they met and made storms. In another tale, Mari was a human who was transformed into a witch with the power to control the weather.
See also: Apollo and Daphne 60–61 ▪ Aeneas, founder of Rome 96–101 ▪ Carna and Janus 121

LIBUŠE THE FOUNDER OF PRAGUE
Czech, 8th century CE

Libuše was the youngest daughter of Duke Krok, a mythical figure who ruled the Czech people benevolently. Libuše was wise and beautiful, and because of this, Krok chose her to be his successor. Libuše also had the gift of prophecy. While looking over the Vltava River, she predicted that this location would one day be home to a great city. Later, a castle was built there, and around it grew the city of Prague. The Council of Prague resented female rule and demanded that Libuše marry, so selected a humble ploughman called Premysl. They were the mythical ancestors of the Premyslid dynasty – rulers of the Czech lands from the 9th century CE until 1306.
See also: The lost city of Atlantis 91 ▪ Aeneas, founder of Rome 96–101 ▪ The founding of Rome 102–05

BALTIC DIVINE TWINS
Lithuanian/Latvian, pre-13th century CE

Dievs and Velns were divine twins who played a major role in the pre-Christian mythology of eastern Europe, around the Baltic Sea. The world was created after a fight between Dievs and Velns on a rock in the middle of the sea, which then became the central point in the universe. Dievs, the personification of light, was a generally benevolent deity. He sometimes descended from the heavens to test humanity's goodness and generosity by walking the earth as an old beggar. Velns, by contrast, was a trickster who often interfered with creation; for example, he created mountains by spitting mud over the earth.
See also: Ahura Mazda and Ahriman 198–99 ▪ The Hero Twins 244–47 ▪ The Dogon cosmos 288–93

HUNOR AND MAGOR
Hungarian, 13th century CE

Nimrod was a biblical king and mighty hunter. In the *Gesta Hungarorum*, a 13th-century epic poem, he had twin sons called Hunor and Magor. While hunting with their followers, they pursued a white stag all the way from Central Asia into Eastern Europe. They decided to remain in the region and married daughters of a local king. Hunor's descendants became the Huns, while Magor's line included the Magyars, who conquered Hungary in the late 9th century CE.
See also: The epic of Gilgamesh 190–97 ▪ The adventures of the Monkey King 218–19 ▪ Fire and rice 226–27

CHERNOBOG
Russian, 12th century CE

In Russian mythology, Chernobog was the deity of death and darkness, and the embodiment of evil. He caused disaster and bad luck. Some believed Chernobog's counterpart was Belobog ("White God"), the deity of sun, light, and fortune. The two gods were thought to be locked in an endless struggle, with Chernobog ruling the winter months while Belobog dominated the summer.
See also: The war of the gods 140–41 ▪ Ahura Mazda and Ahriman 198–99 ▪ Viracocha the creator 256–57

BABA YAGA
Slavic, 18th century CE

Baba Yaga was a hideous cannibal with sharp teeth and a long nose, who was said to lurk deep in the forests of Eastern Europe. She lived in a hut that stood on giant chicken legs, topped with a rooster's head, and surrounded by a fence of human bones. She flew around in a giant mortar, armed with a pestle, which she used to grind down her victims before eating them.
See also: Perseus and Medusa 82–83 ▪ The Mead of Poetry 142–43

TARIEL THE KNIGHT IN THE PANTHER'S SKIN
Georgian, 12th century CE

Set in India and Arabia, this tale follows Tariel, an Indian prince who yearned for his long-lost love Nestan – thought to symbolize Queen Tamar the Great, who ruled Georgia from 1184 to 1213. He set

out to find Nestan with the help of Avtandil, a knight who had served King Rostevan of Arabia. Avtandil had been sent to capture Tariel, the famed "knight in the panther's skin", but was moved by Tariel's story and instead joined his quest. Eventually, they found Nestan, and she and Tariel married in India.
See also: Venus and Adonis 88–89 ▪ Cupid and Psyche 112–13 ▪ Pyramus and Thisbe 124

HAYK THE GREAT
Armenian, 5th century CE

Hayk originally lived in Babylon but fled to escape from the tyrannical rule of the Titan Bel. Hayk and his followers established a village called Haykashen. Bel demanded they return. When Hayk refused, Bel led a huge army against them. Hayk met them in battle and killed Bel with an arrow. Bel's army fled, leaving Hayk and his people to live in freedom. The nation that Hayk founded became Armenia.
See also: The founding of Athens 56–57 ▪ The founding of Rome 102–05 ▪ The legendary foundation of Korea 228–29

ZAHHAK
Persian, 10th century CE

The *Shahnameh* ("Book of Kings") is a 60,000-verse poem that tracks the development of Persia from the mythical era to the 7th century CE. This poem includes the story of Zahhak, a tyrannical ruler who overthrew a great king called Jamshid. Zahhak had two snakes that grew from his shoulders and ate the brains of two men every day. He ruled Persia for 1,000 years, until Kaveh, a blacksmith, led an uprising

that overthrew him. Jamshid's descendant, Fereydun, ascended the throne and Zahhak was imprisoned in a cave for eternity.
See also: Origin of the universe 18–23 ▪ The founding of Rome 102–05 ▪ Marduk and Tiamat 188–89

TENGRI THE CREATOR
Turkic/Mongol, 4th century CE

Many Central Asian peoples, including the Turkic and Mongol, practise a shamanistic religion called Tengriism with the sky god, Tengri, at its centre. It teaches that before creation, the sky god was a pure white goose who flew across an endless ocean. Tengri created a deity called Er Kishi to help him create the universe. Er Kishi was impure, trying to tempt people to do evil, so Tengri sent sacred animals to humans to guide them.
See also: Origin of the universe 18–23 ▪ Ahura Mazda and Ahriman 198–99 ▪ Spider Woman 238–39

ASENA THE GREY WOLF
Turkic, c.7th century CE

The Göktürks were a Turkic people who dominated Central Asia from the 6th to the 8th centuries. When their capital city of Ötüken was captured in 744 CE and their people were slaughtered, only one boy was left alive. He was badly injured, and would have died, but a she-wolf called Asena nursed him back to health. Eventually, he and Asena had ten sons; one of whom was the founder of the Ashina clan, the ruling power of the Göktürks.
See also: The founding of Rome 102–05 ▪ The cattle raid of Cooley 166–67 ▪ Jumong 230–31

KÖROGLU, TURKIC
Turkic, 11th century CE

The figure of Köroglu is common across Central Asian mythology. He was born as Rusen Ali but gained his other name, which means "son of the blind man", because his father was blinded by an evil royal governor. Köroglu was known for his fierce desire for justice and hatred of tyranny, which inspired him to lead a revolt against the governor, launching targeted raids against him before disappearing back into the countryside.
See also: The epic of Gilgamesh 190–97 ▪ The legendary foundation of Korea 228–29 ▪ Jumong 230–31

EPIC OF MANAS
Kyrgyz, collected 18th century CE

More than 500,000 lines long, the *Epic of Manas* is based on Kyrgyz oral tradition. Its hero is Manas, who united the Kyrgyz peoples and led them to independence and prosperity. Manas then conquered neighbouring areas and led campaigns as far afield as Beijing. Still recited by trained performers called *Manaschi*, the epic goes on to tell the story of his son Semetei and grandson Seitek.
See also: Marduk and Tiamat 188–89 ▪ The epic of Gilgamesh 190–97 ▪ The adventures of the Monkey King 218–19

PHA TRELGEN CHANGCHUP SEMPA THE CREATOR
Tibetan (China), date unknown

In Tibetan mythology, one tale seeks to explain the ancestry of the Tibetan people. After a great flood, a monkey named Pha Trelgen Changchup Sempa ("Father Old Monkey Enlightenment-Intention") settled on a Tibetan mountain to lead a life of meditation. A female demon came to the monkey and demanded to marry him. They had six children who, with the waters receding, lived in the forest. After a few years, they numbered 500, and were running out of food. They asked their father for help and, divinely inspired, he taught them the practice of agriculture.
See also: The epic of Gilgamesh 190–97 ▪ The origins of the Baiga 212–13 ▪ Fire and rice 226–27

EPIC OF KING GESAR
Central Asian, 12th century CE

As an infant, Gesar was exiled from the kingdom of Ling to the desert by his cowardly uncle. At the age of 12, Gesar returned to Ling to compete in a horse race that would decide who the next ruler would be. Gesar won and married the daughter of a local chief. He then led a series of victorious campaigns against Ling's enemies, which included man-eating demons.
See also: The labours of Herakles 72–75 ▪ The founding of Rome 102–05 ▪ The adventures of Loki and Thor in Jötunheim 146–47

THE DEVASURA YUDDHA (WARS BETWEEN THE HINDU GODS)
Indian, c.8th century BCE

In Hindu mythology, benevolent, virtuous deities came to be called Devas, and more harmful, demonic gods are called Asuras. The *Rig Veda* and *Ramayana* both include descriptions of the struggle between these two forces. Twelve battles between righteousness and wickedness took place across heaven, earth, and the Underworld. The gods wielded mighty celestial weapons called "astra"; the most fearsome and destructive was the "pashupatastra", an arrow that was capable of destroying all of creation.

See also: The *Ramayana* 204–09 ▪ Durga slays the buffalo demon 210 ▪ The fish-eyed goddess finds a husband 211

EMPEROR BHARATA
Indian, c.8th century BCE

The first book of the Sanskrit epic *Mahabharata* tells the story of Emperor Bharata. His mother Shakuntala was the daughter of a revered sage and a beautiful spirit, and his father Dushyanta ruled a kingdom in northern India. Despite his royal birth, Bharata was not raised at court, but in the forests, where he played with wild animals. As an adult, Bharata succeeded his father as king and through his virtuous rule founded an imperial dynasty that ruled all India. As a result, one of the official names for India is "Bharat".

See also: The game of dice 202–03 ▪ The *Ramayana* 204–09 ▪ The fish-eyed goddess finds a husband 211

THE COWHERD AND THE WEAVER GIRL
Chinese, c.7th century BCE

The Qixi festival takes place on the 7th night of the 7th lunar month. It commemorates the story of Niulang, a cowherd, and the weaver Zhinu, the daughter of the Mother

Goddess. Despite their different professions, they fell in love. The Mother Goddess was furious that her daughter was with a mortal and called Zhinu back to the heavens. When Niulang attempted to follow the weaver, the Mother Goddess tore the heavens apart to separate them, creating the Milky Way. They were only allowed to meet once a year, across a bridge of magpies.

See also: Arachne and Minerva 115 ▪ Pangu and the creation of the world 214–15

LEGEND OF THE WHITE SNAKE
Chinese, 17th century CE

Xu Xian was a boy who accidentally bought some pills that granted immortality. When he tried to swallow the pills, he vomited them into a lake. They were swallowed by a white snake spirit who gained magical powers. Eighteen years later, the snake turned into a woman called Bai Suzhen, who married Xu Xian. They lived happily until he discovered her true nature and died of shock. Bai Suzhen went on a quest and found a herb that would restore her husband to life. When Xu Xian was revived, he fully realized her compassion and loved her again.

See also: Echo and Narcissus 114 ▪ Pomona and Vertumus 122 ▪ Pangu and the creation of the world 214–15

LAC LONG QUÂN AND ÂU CO
Vietnamese, 14th century CE

Lac Long Quân ("Dragon Lord of Lac") was the son of the first king of Vietnam. After he became king, Lac Long Quân married a princess

called Âu Co from a mountain tribe to the north. They had 100 children, but could not be happy together. Âu Co wanted to live in the highlands and Lac Long Quân longed to be by the coast. They took 50 children each and lived in different parts of Vietnam, promising to support each other if necessary. Their children were the ancestors of the people of Vietnam, symbolizing their unity and collective identity.

See also: The legendary foundation of Korea 228–29 ▪ Jumong 230–31

KIVIUQ
Inuit peoples of Canada, Alaska, and Greenland, date unknown

Kiviuq was a shaman said to walk the Arctic eternally. He also used a sled, a kayak, and even the backs of aquatic creatures to travel. His magical powers allowed him to defeat any obstacle in his path. He was once married to a wolf-woman. Sadly, the union ended when her envious mother killed her. She then skinned her daughter and wore her pelt, in an attempt to trick Kiviuq into staying with her.

See also: Orestes avenges Agamemnon 64–65 ▪ Jason and Medea 84–85 ▪ Raven and the whale 242–43

RED HORN
Ho-Chunk of North America, date unknown

The eponymous hero of the *Red Horn Cycle* is one of the sons of the creator god Earthmaker. He gained his name because of his long, braided red hair, but he was also known as "Wears Heads on His

Ears" because of the living human faces grafted on to his earlobes. Red Horn was a great healer and worked to protect humans from the race of giants that plagued them. Along with his brothers, he was challenged to a contest by these giants and, although they won many games, Red Horn and his brothers were killed after losing a wrestling match.

See also: The adventures of Loki and Thor in Jötunheim 146–47 ▪ Spider Woman 238–39 ▪ The first canoe 256–57

IKTOMI THE TRICKSTER
Sioux of North America, date unknown

The son of the creator-god Inyan, Iktomi ("spider") was originally called Ksa ("wisdom"). He was turned into a spider and given his new name for his mischievous ways. Though primarily a spider, Iktomi was a shapeshifter who could take any form, including that of a human, and communicate with animals as well as inanimate objects, such as trees and rocks. As he was physically weak, Iktomi used tricks to survive. While sometimes manipulative, Iktomi was seen by the Lakota Sioux as a patron of ingenuity.

See also: Prometheus helps mankind 36–39 ▪ Arachne and Minerva 115 ▪ Spider Woman 238–39

NANABOZHO THE TRICKSTER
Ojibwa of North America, date unknown

Although Nanabozho was a trickster, his exploits were never malicious. He was the son of a

human woman and the West Wind. Nanabozho was associated with rabbits and was also known as "The Great Hare". His main companion was the wolf spirit Moqwaio, sometimes portrayed as his brother. The Great Spirit sent Nanabozho to teach the Ojibwa the names of the plants and animals, and show them how to fish and use hieroglyphics. He also saved humanity after a great flood by protecting them from water spirits.

See also: Prometheus helps mankind 36–39 ▪ The adventures of Loki and Thor in Jötunheim 146–47 ▪ The epic of Gilgamesh 190–97

EL SILBÓN
Venezuelan/Colombian, 19th century CE

El Silbón ("The Whistler") was a spirit in the form of a thin man 6m (20 ft) tall. While human, he murdered his father to avenge his mother's murder. The spirits of his mother and grandfather punished him by whipping him, rubbing lemons and chillies into his eyes, and setting dogs on him. He was then cursed to wander the world as a spirit for eternity, carrying his father's bones in a sack. As he walked, he whistled a distinctive tune, and preyed on unwary people, womanizers, and drunks.

See also: Prometheus helps mankind 36–39 ▪ Orestes avenges Agamemnon 64–65 ▪ The fate of Oedipus 86–87

THE BASILISCO CHILOTE
Chilean, 16th century CE

The Basilisco Chilote ("the Chilota Basilisk") is a creature in the mythology of the Chilotes, who live

in the Chiloé archipelago in the south of Chile. With the body of a serpent and the head of a rooster, this terrifying creature was said to be hatched from a chicken's egg. If the egg was not burned before the monster hatched, the Basilisco would dig a lair beneath a nearby house. Then it would slowly dehydrate its occupants, feeding remotely on their saliva and moisture. After hatching, it was said that the house above the Basilisco's lair must be burned in order to kill the beast.

See also: The quest of Odysseus 66–71 ▪ The labours of Herakles 72–75 ▪ Theseus and the Minotaur 76–77

SACI THE PRANKSTER
Brazilian, 18th century CE

Saci appeared as a one-legged youth who smoked a pipe and wore an enchanted red cap that gave him the power to appear and disappear at will. He was notorious for his pranks (such as making needles blunt, hiding things, or setting animals loose), but granted wishes to anyone who could steal his cap. His myth was based on a figure from indigenous Guarani mythology adapted by African slaves who were brought to Brazil.

See also: Hermes' first day 54–55 ▪ The adventures of Loki and Thor in Jötunheim 146–47 ▪ The death of Baldur 148–49

GAUCHO GIL
Argentinian, 19th century CE

Antonio Gil was a legendary Argentinian *gaucho* (cowboy) and outlaw said to have been active during the late 19th century. He took from the wealthy to give to the poor, had healing powers, and was immune to bullets. Just before he was to be executed, he promised to continue helping people even after death. The first person he helped was the officer who arrested him, whose child Gil saved from dying of illness. To this day, shrines to Gil exist across Argentina.

See also: Viracocha the creator 256–57 ▪ Hahuba the snake of being 258–59 ▪ The sky makes the sun and earth 260–61

THE QUEEN OF SHEBA
Ethiopian, 6th century CE

While the Queen of Sheba appears in the Bible and Quran in the 6th and 7th centuries CE, the fullest account of her legend is in the *Kebra Nagast*, an Ethiopian epic from 1322. After hearing of King Solomon's wisdom, the queen, Makeda, travelled to Jerusalem to meet him. She returned home pregnant with his child; the boy, Menelik, would become the founder of the Solomonic dynasty that ruled Ethiopia from 950 BCE to 1974.

See also: The epic of Gilgamesh 190–97 ▪ Jumong 230–31 ▪ En-kai and the cattle 285

AISHA QANDISHA
Moroccan, date unknown

Jinn are supernatural beings made of smokeless flame who interact with the material world. They are usually invisible and can be good or evil. In Morocco, Aisha Qandisha was a notorious and powerful jinn. She appeared in the form of a beautiful woman with the legs of a goat, and could cause either fertility and fortune, or death and madness.

When Aisha Qandisha pursued people, it was impossible to run away. They could only survive by plunging a knife into the earth, then using it either to banish her or to negotiate a price for her favour and support.

See also: Fire and rice 226–27 ▪ Ananse the spider 286–87 ▪ The Dogon cosmos 288–93

QUEEN AMINA OF ZAZZAU
Nigerian, 17th century CE

Although the subject of many myths, Amina was a real ruler who reigned over the kingdom of Zazzau in northern Nigeria during the 15th or 16th century. Amina was a great general, highly skilled at leading cavalry. She turned Zazzau into a major power, extending its control over neighbouring areas and trade routes throughout the region. Amina declined to marry and never had children. After each battle, however, she was said to select a lover from amongst her vanquished foes who would be executed after a night with her.

See also: Cybele 116–17 ▪ The descent of Inanna 182–87 ▪ Eshu the trickster 294–97

ADU OGYINAE
Ashanti, date unknown

In Akan mythology, based in Ghana and the Ivory Coast, at the beginning of time all humans lived underground. Then seven men, five women, a dog, and a leopard all crawled out of a hole left by a giant worm, and looked around in terror at their incomprehensible surroundings. Adu Ogyinae, the first of the group to reach the surface, calmed them, one by one,

by laying his hands on them. He led everyone to build the first shelters, but died unexpectedly when he was crushed by a falling tree.

See also: San creation myth 284 ▪ En-kai and the cattle 285 ▪ Ananse the spider 286–87

THE BILOKO
Democratic Republic of Congo, date unknown

The Biloko were dwarves who resided deep in the rainforests of the Congo. They lived inside trees and were covered in grass. While small in size, they had sharp claws and could open their mouths wide enough to swallow a human. The Biloko were highly territorial creatures, preying on those who ventured into their territory. They were able to enchant humans using bells that caused them to fall into a deep sleep – at which point the Biloko devoured them whole.

See also: Origin of the universe 18–23 ▪ Theseus and the Minotaur 76–77 ▪ Ananse the spider 286–87

NYAMINYAMI THE RIVER GOD
Zimbabwean/Zambian, 20th century CE

Nyaminyami was the god of the Zambezi River for the Tonga people. He was usually described as having the body of a snake and a fish's head, and as staining the water red where he swam. Nyaminyami lived underneath a rock and made whirlpools in the water surrounding it, so that no-one could venture near. When the Kariba Dam was built in the 1950s, it separated Nyaminyami from his wife. The project was beset by floods, mishaps, and accidents, which local people attributed to the rage of the river god.

See also: The founding of Athens 56–57 ▪ Perseus and Medusa 82–83 ▪ The fish-eyed goddess finds a husband 211

HUVEANE THE CREATOR
Lesotho/South Africa, date unknown

Huveane was the creator god who made the heavens, the earth, and humanity. Once he had done so, and not wishing to be disturbed by people, he drove pegs into a long pole and used it as a ladder to climb into the sky. As he stepped off each of the pegs, he removed them so that nobody could follow him. Huveane has resided in heaven ever since.

See also: Fire and rice 226–27 ▪ Cherokee creation 236–37 ▪ San creation myth 284

THE RAIN QUEEN
Limpopo of South Africa, 16th century CE

Dzugundini was the daughter of a chief who was forced to flee her home. She escaped to the Limpopo region of northwestern South Africa, and established a tribe called the Balobedu. In this new queendom, the eldest daughter would inherit the throne, and men were not permitted to rule. Dzugundini was famed for her rainmaking ability. Rain queens continued to reign over the Balobedu until the death of Queen Makobo Modjadji VI in 2005.

See also: Cybele 116–17 ▪ The descent of Inanna 182–87 ▪ Eshu the trickster 294–97

RATA AND MATUKU-TANGOTANGO
Maori of New Zealand, c.13th century CE

Rata's father Wahieroa was killed by an ogre called Matuku-tangotango. Seeking revenge, Rata travelled with his companions to find the ogre. While Matuku-tangotango was washing in a stream, Rata killed the ogre, cut out his heart, and roasted it over a fire. He then discovered that his father's bones had been taken by nocturnal goblins called the Ponaturi. Rata and his companions raided the village of the Ponaturi, defeated the goblins, and rescued the bones of Rata's father.

See also: Orestes avenges Agamemnon 64–65 ▪ The fate of Oedipus 86–87 ▪ Tane and Hine-titama 314–15

PELE THE FIRE GODDESS
Hawaiian, date unknown

Pele was the Hawaiian goddess of fire, lightning, dance, wind, and volcanoes. She was also known as *Ka wahine 'ai honua* ("the woman who devours the land"). Pele was born on Tahiti as a daughter to the earth goddess Haumea and the sky father Kane Milohai. Pele was exiled to Hawaii because of her fiery temper and for seducing the husband of her sister. She died when her sister found her and killed her in battle. In death, Pele became a god and took up residence inside Kilauea, a volcano on Hawaii island, where she still lives.

See also: Susanoo and Amaterasu 222–25 ▪ Legend of the five suns 248–55 ▪ Ta'aroa gives birth to the gods 316–17

THE BUNYIP
Australian Aboriginal, date unknown

One of the most fearsome beasts in Aboriginal legend was the amphibious *bunyip* ("devil" or "evil spirit") that lived in lagoons, swamps, and riverbeds. The *bunyip* has been described in a variety of ways; it has been variously said to have the head of a dog or a crocodile; tusks, horns, or a bill; and the body of a hippopotamus, an ox, or a manatee, with at least nine regional variations across Aboriginal Australia. The fierce creature is believed to kill and eat any unwary humans who wander across its territory.

See also: The quest of Odysseus 66–70 ▪ The Dreaming 302–07 ▪ The killing of Luma-Luma 308–09

ISOKELEKEL
Micronesian, 16th century CE

Isokelekel ("shining noble") was a semimythical warrior. He came from the island of Kosrae (now in the Federated States of Micronesia), and in some accounts was the son of the thunder god Nan Sapwe. Isokelekel led an invasion of the island of Pohnpei, almost 500 km (311 miles) away. The local king initially welcomed Isokelekel, but war eventually broke out between them. The mighty Isokelekel triumphed, with his rival running away and transforming into a fish. Isokelekel divided Pohnpei between his sons, from whom the local chiefs trace their lineage.

See also: The many affairs of Zeus 42–47 ▪ Cherokee creation 236–37 ▪ Viracocha the creator 256–57

INDEX

Page numbers in **bold** refer to main entries; those in *italics* refer to captions.

QUOTE ATTRIBUTIONS

ACKNOWLEDGEMENTS

Dorling Kindersley would like to thank Rabia Ahmad, Anjali Sachar, and Sonakshi Singh for design assistance.

PICTURE CREDITS